CHINA BETWEEN PEACE AND WAR

MAO, CHIANG AND THE
AMERICANS, 1945–1947

CHINA BETWEEN PEACE AND WAR

MAO, CHIANG AND THE
AMERICANS, 1945–1947

VICTOR S.C. CHENG

ANU PRESS

'the state of peace appears at times more difficult than the state of war'
George C. Marshall
FRUS, 1946, vol. x: 437

'I still agreed to enter into the discussion. As I see it, this constitutes a concession'
Zhou Enlai
FRUS, 1946, vol. x: 144

ANU PRESS

Published by ANU Press
The Australian National University
Canberra ACT 2600, Australia
Email: anupress@anu.edu.au

Available to download for free at press.anu.edu.au

ISBN (print): 9781760465711
ISBN (online): 9781760465728

WorldCat (print): 1379309094
WorldCat (online): 1379262161

DOI: 10.22459/CBPW.2023

This title is published under a Creative Commons Attribution-NonCommercial-NoDerivatives 4.0 International (CC BY-NC-ND 4.0) licence.

The full licence terms are available at creativecommons.org/licenses/by-nc-nd/4.0/legalcode

Cover design and layout by ANU Press

This book is published under the aegis of the China in the World editorial board of ANU Press.

This edition © 2023 ANU Press

Contents

Acknowledgements	ix
List of abbreviations	xi
Note on sources	xiii
Map 1 Important locations	xv
Map 2 Manchurian theatre	xvii
Introduction	1
1. Negotiating at an uneven table	21
National pride, sovereignty and the Sino-Soviet dispute over Dalian	
2. Rethinking the Chongqing negotiations	47
Concession-making, the trust/distrust paradox and the biased mediator in China's first post–World War II attempt at peace	
3. Civil war in the north-east	77
The rhetorical use of 'decisive war' and the Manchurian gamble	
4. A shattered peace	105
Ambiguous provisions in agreements for ceasefire, the Political Consultative Conference and army nationalisation	
5. Planting radishes in the desert	141
The Nationalists' handling of the negotiations for Sino-Soviet economic cooperation in Manchuria	
6. 'China's Madrid'	171
The synonym of civil war	
7. Towards an all-out civil war in China	199
Short-term solutions, long-term success and the veto players	
Conclusion	241
Bibliography	249
Index	283

Acknowledgements

This book originated in my dissertation prepared at the University of Melbourne. I am indebted to my thesis supervisor Antonia Finnane and associate supervisor Stephen L. Morgan for their advice and help. Over the long course of revising the dissertation into this book, some of the ideas were further trialled in articles written at Lund University and The Australian National University. The final version of the manuscript was mostly completed at ANU. I am grateful for the support offered by these institutions. I have benefited enormously from the mentorship and unreserved help of Kamaruding Abdulsomad, Edward Aspinall, Geremie R. Barmé, Anita Chan, Greg Fealy, John Fitzgerald, Ben Kervliet, Ben Hillman, Chi-kong Lai, Hoiyee Lau, Luigi Tomba, Regina Trillo, Timothy Tsu, Jonathan Unger, Crystal Woo and Haiqing Yu.

My special thanks are extended to CartoGIS Services of ANU for providing the maps in the book and the staff of the Australian Centre on China in the World Matthew Galway and Sharon Strange for volunteering their time.

My gratitude goes as well to my students, especially to Jie Bai, Adala Chan, Irene Chuon, Brooke Churchman, Julian Coady, Aaron Dennis, Montserrat Lopez Jerez, Wai Ki Kam, Yu-ping Luk, Nicole O, Katrina Osborne, Kori Rutcosky and Hugo Velazquez. Some of them offered practical support even years after their graduation. The inspiring questions they asked and the experiences they shared with me across a variety of fields make me understand why the guide to negotiation and mediation is often antecedent events rather than theories developed in the ivory tower of academia. To all I offer my heartfelt thanks.

I could not have completed this book without help from many librarians, archivists, language specialists and journalists. I especially wish to thank Irina Chou, Darrell Dorrington, Cathryn Game, Di Pin Ouyang, Dayaneetha De Silva, Wan Wong, Bick-har Yeung and my lifetime friend Chen Ping-hsun for facilitating my research.

I would like to express my deepest gratitude also to the following individuals. My parents and Alice disguised their worry for me. Their love gave me the serenity and spirit to write this book. Samuel W.K. Chan, who also made critical comments on my draft, helped me to locate some of the rare source materials. Samuel's constant concerns over my progress have been a powerful source for me to stay on course and reach the finishing line.

This volume is a tribute to my good friend Professor Shui-Lung Tsang. It has now been two decades since Lung's passing, but his works on history still live. I promised Lung, on the day I saw him off, to stay healthy and tell his tale: all academics deserve a fairer workplace. I keep my promise.

Victor S.C. Cheng

List of abbreviations

CC	The Central Committee
CCNE	Circulating Currency for the Nine Provinces of the North-East
CCP	Chinese Communist Party
CEC	Central Executive Committee
CMC	Central Military Commission
CRDC	Committee for the Reviewing of the Draft Constitution
GMD	Guomindang, Kuomintang or Chinese Nationalist Party
KMT	Kuomintang, Guomindang or Chinese Nationalist Party
LST	landing ship, tank
MPR	Mongolian People's Republic
NEB	North-East Bureau
NEDUA	North-East Democratic United Army
NEHQ	North-East Headquarters
NEPAA	North-East People's Autonomous Army
PCC	Political Consultative Conference
PLA	People's Liberation Army
PRC	People's Republic of China
UNRRA	United Nations Relief and Rehabilitation Administration

Note on sources

Full bibliographical information is given in the Bibliography. The following special terms and abbreviations are used in shortened citations in the footnotes after a first citation:

AH	Academia Historica (Guoshiguan)
CAM	Miscellaneous Chinese Army Moves
CBIT	Records of US Army Forces in the China–Burma–India Theaters of Operations
CC	Central Committee
Chairman	Records of the Chairman
Chiang Diary	*Chiang Kai-shek diaries 1917–72*
Chongqing tanpan	Zhonggong Chongqing shiwei dangshi gongzuo weiyuanhui, Chongqing Shi zhengxie wenshi ziliao yanjiu weiyuanhui and Hongyan geming jinian guan, ed. *Chongqing tanpan jishi*
CMC	Central Military Commission
CT	Records of Headquarters US Forces, China Theater
DOSIAC	Records of the US Department of State Relating to the Internal Affairs of China
FRUS	United States Department of State, *Foreign Relations of the United States: Diplomatic Papers, the Far East, China*
HQCT	China Theater Administrative, Shanghai, China
Huang Yanpei riji	*Huang riji*
JCS	Records of the US Joint Chiefs of Staff

Junshi	Zhonggong zhongyang wenxian yanjiushi and Zhongguo renmin jiefangjun junshi kexue yuan, ed. *Mao Zedong junshi wenji*
JZZW	*Jiang Zhongzheng zongtong wenwu*
Leahy	Admiral Leahy, 1942–48
Liaoshen	Zhonggong zhongyang dangshi ziliao zhengji weiyuanhui, Zhongguo renmin jiefangjun Liaoshen zhanyi jinianguan jianguan weiyuanhui and Liaoshen juezhan bianshen xiaozu, ed. *Liaoshen juezhan*
Liu nianpu	Zhonggong zhongyang wenxian yanjiushi, ed. *Liu Shaoqi nianpu 1898–1969*
Manchuria	Zhang, Jia'ao, *Last Chance in Manchuria: The Diary of Cheung Kia-ngau*
Mao nianpu	Zhonggong zhongyang wenxian yanjiushi, ed. *Mao Zedong nianpu, 1893–1949*
NAA	National Archives Administration, National Development Council, Taipei
NACP	National Archives, College Park
QZ	Quanzong
RG	Record Group
Tanpan shi	Yang Shengqing ed., *Zhongguo gongchandang tanpan shi*
Wang riji	*Wang Shijie riji*
Xiong Papers	*Hsiung Shih-hui Papers*
Zhonggong	Zhongyang dang'anguan, ed. *Zhonggong zhongyang wenjian xuanji*
Zhonghua Minguo	Qin Xiaoyi, ed. *Zhonghua Minguo zhongyao shiliao chubian—Dui ri kangzhan shiqi*
Zhou 1946	Zhonggong zhongyang wenxian yanjiushi and Zhonggong Nanjing Shi weiyuanhui, ed. *Zhou Enlai yijiusiliu nian tanpan wenxuan*
Zhou nianpu	Zhonggong zhongyang wenxian yanjiushi, ed., *Zhou Enlai nianpu*
zuozhan riji	Zhongguo dier lishi dang'anguan, ed. *Kangri zhanzheng shiqi Guomindang jun jimi zuozhan riji*

Map 1 Important locations

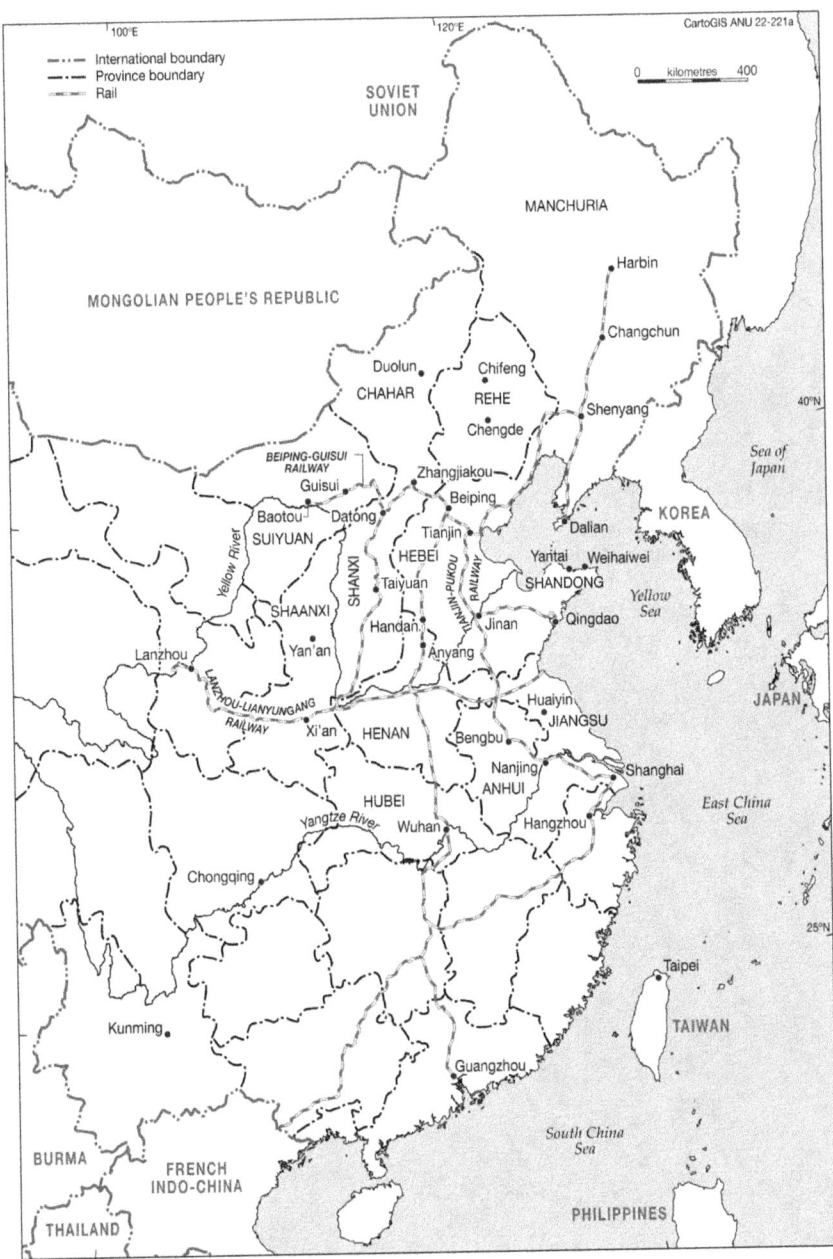

Source: ANU CartoGIS Services.

Map 2 Manchurian theatre

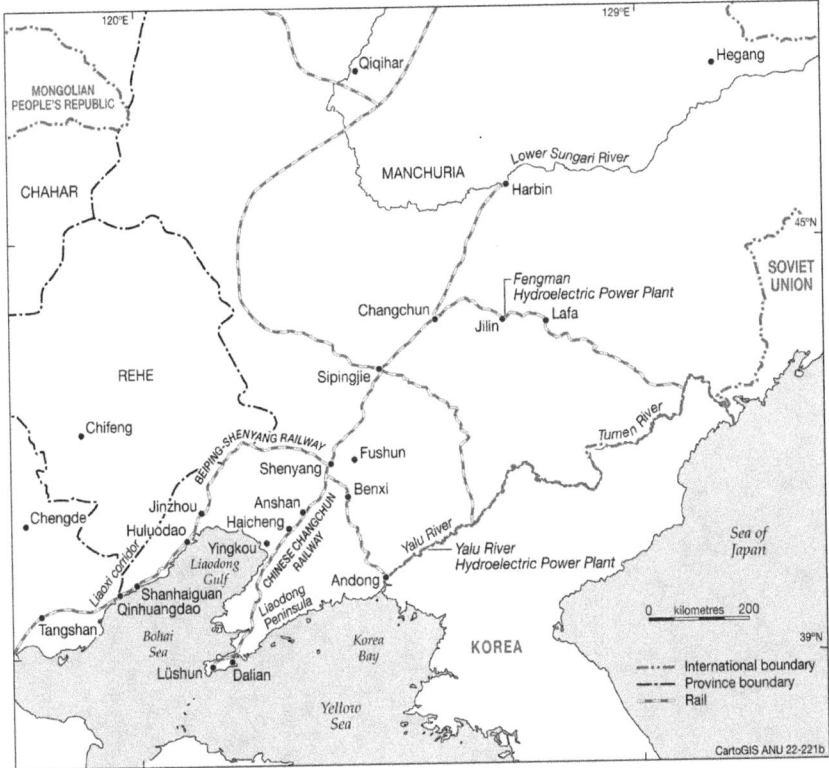

Source: ANU CartoGIS Services.

Introduction

Following the end of World War II, China was plunged almost immediately into a second, even more fateful conflict: the Civil War of 1945–49. In this conflict's early phases, some of the action took place not on the battlefield but around the negotiating table. This book is about those negotiations, in the context of the developing theatre of war. The received wisdom among historians about these negotiations is that the differences between the two belligerent parties in the Chinese Civil War—the Guomindang (GMD; Kuomintang, or Chinese Nationalist Party) and the Chinese Communist Party (CCP)—were irreconcilable,[1] and that the failure of the peace talks was somewhat predetermined,[2] not least by virtue of the wholesale failure of US foreign policy towards China,[3] exemplified by the Americans' unsuccessful mediation efforts to establish lasting peace.[4] A separate set of negotiations was carried out early in this period, in which the GMD government negotiated with the Soviet Union over the recovery of Manchuria. This greatly influenced the subsequent outbreak of the civil war and is often considered in the context of Soviet–US rivalry.[5]

---

1   Francis Yi-hua Kan, 'The irreconcilable Chinese rival regimes and the weakening of the policies of neutrality of the Great Powers', *Civil Wars* 3, no. 4 (2000): 85–104.
2   Wang Chaoguang, 'Zhan yu he de bianzou: Chongqing tanpan zhi Zhengxie huiyi qijian de Zhongguo shiju yanbian' [A variation on war and peace: The evolution of China's political situation from the Chongqing negotiations to the Political Consultative Conference], *Jindaishi yanjiu* [Modern Chinese History Studies] 1 (2002): 14–42.
3   See, for example, Simei Qing, *From Allies to Enemies: Visions of Modernity, Identity, and US–China Diplomacy, 1945–1960* (Cambridge, MA: Harvard University Press, 2007), 57–84; Tang Tsou, *America's Failure in China, 1941–50* (Chicago: University of Chicago Press, 1963), *passim*.
4   Kan, 'Irreconcilable Chinese'; Yang Shengqing ed., *Zhongguo gongchan dang tanpan shi* [A history of negotiations of the Chinese Communist Party] (Beijing: Zhongyang wenxian chubanshe, 2005), 388 (hereafter *Tanpan shi*).
5   See, for example, Odd Arne Westad, *Cold War and Revolution: Soviet–American Rivalry and the Origins of the Chinese Civil War, 1944–1946* (New York: Columbia University Press, 1993), 1, 31–56, 99–117; Steven I. Levine, 'Soviet–American rivalry in Manchuria and the Cold War', in *Dimensions of China's Foreign Relations*, ed. Chün-tu Hsüeh (New York: Praeger Publishers, 1977), 10–43.

It is a matter of record that the negotiations and agreements that promised to terminate the civil war, de-escalate international tension and simultaneously foster cooperation were all part of a failed attempt at peace. The results seem speak for themselves: a full-scale civil war in China that fed into the rivalry between the Cold War superpowers.

The main interest of this book is twofold. First, it offers an account of what the interested parties were really negotiating about. Second, it provides a reassessment of the early phase of the civil war through the lens of the negotiations. It concerns how the negotiators and mediators strove for progress over the bargaining table when China teetered between peace and war in the immediate aftermath of World War II.

In retrospect, many historians assume that the negotiations were doomed to failure from beginning to end. But negotiations do not take place 'in retrospect'. At the time, the effort to negotiate a peaceful resolution to the conflict between the GMD and CCP was taken very seriously by all sides. Chiang Kai-shek devoted substantial space in his diary to the ongoing twists and turns of the negotiations and the Communist leaders also discussed them at length in their internal communications. The United States was so committed to the negotiations that it dispatched to China one of America's most respected and influential figures, George C. Marshall, who had commanded the US armed forces during World War II, to lead the negotiations.

This book reveals how the negotiators understood the nature of their job. Negotiation is not always about assessing the chance of a comprehensive settlement; rather, it is often a series of continuous efforts of seeking even the smallest compromise that could reduce further escalation of the conflict. By moving away from a retrospective outcome-oriented historical analysis, the book shows that the debates, disagreements and compromises of the negotiations are more significant to our understanding of China's post-war struggle between peace and war than previously thought.

As battlefield correspondent Dewitt Mackenzie noted in 1946, the local dynamics of the Chinese Civil War had turned it into a world threat in light of the totalising view of international politics.[6] At present, scholars have

---

6   Dewitt Mackenzie, 'Chinese civil war is seen as world threat', *Kentucky New Era*, 19 July 1946.

sought to understand civil wars from a variety of aspects rather than relegating them to the margins of international political studies.⁷ Nevertheless, negotiations to resolve the Chinese Civil War remain a neglected topic.

This contrasts sharply with research into the Chinese Civil War's battle engagements, which attract enormous research interest. The major campaigns fought after the complete breakdown of the peace talks, particularly the massive operations that occurred in 1948 and 1949, have prevailed in academic discussions of Chinese Civil War history. In part, this is because they are considered decisive for the CCP's conquest of the mainland and the founding of the CCP-led People's Republic of China (PRC).⁸

Peace negotiations and war are often two sides of the same coin. World War I, for instance, was 'a diplomatically botched negotiation', as American diplomat Richard Holbrooke has said.⁹ If the combat operations of the Chinese Civil War require in-depth analysis, it seems reasonable to ask if there was more to the negotiations than their outcome.

This book examines a number of interrelated themes. While it studies the two civil war rivals' use of concessions, ambiguous treaties and short-term solutions as negotiation strategies, the book intervenes in the discussion of the American peacemakers' mediation efforts under conditions of bias. The book goes beyond the often inconclusive debates over infractions of international treaties. It draws attention to the GMD government's predicament, from a position of weakness, in maintaining a cooperative relationship with the powerful Soviet Union in both treaty negotiations and post-treaty stages. It demonstrates how the Nationalists' handling of the Soviets at the negotiating table affected their war efforts against the CCP.

As the unfolding negotiation dynamics and the escalation of military confrontation on the battlefield were closely related, this book also explores the military conflicts that ultimately plunged China into what is considered the world's largest military engagement of the seven-plus decades since

---

7   Caroline Kennedy-Pipe and Clive Jones, 'An introduction to civil wars', *Civil Wars* 1, no. 1 (1998): 1–15.
8   See, for example, Harold M. Tanner, *Where Chiang Kai-shek Lost China: The Liao–Shen Campaign, 1948* (Bloomington, IN: Indiana University Press, 2015); Larry M. Wortzel, 'The Beiping–Tianjin campaign of 1948–1949: The strategic and operational thinking of the People's Liberation Army', in *Chinese Warfighting: The PLA Experience since 1949*, ed. Mark A. Ryan, David M. Finkelstein and Michael A. McDevitt (Armonk, NY: M.E. Sharpe, 2003), 56–72.
9   Quoted in Richard Bingley, *The Security Consultant's Handbook* (Ely, Cambridgeshire: IT Governance Publishing, 2015), 67.

World War II.[10] It highlights the contradictory role of political leaders who were micro-managing both military and peace efforts, including their struggle to connect political objectives and military power, rhetorical use of the 'decisive war' concept, and the pursuit of radical military and political goals at the expense of a negotiated peace.

These central themes frame this book's inquiry into a period with an entwined history of warfare and peace negotiations in post-war China until the fighting escalated into a full-blown civil war in 1947. The civil war began in August 1945 when the Soviet invasion of Manchuria[11] precipitated the Japanese surrender and ended China's eight-year-long war against the Japanese invaders. Japan's sudden surrender in August 1945 reignited the civil war between the ruling GMD, led by Chiang Kai-shek, and its armed opposition, Mao Zedong's CCP, in a race for post-war territorial recovery, despite their conflict-laden wartime alliance against Japan that had existed since 1937. The two old foes nevertheless entered into the US-sponsored peace talks owing to domestic and international constraints. In a bid to recover Manchuria from Soviet Red Army occupation, the GMD government was simultaneously deadlocked in a negotiating conflict with the powerful Soviets, where it was disadvantaged. The GMD–CCP peace talks gained momentum in early 1946. Progress at the negotiating table kindled hopes for permanent peace in China, which culminated in a truce agreement and a range of multiparty resolutions for a power-sharing government. Hopes for peace were disappointed, however. Escalation of the military situation in Manchuria and China proper[12] quickly ensured that the ceasefire became a dim memory. The peace efforts unravelled in mid-1946 and collapsed completely in early 1947, after the outbreak of full-scale civil war and after the Nationalists terminated discussions with the Soviets over Manchuria.

---

10 Odd Arne Westad, *Decisive Encounters: The Chinese Civil War, 1946–1950* (Stanford, CA: Stanford University Press, 2003), 1.
11 'Manchuria' is a term used in historical geography of China as a convenient designation of a geographical area in the north-east of China and parts of today's Inner Mongolia Autonomous Region. 'Manchuria' and 'the north-east' are used interchangeably in this book.
12 'China proper' is a term used in the historical geography of China as a convenient designation of regions to the south of the Great Wall, excluding Manchuria, Mongolia, Tibet and Xinjiang.

The conceptual basis of the book

Through studying the negotiations that took place in post–World War II China, this book reviews an abundance of original negotiation meeting records. Despite many of these documents being published, an enormous wealth of knowledge about peacemaking in these records remains relatively unexplored. In particular, the significance of some of the creative ideas proposed by the negotiators to break impasses was not recognised until decades later. Clearly, these ideas are best understood in light of subsequent advances in the study of negotiation.

Notably, some of the negotiation concepts in these records have been mentioned by media outlets using names that have become popular nowadays (e.g. 'highball tactics' and 'third-party intervention'), in accordance with the global use of negotiation and mediation as alternatives to litigation and armed conflict. This book examines these historical negotiation records through the lens of the modern literature on negotiation and mediation. This literature provides a conceptual basis for the book's historical inquiry, given that negotiation and mediation have never been specialised knowledge intended only for a small group of political scientists, mathematicians and game theorists.

This book cites conceptual studies on negotiation from authors who acquired expertise in studying how conflicts are resolved in a variety of areas and who come from a variety of academic disciplines, including business, law, political science, international relations, social psychology, anthropology and, more narrowly, specific areas such as clinical nursing. These studies provide insights into the book's historical research about the complex relationships between peace, war and conflict management. Peace negotiations and mediations certainly differ from those that occur in commercial, legal and community disputes, but many basic strategies and tactics—such as seeking mutual concessions and compromises—are pertinent to a variety of negotiation settings.[13]

---

13 Roger Fisher, William Ury and Bert Spector, 'An interview with Roger Fisher and William Ury', *Academy of Management Executive* 18, no. 3 (2004): 101.

The writings on negotiation are voluminous. They take different approaches,[14] and tend to highlight one or another aspect of negotiation and mediation.[15] Increased integration and the emergence of new perspectives over recent decades in this vibrant field have blurred the lines that separate different approaches.[16]

The massively complex negotiations in the Chinese Civil War simply cannot be understood through foregrounding a particular negotiation 'style'[17] or the viewpoint of a single side,[18] as in some previous studies. At different times in the Civil War negotiations, as the various parties shifted their ground and the mediators shifted their tactics, one or another of the writings on negotiation becomes most relevant as explanatory analysis, and I will introduce this writing at that juncture of the book.

This book reveals that the raucous haggling at the negotiating table was matched by military decisions and actions on the battlefield. A key component of the book studies these military operations, as what occurred on the battlefield affected the negotiation process. The following chapters show that while the two belligerents tried using the outcomes on the battlefield to gain leverage at the bargaining table, the increasing escalation

---

14 There were few attempts to categorise the approaches in the study of negotiation in the 1980s and 1990s. See Jacob Bercovitch, 'Problems and approaches in the study of bargaining and negotiation', *Political Science* 36, no. 2 (1984): 125–44; Anatol Rapoport, *The Origins of Violence: Approaches to the Study of Conflict* (New York: Paragon House, 1989); Linda L. Putnam, 'Challenging the assumptions of traditional approaches to negotiation', *Negotiation Journal* 10, no. 4 (1994): 337–46. Recent studies place less emphasis on identifying different approaches to the study of negotiation as they actually inform one another and each perspective is limited when standing alone. See Roy J. Lewicki, Bruce Barry and David M. Saunders, *Negotiation*, 6th edn (New York: McGraw-Hill, 2010), 3.
15 A single aspect of the same negotiation cases could be studied concurrently from several partly contending but partly overlapping and complementary approaches, bringing different perspectives on the same topic. This trend is still emerging. See, for example, I. William Zartman ed., *International Multilateral Negotiation: Approaches to the Management of Complexity* (San Francisco, CA: Jossey-Bass, 1994), 213–22. Similarly, a re-evaluation of an existing negotiation concept could pioneer new approaches. See, for example, Daniel Druckman, 'Turning points in international negotiation: A comparative analysis', *Journal of Conflict Resolution* 45, no. 4 (2001): 519–44.
16 To illustrate with one example, the behavioural decision-making perspective integrates with the social psychology of negotiation. See Max H. Bazerman, Jared R. Curhan and Don A. Moore, 'The death and rebirth of the social psychology of negotiation', in *Applied Social Psychology*, ed. Marilynn B. Brewer and Miles Hewstone (Malden, MA: Blackwell Publishing, 2004), 268–300.
17 A previous study on the PRC's diplomatic negotiation history after 1949 has tried to identify whether there was a distinctive 'Chinese style' of negotiation. The conclusion of the study is not persuasive. It finds that the Chinese style of negotiation was 'neither so unique as to completely obviate Western negotiating experiences and concepts, nor so characterless to be undifferentiated'. See Alfred D. Wilhelm, *The Chinese at the Negotiating Table: Style and Characteristics* (Washington, DC: National Defense University Press, 1994), 4, 18, citation from 203.
18 See *Tanpan shi*.

of conflict injected urgency into negotiations. The existing literature on warfare offers a basis for assessments. However, the book studies a period of Chinese history when the tug of war at the negotiating table and bloodshed on the battlefield reduced every negotiating proposal to a temporary status. As B.H. Liddell Hart noted in his study of military strategy, 'the one constant factor is that means and conditions are invariably inconstant'.[19]

As the unpredictability of war is somewhat inevitable, some of the military decision-making discussed here defies the modern logic of risk-taking. While previous studies on military affairs are useful for studying these decisions, the military decisions of the two antagonists enrich our understanding of wartime fighting, including less studied aspects of guerrilla warfare and the concept of a decisive war.

The historical evidence of the book

This book is about two important aspects of the history of the Chinese Civil War—the military and the politics between the rival parties, as revealed in the negotiations—and primary source materials are at its core. Studies on the history of negotiations are often limited by a lack of historical records,[20] but the empirical findings of this book are supported by the availability of many original records of conversations at negotiation meetings, either in the official documented historical record or preserved in the personal diaries and chronological biographies of individual negotiators. With the exception of the editors' comments in these biographies, the sources present the negotiation strategies and tactics of the negotiators and the mediators without hindsight.

---

19 B.H. Liddell Hart, *Strategy*, 2nd rev. edn (London: Signet, 1974), 4.
20 Wilhelm, *The Chinese at the Negotiating Table*, xxxiii.

For example, this book reviews the original negotiation meeting conversation records of the GMD–CCP negotiations in late 1945, as documented and approved by both parties.[21] Despite the complete set of these conversation records[22] or synopses[23] of these meeting being published, these documents remain essentially unstudied.

The GMD–CCP negotiations became tripartite in 1946 when the American mediators directly participated in the negotiations and were responsible for keeping detailed conversation records of the meetings. The Americans organised comprehensive clerical services. Two stenographers alternated, conducting live record-keeping in English of the participants' (or translators') discussions during negotiation sessions. The two disputed parties received carbon copies of the initial record immediately following the meeting. This was before the record was thoroughly checked and typed in its final form, as a correct record of the conference for all participants to approve. The two belligerent parties were free to arrange their respective Chinese translations from the original English minutes for their own reference.[24] The Americans were even responsible for drafting proposals in both English and Chinese in some cases, particularly when the two parties used the Americans as intermediaries to convey demands without holding meetings.[25]

---

21   Qin Xiaoyi ed., *Zhonghua Minguo zhongyao shiliao chubian—Dui ri kangzhan shiqi* [A first selection of important historical materials of the Republic of China—The period of the war of resistance against Japan] (Taipei: Zhongguo Guomindang zhongyang weiyuanhui dangshi weiyuanhui, 1981), 7, book 2: 60, 68 (hereafter *Zhonghua Minguo*); Zhonggong zhongyang wenxian yanjiushi [Research office for documentation of the Central Committee of the CCP] ed., *Zhou Enlai nianpu, 1898–1949* [The chronological biography of Zhou Enlai, 1898–1949] (Beijing: Zhongyang wenxian chubanshe, 1989), 621 (hereafter *Zhou nianpu*).
22   *Zhonghua Minguo*, 7, book 2, 45–97; Zhang Jiuru, *Hetan fuzhe zai Zhongguo* [The disastrous road towards peace talks in China] (Taipei: Lianjing chuban shiye gongsi, 1981), 134–45.
23   Zhonggong Chongqing shiwei dangshi gongzuo weiyuanhui [Committee of party history of the CCP Chongqing branch], Chongqing Shi zhengxie wenshi ziliao yanjiu weiyuanhui [Literary–historical source materials study committee—An affiliate of the Chinese People's Political Consultative Conference, Chongqing branch] and Hongyan geming jinian guan [Hongyan Village Revolutionary Memorial Hall] eds, *Chongqing tanpan jishi* [The true story of Chongqing negotiations] (Chongqing: Chongqing Chubanshe, 1984), 189–228 (hereafter *Chongqing tanpan*).
24   United States Department of State, *Foreign Relations of the United States: Diplomatic Papers, the Far East, China* (Washington, DC: United States Government Printing Office, 1967–72), 1946, 9: 26–39, 43–59, 59–75, 1025–33, esp. 38, 43, 59; 10: 310–11 (hereafter *FRUS*).
25   Ibid., 1099–101.

INTRODUCTION

The complete set of recorded conversations about the US-brokered GMD–CCP peace talks of 1946 was later published in a diplomatic papers series by the US government. Although this set of documents is easily accessible to the general public, an enormous wealth of knowledge within the texts about making peace remains untapped.

Since the 1980s, the PRC has gradually released a significant amount of source material comprising original telegrams, correspondence and internally circulated documents of various types. These have revised and enriched our understanding of the civil war's history. They were published as documentary collections, personal chronological biographies and the collected writings of individual Chinese statesmen and generals.[26] Included in this material is the eighteen-volume selected documentary collection of the Central Committee of the CCP, covering the period of the Chinese Communist movement from 1921 to 1949.[27] The collection contains a large number of original documents pertaining to important political and military decisions of the CCP leadership.

This group of historical records is accompanied by a substantial number of personal diaries, memoirs and oral histories on the civil war. The Japanese World War II admiral Takagi Sokichi once took a sceptical position towards the reliability of the official military records,[28] and his scepticism should not be overlooked. However, the use of personal diaries, narratives and memoirs in historical studies is not without problems for researchers. Some scholars therefore have based their research entirely on the documents of organisations and governments, on the basis that memoirs and diaries can often be misleading.[29] This book takes a more comprehensive approach and

---

26 See, for example, Zhonggong zhongyang wenxian yanjiushi and Zhongguo renmin jiefangjun junshi kexue yuan [PLA academy of military science] eds, *Mao Zedong junshi wenji* [Collected military papers of Mao Zedong] (Beijing: Junshi kexue chubanshe and Zongyang wenxian chubanshe, 1993) (hereafter *Junshi*); Zhonggong zhongyang wenxian yanjiushi ed., *Liu Shaoqi nianpu 1898–1969* [The chronological biography of Liu Shaoqi, 1898–1969] (Beijing: Zhongyang wenxian chubanshe, 1996) (hereafter *Liu nianpu*).
27 Zhongyang dang'anguan [Central party archives] ed., *Zhonggong zhongyang wenjian xuanji* [Selected documents of the Central Committee of the CCP] (Beijing: Zhongyang dangxiao chubanshe, 1989–92) (hereafter *Zhonggong*).
28 Hiroyuki Agawa, *The Reluctant Admiral: Yamamoto and the Imperial Navy*, trans. John Bester (Tokyo: Kodansha International, 1979), 365.
29 See, for example, Li Yuzhen, 'Chiang Kai-shek and Joseph Stalin during World War II', in *Negotiating China's Destiny in World War II*, ed. Hans Van de Ven, Diana Lary and Stephen MacKinnon (Stanford, CA: Stanford University Press, 2015), 141–55.

considers official records, along with personal diaries, memoirs and oral interview testimonies, as vital primary sources. Together, they form a useful set of cross-references.

Perhaps the most revealing source materials on the Chinese Civil War in the personal records are the personal archives—particularly the diary—of Chiang Kai-shek.[30] Many of the political and military leaders of modern China kept diaries, but they created this personal space in various ways. Some of them are just a concise record of events with very little personal feelings about or reflections on what had happened.[31] Chiang's personal diaries, which are located today at the Hoover Institution library at Stanford University, are quite different and stand out in their value. I spent many fruitful days at the Hoover Institution reading through them.

Chiang's voluminous diaries not only keep a record of events but also preserve substantial comments on planning and decision-making, analyses of his enemies and allies, and personal impressions of the occurrences recorded. Chiang was a meticulous diary keeper. The events he recorded and omitted from his diary have the power either to shape or to shade our historical understanding.[32] In many cases, Chiang used his diary to review incidents that had occurred months, years or even decades previously. As these diary entries were written with hindsight, Chiang's diary operates simultaneously as his memoir. Chiang did not write a diary to record the moment; he wrote it for meaning and insight. In this sense, the diary tells Chiang's version of a story of the world in which he was living, and he was determined to take possession of that world. The style of Chiang's diary makes for a captivating political biography.[33]

Making Chiang's diary even more interesting and challenging to historians, he compiled lengthy retrospection logs at weekly, monthly and yearly intervals over the period under study. Chiang's diary also includes a large collection of his written notes. Some of these pieces read more like full-length articles than random notes. The retrospective sections and fragmented pieces of handwriting gave Chiang more opportunity to judge the same

---

30 *Chiang Kai-shek Diaries, 1917–72*, Hoover Institution Archives, Stanford University (hereafter *Chiang Diary*).
31 See, for example, Pi Dingjun, *Pi Dingjun riji* [The diaries of Pi Dingjun] (Beijing: Jiefangjun chubanshe, 1986).
32 R. Keith Schoppa, 'Diaries as historical source: Goldmines and/or slippery slopes', *Chinese Historical Review* 17, no. 1 (2010): 31–6.
33 See, for example, Jay Taylor, *The Generalissimo: Chiang Kai-shek and the Struggle for Modern China* (Cambridge, MA: Belknap Press of Harvard University Press, 2009).

issue at several levels of consideration, but they also placed Chiang directly in a world of hindsight and outcome bias. Put simply, a diary entry might disclose Chiang's initial assessment of an incident right after it occurred, but a different opinion on the same matter might be noted in a retrospection log written a few days later after reflection.

Among the published source materials related to the Chinese Civil War, the recently published major events chronology of Chiang Kai-shek has been an underrated primary source.[34] It is a series about Chiang's personal, political and military life in mainland China from 1927 to 1949. It contains scans of the original handwritten manuscripts by Chiang's secretaries, comprising a miscellany of documents, including correspondence, telegrams and decrees in chronological order. Excerpts from Chiang's diaries constitute the narrative text structure.

The chronology's diary excerpts were heavily edited in order to construct a positive image of Chiang.[35] Nevertheless, it remains an important primary source for this book's research on a number of fronts. First, it retains a considerable number of telegrams and correspondence not available in Chiang's personal archives currently open to the public. The specificity of these documents gave the compilers of the chronology very little room to alter the original text.[36] The incoming telegrams preserved in the chronology are of particular value. Although some of the original/carbon copy drafts of these telegrams may still be found in other related archives, many are not fully dated and readers must refer to Chiang's chronology for the exact dates they were sent or received. Nevertheless, even a voluminous chronology is unable to fully cover the flurry of handwritten orders, letters and confidential cables that Chiang sent to his subordinates daily. Although a certain amount of this immense bundle of outgoing messages is preserved in Chiang's personal archives, many of these original documents were either undated or not fully dated. The contextualising words written by the compliers of Chiang's chronology therefore become a useful tool to verify these records.

---

34 *Jiang Zhongzheng zongtong dang'an: Shilüe gaoben* [The Chiang Kai-shek collections: The chronological events] (Taipei: Academia Historica, 2003–13), 82 vols and two supplementary vols to vols 40 and 42 published in 2015 (hereafter *Shilüe*).
35 Grace C. Huang, 'Creating a public face for posterity: The making of Chiang Kai-shek's Shilüe manuscripts', *Modern China* 36, no. 6 (2010): 617–43.
36 Ibid., 630.

Certain sentences in Chiang's original diaries subsequently were covered up by ink to conceal what he had written, and the current copies of the diaries received further redaction before being opened to public access. The redaction of Chiang's diaries makes the chronology a vital reference for Chiang's view of the respective historical incidents. Regarding the redaction of Chiang's diary and the extensive editing of his major events chronology, this book studies them against the backdrop of historical events and uses them in a more analytical manner, with reference to other historical documents.

While Chiang's diaries at Stanford are uniquely informative, I also secured valuable primary source materials, including handwritten diaries, through research in the archives at the Rare Book and Manuscript Library at Columbia University in New York. In addition, I found important information in the National Archives of the United States in College Park, Maryland; the Second Historical Archives of China in Nanjing; the archives of the Academia Historica and the Chinese National Army archives at the now defunct Bureau of Historical Compilation and Translation in Taipei.

Structure of the book

This book is not a chronological history of the Chinese Civil War. It is structured chronologically simply to ensure that the complex historical events are comprehensible to readers and that they can easily follow the unfolding historical events and understand how conclusions are drawn at the end of each chapter. To this end, the book's analytical paragraphs provide the necessary support for the accounts of historical events. Most of these analytical passages and comments are written with reference to (as discussed) current negotiation literature. To meet the above objectives, the book is organised into one introductory chapter, seven content chapters and one concluding chapter.

Chapter 1, 'Negotiating at an uneven table', is one of two chapters discussing the Nationalists' struggle to negotiate with the Soviets over Manchuria, which unfolded against the backdrop of the Anglo-American–Soviet secret deal at Yalta, the Soviet Red Army occupation of Manchuria and the end of World War II. The discussion centres on the Nationalists' negotiating behaviour in dealing with their stronger Russian opponents. Of particular interest here is the notion that a weak party enjoys fewer margins for error than a strong party in diplomatic negotiations. As Kenneth Waltz argues,

INTRODUCTION

the strong 'can do the same dumb things over again' and 'can hold back until the ambiguity of events is resolved without fearing that the moment for effective action will be lost'. In contrast, the weak party manoeuvres 'on narrow margins. Inopportune acts, flawed policies, and mistimed moves may have fatal results.'[37]

The chapter begins by looking at how the GMD government sacrificed key national interests in pursuit of a treaty of friendship with the Soviet Union in 1945. Notwithstanding the pragmatic origins of this appeasement policy, the Nationalists went on to clash with the Soviets at the treaty's implementation stage over the GMD government's military takeover of Manchuria from the Soviet Red Army, particularly the GMD's initial landing of troops at the Manchurian port of Dalian (Dairen). The chapter probes how contentious issues involving national pride and territorial sovereignty pushed the weak GMD government to drift from its accommodating negotiation strategy and stumble into an unwanted treaty dispute with the Soviet Union, one it had desperately sought to avoid at the outset.

Chapter 2, 'Rethinking the Chongqing negotiations',[38] rethinks what are perhaps the most important attempts at making peace in modern Chinese history: the first post-World War II peace talks convened in China's wartime capital Chongqing in autumn 1945 between the GMD and the CCP. Previous studies treated the American-sponsored peace conference as a sideshow to the subsequent full-blown civil war. Many scholars believe that the Chongqing negotiations were meaningless,[39] or, more precisely, that the peace talks are overrated and do not deserve historical prominence.[40] Maochun Yu remarks that both parties simply went 'for a reluctant and pretentious peace talk'.[41] Some believe that the leaders of both camps were pressured to prioritise military options; this implies that war became the dominant theme and that negotiations were of secondary importance.[42]

---

37 Kenneth N. Waltz, *Theory of International Politics* (Boston: McGraw-Hill, 1979), 194–5.
38 The chapter is revised from my journal article 'Rethinking the Chongqing negotiations of 1945: Concession-making, the trust/distrust paradox, and the biased mediator in China's post-war transitions', *Journal of Chinese Military History* 9 (Brill, 2020): 168–203.
39 O. Edmund Clubb, *Twentieth Century China*, 2nd edn (New York: Columbia University Press, 1972), 260; Theodore H. White and Annalee Jacoby, *Thunder Out of China*, 2nd edn (New York: William Sloane, 1961), 288.
40 Deng Ye, 'Lun Guogong Chongqing tanpan de zhengzhi xingzhi' [On the political nature of the Chongqing negotiations between the GMD and the CCP], *Jindaishi yanjiu* 1 (2005): 30–64.
41 Maochun Yu, *OSS in China: Prelude to Cold War* (New Haven, CT: Yale University Press, 1996), 240.
42 Christopher R. Lew, *The Third Chinese Revolutionary Civil War, 1945–49: An Analysis of Communist Strategy and Leadership* (New York: Routledge, 2009), 19; Wang Chaoguang, 'Zhan yu he'.

The focus of this chapter, however, is not the two belligerent parties' initial intent to enter talks but the interaction dynamics over the negotiating table that shaped the negotiation process of the Chongqing peace talks. The chapter's conclusions overturn previous scholars' preconceptions.

The chapter begins with a brief overview of the intertwined prior history of the two civil war rivals' on-going armed conflicts, peace initiatives and their fragile anti-Japanese alliance, from the late 1930s through to the end of World War II. The two antagonists engaged in comprehensive peace talks against the backdrop of these changing domestic and international environments. It finds that while the two parties fought each other fiercely on the battlefield, they adopted unsystematic piecemeal solutions to prevent the armed conflict from spreading and to avoid the complete breakdown of their wartime cooperation. Although the post–World War II race for territorial recovery between the two triggered a new bout of civil war, the chapter shows that a peace deal was needed for both parties in the post-war environment. Therefore the real challenge for the two belligerent sides and their American mediator during the peace talks in Chongqing was not securing peace in China once and for all. Rather, it was whether they could pick up where the two parties had left their awkward wartime alliance.

The core of the chapter examines hitherto unexplored aspects of the negotiations in Chongqing in 1945: the debates, disagreements and compromises, and the American mediator's attempt, from an inherently biased position, to alter the dynamics of the peace talks. It contends that the history of the Chongqing negotiations, although they lasted only six weeks, is more important to our understanding of China's struggle between peace and war in the post–World War II era than previously acknowledged.

The two belligerent parties reached an interim peace accord in October 1945 at the end of the Chongqing negotiations, and agreed to continue negotiations to find a more permanent resolution. Both sides seemed eager to prove that negotiations could still proceed even as fighting continued, particularly in the region the treaty did not mention: Manchuria. Chapter 3, 'The civil war in the north-east', focuses on the race between the two belligerents to repossess Manchuria. It investigates the military decision-making of both parties when they met on the battlefield, in a region where troop deployment proved logistically challenging. It reconsiders two common beliefs about the onset of the Chinese Civil War. Some believe that if Chiang had not gambled his best troops in Manchuria but had rather sent them to the North China battlefield at the outset, the Nationalists' debacle in China could have been avoided.[43] Others argue that had Chiang driven his armies to Manchuria more quickly, they would have fared more successfully.[44] This chapter addresses important and hitherto unstudied military documents and finds that both beliefs about Chiang's decision-making in 1946 are moot points: the Nationalist strategists and their American advisers had already thoroughly debated and decided on the best military strategy for the GMD in Manchuria in 1945.

A second popular notion emerges from previous studies' rather loose use of the term 'decisive war' in attempts to offer a parsimonious explanation of the CCP's civil war strategy.[45] Claims have been made that Mao tried to push his armies to conjure up 'a single, climactic decisive battle'[46] against Chiang's elite corps in Manchuria in the winter of 1945, which some believe represented a turning point in Mao's military thought.[47] This chapter explores the contradictory role of political leaders in war management and contends that while Mao was not a perfect military planner, he did not order his armies to launch a final decisive battle against the Nationalists' US-armed armies during that period. Although Mao used the phrase 'decisive battle' in his proclamations, this was merely political rhetoric designed to construct an atmosphere of optimism at the beginning of the war.

Chapter 4, 'A shattered peace', probes the much-discussed yet little-understood mission of General George C. Marshall of the US Army to mediate an end to the Chinese Civil War. Previous studies have treated the mission and the ambiguous agreements it endorsed as manifest failures. One widely held assumption among scholars has been that Marshall's effort to mediate the end of the Chinese Civil War was doomed to failure from the start due to ill-formulated targets at the mission's outset. The US support of

---

43 See, for example, Arthur Waldron, 'China without tears: If Chiang Kai-shek hadn't gambled in 1946', in *What If? The World's Foremost Military Historians Imagine What Might Have Been*, ed. Robert Cowley (London: Macmillan, 2000), 377–91.
44 Wang Chaoguang, 'Guogong neizhan chuqi de Dongbei zhanchang yu Jiang Jieshi de junshi jueche' [The Manchurian theatre in the initial stage of the Chinese Civil War and the military decision-making of Jiang Jieshi], in *Jiang Zhongzheng riji yu minguo shi yanjiu* [Jiang Jieshi's diaries and the study of Republican Chinese history], ed. Lü Fangshang (Taipei: Shijie datong, 2011), 530–2.
45 Victor Shiu Chiang Cheng, 'Imagining China's Madrid in Manchuria: The Communist military strategy at the onset of the Chinese civil war, 1945–1946', *Modern China* 31, no. 1 (2005): 72–114; Shiu Chiang Cheng, 'The escalation of hostilities in Manchuria, 1945–47: A study of strategic realities and normative guidelines in military conflict in the context of the Chinese Civil War' (PhD diss., University of Melbourne, 2002).
46 Harold M. Tanner, *The Battle for Manchuria and the Fate of China: Spring, 1946* (Bloomington, IN: Indiana University Press, 2013), 67.
47 Lew, *Chinese Revolutionary Civil War*, 30.

the Nationalist regime via military aid, the attempt to induce a GMD–CCP reconciliation for a democratic government and the reluctance of military involvement in support of American policy objectives in China were shown to be self-contradictory and untenable.[48] It is also believed that the deterioration of relations between the Soviet Union and the United States at that time did more to hasten the collapse of the mission.[49] Even those who do not believe that the failure of the Marshall mission was predetermined argue that the collapse of the mission lived on in Truman's pre-set policy choices on China.[50] The criticisms about Marshall's failure are merited in the realm of foreign policy studies, but they all face 'the danger of ascribing greater consistency and internal cohesiveness to a policy than it may actually have had'.[51] As Tang Tsou admitted, many of these hypotheses can be neither proved nor disproved.[52]

Three distinctive aspects set this chapter apart from the existing literature. First, it explores the interplay between Marshall and his Chinese counterparts at the negotiating table. Second, the chapter studies Marshall's attempt to use his biased mediating stance as leverage in his push for agreements and the two biggest threats he faced: the propensity of the belligerent parties to want to get a bigger piece of the post-conflict pie at gunpoint, and discontent over the implementation of ambiguous agreements. Third, the chapter studies the Political Consultative Conference—a multiparty peace forum that Marshall did not intend to involve—and the ambiguous resolutions it adopted. The chapter contends that the ambiguously written agreements made it possible for a compromise resolution to the conflicting interests of the CCP and the GMD. Ambiguous treaties are not uncommon in peace negotiations, but the chapter highlights the significance of continuing efforts from all signatory parties to build a cooperative post-treaty relationship by eliminating the possibility of exploiting ambiguities within the agreements for partisan purposes.

---

48   Tsou, *America's Failure in China*, 349–440. Also, Wang Chen-main, 'Marshall's approach to the mediation effort', and Zhang Suchu, 'Why Marshall's mission failed', in *George C. Marshall's Mediation Mission to China, December 1945–January 1947*, ed. Larry I. Bland (Lexington, VA: George C. Marshall Foundation, 1998), 21–43, 45–62.
49   Daniel Kurtz-Phelan, *The China Mission: George Marshall's Unfinished War, 1945–1947* (New York: W.W. Norton, 2018), 295.
50   Qing, *From Allies to Enemies*, 57–62, 88–94.
51   Levine, 'Soviet–American rivalry', 25.
52   Tsou, *America's Failure in China*, 398–400.

While China was experiencing a troubling escalation of GMD–CCP military conflict in the north-east, the GMD leaders had a fight on their hands over the dispute with the Soviets regarding the possession of former Japanese industrial assets, minerals and energy resources in Manchuria. The Soviets were dismantling these and sending them to the USSR. The disagreement was a moot question that had no direct bearing on the issues being discussed during the treaty of friendship negotiations between the two governments. However, it initiated a dangerous slide towards a new round of disputes in the backdrop of the GMD–Soviet political tussle over Dalian. The Soviets regarded all enemy assets as war booty of the USSR's Red Army, but the Nationalists claimed the wholesale confiscation of Japanese-owned properties as war reparations to China. As will be observed, the Soviets offered, amid a negotiating stalemate, to negotiate an exclusive joint venture enterprise in cooperation with China for all major Manchurian industries and mines.

Chapter 5, 'Planting radishes in the desert', continues to explore the Nationalists' experience against the stronger Soviet opponents at the uneven negotiating table: their disagreement with the Soviets over former Japanese factories and other Japanese assets in Manchuria that the Soviets were dismantling and shipping to Russia, which sparked a dangerous slide towards a new round of disputes. Previous studies have argued that the Soviet Union was fundamentally hostile towards the Chinese Nationalist government and hinted that what Moscow actually sought was to establish neo-colonialist economic domination over this key Chinese region.[53] This chapter tells an entirely different story. The Soviets were unwilling to escalate the conflict even when facing the Nationalists' hostile acts, and Moscow was evidently less interested in rolling the dice to determine war. The chapter examines the transitional arrangements hatched by the GMD leaders that attempted to break the impasse, particularly Chiang's intriguing multi-billion GMD government-issued Circulating Currency for the Nine Provinces of the North-East (*Dongbei jiusheng liutong quan* 東北九省流通券) cash pay-out plan, ignored by existing scholarship. Analysing hitherto little studied historical records, the chapter shows that the dispute's complexity was greater than it appeared and that elements of common interest for an economic joint-venture deal between the two disputants were never beyond reach.

---

53 Ibid., 338.

Without workable post-treaty relations with the Soviet Union, the GMD forces failed to secure a cooperative takeover from the withdrawing Soviet forces in Manchuria. The CCP captured Manchurian cities along the main railway with ease, including the transportation hub of Sipingjie. When Chiang sent his elite corps to capture the city, the two warring parties clashed in the first major battle of the Chinese Civil War. The civil war in Manchuria, fought on the cusp of spring and summer in 1946, has long attracted attention from scholars and writers alike. It fascinates many, in part because the Chinese Communists seemed to be moving away from their signature mobile guerrilla warfare strategies, instead massing troops in positional warfare during this period. By the time their success seemed unlikely, Mao ordered his troops to make a protracted defence of Sipingjie, citing the Republicans' defence of Madrid during the Spanish Civil War of 1936–39 as a parallel to the Chinese struggle. Chiang, on the other hand, mobilised his best troops in a bid to wipe out the enemy and take control of large cities along the main rail transport artery. Both Mao's vision and Chiang's military gamble were, however, negated by reality. The battle concluded in May 1946, but this was an anti-climax. While Mao's forces staged a morale-sapping withdrawal after suffering disproportionate casualties, Chiang's crack troops not only failed to eliminate the enemy's main forces but were also stretched painfully thin.

A thriving scholarly literature on the 1946 battle of Sipingjie has emerged in recent years. Although some consider the battle a missed opportunity for the GMD to completely eliminate the CCP's Manchurian field forces,[54] a number of analysts have studied the battle from the perspective of the CCP leadership's decision-making. Some believe the battle was just a miscalculation of the CCP leaders in their decision-making, but some severely criticise Mao's enthusiasm for following Moscow's instructions.[55] Alternatively, some blame Mao's field commander Lin Biao for his command failures[56] and for clouding Mao's judgement,[57] and argue otherwise: that the battle was fought under 'unique' political and historical conditions, exonerating Mao for its

---

54   Cheng, 'China's Madrid', 75.
55   See, for example, Bai Xianyong and Liao Yanbo, *Beihuan lihe sishi nian: Bai Chongxi yu Jiang Jieshi* [Forty years of sorrow and joy: Bai Chongxi and Chiang Kai-shek] (Taipei: Shibao Chuban, 2020), vol. 2, 29–75.
56   Westad, *Decisive Encounters*, 40; Michael M. Sheng, *Battling Western Imperialism: Mao, Stalin, and the United States* (Princeton, NJ: Princeton University Press, 1997), 130–4.
57   Yang Kuisong, 'Yijiusiliu nian Guo-Gong Siping zhi zhan ji qi muhou' [The KMT–Communist battle at Sipingjie in 1946: Behind the scenes], *Lishi yanjiu* [Historical research] 4 (2004): 149.

failure.⁵⁸ A synthesis study finds that a number of normative and material factors, as highlighted by Mao's 'Madrid' analogy, had led to an increased acceptance of risk among the CCP leaders at the onset of the Chinese Civil War.⁵⁹ Recent research on the battle of Sipingjie emphasises the significance of a symbolic 'Madrid' in Mao's strategic behaviour.⁶⁰

Chapter 6, 'China's Madrid', studies the transition from the breakdown of ceasefire negotiations to the escalation in fighting in Manchuria. It brings a new perspective to the battle of Sipingjie, against the backdrop of the loss of prestige of the US-sponsored truce supervision system. It demonstrates, for instance, that Mao's strategy in this period shifted from the paradigm of offensive accommodation to a defensive accommodation mode of warfare, and a plan for defending the status quo, before moving into a quasi-withdrawal appeasement approach. Chiang, on the other hand, relied on an ultra-conservative war plan merely to exert symbols of power for his government in Manchuria. The events in Manchuria suggest that the GMD was incapable of winning a full-blown civil war against the CCP, but Chiang's tough stance proved to be an obstacle for Marshall's continued efforts to broker a political settlement.

Chapter 7, 'Towards an all-out civil war', starts in mid-1946 when the escalation of military confrontations finally drove China into a full-scale civil war. It examines the growing scepticism of the two belligerent parties regarding prospects for the peace talks, which helped to ensure that the fighting quickly developed into an unlimited civil war. In examining some of the most brutal battles of this period, which tore off the ideological masks of the two armed factions and revealed their military core, this chapter discusses how leaders of both warring parties and their American mediators were almost simultaneously held hostage by the war. Studying the US arms embargo, designed to curb Chiang's military ambitions, the chapter contends that no single country in the post-war Western bloc could prop up the Nationalists' huge army.

---

58 Hu Zhefeng, 'Shilun Siping baoweizhan zhong de Mao Zedong yu Lin Biao' [Mao Zedong and Lin Biao in the battle of defence of Sipingjie: An elaboration], *Junshi lishi yanjiu* [Military history studies] 4 (1996): 1–12.
59 Deng Ye, 'Dongbei wenti yu Siping juezhan' [The question of north-east China and the decisive battle at Sipingjie], *Lishi yanjiu* 4 (2001): 57–71; Chen Lian, 'Jiefang zhanzheng guodu jieduan Zhonggong zhongyang lüequ Dongbei de zhanlüe fangzhen yu bushu' [The strategic principle and disposition of the Central Committee of the Communist Party of China on capturing the north-east in the transition period of the War of Liberation], *Junshi lishi* [Military history] 2 (2002): 53–7.
60 Cheng, 'China's Madrid'.

When the collapse of the negotiations seemed imminent, minor parties across China's left–right political spectrum formed a coalition, entering the peace talks as messengers of peace in the dying days of Marshall's mediation mission in late 1946. The coalition's plea for peace was unavailing. Previous studies of the group's mediation efforts attribute its failure to influence the negotiation outcome to the internal weaknesses of the group regarding certain issues, including the motivations behind their prioritisation of their own interests, a lack of mass public support, and military power.[61] This chapter refers to a renewed 'veto players' concept, initially developed for analysing political institutions in the study of multiparty bargaining in civil wars. It treats the coalition as un-armed legitimate signatories of the resolutions adopted by the Political Consultative Conference, whereas the two heavily armed major parties, who possessed military power strong enough to veto peace accords unilaterally and fight again, were the only two 'veto players' in the Chinese Civil War.[62] The final mediating efforts by the minor parties were cut short by the intense political manoeuvring of the two major parties. The chapter examines the difficulties in accommodating the political and military ambitions of the two major parties to the multiparty bargaining environment and shows how these obstacles motivated them to plunge deeper into all-out war.

The final chapter, 'Conclusion', summarises the themes that have emerged in the book and explores the book's main arguments in further detail.

---

61 Tanner, *The Battle for Manchuria*, 8, 143, 177.
62 Roger B. Jeans, 'Last chance for peace: Zhang Junmai (Carsun Chang) and third-party mediation in the Chinese Civil War, October 1946', in *Marshall's Mediation Mission*, ed. Bland, 293–325; Lloyd E. Eastman, 'China's democratic parties and the temptations of political power, 1946–1947', in *Roads Not Taken: The Struggle of Opposition Parties in Twentieth-Century China*, ed. Roger B. Jeans (Boulder, CO: Westview Press, 1992), 189–99.

1

Negotiating at an uneven table

National pride, sovereignty and the Sino-Soviet dispute over Dalian

In the mid-1960s, during a private chat with Beijing's deputy mayor Wu Han, Mao staunchly defended his arch-rival Chiang Kai-shek against criticism by recognising that Chiang's insistence on the indivisibility of China against foreign encroachments had contributed to China's national integrity. It was quite exceptional for Mao to speak out in support of Chiang. This only lends weight to Guy Alitto's observation that even 'the most fervent of the reputable vilifiers' against Chiang have to recognise Chiang as one of the foremost promoters of China's political independence and territorial integrity.[1]

As Chiang's brother-in-law Song Ziwen (T.V. Soong) confided to Stalin during their treaty negotiations in 1945, the GMD itself had created the all-pervasive nationalist climate in China. The Chinese people had been imbued with the idea of territorial integrity since the time of GMD's founding father Sun Yat-sen, which made it extremely difficult for leaders like Song to abandon the moral high ground in international negotiations.[2] GMD leaders had been relentless, riding a tiger of their own creation since

---

1   Li Zhisui, *The Private Life of Chairman Mao: The Memoirs of Mao's Personal Physician*, trans. Hung-chao Tai (London: Random House, 1994), 441; Guy Alitto, 'Chiang Kai-shek in Western Historiography', in *Proceedings of Conference on Chiang Kai-shek and Modern China*, ed. Compilation Committee of Proceedings of Conference on Chiang Kai-shek and Modern China (Taipei: China Culture Service, 1987), 1: 725.
2   Record of Stalin–Song meeting, 2 July 1945, *T.V. Soong Papers*, Hoover Institution Archives, Stanford University, Folder 3, Box 63.

the 1920s: simultaneously exploiting mass nationalism, turning it into an anti-imperialist groundswell against foreign interests while forging ties with foreign powers to fulfil a 'nation-state-building impulse'.[3] History seems to endorse this view. Following Japan's invasion of Manchuria and the creation of the Manchukuo puppet state in 1932, Chiang's regime had pursued peace with the Japanese via a series of treaties unfavourable to China.[4] Chiang's method of prioritising the counterinsurgency against their domestic Communist enemy over fighting Japan's aggression was like introducing a Trojan horse into his regime. His overall policy regarding Japan was vehemently criticised, both domestically and internationally, for being weak.[5] In 1936, Chiang was kidnapped at Xi'an by two of his own generals, who forced him to acknowledge national sentiment and terminate the anti-Communist campaign, in support of an anti-Japanese united front with the CCP. Although Chiang's negotiators had held talks with the Chinese Communists for an anti-Japanese alliance before the mutiny, the Xi'an Incident prompted changes in the GMD's wartime foreign and domestic policy alignments, paving the way for total war against Japan from 1937 to 1945.[6]

The GMD's policy during the post-war Sino-Soviet negotiations over Manchuria deserves attention here. In August 1945, during the closing days of World War II, the GMD signed a friendship treaty with the Soviet Union, under the framework of an Anglo-American–Soviet secret deal, at Yalta. In a bid to secure post-war reclamation of the territory, the Nationalists yielded to Soviet demands to concede Outer Mongolia and some vital Chinese interests in Manchuria. Despite the treaty, GMD leaders proceeded to clash with the Soviets in the immediate aftermath of the Allied victory over Japan. The origins of the dispute lay in the re-establishment of Chinese sovereignty over Manchuria, in particular over the Nationalists' plan to land troops at the strategic seaport of Dalian. Disagreement over Dalian, as well as the extent and manner of Sino-Soviet economic cooperation in Manchuria, soon developed into a stalemate between China and the Soviet Union. This eventually resulted in the GMD losing the race against the CCP to recover Manchuria.

---

3   Michael G. Murdock, 'Exploiting anti-imperialism: Popular forces and nation-state-building during China's northern expedition, 1926–1927', *Modern China* 35, no. 1 (2009): 70.
4   So Wai Chor, 'The making of the Guomindang's Japan policy, 1932–1937: The role of Chiang Kai-shek and Wang Jingwei', *Modern China* 28, no. 2 (2002): 213–52.
5   David Scott, *China and the International System, 1840–1949: Power, Presence, and Perceptions in a Century of Humiliation* (Albany, NY: State University of New York Press, 2008), 244–6.
6   Hans van de Ven, *China at War: Triumph and Tragedy in the Emergence of the New China, 1937–1952* (London: Profile Books, 2017), 60–4.

The dispute over Dalian has been viewed from a 'US–GMD versus Soviet–CCP' dichotomy: Chiang's insistence on sending his armies to Dalian was deliberately aimed at pleasing the Americans, who wished to break the Soviet stranglehold on the port.[7] Arne Westad, who believes that Chiang clashed with the Soviets over Dalian for American support, also argues that the GMD leader's deal with Stalin was an act of political expediency and that Chiang was too shrewd a politician to be taken in by either the Americans or the Soviets without weaving in his own foreign policy. In dealing with the Soviets during the treaty negotiations in July and August 1945, Chiang was aware that Washington would favour its own interests: China had to decide its own foreign policy even if Chiang had been reporting to Washington on progress at the negotiating table.[8] Chiang's skill in dealing with the Great Powers (i.e. the US and USSR) has been widely recognised, and some even argue that Chiang was motivated solely by rational–strategic interests regarding policy choices.[9]

So how did a perspicacious leader like Chiang allow a disagreement (one that emerged only after the signing of the treaty) to throw GMD–Soviet relations off course, ultimately scuttling his bid for a favourable post-war arrangement over Manchuria? This chapter tracks the policies and decisions of the GMD leaders and the negotiating behaviour of the GMD interlocutors. It argues that it was national pride and sovereignty, rather than the interplay of Great Power politics *per se*, that foiled Chiang's plans for reclaiming north-east China.

The Sino-Soviet Treaty

China acquired Great Power status under US auspices during the Allied summits in 1943.[10] However, when the United States sought Soviet entry into the Pacific War, China was excluded from the Yalta Conference in February 1945, where the United States, Britain and USSR secretly agreed that the Soviet Union would enter the war against Japan. In return, the Soviets received tacit approval from the Americans and British to, among

---

7   Westad, *Cold War and Revolution*, 112.
8   Ibid., 46–8, 56.
9   Taylor, *Generalissimo, passim*; John W. Garver, *Chinese–Soviet Relations, 1937–1945: The Diplomacy of Chinese Nationalism* (New York: Oxford University Press, 1988), 228–9, 271; Li Yuzhen, 'Chiang Kai-shek and Joseph Stalin', 142.
10 Scott, *China and the International System*, 268–74; Wilson D. Miscamble, *From Roosevelt to Truman: Potsdam, Hiroshima, and the Cold War* (Cambridge, NY: Cambridge University Press, 2007), 267.

other interests in the North Pacific, gain control over Manchurian railways and major ports and a nominally independent Outer Mongolia. The agreement was made without Chiang's knowledge, but Chiang, who was supreme allied commander in China, would be compelled to go along with it.[11]

Chiang felt that the best available foreign policy option for China under the circumstances was to maintain the policy of non-involvement in the face of Soviet–US rivalry. Chiang hoped that this policy would buy him two to three years to unify China before the Soviets turned to support the CCP.[12] Accordingly, in late June 1945, Chiang sent a delegation led by premier-cum-foreign minister Song Ziwen to Moscow to negotiate a friendship treaty with the Soviet Union. The negotiations dragged on into August. On 8 August, the USSR declared war on Japan and launched the Red Army's invasion of Manchuria.[13] A massive Soviet force invaded Manchuria and rapidly overran China's north-east. They succeeded in forcing the Japanese troops to capitulate, thus bringing the Pacific War to a swift end on 15 August, precipitating Japan's unconditional surrender.[14] The following paragraphs will prove that Chiang had been hoping for this war even before World War II.

The Soviet invasion of Manchuria forced the GMD negotiators to seek an early agreement before Manchuria was completely overrun by the Red Army. The prospect of not reaching a deal with the Soviets was politically unacceptable for the Nationalists, although the Soviets also were equally insistent that the treaty be signed quickly.[15] Exploiting Soviet leverage to the fullest, Stalin and his foreign minister Molotov were able to persuade Song and his associates of the deal's value, thereby softening the GMD's bargaining stance. Stalin adeptly set the stage, making Song haggle intensely for every concession he made. This gave Chinese negotiators the

---

11 For the full text of the agreement, see 'Yalta Agreement on the Kuriles: Text of the agreement', *Department of State Bulletin* 14, no. 347 (1946): 282–3. On the Yalta Agreement, see Fraser J. Harbutt, *Yalta 1945: Europe and America at the Crossroads* (New York: Cambridge University Press, 2010), 299; Taylor, *Generalissimo*, 300–1; Westad, *Cold War and Revolution*, 28–30; Steven I. Levine, *Anvil of Victory: The Communist Revolution in Manchuria, 1945–1948* (New York: Columbia University Press, 1987), 29.
12 *Chiang Diary*, 28 July 1945, Chiang's handwritten notes, Folder 1, Box 44.
13 Wang Shijie, *Wang Shijie riji* [The diary of Dr Wang Shih-chieh] (Taipei: Academia Sinica, 1990), 8 August 1945, 5: 143–5 (hereafter *Wang riji*); Taylor, *Generalissimo*, 314.
14 Nakayama Takashi, *Manshū, 1945.8.9. Sorengun shinkō to Nihongun* [Manchuria, 9 August 1945: The Red Army against the Japanese forces] (Tokyo: Kokusho kankokai, 1990), 34.
15 Xiong's diary, 8, 10–14 August 1945, *Hsiung Shih-hui Papers*, Rare Book and Manuscript Library, Columbia University, Box 13, portfolio 2: Diaries, 1943–1946, Microfilm Reel #95–2031 (hereafter *Xiong Papers*); *Wang riji*, 6–14 August 1945, 5: 141–52; Westad, *Cold War and Revolution*, 38–42.

impression that some Soviet concessions were more valuable than they actually were. For instance, Song accepted Stalin's support for a Chinese civil administration in Dalian as a major Soviet concession.[16]

During the Moscow talks, Stalin also made several verbal promises, such as maintaining a no-arms-supply policy to the CCP and banning cross-border firearm sales to the Muslim rebels in Xinjiang.[17] Notably, however, the final text of the treaty did not contain any of these assurances. Some treaty clauses were too vague to signify a clear and unambiguous agreement. Jay Taylor argues that the ambiguous wording of the Soviet pledge to support the Nationalist government posed a particular problem for treaty implementation.[18] However, recent studies of international political agreements have found that ambiguous treaties are not uncommon; this is because negotiators often need to determine a settlement through a maze of conflicting interests between the disputing parties. In ratifying an ambiguous agreement, political leaders need the courage to achieve a mutually acceptable interpretation of the agreement in the implementation stage, rather than blaming ambiguous wording in treaty clauses for implementation failures.[19] Chiang might not have had the foresight of modern negotiation analysts, but he was pleased with the outcome. He knew that the most important concession he had made—the independence of Outer Mongolia—conflicted ideologically with the GMD's reunification goal.[20] However, as he confided to his foreign-minister-in-waiting, Wang Shijie, the disagreement over Mongolia 'was not worth the misgivings'.[21]

First, the former northern region of China had been under Soviet control since the 1920s and had proclaimed separate statehood as the Mongolian People's Republic (MPR) in 1924. The ties between the two nations were further strengthened in 1936 when Moscow and Ulan Bator signed a ten-year mutual assistance pact, paving the way for the MPR's complete

---

16 *Wang riji*, 10 August 1945, 5: 147–8; Garver, *Chinese–Soviet Relations*, 226; Westad, *Cold War and Revolution*, 42, 51, 193–4, fn. 78.
17 Record of Stalin–Song meeting, 9 July 1945, *T.V. Soong Papers*, Folder 3, Box 63; *Wang riji*, 11 July 1945, 5: 120–1.
18 Taylor, *Generalissimo*, 314.
19 Dražen Pehar, 'Use of ambiguities in peace agreements', in *Language and Diplomacy*, ed. Jovan Kurbalija and Hannah Slavik (Msida: DiploProjects, 2001). Chapter 4 offers further discussion of the role of ambiguous agreements in conflict transformation.
20 Westad, *Cold War and Revolution*, 40.
21 Quotation translated from *Wang riji*, 25 July 1945, 5: 130–1. For the Song–Stalin negotiations over the Mongolian issue, see meeting records, 2, 7 and 9 July 1945, *T.V. Soong Papers*, Folder 3, Box 63.

Sovietisation.²² Second, before World War II, Chiang had recognised that Soviet control of the MPR was not entirely against China's national interests as it offered a counterbalance to Japanese aggression. He believed that Moscow's hegemony over the MPR's affairs would ultimately lead it to wage war with Japan. For Chiang, a Soviet–Japanese war could open a window of opportunity from which he might benefit; additionally, it would be a disaster for China if the Soviet Union and Japan delayed war against each other. Chiang held to his judgement throughout World War II, even though he might not have thought that war between Japan and the USSR would finally break out in August 1945.²³ Hence, during the 1945 Moscow negotiations, although Chiang was sensitive to popular nationalist sentiment over Outer Mongolia, he was willing to recognise its independence.²⁴

In the Nationalists' political calculations, the worst-case scenario was a Soviet occupation of Manchuria *without* any prior agreement. The GMD leaders thought that a formal treaty with the Soviets would legally restrain the USSR from normalising relations with the CCP, keeping the GMD's programs of quelling the Communists and Manchuria's recovery on course.²⁵ The GMD leadership's strategy during the Moscow talks was 'to pursue the possible, rather than the preferred'.²⁶

Nevertheless, the GMD's leaders had no desire to be linked to the calumny of forfeiting China's sovereign rights in a humiliating treaty.²⁷ In the midst of the negotiations, Song desperately sought another leader with whom to share the blame. Chiang turned to Wang Shijie, head of the Central Propaganda Department, coaxing him to replace his lead negotiator Song as foreign minister and sending him to join Song at the final stage of the Moscow talks. Chiang cloaked his moves in the façade of a cabinet reshuffle

---

22 Sharad K. Soni, *Mongolia–China Relations: Modern and Contemporary Times* (New Delhi: Pentagon Press, 2006), 90, 97; Elena Boikova, 'Aspects of Soviet–Mongolian relations, 1929–1939', in *Mongolia in the Twentieth Century: Landlocked Cosmopolitan*, ed. Stephen Kotkin and Bruce A. Elleman (Armonk, NY: M.E. Sharpe, 1999), 114–15.
23 *Shilüe*, 1 April and 2 May 1936, 36: 222–5, 501; *Chiang Diary*, 7 April 1936, Folder 12, Box 38; 31 July 1943, Folder 6, Box 43.
24 Garver, *Chinese–Soviet Relations*, 229; *Chiang Diary*, the retrospection log after entry 7 July 1945, Folder 8, Box 44.
25 *Wang riji*, 4–5 August 1945, 5: 138–41.
26 Janice Gross Stein uses this phrase in 'Prenegotiation in the Arab–Israeli conflict: The paradoxes of success and failure', in *Getting to the Table: The Process of International Prenegotiation*, ed. Janice Gross Stein (Baltimore, MD: Johns Hopkins University Press, 1989), 191.
27 Hurley to Truman and Byrnes, 20 July 1945, in *The Conference of Berlin (The Potsdam Conference), 1945*, US Department of State (Washington, DC: Government Printing Office, 1960), 2: 1225–7.

designed to place Wang in the front line.[28] Wang was thus dragooned into representing the GMD to sign a treaty with unfavourable terms dictated by Stalin and accepted by Song and Chiang. The Nationalists calculated that the treaty could lead to post-war cooperation with the Soviets, if it did not attract overwhelming domestic criticism and if the Soviets reciprocated Chiang's sweeping concessions. Wang noted that if Chinese public opinion turned against the USSR over the treaty, the Sino-Soviet relationship could be thrown off course and the GMD would be forced to accept a one-sided deal.[29] In contrast, Song seemed to believe in the adage that the real negotiations would only begin once the treaty was signed. During the final stage of the Moscow talks, Song used the prophetic phrase 'a life sentence', hinting to his fellow delegate Xiong Shihui (widely tipped as Chiang's favourite to be the new chief executive of Manchuria working with the Soviets on treaty implementation) about the difficulties ahead regarding negotiations with the Soviets.[30]

The negotiations were completed on 14 August 1945 when both sides signed the China, Soviet Union Treaty of Friendship and Alliance (hereafter the Sino-Soviet Treaty). As Chiang had authorised Song to concede to Soviet demands,[31] the treaty was constructed within the framework of Yalta and formulated very much on Soviet terms.[32] Stalin thus emerged victorious by securing GMD recognition of Outer Mongolia's independence and the primacy of Soviet interests in Manchuria. These interests included control of Lüshun as a naval base, opening Dalian as a commercial free port, and joint Sino-Soviet ownership and operation of the Chinese Changchun Railway. In contrast, the GMD received nothing tangible in return, essentially obtaining a Soviet pledge of support and respect for China's full sovereignty over Manchuria.[33]

The recovery of Manchuria thus became the key component of the GMD's post-war strategy. Internationally, the GMD needed to prove it was capable of protecting China's sovereign rights.[34] Domestically, the GMD was facing

---

28   *Wang riji*, 24–25, 27–31 July 1945, 5: 129–39; Jiang Yongjing, 'Cong Wang Shijie riji kan Zhongsu mengyue de qianding' [The Sino-Soviet treaty in perspective: The diaries of Wang Shijie], *Zhuanji wenxue* [Biographical Literature] (Taipei) 56, no. 6 (1990): 29–36.
29   *Wang riji*, 24–25, 27–31 July, 1 and 4 August 1945, 5: 129–39.
30   Xiong's diary, 8 August 1945, *Xiong Papers*, Box 13, portfolio 2.
31   Chiang Kai-shek to Song and Wang Shijie, 13 August 1945, *Zhonghua Minguo*, 3, book 2: 649.
32   Levine, *Anvil of Victory*, 29–31.
33   'Sino-Soviet Treaty of Friendship and Alliance: Treaty of Friendship and Alliance between the Republic of China and the USSR', *Department of State Bulletin* 14, no. 345 (1946): 201–8.
34   Westad, *Cold War and Revolution*, 16.

a strong challenge from the CCP to recover Manchuria. As will be discussed further in the following chapters, the GMD and the CCP had formed an uncomfortable wartime alliance in 1937. While conducting the war against Japan together, these two armed forces clashed under the banner of a 'United Front', with heightened tensions between the two parties towards the end of World War II. The CCP started a race against the GMD for the recovery of Manchuria immediately after the Soviet incursion in August 1945. This was done by deploying a substantial number of troops to the north-east. Chiang urgently needed to control Manchuria to stop the CCP from collaborating with the Soviets and extending its base into the north-east. Manchuria had become the destination of Chiang's nationalist revolution.[35]

Dispute over Dalian

The most direct way for the GMD to reclaim Manchuria was to negotiate with the Soviets to take the entire region from the Red Army. A new GMD organisation, the North-East Headquarters (NEHQ) of the Military Affairs Commission, was established by the end of August 1945 for this purpose.[36] The NEHQ's key positions were drawn from influential figures in the GMD government: Xiong Shihui, Zhang Jia'ao and Chiang Ching-kuo.

Xiong was appointed director of the NEHQ and concurrently chairman of its Political Affairs Commission, making him the GMD's top bureaucrat and later chief negotiator with the Soviets in Manchuria. Xiong was Chiang's long-time military and political associate and was in charge of post-war reconstruction. Xiong's experience in international negotiations came largely from his appointment in 1942 as chief of a Chinese military mission to the United States—a GMD lobby group sent to Washington to obtain American aid.[37] During his tenure in the United States, Xiong expressed indignation over what he perceived as his American counterparts' discriminatory attitude towards the Chinese.[38] At times, Xiong found it

---

35   Chiang's speech delivered on 18 September 1945, *Zhonghua Minguo*, 7, book 1: 69–74.
36   *Guomin zhengfu zhuxi Dongbei Xingyuan gongzuo baogao* [The Nationalist government chairman's report: The North-east Headquarters] (n.p., March 1947), 2–4.
37   See Yu Ying-shih's preface in *Haisangji: Xiong Shihui huiyilu, 1907–1949* [An insider's account of modern Chinese history: Memoirs of governor and general Hsiung Shih-Hui, 1907–1949], Xiong Shihui, ed. Hong Chaohui (New York: Mirror Books, 2008), 9–21; Howard L. Boorman ed., *Biographical Dictionary of Republican China* (New York: Columbia University Press, 1967–79), 2: 112–16.
38   Xiong's diary, 1 August 1942, *Xiong Papers*, Box 13, portfolio 1: Diaries, 1930–1942, Microfilm Reel #2006–1010.

difficult to manage the conflicting demands of defending national pride and depersonalising petty issues in order to establish good working relationships with the Americans. As an example, in September 1942, when Xiong visited American politician Wendell Willkie in New York, he stormed out of the latter's office even before the meeting started because he believed that Willkie had failed to practise proper etiquette. This later proved to be nothing other than a simple misunderstanding.[39] As mentioned, Xiong had been part of the GMD delegation in Moscow for the Sino-Soviet treaty negotiations, although he had not participated in the actual negotiations and was received coldly by Soviet officials.[40] Later, in a more combustible context, Xiong's testiness with his international counterparts caused friction at the negotiating table.

Zhang Jia'ao, a leading banker and economist, was appointed chairman of NEHQ's Economic Affairs Commission. Zhang had a successful record of representing the GMD government in negotiating with foreign interests during the 1930s. However, given that Zhang had only held junior-level ministerial positions in Chiang's cabinet—and his brother Zhang Junmai (Carsun Zhang) was the co-founder of China's political third force (the China Democratic League)—he was certainly not one of Chiang's cronies. Rather, Zhang was someone over whom Chiang tried to exert some control, due to Zhang's influential position in China's finance and banking sector and his connections to Chiang's political foes.[41] The post of special envoy for foreign affairs of the NEHQ was reserved for Chiang's eldest son, Chiang Ching-kuo, who had studied and worked in the Soviet Union.[42] As Chiang Kai-shek's top adviser on Soviet policy, Chiang Ching-kuo played a role in persuading his father to negotiate the Soviets into cooperation.[43]

Despite the urgency of recovering Manchuria, Chiang Kai-shek's government now wasted precious time on other matters, including re-demarcating the Manchurian provinces and NEHQ staffing. Hence, key NEHQ

---

39 Xiong, *Haisangji*, 355–6.
40 Guo Dequan, 'Zhongsu youhao tongmeng tiaoyue qianding jingguo' [An account of the signing of the Sino-Soviet treaty], *Zhuanji wenxue* (Taipei) 35, no. 2 (1979): 30–2.
41 Boorman ed., *Biographical Dictionary*, 1: 26–35; Levine, *Anvil of Victory*, 47.
42 Yao Songling ed., *Zhang Gongquan xiansheng nianpu chugao* [A draft chronological biography of Zhang Jia'ao] (Taipei: Zhuanji wenxue chubanshe, 1982), 1: 513; Chiang Ching-kuo, 'Wo zai Sulian de shenghuo' [My life in the Soviet Union], in *Jiang Jingguo xiansheng quanji* [The collected works of Jiang Jingguo], ed. Jiang Jingguo xiansheng quanji banji weiyuanhui [The editorial group of the collected works of Jiang Jingguo] (Taipei: Government Information Office, 1991), 1: 1–90.
43 Jay Taylor, *The Generalissimo's Son: Chiang Ching-kuo and the Revolution in China and Taiwan* (Cambridge, MA: Harvard University Press, 2000), 130.

officials were not ready for Manchuria until mid-October.[44] In contrast, in September Moscow informed Chongqing that it had appointed Marshal Rodion Yakovlevich Malinovsky, a Soviet Army commander during the invasion of Manchuria, as its delegate plenipotentiary to negotiate with the GMD over the Red Army's withdrawal. The Soviets also proposed a time frame, 10–15 October, and a place, Changchun (the old capital of Manchukuo). The Nationalists reacted by appointing Xiong as their representative in Manchuria.[45] Preliminary negotiations between the GMD officials and the Soviet ambassador, Appolon Alexandrovich Petrov, began in late September in Chongqing. Attempting to manipulate the boundaries and agenda during this pre-negotiation stage, both parties made unilateral moves without consulting each other. On 26 September, Petrov informed Zhang Jia'ao that the Red Army's headquarters in Manchuria had begun issuing its own army scrip. Next, the Soviets endeavoured to ensure GMD acknowledgement of Soviet control of the Chinese Changchun Railway. From the GMD's perspective, Petrov's move indicated the Soviets would not countenance the return of Manchuria to China unless their own interests were satisfied.[46]

Although details were noticeably absent in the terms of the Sino-Soviet Treaty, the Nationalists were committed to putting the Soviets on notice regarding China's intention to land its armies in the most effective location and reclaim China's sovereignty over Manchuria. Clearly, a successful and glorious takeover would satisfy China's national pride. Without persuading the Soviets into countenancing bilateral solutions to the issues, Chongqing bluntly informed Moscow (via a memorandum on 1 October) that the Chinese government had decided the GMD armies, with US aid, would disembark in Dalian. The memorandum did not acknowledge that the Soviets, as one of the signatory parties of the GMD–Soviet pact, had an equal right to provide their own interpretation of the treaty. Neither did it show any intention to develop a positive treaty partnership with Moscow. In other words, the GMD adopted a hard-line approach that was not conducive to post-treaty cooperation.[47]

---

44 Tian Yushi, 'Dongbei jieshou sannian zaihuo zuiyan' [An avowal of guilt: The three-year misfortunes in the takeover of Manchuria], *Zhuanji wenxue* (Taipei) 35, no. 6 (1979): 23–4; Chang Yu-fa and Shen Sung-chiao eds., *Tung Wen-ch'i xiansheng fangwen jilu* [The reminiscences of Mr Tung Wen-ch'i] (Taipei: Institute of Modern History, Academia Sinica, 1986), 282–6.
45 Zhang Jia'ao, *Last Chance in Manchuria: The Diary of Cheung Kia-ngau*, ed. Donald Gillin and Ramon Myers (Stanford, CA: Hoover Institution Press, 1989), 66 (hereafter *Manchuria*).
46 Ibid., 67–8.
47 Ministry of Foreign Affairs to Soviet Embassy in China, 1 October 1945, *Zhonghua Minguo*, 7, book 1: 117.

Manchuria's international port Dalian was the GMD's preferred debarkation site. The port's railways connected it to the rest of the north-east, and the harbour was capable of accommodating US deep-draft cargo ships, particularly the Liberty ships (around 10,000 tonnes). Notably, the GMD government did not have a modern transport capacity and had to rely on the United States.[48] The Americans were using Liberty ships and tank landing ships (LST) to assist GMD troop movement.[49] However, Chinese navigation specialists had already noted in 1943 that the Liberties were too large to enter most Chinese ports.[50] While Dalian was unmistakably the best choice for the Nationalists, the city and its seaport, located at the tip of the Liaodong Peninsula, had been occupied by Soviet troops since late August.[51] This meant that the GMD had to reach an understanding with the Soviets before it could send its troops in. Despite this, Chongqing chose to act unilaterally, inviting Moscow's immediate rebuff.

Moscow insisted that Dalian was a commercial port according to the Sino-Soviet Treaty and should not be used for military purposes. The Soviets wasted no time in clarifying their stance: on 6 October, Moscow expressed its objection to the proposed GMD troop landing to Chiang's government.[52] The GMD leaders held a round of internal conferences in late September but failed to find an acceptable bargaining range on key issues for the upcoming negotiations on Manchuria.[53]

When Xiong Shihui and his cohort arrived in Changchun on 12 October 1945, they discovered that the entire city was living under a strong Soviet military presence.[54] The GMD takeover personnel immediately received reports from local informants about the Soviets' planned removal of crucial industrial equipment in the region. The officials, perceiving these plans as

---

48   Record of conversations between Wang Shijie and Petrov, 25 October 1945, *Zhonghua Minguo*, 7, book 1: 125; Westad, *Cold War and Revolution*, 93.
49   Col. R.W. McNamee to Col. Hayman, 9 April 1946 and Minutes of Fourth Liberty Ship Coordination Meeting, 28 March 1946, 'Miscellaneous Chinese Army moves' (hereafter CAM); Records of the Special Staff (hereafter SS); Records of Headquarters US Forces, China Theater (hereafter CT); Box 687; Records of US Army Forces in the China–Burma–India Theaters of Operations (hereafter CBIT); Record Group (hereafter RG) 493; National Archives, College Park (hereafter NACP).
50   Xiong, *Haisangji*, 433.
51   I.I. Lyudnikov, 'Internationalist assistance', in *Soviet Volunteers in China, 1925–1945: Articles and Reminiscences*, trans. David Fidlon (Moscow: Progress Publishers, 1980), 305–12.
52   Fu Bingchang to Ministry of Foreign Affairs, 7 October 1945, *Zhonghua Minguo*, 7, book 1: 119.
53   *Manchuria*, 66, 87.
54   *Manchuria*, 12 October 1945, 72–3.

Soviet infringements of China's sovereignty, felt insulted and humiliated. Not surprisingly, the diaries and memoirs of the GMD delegation emphasised their experience of injustice.[55]

On the evening of 12 October, the NEHQ trio, Xiong, Chiang Ching-kuo and Zhang Jia'ao, prepared a three-point agenda for their first formal negotiation with Marshal Malinovsky, scheduled for the following day. The agenda demonstrates a strong commitment to continue the GMD's strategy in the Sino-Soviet Treaty, emphasising the pursuit of a negotiated settlement rather than Chiang Kai-shek's preferred solution. The agenda included requesting Soviet cooperation to return regional transportation to normal, reopen airfields to the GMD and supply military aircraft and army uniforms to the NEHQ. The sensitive issue of the GMD's proposed troop entry to Dalian was deliberately bypassed.[56]

The agenda presented a position of moderation to the Soviets, but as it did not concede any ground, the GMD negotiators could still begin haggling for China's primary interests at the time of their choosing. The agenda represented a negotiation style that purposely delayed the presentation of opening positions while gaining time to learn more about the rival's real position: the 'flanking manoeuvre' of a weaker party.[57] By seeking Soviet donations-in-kind for transport and clothing for its takeover personnel, the GMD also showed deference to the Soviet Union—a tactical move to alleviate Soviet sensitivities over the ongoing US–GMD alliance. In other words, this was a gesture from the Nationalists to the Soviets that the GMD would pursue its interests in a way that respected the Great Power status of the USSR. The implication of such a deferential gesture was that the GMD accepted its asymmetrical relations with the Soviet Union.[58]

However, the situation began to unravel when Xiong called on Malinovsky at the Soviet Army headquarters on 13 October for a courtesy visit before the scheduled start of the negotiations—a development that completely altered the GMD's approach. Malinovsky did meet with Xiong at his headquarters

---

55   Dong Yanping, *Su e ju dongbei* [Soviet Russia's invasion of north-east China] (Taipei: Chinese Library, 1965), 2–6; Xiong, *Haisangji*, 493; Wu Huanzhang, 'Kangzhan shengli hou jieshou dongbei de huiyi, shang' [Recollections of the takeover of north-east after the end of the War of Resistance against Japan, Part 1], *Zhuanji Wenxue* (Taipei) 24, no. 2 (1974): 33–9.
56   *Manchuria*, 12 October 1945, 72–3.
57   Raymond Cohen, *Negotiating across Cultures: International Communication in an Interdependent World*, rev. edn (Washington, DC: United States Institute of Peace Press, 1997), 86–7.
58   Brantly Womack, 'Asymmetry and systemic misperception: China, Vietnam and Cambodia during the 1970s', *Journal of Strategic Studies* 26, no. 2 (2003): 92–119.

compound, but the Soviet marshal did not pay Xiong a courtesy 'return visit' as traditional Chinese etiquette required. Instead, Malinovsky told Xiong simply to return in about two hours time with his delegation for the first plenary meeting of the two parties. Xiong felt that Malinovsky had failed to properly acknowledge his status as the senior Chinese bureaucrat in Manchuria and was clearly offended. In his memoir some twenty years later, Xiong recalled with bitterness that the Soviet marshal was boorish and arrogant.[59]

Perceived injustice is a breeding ground for conflict. The feeling of not being treated with due respect had a great influence on Xiong's subsequent negotiation strategy.[60] In his first official meeting soon after with Malinovsky, one that Chiang Ching-kuo and Zhang also attended, Xiong made two crucial statements that were incompatible with the original agenda that Chiang Ching-kuo and Zhang had agreed upon. First, Xiong enquired about the schedule for the Soviet forces' evacuation and, in violation of the spirit of the original agenda, he informed the Soviets of the GMD's intention to land its troops not just in Dalian but also at other Manchurian ports. He also requested Soviet support for the GMD troop disembarkations.[61]

If Xiong's intention was to demonstrate China's uncompromising stance over Manchuria, he could consider his approach a success, as he received a tough response from Malinovsky. The Soviet marshal told Xiong that any dispute over Dalian should be settled between the two governments, intentionally skirting the issue. Malinovsky also rejected Xiong's request for Soviet assistance to transport troops. Nevertheless, he indicated that if the GMD armies intended to disembark at Yingkou and Huludao, this was negotiable.[62]

The port of Yingkou provided maritime access to the Manchurian Plain, with the regional industrial and business centre Shenyang within striking distance. Huludao was a domestic deep-water seaport situated on a cape extending into the Liaodong Gulf just outside the strategic Manchurian

---

59   Xiong, *Haisangji*, 493.
60   For a useful analysis of the relationship between conflict and justice, see Morton Deutsch, 'Justice and conflict', in *The Handbook of Conflict Resolution: Theory and Practice*, 2nd edn, ed. Morton Deutsch, Peter T. Coleman and Eric C. Marcus (San Francisco, CA: Jossey-Bass, 2006), 43–68.
61   *Manchuria*, 13 October 1945, 73–7; Xiong's diary, 13 October 1945, *Xiong Papers*, Box 13, portfolio 2; Dong Yanping, 'A report of the military mission of the Republic of China on the negotiations with the Soviet military authorities for the withdrawal of Soviet troops from the north-eastern provinces', c. 1946, 8–9, *Xiong Papers*, Box 3.
62   *Manchuria*, 13 October 1945, 73–7; Dong Yanping, 'Report', 8–9.

town of Jinzhou, located in the land transport corridor connecting Manchuria and China proper. Malinovsky nonetheless declared that he had no knowledge about the harbour conditions in these two places.[63] At that point, the two parties did not resolve the dispute over Dalian immediately by negotiating for possible transitional arrangements. The meeting ended in a stalemate, and Xiong left empty-handed. Xiong recorded his 'revised' meeting agenda in his diary entry for Saturday 13 October 1945, but he did not state whether it was supported by Chiang Ching-kuo and Zhang Jia'ao before the meeting.[64] In a report to his father, Chiang Ching-kuo clearly revealed his concern over the negotiation stalemate.[65] Zhang, on the other hand, was sceptical about Xiong's decision to raise the Dalian issue at the start of negotiations.[66]

Negotiating at an uneven table

Moscow was alarmed. On 15 October, the Soviet government sent a communiqué to Chongqing, reiterating its opposition to any GMD troops entering Dalian.[67] When Chiang Kai-shek received Moscow's stern message, he also obtained a scathing report from Changchun about Soviet encroachment in China's national interests and sovereign rights in Manchuria.[68] In a handwritten directive to Xiong and Zhang on 16 October, Chiang Kai-shek apparently realised that his preferred settlement of the Dalian issue was almost unattainable and that a change of plan was necessary. He told Xiong and Zhang that he had already made arrangements to prioritise sending armies overland, and he expected that these army units would reach Shenyang before 20 November. Diplomatically, however, Chiang refused to seek a bilateral solution to the dispute with the Soviets. He insisted that the military sea transport destined for Manchuria would be executed as planned and that his troops would disembark at Dalian.[69]

---

63   *Manchuria*, 13 October 1945, 73–7; Dong Yanping, 'Report', 8–9.
64   Xiong's diary, 13 October 1945, *Xiong Papers*, Box 13, portfolio 2; cf. Shigeo Nishimura, 'Cong Xiong Shihui riji kan Guomin zhengfu jieshou Dongbei shi "xianchang" de zhengzhi maodun' ['On-the-scene' political conflict of the Chinese Nationalist government's takeover of Manchuria: From the perspective of Xiong Shihui diary], in *Zhanhou Dongbei jieshou jiaoshe jishi—yi Zhang Jia'ao riji wei zhongxin* [True story of the post-war negotiation for the takeover of Manchuria: From the perspective of Zhang Jia'ao diary], ed. Takushu Ihara (Beijing: Zhongguo renmin daxue chubanshe, 2011), 197.
65   Chiang Ching-kuo to Chiang Kai-shek, 13 October 1945, *Zhonghua Minguo*, 7, book 1: 122–3.
66   *Manchuria*, 21 October 1945, 87–8.
67   *Zhonghua Minguo*, 7, book 1: 123.
68   *Manchuria*, 14 October 1945, 76.
69   Chiang to Xiong and Zhang, 16 October 1945, attached in Zhang's diary entry of 19 October 1945, *Manchuria*, 84.

1. NEGOTIATING AT AN UNEVEN TABLE

Simultaneously, reports about the Soviets disarming the Japanese puppet forces and transferring Japanese weapons to the pro-CCP elements continued to flow to Xiong.[70] At their second formal meeting with the Soviets on 17 October, Xiong and his team still pushed for Soviet military support for two GMD armies to enter Dalian and advance into the Manchurian hinterland after landing.[71] In addition, Xiong notified the Soviets of the GMD's intention to send another two armies overland into Manchuria and requested that the Soviet forces restore the Manchurian railway sector southbound to Shenyang.[72]

Malinovsky did not respond directly to Xiong's untiring appeals to send troops to Dalian. Rather, he replied adroitly that the Soviet forces would begin a phased withdrawal from Manchuria from mid-November (to be completed in early December). However, he simultaneously ruled out the possibility of a joint GMD–Soviet forces rendezvous. In a proclamation to which Malinovsky adhered as stipulated, he informed his Chinese counterpart that the GMD forces would take over the defence only after Soviet troops had withdrawn. This effectively disregarded the Soviets' responsibility to assist the GMD forces entering Manchuria.[73]

Xiong and his team seemed to realise, at that particular juncture, that they were negotiating at an uneven table, and the Soviets remained unperturbed by their attempts to make an issue of Dalian. Existing records show that Xiong now tried to shift the focus of the troop-landing dispute by declaring that the GMD forces would seek alternative disembarkation points. Malinovsky was keen to show his GMD counterparts that the Soviets were manipulating the terms. The Soviet marshal told Xiong he was inclined to accept GMD troop entry to these ports, but the Red Army would not be able to offer assistance.[74] In an attempt to persuade the Nationalists to send their troops by an overland route to Shenyang via Chengde, the provincial capital of Rehe Province, Malinovsky pledged to restore the main railway. He stressed that non-GMD Chinese forces would not be allowed to remain in the line of communication.[75] In doing so, Malinovsky kept secret the deal he had made with the CCP just a few weeks previously. As part of this deal, the Red Army had promised to let the CCP take control of Chengde.[76]

---

70 Xiong's diary, 16–17 October 1945, *Xiong Papers*, Box 13, portfolio 2.
71 *Manchuria*, 17 October 1945, 78–83.
72 Dong Yanping, 'Report', 9.
73 Yao Songling ed., *Zhang Gongquan*, 17 October 1945, 1: 522–6; Dong Yanping, 'Report', 9–11.
74 Dong Yanping, *Su e ju Dongbei*, 12.
75 *Manchuria*, 17 October 1945, 79–80.
76 The Central Committee (hereafter CC) of the CCP to the Chongqing delegation, 26 September 1945, in *Zhonggong*, 15: 295–6.

It should be noted here that certain items raised in Malinovsky's response, such as supporting GMD troop transport via overland routes, were compatible with the GMD's initial proposal. The problem for the two parties was that they failed to explore more common ground. At the end of the meeting on the troop-landing issue, Xiong completed a full circle, from pressing for Dalian to accepting alternative ports again. In making his final statement, Xiong argued that the Chinese government had decided to dispatch armies to Manchuria via sea to Dalian because of its superior harbour. Xiong dropped his last bombshell before the end of the meeting by telling the Soviets to take full responsibility for maintaining local security before their withdrawal—a tart reminder that the Soviet forces was not trying hard enough to suppress the CCP combatants. Dong Yanping, Xiong's deputy chief of staff, who also attended the negotiations, recalled that Xiong's final statement was designed to clarify the duties of the two parties: a pre-emptive measure against possible Soviet interference in regional politics.[77]

In Chongqing, Chiang Kai-shek decided to intervene after learning that his demands had not been met. On 18 October, Chiang summoned Petrov to a meeting. Chiang recommended, for Stalin's urgent consideration, that the GMD armies be allowed to land at Dalian.[78] Following the example set by Chiang Kai-shek, Xiong went to see Malinovsky on 19 October and expressed his government's staunch position on sending troops to Dalian.[79] Malinovsky snubbed Xiong by advising him to return to Chongqing to acquaint his government with Soviet opinion, so that the negotiations would run smoothly.[80] Xiong flew back to Chongqing to report to Chiang on 21 October.[81]

While Malinovsky used his sarcasm to pressure Xiong at the expense of their working relationship, his vice chief of staff Pavlovsky went one step further. As agreed by both parties on 17 October, Pavlovsky would confer with Dong on military affairs.[82] Starting 20 October, the pair held meetings for two days, during which the disagreement over Dalian once again sparked a barrage of unfriendly exchanges. For instance, Pavlovsky connected the Dalian issue with the Soviets' prime concern, its naval base at Lüshun. He pronounced that Dalian was within a restricted zone of the Soviet naval

---

77 Dong Yanping, *Su e ju Dongbei*, 13.
78 Record of conversation between Chiang and Petrov, 18 October 1945, *Shilüe*, 63: 201–6.
79 Xiong's diary, 19 October 1945, *Xiong Papers*, Box 13, portfolio 2.
80 *Manchuria*, 19 October 1945, 84.
81 Dong Yanping, 'Report', 13.
82 Ibid., 11.

base and therefore Chinese officials would not be allowed to enter. The Soviet also rejected Dong's request for winter gear for the GMD armies. Given that, in an asymmetric bilateral relationship, the stronger party has more incentive to show graciousness in a climate of friendship rather than hostility, Pavlovsky's show of toughness indicated that the Soviets intended to sanction the GMD over their differences. In turn, Dong restated China's right to land its armies in Dalian and take over its civil administration. Dong's perseverance over Dalian certainly was in line with Chiang Kai-shek's policy, but this approach substantially limited the latitude for GMD negotiators to compromise. When Pavlovsky reiterated the Soviet position that they would allow GMD troops to enter Manchuria via alternative ports, Dong was noncommittal.[83]

In a letter to his father, Chiang Ching-kuo noted that this tactic of insisting on landing at Dalian was not helping to solve the dispute. Nevertheless, the attraction of applying such a tactic, as he also discovered, was that it would help the GMD maintain what they believed was a solemn and just stand.[84]

While his negotiators struggled to find a balance between national pride and resolving the dispute over Dalian with their Soviet counterparts, Chiang Kai-shek was about to make China's sovereignty a much bigger issue. He summoned Petrov again on 23 October. During this meeting, the Soviet ambassador conveyed Stalin's personal message to Chiang Kai-shek: it would contravene the treaty if GMD troops entered Dalian. Chiang Kai-shek responded, without tactful circumlocutions, that Dalian *was* Chinese territory and that it would be a true violation of the treaty if his armies could not use it as a port of entry.[85] By analysing the dispute from the perspective of sovereign rights, in his position as China's paramount leader, Chiang's statement virtually turned the Dalian issue into a fundamental and irreconcilable dispute between China and the Soviet Union. As Raymond Cohen cogently argues, issues concerning territorial sovereignty are extremely sensitive in political negotiations. Negotiators must manage these issues skilfully, as they risk derailing the entire process.[86] Chiang was indeed aware of the great risk he was taking, as he appeared more conciliatory immediately after his harsh statement. He told Petrov that he wanted to disengage from their disagreement on the treaty and its legality. He further

---

83   Ibid., 12–15. Also, *Manchuria*, 22 October 1945, 88.
84   Chiang Ching-kuo to Chiang Kai-shek, 22 October 1945, in *Jiang Jingguo xiansheng quanji*, ed. Jiang Jingguo xiansheng quanji banji weiyuanhui, 15: 338–9.
85   *Chiang Diary*, 23–24 October 1945, Folder 11, Box 44.
86   Cohen, *Negotiating across Cultures*, 65.

recommended that Stalin consider their personal relationship and the spirit of the Sino-Soviet alliance, and allow the GMD armies to use Dalian as their port of entry to Manchuria.[87]

To Chiang Kai-shek's disappointment, he did not have much to cling to in terms of personal ties with Stalin, as distrust between the two leaders ran high towards the end of World War II. Chiang Kai-shek's relationship with Stalin had been good when the Soviet Union augmented its aid to China, helping to resist Japan in 1938, but since then their relationship had spiralled downwards. Chiang's distrust of the Soviet Union grew after the latter signed the Treaty of Non-Aggression with Germany in 1939. Stalin too had begun to think about pressuring Chiang in support of the CCP after the Soviets' decisive victory against the Germans in 1943. Mistrust between the two became apparent when both Stalin and Chiang would agree to attend the Allied summit meetings only if the other party was excluded.[88]

Not surprisingly, the Soviets reacted to Chiang Kai-shek's strong statement more rapidly than to his personal plea to Stalin. On 24 October, the Soviet forces in Manchuria raided the GMD party branch headquarters in Changchun and arrested the branch staff officers for violation of the propaganda code (although the detained personnel were released the following day after receiving a stern warning to end all anti-Soviet activities).[89] Watching his government's relationship with the Soviets suffer yet another serious setback, Chiang Kai-shek instructed his Foreign Ministry officials on 25 October to notify Petrov that the GMD armies would land at Huludao and Yingkou until the Dalian issue was settled.[90] To control the damage, Chiang Kai-shek advised Xiong to restrain the activities of their hardliners in Changchun.[91] Having shifted their support to the CCP, the Soviets were in no mood to be conciliatory and continued to wield their power to blunt Chiang's moves to recover Manchuria. On 27 October 1945, a CCP-controlled municipal government was established in Dalian under the aegis of Soviet forces.[92]

---

87 *Chiang Diary*, 24 October 1945, Folder 11, Box 44.
88 Taylor, *Generalissimo*, 156–7, 167–8, 241–2; Li Yuzhen, 'Chiang Kai-shek and Joseph Stalin'.
89 *Manchuria*, 24–25 October 1945, 88–9.
90 Record of conversation between Wang Shijie and Petrov, *Zhonghua Minguo*, 7, book 1: 125.
91 Chiang Kai-shek to Xiong, 26 October 1945, *Zhonghua Minguo*, 7, book 1: 128.
92 Zhonggong zhongyang dangshi ziliao zhengji weiyuanhui [Committee for compiling materials on party history of the Central Committee of the CCP], Zhongguo renmin jiefangjun Liaoshen zhanyi jinianguan jianguan weiyuanhui [The founding committee of the PLA's Liaoshen Campaign Museum] and Liaoshen juezhan bianshen xiaozu [The editorial group of Liaoshen juezhan] eds, *Liaoshen juezhan* [The Liaoshen Campaign] (Beijing: Renmin chubanshe, 1988), 2: 595 (hereafter *Liaoshen*).

Landing attempts

Thus, after almost two weeks of heated exchanges with the Soviets, Chiang Kai-shek was forced to relinquish the plan to use Dalian. He instead staked his hopes on Huludao and Yingkou, in the vain hope that his troops could disembark at either of these alternative ports. But the change of plan did not automatically put the GMD–Soviet negotiations on an even keel. On 24 October 1945, a contingent of the US Navy's Seventh Fleet started transporting the GMD Thirteenth Army (hereafter 13A) from Hong Kong to provisional debarkation ports in Manchuria, but the American commanders in charge of troop movement did not know exactly where they were supposed to land.[93]

Operating under such uncertainty, the US Navy conducted reconnaissance missions for possible landing sites along the Manchurian coastline, including at Lüshun–Dalian: some US naval crew disembarked at Dalian,[94] and another small boat with the US flag prominently displayed approached the port of Huludao, where it was fired upon by suspected pro-CCP troops on the shore.[95] The Soviets protested through Malinovsky to Xiong in Changchun on 29 October against American military activities in the Lüshun–Dalian zone. The Soviets quickly issued a disclaimer that they were unable to ensure a safe disembarkation of the GMD armies at Huludao.[96] Thus, Yingkou seemed to be the last entry point in Manchuria available for the GMD, given that the port facilities in Andong (China's northernmost port, which borders North Korea on the Yellow Sea) were substandard, according to the Soviets.[97] Despite its geographical advantage, Yingkou was a small river port and could not accommodate large-capacity troop carriers.

When Du Yuming, NEHQ's newly appointed overall commander of the GMD's Manchurian forces, met Malinovsky on 28 October, the Soviet marshal behaved differently from the way he had with Xiong. This meeting passed amicably, as Malinovsky was open to Du's proposal to use Yingkou as

---

93   Chen Tsun-Kung and Chang Li eds, *Shijue xiansheng fangwen jilu* [The reminiscences of General Shih Chueh] (Taipei: Institute of Modern History, Academia Sinica, 1986), 207; Daniel E. Barbey, *MacArthur's Amphibious Navy: Seventh Amphibious Force Operations, 1943–1945* (Annapolis, MD: United States Naval Institute, 1969), 338.
94   Lyudnikov, 'Internationalist assistance', 305–12.
95   Chiang Kai-shek to Chiang Ching-kuo, 29 October 1945, *Zhonghua Minguo*, 7, book 1: 130; Barbey, *MacArthur's Amphibious Navy*, 339–40.
96   *Manchuria*, 29 October 1945, 93–8; Dong Yanping, 'Report', 17.
97   Xiong, *Haisangji*, 497.

a landing site.[98] Xiong took full advantage of Du's success. On 31 October, Xiong struck a deal with Pavlovsky, in which it was agreed that the Soviet garrison forces at Yingkou would secure the port until 10 November in support of GMD troop entry.[99]

After an exchange of fire with the CCP forces at Huludao had become menacingly close, the US Navy commanders were on high alert. Despite their image of promoting unqualified support for the GMD regime,[100] the US Navy was careful to pursue Washington's policy of providing assistance to the GMD without becoming involved in armed conflicts with the CCP.[101]

On 2 November, Daniel Barbey, commander of the US Seventh Amphibious Force, anchored his flagship some 30 kilometres off the Yingkou waterfront in an attempt to coordinate with the local Soviet forces to disembark the GMD troops. Two days later, a prearranged meeting with Soviet Army officers came to an abrupt end after Barbey, Du and a GMD reconnaissance party were fired upon by unidentified gunmen at Yingkou's dock area. Barbey soon received reports that the Soviet troops had decamped and that the port had been captured by pro-CCP forces.[102] The landing was therefore abandoned.[103]

Meanwhile in Changchun, during a meeting with his GMD counterparts on 5 November about the Soviets' early withdrawal from Yingkou before the prior agreed date, Malinovsky delivered a convoluted diplomatic statement. The Soviet marshal stated that his men had pulled out of Yingkou because they were outnumbered by the influx of strong CCP regular combat units

---

98 Du Yuming, 'Guomindang pohuai heping jingong Dongbei shimo' [An account of the Nationalists' peace agreement violations and the offensive into the north-east], in *Liaoshen zhanyi qinliji : Yuan Guomindang jiangling de huiyi* [Personal accounts of the Liaoshen Campaign by former Guomindang generals], ed. Zhongguo renmin zhengzhi xieshang huiyi quanguo weiyuanhui wenshi ziliao yanjiu weiyuanhui Liaoshen zhanyi qinliji shenbianzu [The editorial group of 'The Personal Accounts of the Liaoshen Campaign' of the literary–historical source materials study committee of the national committee of the Chinese People's Political Consultative Conference] (Beijing: Zhongguo wenshi chubanshe, 1985), 519–20.
99 Xiong to Chiang Kai-shek, 31 October 1945, *Zhonghua Minguo*, 7, book 1: 134.
100 Edward J. Marolda, 'Through a long glass: US naval leaders and the Chinese Civil War, 1945–1950', *Journal of Strategic Studies* (UK) 15, no. 4 (1992): 528–47.
101 Barbey, *MacArthur's Amphibious Navy*, 338.
102 China Theater Administrative, Shanghai China (hereafter HQCT) to War Department, 9 November 1945, 8–11, Folder 'China (1945)'; Records of the Chairman (hereafter Chairman); Admiral Leahy, 1942–48 (hereafter Leahy); Folders nos 11–13 (hereafter 11–13); Box 3, Records of the US Joint Chiefs of Staff (hereafter JCS); RG 218; NACP.
103 HQCT to War Department, 6 November 1945, Folder 'China (1945)'; Leahy; 11–13; Box 3, JCS; RG 218; NACP.

into the area. The justification for the Soviet forces' disengagement was, according to Malinovsky, the principle of non-intervention in China's internal affairs. The meeting ended in discord after Xiong retaliated by blaming the GMD armies' failure to land at Dalian and Yingkou on Soviet non-cooperation. After the meeting, key GMD negotiators attributed the diplomatic setback, with near-unanimity, to Soviet antipathy towards US involvement in Manchurian affairs.[104]

Eventually, on 7 November the US Seventh Amphibious Force landed the GMD Fifty-Second Army (hereafter 52A) at Qinhuangdao (the nearest deep-water port to Manchuria in China proper) to join the GMD 13A, which had disembarked there earlier.[105] Qinhuangdao was a less desirable port at which to disembark the GMD armies due to the lengthy rail transportation necessary to move troops into Manchuria, and the presence of strong CCP forces along the way. The port was too small for a main troop embarkation point, and the berth was congested.[106]

The GMD's bid to move its troops quickly into Manchuria with the US Navy's help was thus dashed completely. In reviewing the cascade of events in its sea-transport operations in Manchuria, US officials were punctilious in avoiding a repetition of incidents that would have embroiled the United States in the centre of the conflict between the GMD, the CCP and the Soviet Union.[107] The commander of the US forces in China and chief of staff to Chiang, Albert C. Wedemeyer, sent a memorandum to Chiang on 10 November, concerning the founding of a pro-GMD American Military Advisory Group. In the memorandum, Wedemeyer commented scathingly that the United States would consider severing military aid if the GMD government continued to use American aid to fund its war efforts against the CCP.[108]

---

104 Chiang Ching-kuo to Chiang Kai-shek and Xiong to Chiang Kai-shek, 5 November 1945, *Zhonghua Minguo*, 7, book 1: 138, 140–3; Chiang Ching-kuo to Chiang Kai-shek, 6 November 1945, *Shilüe*, 63: 430–2.
105 Yang Jingbin ed., *Wushierjun kanluan zhanyi jishi* [True history of the 52nd Army in bandit suppression battles] (Taipei: Beida shuju, n.d.), 3–4; Shi Jue to Chiang Kai-shek, 2 November 1945, *Jiang Zhongzheng zongtong wenwu* [President Chiang Kai-shek cultural relic], 002-020400-00001-052, Academia Historica [Guoshiguan] (hereafter *JZZW*).
106 Minutes of Fourth Liberty Ship Coordination Meeting, 28 March 1946; CAM; SS; CT; Box 687; CBIT; RG 493; NACP.
107 HQCT to War Department, 9 November 1945, 13–14; Folder 'China (1945)'; Chairman; Leahy; 11–13; Box 3; JCS; RG 218; NACP.
108 Wedemeyer to Chiang Kai-shek, 10 November 1945, *Shilüe*, 63: 499–522.

Trying to 'flog a dying horse'

When Wang Shijie departed for Moscow for the final round of the Sino-Soviet treaty negotiations in August 1945, his daughter Wang Qiuhua wrote a touching goodbye message on a small sheet of blotting paper that she left inside his diary. She quoted Hamilton Mabie: 'Don't be afraid of opposition. Remember, a kite rises against, not with, the wind.'[109] Wang Qiuhua's choice of encouraging words for her father succinctly concurred with the view that you should refuse to negotiate if your counterpart requests something you cannot support.[110] This view, to a certain extent, explains the actions taken by tens of thousands of nationalist-minded Chinese, who were emotionally unprepared to accept the unfavourable treaty that the GMD government signed with the Soviet Union, and expressed their anger in a nationwide anti-Soviet protest in early 1946.[111]

However, it is vital for the weak to have moral courage in reaching agreements with stronger parties on the basis of interests, not positions.[112] During the Sino-Soviet treaty negotiations, Chiang Kai-shek and his interlocutors were rationally prepared to abandon pursuit of the preferred and settle for the possible. Walking away from the GMD's position on China's sovereign right over Outer Mongolia, the prediction Chiang Kai-shek had made before World War II materialised: a full-scale military confrontation between the USSR and Japan—the 1905 Russo-Japanese War, déjà vu—but the Soviets and Chinese Nationalists were on the winning side this time. Most importantly, Chiang won a Soviet pledge of support for the GMD's post-war control of Manchuria. Chiang Kai-shek and his negotiators were nonetheless aware that accepting a weak treaty could spark popular as well as internal discontent. In this sense, the GMD's greatest sacrifice in signing the treaty was not Chinese sovereignty over a breakaway landlocked border region or Russian privileges in Manchuria, but the sidestepping of their emotional and ideological responsibilities to the Chinese people.

---

109 *Wang riji*, 8 August 1945, 5: 140–1.
110 Jay Conrad Levinson, Mark S.A. Smith and Orvel Ray Wilson, *Guerrilla Negotiating: Unconventional Weapons and Tactics to Get What You Want* (New York: John Wiley & Sons, 1999), 22.
111 This incident is discussed further in chapter 5.
112 Phyllis Beck Kritek, *Negotiating at an Uneven Table: Developing Moral Courage in Resolving Our Conflicts* (San Francisco, CA: Jossey-Bass, 1994), *passim*; Fisher, Ury and Patton, *Getting to Yes*, 41–57.

Making concessions is a high-stakes game in international treaty negotiations. Concession-making cannot be haphazard. This can put the concession-maker on the spot if the other party is unable to reciprocate proportionally.[113] Chiang Kai-shek and his interlocutors were left exposed by the substantial concessions they had made in the treaty, even as Chiang resorted to shift the blame onto Wang, to protect his brother-in-law Song. The political reality for the Nationalists after the treaty was that if the Soviets did not reciprocate Chiang Kai-shek's concessions by making good their promise to support the Nationalists' bid for Manchuria, it would be extremely difficult for the GMD to shed its weak-kneed image.

The GMD leaders were also aware that the real haggling would start after the Sino-Soviet Treaty was signed. In the lead-up to the post-treaty negotiations held in Changchun, GMD officials tried desperately to obtain Soviet support for the GMD's troop entry into Manchuria, particularly at Dalian. Unfortunately, their attempts failed even before the game began. The GMD's unilateral moves triggered a treaty interpretation dispute between Moscow and Chongqing. As a result, the GMD negotiators were forced to begin talks in Changchun without a prior agreement with their Soviet counterparts on whether the issues under dispute were negotiable.

Further, chief negotiator Xiong did not establish a good working relationship with his Soviet counterpart Malinovsky. As Cohen has remarked, 'all negotiations involve a problem-solving element and a relationship element',[114] but it is always advisable to be 'hard on the problem but easy on the people' when entering into any negotiating situation.[115] The lack of rapport between the Soviets and the Chinese at the Changchun negotiations proved detrimental to the outcome. First, it encouraged univocal and exclusivist rhetoric from both parties in expressing their respective views on principle disagreements. Second, both parties presented tough opening stances at the onset of negotiations. Moreover, the situation encouraged the Soviets to sanction the Nationalists at a time when the GMD–Soviet relationship was at a low point.

---

113 Lewicki, Barry and Saunders, *Negotiation*, 52–3.
114 Cohen, *Negotiating across Cultures*, 69.
115 Levinson, Smith and Wilson, *Guerrilla Negotiating*, 10.

Xiong later blamed Malinovsky's personal style. Indeed, foreign policy under Stalin has been criticised for its crudeness and excessive shrewdness, which worked against overall Soviet foreign policy objectives.[116] Nevertheless, Xiong failed to acknowledge that the USSR's foreign policy process, like that of all superpowers, was awfully messy. While the superpowers are giants in world politics, they usually have troubled lives. For Xiong, negotiating with the Soviets was similar to facing a dilemma: a dilemma cannot be resolved but must be managed. Xiong was the lead negotiator of a weaker party, which means that he had to deal with the situation skilfully, however harrowing this might be.[117]

There is no winning formula for effective negotiation, and the tough stance that Xiong took by addressing the dispute over Dalian at the start of the Changchun negotiation might not justify criticism in itself. However, as Xiong's belligerence was instantly mirrored by Malinovsky, Zhang and Chiang Ching-kuo's more moderate initial position could have been more prudent. Recent studies have demonstrated that when an opposing party does not mirror a moderate opening stance, this is likely to create constraints regarding its response.[118]

Once the process is underway, upholding negotiation positions does not usually lead to conflict resolution.[119] In the face of relentless Soviet rejection, the GMD's interest in Dalian (attached to its initial negotiating position) dwindled. The Nationalist leaders were interested in sending troops to Dalian for its geographical advantage, superior harbour conditions and easy rail system access. Most significantly, GMD troop entry into Dalian would have produced enough glory to satisfy China's national pride. None of the above advantages were possible without full Soviet support, however. Ultimately, the GMD's insistence on sending its forces to Dalian was tantamount to pursuing a hollow position.

Yet Chiang Kai-shek had also called for preparations to move the troops overland as soon as the negotiations reached an impasse in Changchun, clearly demonstrating that he knew the GMD forces had no real chance of entering via the sea. Hence, Chiang's instructions to his negotiators to uphold their position on territorial integrity regardless of Soviet objections,

---

116 Westad, *Cold War and Revolution*, 55; John R. Deane, *The Strange Alliance: The Story of American Efforts at Wartime Co-operation with Russia* (London: John Murray, 1947), 92–3.
117 For the challenges of being a Great Power, see Waltz, *Theory of International Politics*, 183–92.
118 Lewicki, Barry and Saunders, *Negotiation*, 50.
119 See, for example, Fisher, Ury and Patton, *Getting to Yes*, passim.

and his disturbing lectures to Petrov on Chinese sovereign rights, were astonishing examples of refusing to make further concessions before the Soviets reciprocated the major concessions he had made in the Sino-Soviet Treaty. In other words, Chiang Kai-shek needed to reconcile his stance in the current negotiation with the compromises he had made in the past.

Chiang Ching-kuo's letter to Chiang Kai-shek verifies the claim that the vulnerable often find 'a false security' in using perseverance to create an image of greater independence and power, even at the risk of self-defeat.[120] The problem is that such an approach does not improve the negotiating leverage of the weaker party. In the GMD's case, its insistence on haggling over Dalian from the high moral ground of sovereignty and territorial integrity invoked a heavy-handed reprisal by the Soviet forces against GMD activities in Changchun and ultimately cleared the way for the Soviets to shift their support to the CCP. Perhaps the GMD's predicament is best described by Cohen's description of the relations between American political negotiators and their international counterparts: Chiang Kai-shek's plan to negotiate with the Soviets for the recovery of Manchuria was scuttled by 'the twin rocks of pride and sovereignty'.[121]

As the Sino-Soviet negotiations spun out of the GMD's control, it also became more difficult for GMD leaders to manoeuvre at the interstices of Great Power competition. Chiang Kai-shek's overt reliance on US logistical support for GMD troop deployment to Manchuria was incompatible with the position of non-involvement that he intended to establish in the face of US–Soviet global rivalry. When the United States was alarmed by the ever-escalating situation in Manchuria, fearing it could be embroiled in direct confrontations with the Soviet Union, it resorted to threatening the GMD to adopt a crisis avoidance stance as a condition of continuing to receive US military aid.

Meanwhile, the CCP emerged from the GMD–Soviet dispute over Dalian as a beneficiary. As the GMD armies were prohibited from entering the Lüshun–Dalian zone, the major shipping routes between the Liaodong Gulf and the CCP base areas in the eastern China coastal province of Shandong were laid open to the CCP. The huge influx of CCP combatants from the sea soon proved a major threat to Chiang Kai-shek's attempt to exert control over Manchuria.

---

120 Kritek, *Negotiating at an Uneven Table*, 105.
121 Cohen, *Negotiating across Cultures*, 65.

Losing his initiative in the race for territorial recovery in Manchuria against the CCP, Chiang Kai-shek was forced to land his two armies at Qinhuangdao and move them into the north-east via an overland route. Chiang was, however, cautious about the combat risk that his armies would face. Du was instructed on 7 November to secure the land transport corridor between Shanhaiguan at the coastal end of the Great Wall in China proper to the Manchurian city of Jinzho, without pushing his elite forces further to the north.[122]

Chiang noted that the unfavourable situation had forced him to shift his focus from the north-east to China proper before he could make a final effort to show an optimistic face regarding the problems in Manchuria. As he noted, this would be to 'make a last try to save the dying horse'.[123] Discussing people's different perceptions of negotiation before and after a crisis, William Zartman laments that people 'only lock the stable door after the horse has bolted'.[124] In GMD's case, the champion race horse in Chiang Kai-shek's stable lay dying after being mortally injured on the racecourse, but Chiang kept flogging it as long as he saw some movement.

---

122 Du, 'Guomindang pohuai heping', 521–35; Guofangbu shizhengju [Bureau of historical compilation and translation, Ministry of Defense] ed., *Kanluan zhanshi* [A history of rebellion suppression] (Taipei: Guofangbu shizhengju, 1975–84), 4: 27. Also, Wedemeyer to Eisenhower, 26 November 1945, *FRUS*, 1945, 7: 679–84.
123 Citation translated from *Shilüe*, 63: 436. For further reference, see *Chiang Diary*, 7 November 1945, Folder 12, Box 44.
124 William I. Zartman, 'Prenegotiation: Phases and functions', in *Getting to the Table*, ed. Stein, 17.

2

Rethinking the Chongqing negotiations

Concession-making, the trust/distrust paradox and the biased mediator in China's first post–World War II attempt at peace

While the GMD–Soviet negotiations over Manchuria continued to be a focus of increased international attention, it was the Chinese Nationalist–Communist negotiations that drew most concern domestically. In autumn 1945, World War II and China's war against Japan had barely ended. At this point, the race for territorial recovery after the Japanese surrender between the GMD and the CCP was about to trigger a new round of civil war in China. To avert this, Mao and his men from their headquarters in Yan'an were invited to attend the highly anticipated peace talks with Mao's arch rival Chiang and top-ranking GMD officials in Chongqing in late August. During his stay in Chongqing, Mao sent his negotiators to attend most official meetings while he stayed aloof from the gruelling negotiations held behind closed doors. Except for holding private talks with Chiang, Mao maintained appearances on most public occasions. He endeavoured to lobby senior government officials, leaders of the minor parties, and non-partisans in personal talks and informal meetings.[1]

In late September, when the negotiation had already passed the halfway mark, one of the minor party leaders, Jiang Yuntian, was invited for a private talk with Mao. When the pair met, Mao revealed that the negotiation had so

---

1 *Chongqing tanpan*, 91–132.

far been disappointing: disagreements on the armed forces ratio of the two rival armies and the authority of the CCP-held areas had created an impasse. Although a private meeting with Mao might have been a godsend to Jiang, he did not treat Mao with adulation. On the contrary, Jiang unreservedly criticised the political ethics of the two major parties, including their relentless pursuit of military power and carving up of territories for self-serving purposes. For Jiang, this wheeling and dealing was merely delaying the inevitable.[2]

Throughout the meeting, Jiang Yuntian created some embarrassing moments that Mao found difficult to ignore, despite his clever quips and buffoonery. On one occasion, Jiang asked Mao if he would relinquish military power in favour of a democratic political system akin to that of Western countries. Mao did not respond directly, instead replying, 'Just think that if I can rely solely on my political skills to assume power, why do I have to bear the financial burden of maintaining hundreds of thousands of troops?'[3]

An awkward alliance

Mao's response to Jiang Yuntian's query provides a critical reflection on the relationship between the GMD and the CCP, which had been based on talking peace and making war since the 1920s. Previous research has been devoted to the military conflict between the two parties: the civil war from 1927 to 1936, the simultaneous internal strife amid their wartime alliance against Japan, and the CCP's military and base (Liberated Areas) expansion during the war with Japan from 1937 to 1945.[4]

However, little attention has been paid to each party's efforts to reduce tension. In particular, the survival of their awkward wartime united front from 1937 to 1945 has been considered as either a miracle or a patriotic act.[5] Existing historical records show that there was no miracle: in an attempt to

---

2   Jiang Yuntian, *Zhongguo jindaishi zhuanliedian* [The turning point of modern Chinese history] (Hong Kong: Youlian chubanshe, 1976), 1–2.
3   Jiang Yuntian, *Zhongguo jindaishi*, 1–2, citation translated from page 4.
4   See, for example, William Wei, *Counterrevolution in China: The Nationalists in Jiangxi during the Soviet Period* (Ann Arbor, MI: University of Michigan Press, 1985); Gregor Benton, *New Fourth Army: Communist Resistance along the Yangtze and the Huai, 1938–1941* (Berkeley, CA: University of California Press, 1999); Sherman Xiaogang Lai, *A Springboard to Victory: Shandong Province and Chinese Communist Military and Financial Strength, 1937–1945* (Leiden: Brill, 2011); van de Ven, *China at War*.
5   Tien-wei Wu, 'The Chinese Communist movement', in *China's Bitter Victory: The War with Japan, 1937–1945*, ed. James C. Hsiung and Steven I. Levine (Armonk, NY: M.E. Sharpe, 1992), 98–103.

avoid a split, high-level officials, negotiators and army officers from both parties engaged in countless negotiations and side conversations. These negotiations were tough because the major differences between the two parties on issues including political ideologies, the autonomy and expansion of the CCP's Liberated Areas, and the armed forces were too significant for a comprehensive resolution.[6]

From 1937 to 1943, both parties had proposed a range of local stop-gap arrangements either to defer the crisis or to stop the fighting from spreading. These temporary measures included sending a civilian commissioner (*zhuanyuan* 專員) to the key conflict zone,[7] separating the two forces via demarcation of war zones on a case-by-case basis,[8] the redeployment of troops[9] and promoting bilateral liaison between the parties.[10] Many of these creative conflict management approaches were implemented either partially or not at all. However, as Wise argues, the principles and concepts from previously failed plans became the precedents for subsequent negotiations.[11]

---

6   Yang Shengqing ed., *Tanpan shi*, 110–63; Yang Kuisong, *Shiqu de jihui? Kangzhan qianhou Guogong tanpan shilu* [Lost opportunity? A true record of the GMD–CCP negotiations during the period before and after the War of Resistance] (Guilin: Guangxi Shifan Daxue chubanshe, 1992), 78–114; *Zhonghua Minguo*, 5, book 1: 432–502, book 2: 55–199, book 3: 9–49.
7   *Tanpan shi*, 205–9. This idea began with Zhou Enlai's proposal of forming joint fact-finding teams to the conflict zone in his letter to Chiang Kai-shek on 25 January 1939. See Zhou Enlai, *Zhou Enlai shuxin xuanji* [Selected correspondence of Zhou Enlai] (Beijing: Zhongyang wenxian chubanshe, 1988), 166–71.
8   Xiao Jinguang, *Xiao Jinguang huiyilu* [The memoirs of Xiao Jinguang] (Beijing: Jiefangjun chubanshe, 1987), 264–6; Zhonggong zhongyang wenxian yanjiushi ed., *Zhu De nianpu (xinbian ben) 1886–1976* [The chronological biography of Zhu De, new edn, 1886–1976] (Beijing: Zhongyang wenxian chubanshe, 2006), 956.
9   Liu Gangfu, 'Huiyi wo he Gao Jingting tanpan dacheng xieyi de jingguo' [An account of my experiences in negotiating and reaching an agreement with Gao Jingting], in *Anhui Wenshi ziliao* [Literary–historical source materials of Anhui], ed. Zhengxie Anhui Sheng weiyuanhui wenshi ziliao yanjiu weiyuanhui [The literary–historical source materials study committee—An affiliate of the Anhui Provincial Committee of the Chinese People's Political Consultative Conference] and Anhui Sheng shehui kexueyuan lishi yanjiusuo [Institute of historical studies, Anhui academy of social sciences] (Hefei: Anhui renmin chubanshe, 1986), 25: 17–30.
10 Shi Peimei and Zhen Zaiming, 'Deng Baoshan zai Yulin he Zhonggong tuanjie kangri de pianduan' [A page in the history of Deng Baoshan's anti-Japanese alliance with the CCP in Yulin], in *Gansu wenshi ziliao xuanji* [A selection of literary–historical source materials of Gansu], ed. Zhongguo renmin zhengzhi xieshang huiyi Gansu Sheng weiyuanhui wenshi ziliao yanjiu weiyuanhui [The literary–historical source materials study committee of the Gansu provincial committee of the Chinese People's Political Consultative Conference] (Lanzhou: Gansu renmin chubanshe, 1987), 25: 112–19.
11 Laura Wise, 'Territorial power-sharing and inclusion in peace processes', PA-X Report, Power-sharing Series (Edinburgh: Global Justice Academy, University of Edinburgh, 2018), 31–2, retrieved 25 May 2022; www.politicalsettlements.org/wp-content/uploads/2018/07/2018_Wise_PA-X-Territorial-Power-Sharing-Report.pdf. Wise's report was written for the Political Settlement Research Programme run by a consortium of seven peace, justice and conflict resolution organisations and universities in Europe and Africa. The report is based on PA-X—a peace agreements database from 1990 to the end of 2019.

In other words, the two disputed parties had been negotiating to cut a large and complex issue into smaller and more manageable units at a time when a comprehensive resolution of their ongoing conflict was still remote. While the 'fractionating'[12] approach made both parties focus on small and separate issues rather than their major differences, it helped China avert a full-blown civil war during its conflict with Japan. As long as the leaders of the two parties still believed a weak united front was better than a total split, China lived to fight another day. In the end, China achieved a bitter victory over Japan amid a conflict-laden GMD–CCP wartime cooperation.

The United States—China's major wartime aid program provider and the most important ally of the GMD government—was increasingly apprehensive about the negative impact of infighting on China's war effort. As a result, the United States offered to facilitate a comprehensive reconciliation between the two parties.[13] The US intervention, however, resulted in futile mediation attempts in late 1944 by Patrick J. Hurley, the presidential emissary and later the US ambassador to China. A crucial part of the US government's action plan was to sustain Chiang's rule.[14] From the CCP's perspective, this approach rendered Hurley a biased mediator. For the CCP, the United States was a capitalistic country, one that would recognise the GMD as the only legitimate government of China.[15]

As one of the main purposes of Hurley's mission was 'to unify all the military forces in China' against Japan,[16] his mediation approach was fairly ambitious. It forced the leaders of both parties to settle their differences over the most contentious issues in their relationship—such as political power sharing and the command of troops—where the room for concessions had been very narrow.[17] It is therefore not unexpected that the US-brokered negotiation was deadlocked from the outset before it broke off in February 1945.[18] Hence, when the Japanese surrendered on 15 August 1945, the hostile negotiation situation meant that the two parties were unable to resolve their issues, with the surrender exacerbating the difficulties.

---

12 Roger Fisher, 'Fractionating conflict', *Daedalus* 93, no. 3 (1964): 920–41.
13 Hull to Gauss, 14 July, *FRUS*, 1944, 6: 245.
14 Hurley to Roosevelt, 10 October, *FRUS*, 1944, 6: 166–70.
15 Chen to Vincent, 24 January; Hurley to Stettinius, 19 February, *FRUS*, 1945, 7: 185, 234–6.
16 US Department of State, *The China White Paper, August 1949*, 1: 71 (hereafter *China White Paper*).
17 Immanuel C.Y. Hsü, *The Rise of Modern China*, 4th edn (Oxford: Oxford University Press, 1990), 605–6.
18 *Tanpan shi*, 269–94.

Japan's surrender rekindled the civil war between the CCP and the GMD, as both parties asserted the right to claim Japanese-occupied territories in China. Making use of their enhanced military might, the CCP intensified the campaign for territorial expansion in order to achieve a satisfactory post-war settlement.[19] The bulk of the GMD forces, on the contrary, were still deployed in south-west China in the immediate aftermath of the war. They were placed at a significant disadvantage in the race for territorial recovery against the CCP, which was based in rural areas close to Japanese-controlled territories in eastern and northern China—the nation's political and economic centre.

When the victory over Japan was already in sight in June 1945, the CCP's regional bureaux were instructed to intensify the campaign for territorial expansion in order to achieve a satisfactory post-war settlement.[20] On 11 August, Yan'an issued the first directive to its forces respecting surrender of Japanese armies. The order asserted the CCP's right to accept enemy surrender independently. As it turned out, this was only the first of seven instructions Yan'an delivered to its armies on the eve of Japan's surrender. Yan'an's Seven Orders of the Day directed the CCP forces to take control of, or make troop movements into, the strategically important provinces in North China and Manchuria.[21] If the CCP forces acted according to these orders, the entire nation, except the GMD's wartime power base in south-west China, could have been under their control.

For Chiang, the situation was certainly not good, but it was not entirely hopeless. In North China, for instance, the GMD commander Fu Zuoyi maintained well-trained cavalry from his Hetao region of the Yellow River garrison in the province of Suiyuan.[22] The provincial ruler Yan Xishan and his armies in Shanxi were strong supporters of Chiang's government.[23] In early October, around 20,000 US Marines landed on China's east coast and took control of Beiping (known as Beijing after September 1949) and Tianjin before airlifting Chiang's troops into the two cities.[24] All these Nationalist

---

19   Cheng, 'China's Madrid', 76.
20   CC directive to Hunan–Hubei–Jiangxi Branch Committee, 24 June 1945, *Zhonggong*, 15: 171–3.
21   Hurley to Byrnes, 12 August 1945, *FRUS*, 1945, 7: 514–15; *Zhonggong*, 15: 217–25.
22   Geng Routian, *Zhonggou jiaofei kanluan zhanshi yanjiu* [A study of the history of bandit suppression in Republican China] (Taipei: Lujun zongsilingbu, Guofangbu zuozhan canmou cizhang shi, 1981), 2: 30–3.
23   Guofangbu shizhengju ed., *Kanluan*, 2: 15.
24   Guo Tingyi, *Zhonghua Minguo shishi rizhi* [A chronological history of Republic of China] (Taipei: Academia Sinica, 1984–85), 4: 398–411.

armies showed growing resolve to scramble for control of territories against the Chinese Communists, but they needed urgent troop reinforcements to counter the continued influx of their enemies.

Military uncertainty created chaos. Some GMD-aligned militia groups had entered the Japanese-occupied areas without prior authorisation from Chiang's government. The unauthorised troop movement by the two opposing Chinese parties prompted the Japanese to register a complaint with Supreme Commander of the Allied Powers Douglas MacArthur stating that forces from both Yan'an and Chongqing had created confusion. This meant that the Japanese armies had difficulty surrendering according to the terms and conditions stipulated in the Potsdam Declaration. The Japanese complaint was made against both parties, but the embarrassment of receiving a complaint from a defeated nation was reserved for Chiang's regime.[25] The GMD was losing the race for territorial recovery, even on paper. Not surprisingly, Chiang tried to persuade Mao to visit Chongqing and settle their differences via negotiation.

Chiang sent three consecutive invitations to Mao for a summit meeting. Mao finally agreed on 24 August 1945.[26] Some believe that Mao accepted Chiang's invitation because of foreign pressure, particularly advice from Stalin.[27] Others contend that Mao met Chiang mainly because of domestic considerations and that he was more concerned about US, rather than Soviet, attitudes.[28] Mao, however, admitted that he agreed to negotiate due to all major powers disapproving of a civil war in China.[29]

Foreign pressure might have had an impact on Mao's decision-making, but the growing dilemma of the CCP's military strategy towards the end of World War II was also a contributing factor that prompted Mao to seek a *modus vivendi* with Chiang. For instance, the CCP's force-concentrated offensives against the GMD armies were subject to local resentment even before the Japanese surrender. Force concentration was important to Mao's

---

25 Chiang to He Yingqin and Xu Yongchang, 22 August 1945, *JZZW*, 002-020300-00027-038; *Chiang Diary*, 22 August 1945, Folder 9, Box 44.
26 *Zhonghua Minguo*, 7, book 2: 23–9.
27 Sheng, *Battling Western Imperialism*, 103–4; Dieter Heinzig, *Soviet Union and Communist China, 1945–1950: The Arduous Road to the Alliance* (Armonk, NY: M.E. Sharpe, 2004), 64–73.
28 Hu Qiaomu, *Hu Qiaomu huiyi Mao Zedong* [Hu Qiaomu remembers Mao Zedong], rev. and enl. edn (Beijing: Renmin chubanshe, 2003), 397–8.
29 Mao Zedong, 'On peace negotiations with the Kuomintang—Circular of the Central Committee of the Communist Party of China', 26 August 1945, in *Selected Works of Mao Tse-Tung*, Mao Zedong (Beijing: Foreign Languages Press, 1961–65), 4: 47–51.

guerrilla army to win significant battles against the GMD. While a guerrilla army may concentrate large forces for a specific operation, the concentrated guerrilla units should disperse swiftly upon completion of an operation.[30] The CCP's case nevertheless shows that once battles intensified, there was no guarantee of how soon the fighting would end; the concentrated army units had to seize food from peasants within the warring lands to replenish the armies' dwindling food supplies.

In a large-scale military conflict against the GMD in the eastern coastal province of Zhejiang, which took place just months before the Japanese surrender, the CCP amassed an army of nearly twenty thousand men in an area that extended over 250 square kilometres at the Tianmu Mountain (approximately 80 kilometres west of Hangzhou). The combat lasted for five months from February to June 1945, but the local peasant economy was ruined in the first three months of fighting. In the campaign's final stage, the food source of the poorest farm labourers was wiped out completely after they yielded to the CCP troops' extortion demands. A report written by the campaign's CCP commander reveals that the depredation caused by food seizures had a profound negative impact on the civil population, dealing a gargantuan blow to the mass-based revolution for communism.[31] The operations of CCP forces in 1945 show that a peace deal was needed for the Chinese Communists: Mao did not simply go to Chongqing on Stalin's order to humour the Americans.

The stalemate

Shortly after Mao agreed to meet Chiang, he wrote a carefully worded letter to Wedemeyer. Wedemeyer and his team provided military intelligence analysis in support of the US Embassy in China, but were not involved in Hurley's mediation between the CCP and GMD.[32] As Wedemeyer played no part in the negotiations, Mao's letter was written in reply to Ambassador

---

30 United States Department of the Army, *US Army Guerrilla Warfare Handbook* (New York: Skyhorse, 2009), 87.
31 Su Yu to CC, Central Military Commission (CMC) and East China Bureau of CC, 18 April 1948, in *Yudong zhanyi* [The eastern Henan campaign], ed. Zhonggong Kaifeng shiwei dangshi bangongshi [Office of party history of the Kaifeng City branch committee of the CCP] and Zhonggong Shangqiu diwei dangshi bangongshi [Office of party history of the Shangqiu County branch committee of the CCP] (Zhengzhou: Henan renmin chubanshe, 1988), 31–5.
32 Hurley to Byrnes, 9 June, *FRUS*, 1945, 7: 406–10; Albert C. Wedemeyer, *Wedemeyer Reports!* (New York: Holt, 1958), 345–6.

Hurley's request to visit Yan'an. It essentially demanded that Hurley come to Yan'an and escort Mao to Chongqing in the same plane.[33] Mao might not have been worried that Chiang's secret agents would assassinate him in mid-air, as Chang and Halliday have suggested.[34] But Mao's assurance-seeking from the Americans (who were biased towards the Nationalists) regarding his safety in Chongqing shows the advantage a partial peace-broker possesses over the least favoured side in peace negotiations.[35] In the CCP's case, the United States unquestionably sided with the GMD. Mao certainly would not have treated Hurley as an ally, but the American had more leverage (e.g. in the form of military aid) over Chiang and was less likely to misrepresent the intention of 'their side'.

Accompanied by Hurley and the GMD negotiator Zhang Zhizhong, Mao and his party arrived at Chongqing on 28 August 1945 on a US military aircraft.[36] Such an arrangement further confirmed the American's role as the negotiation's facilitator, and, in particular, Hurley's position as a mediator. Hurley adjusted his approach as soon as the negotiations commenced. He acted as a passive peacemaker and allowed the negotiators from both parties to enter direct talks. While being a respectful third party for most of the negotiations, the American was apprised of the talks' progress by both parties.[37] As the analysis of this chapter unfolds, it reveals that Hurley was not sent to China only to collect and provide information.

Mao's arrival marked the beginning of a six-week-long summit between the two disputed parties. The peace talks took place on two levels. One level comprised summit meetings in which Chiang and Mao met in face-to-face discussions. Chiang and Mao met on no fewer than ten occasions during the latter's visit, but only six were private discussions. The rest of the meetings consisted of informal discussions during social functions, courtesy calls and photo opportunities.[38] At another level, the most effective representatives from each party held rounds of negotiations behind closed doors.

---

33 Zhonggong zhongyang wenxian yanjiushi ed., *Mao Zedong nianpu 1893–1949* [The chronological biography of Mao Zedong, 1893–1949] (Beijing: Renmin chubanshe and Zhongyang wenxian chubanshe, 1993) (hereafter *Mao nianpu*), 3: 13.
34 Jung Chang and Jon Halliday, *Mao: The Unknown Story* (London: Jonathan Cape, 2005), 296.
35 Renato Corbetta and Molly M. Melin, 'Exploring the threshold between conflict management and joining in biased interventions', *Journal of Conflict Resolution* 62, no. 10 (2018): 2209.
36 *Xinhua ribao* (Xinhua daily), 29 August 1945, Chongqing.
37 'The Chinese Ministry of Information to the American Embassy', 2–3 September and Zhou to Hurley, 16 September, *FRUS*, 1945, 7: 455–65.
38 *Shilüe*, 62: 363–744, 63: 2–123.

Chiang dispatched a team of four to lead the negotiations. They were Zhang Qun, Wang Shijie, Zhang Zhizhong and Shao Lizi. While all four were prominent members of the GMD, Zhang Qun was also a strong supporter and loyal friend of Chiang.[39] Wang, Shao and Zhang Zhizhong had been regular participants in the two-party peace talks. Ultimately, Foreign Minister Wang attended only the pre-negotiation discussions, leaving for an overseas diplomatic assignment just before formal negotiations began.[40]

Mao sent his deputy Zhou Enlai as chief negotiator. Zhou's role was supported by Wang Ruofei. Wang had been negotiating with the Nationalists in Chongqing with Zhou since 1944. Wang had once been arrested, ferociously interrogated by Chiang's secret agents, and imprisoned for more than five years at notorious GMD prisons. During his trials and imprisonment, Wang stubbornly resisted authority even when threatened at gunpoint. Wang's uncompromising stance towards the Nationalist law enforcers was applauded by his fellow inmates.[41] When he applied the same attitude at the peace talks, it caused some trouble for Zhou.

Although Chiang and Mao sent experienced negotiators to set the stage for bargaining, both parties held firm, showing no sign of making early concessions. Chiang, who was keen to recover lost ground in his race for territorial recovery against the CCP, intended to play tough, particularly on military issues.[42] Mao, on the other hand, unveiled his negotiation policy to his comrades before departing for Chongqing. He even indicated that he was prepared to make negotiation trade-offs with the GMD.[43] However, as Mao had stepped up his war talk against the GMD towards the end of the war, he was in no mood to ingratiate himself with Chiang.[44]

The CCP interlocutors took the initiative and, in the meeting held on 3 September, made a rather aggressive opening bid.[45] Two extremely controversial and divisive topics existed within the proposal. On issues concerning the post-war army reorganisation, they demanded that the CCP retain an army of forty-eight divisions. In seeking recognition of

---

39 'Annex', Wallace to Roosevelt, 10 July, *FRUS*, 1944, 6: 240–4.
40 *Wang riji*, 28 August and 4 September 1945, 5: 161, 168–9.
41 Chen Zhiling and He Yang, *Wang Ruofei zhuan* [Biography of Wang Ruofei] (Shanghai: Shanghai renmin chubanshe, 1986), 112–58, 257–63.
42 *Chiang Diary*, 20 August 1945, Folder 9, Box 44.
43 Mao, 'On peace negotiations', 49.
44 Mao, 'Situation and our policy after victory over Japan', 13 August 1945, in *Selected Works*, Mao, 4: 11–26.
45 *Wang riji*, 3 September 1945, 5: 164.

the Liberated Areas, they presented the GMD with a *fait accompli*. Zhou and Wang requested that CCP officials be appointed, among other crucial local government positions, as the administrative heads of five major provinces in North China on the grounds that they had already seized an unassailable position in these provinces.[46] In political settlement parlance, the CCP considered territorial power-sharing (e.g. delegation of a central government's power to local groups who declare rule of a particular geographical area) as one of its preferred mechanisms for resolving conflict.[47]

The danger of the fait accompli tactic is that it might push the opponent's loss aversion to an extreme position.[48] From the CCP's perspective, however, Zhou merely presented indisputable facts to the Nationalists.[49] Seething with rage after discovering Zhou's proposal, Chiang threatened to make it available to the public. That move would certainly have derailed the negotiation before it had started, but Chiang soon changed his mind after seeking counsel from his negotiators.[50] However, he did not stop Wang Shijie from writing a personal letter to Mao, pleading for a compromise.[51]

According to some scholarship, acknowledging and engaging with the pre-existing territorial claims of local armed groups is a useful tool for risk mitigation in peace negotiations. This is because a non-state actor may think it unnecessary to negotiate with a central government over the issue, as it would already have established *de facto* control over the territories.[52]

However, Chiang did not view Zhou's extreme claims as a compromise mechanism that would resolve the peace talks' central sticking points. Chiang's negotiators rejected Zhou's two major demands outright, claiming that the Liberated Areas were now irrelevant and that the maximum number of CCP armed forces divisions to which the government could give consent was twelve.[53] From 4 to 11 September, the negotiators engaged in four

---

46 'Chinese Ministry of Information to the American Embassy', 3 September, *FRUS*, 1945, 7: 457–9; *Zhonghua Minguo*, 7, book 2: 39–41, 45–55.
47 Isak Svensson, 'Who brings which peace? Neutral versus biased mediation and institutional peace arrangements in civil wars', *Journal of Conflict Resolution* 53, no. 3 (2009): 464–5; Wise, 'Territorial power-sharing', 1.
48 Robert Jervis, *The Meaning of the Nuclear Revolution: Statecraft and the Prospect of Armageddon* (Ithaca, NY: Cornell University Press, 1989), 170.
49 Deng Ye, 'A new exploration into the background and basic themes of the Chongqing negotiations', *Social Sciences in China* 2 (2006): 115–27.
50 *Chiang Diary*, 4 September 1945, Folder 10, Box 44.
51 *Wang riji*, 4 September 1945, 5: 168–9.
52 Wise, 'Territorial power-sharing', 5, 29.
53 'Chinese Ministry of Information to the American Embassy', 3 September, *FRUS*, 1945, 7: 459–62.

feisty debates, but failed to make headway in ending the military stand-off.⁵⁴ The CCP negotiators called for a rational and equitable reorganisation of all armed forces nationwide, and they were firm on their forty-eight division demand. The GMD representatives argued that this number was excessive for a standing regular army in peace time. They insisted that their twelve-division offer was the best the CCP could obtain.⁵⁵ Chiang and Mao therefore needed to resolve the stalemate face to face.

The game changer

Chiang and Mao held a constructive meeting on 12 September. Mao promised a further reduction of his army to twenty-eight divisions.⁵⁶ The offer was by far the biggest concession since the negotiations had begun. Mao's abrupt reversal of his position might have been surprising, but it can be viewed as a strategic concession to break the impasse.

First, Mao did not specify how long it would take to reduce his armies to the number he proposed. Given the size of the CCP military, Mao could have been discussing a topic for the distant future. Second, the CCP regular forces could be used as fully fledged guerrillas operating in small units, thanks to their outstanding deployment capabilities. Conversely, the CCP guerrilla teams could conduct regular or mobile warfare after proper force concentration and enhancement in both organisation and weaponry.⁵⁷ Once these forces played havoc with the Nationalists, their whereabouts and exact numbers would be undetectable, let alone subject to decommissioning. Mao could have reduced the official numbers in his regular armies without reducing the actual quantity of his troops.

Of course, even the smallest change in force deployment would affect Mao's military strategy, but this could not possibly outweigh the benefits for his negotiation game plan. For Mao, the official figures of active army divisions and the actual number of troops in an army unit were different things.

---

54 *Zhonghua Minguo*, 7, book 2: 45–73; *Chongqing tanpan*, 191–204.
55 'Chinese Ministry of Information to the American Embassy', 3 September, *FRUS*, 1945, 7: 457–9, 459–62.
56 *Chiang Diary*, 12 September 1945, Folder 10, Box 44.
57 Cheng, 'China's Madrid', 74–5.

No matter how he decided to organise them, he would not give them away easily. 'The arms of the people, every gun and every bullet, must all be kept, must not be handed over', Mao emphasised.[58]

The actual number of the CCP forces is interesting. The CCP representatives started the negotiations claiming they had a regular force of 1,200,000 men (more than eighty army divisions), using this to support their demand to retain at least forty-eight divisions.[59] Historical evidence, however, shows that the CCP leaders had different versions of the account regarding the actual number of their armed forces.

A CCP Central Committee directive in July 1944 stated that it had only 470,000 regular (fewer than forty army divisions) and 2,100,000 militia troops. Notably, the same directive stated specifically that the current policy of army streamlining was still in force. Regional commanders were instructed to maintain the existing size of the regular army for one year before considering any aggressive army expansion program.[60] Astonishingly, when the CCP leaders negotiated with the Americans in a bid to obtain US arms in December 1944, they claimed they had an army of 650,000 men and a militia force of 2,500,000 combatants.[61] In September 1945, the CCP negotiators required statistical data to support their claim of a one-million-plus army. Their comrades in Yan'an passed on the numbers they needed—the CCP had a staggering 1,270,000 regular troops.[62]

For the GMD, the figures provided by the CCP were palpably spurious. According to the statistical figures provided by the GMD Board of Military Operation (*junlingbu* 軍令部) on 20 February 1945, the CCP had a standing army of 619,800 men, out of which only 434,780 were properly trained and organised.[63] Therefore, from the GMD's perspective, the CCP was using a 'highball' negotiation tactic (an outrageous bid that was impossible to justify),[64] and they questioned the validity of the CCP's claim from the start. Zhang Zhizhong queried, 'How it is possible that your army expands so quickly?'[65] Questions of this kind put Zhou and Wang

---

58   Mao, 'On the Chungking negotiations', 17 October 1945, in *Selected Works*, Mao, 4: 57.
59   *Zhonghua Minguo*, 7, book 2: 51; *Chongqing tanpan*, 191–6.
60   CC directive, recipients unavailable, 1 July 1944. The content of the directive suggests that the addressee was the regional military bureaux. See *Zhonggong*, 14: 261–7.
61   Yu, *OSS in China*, 186–7.
62   Yang Kuisong, *Shiqu de jihui*, 214.
63   *Zhonghua Minguo*, 5, book 4: 429–30.
64   Lewicki, Barry and Saunders, *Negotiation*, 61–9.
65   *Zhonghua Minguo*, 7, book 2: 57; *Chongqing tanpan*, 198.

2. RETHINKING THE CHONGQING NEGOTIATIONS

Ruofei on the spot, and they tried to avoid discussion of issues related to their forces' complement. It would have been awfully embarrassing for them if they were forced to clarify that the CCP had not incorporated the surrendered Japanese puppet troops (i.e. the Collaborationist 'Chinese' Army) into its army.[66] As of September 1945, Yan'an initiated a new round of army expansion. The mobilisation of Japanese puppet forces to join the CCP regular army was one of the program's main components.[67]

The Nationalists' query demonstrates the risk of using a 'highball' offer in negotiations. As it intends to push the opening offer of the other party closer to or beyond the resistance point, the opponent might abandon the negotiations, deeming them a waste of time.[68]

While the Nationalist negotiators tried to undermine the credibility of the CCP's forty-eight army division opening bid, Mao's twenty-eight division offer, by contrast, instantly made their strident pronouncements seem weak. Mao did not ask Chiang to accept his concession on a quid pro quo basis, but this was not necessary. The timing and size of Mao's concession had automatically pressured Chiang to reciprocate with a sizeable cut of his 350-plus army divisions.[69] In a worst-case scenario, if Chiang did not respond commensurately, Mao could walk away from the commitment with good reason.

Mao had made a significant concession in one jump. This decisive move imbued him with a moral superiority and allowed him to claim that the twenty-eight-division plan was the best and most reasonable final offer: one he must stick to. A moral victory would give Mao an edge in winning 'the sympathy of … the middle-of-the-roaders within the country', which was what he had originally planned.[70]

Mao's strategy of using one significant concession to place his party in an unassailable negotiating position was also employed by his negotiators against their American counterparts headed by Henry Kissinger in the 1970s. Kissinger soon learnt the lesson from the Chinese that, even though a concession might look significant initially, it actually amounted to less than

---

66 *Zhonghua Minguo*, 7, book 2: 57, 86–9; *Chongqing tanpan*, 196–201, 212–13.
67 The Secretariat of the CC to regional bureaux, 21 September 1945, *Zhonggong*, 15: 288–90.
68 Lewicki, Barry and Saunders, *Negotiation*, 61–9.
69 Guofangbu shizhengju ed., *Kanluan*, 2: 171.
70 Mao, 'On peace negotiations', 49.

a string of piecemeal concessions. In his memoirs, Kissinger used the term 'pre-emptive concession' to describe this particular negotiating approach he learnt from PRC interlocutors in the 1970s.[71]

At times, negotiators need to shape their own rules for tactical battles. For the Nationalists, the reality was that even a partial decommissioning of Mao's highly flexible armies was a long shot, but if they could entice Mao to deploy some of his elite troops in the guerrilla theatres of operation and let him win the propaganda battle—the CCP had made genuine attempts to reduce its armed forces—a full-scale civil war might be delayed, if not averted. Soon after Mao made the concession, Shao urged Zhou to send the remaining CCP troops outside the government-endorsed quota to open up wasteland and complete construction projects.[72] Shao's idea was tantamount to an implicit approval that the CCP could keep its excess forces as station troops.

Mao's commitment to reconciliation was short-lived, however. He reneged on his offer soon after by sending Zhou to inform Zhang Qun that the number of army divisions he intended to retain was forty-eight, not twenty-eight.[73] In other words, the promise Mao made in his previous meeting with Chiang was nothing but a glitch. Existing civil war records do not provide direct evidence for the reasons behind Mao's abandonment of this commitment, but the usually tight-lipped Wang Ruofei revealed some hints about the answer. Wang told Zhang Qun that the difficulty for them to commit to a more cooperative approach was that they would have a hard time persuading their comrades in Yan'an to accept it.[74]

The withdrawal of commitments is not uncommon in negotiation, but the party who reverses a commitment must plan it carefully. In Mao's case, it was not the retraction of his commitment but the way he and his associates handled the situation that did the damage. Importantly, they did not give Chiang any indication that the conditions under which Mao's commitment applied had changed before calling it off. Neither did they take the time to let the issue die silently, and Mao also failed to send his eloquent deputies to deliver a more prudent restatement of his commitment (e.g. by establishing more conditions).[75]

---

71 Kissinger, *White House Years*, 752.
72 *Zhonghua Minguo*, 7, book 2: 83; *Chongqing tanpan*, 208.
73 *Chiang Diary*, 17 September 1945, Folder 10, Box 44.
74 *Zhonghua Minguo*, 7, book 2: 81.
75 Lewicki, Barry and Saunders, *Negotiation*, 59–60.

From Chiang's perspective, Mao lost all credibility when he abandoned his promise. Chiang's diary shows that he was offended by Mao's act. Chiang later noted that he sought punishment of the Chinese Communists in a most severe manner.[76] Chiang's expression, in addition to the overblown anti-Communist rhetoric recorded in his diaries during that period, provided a niche for some writers to claim that Chiang had come close to arresting Mao in early October 1945.[77] Although forgiveness was not the forte of either man, they held at least five more meetings afterward, before Mao departed on 11 October. However, either these meetings were mere courtesy calls or both men engaged in discussions without making commitments.[78]

A night with Ambassador Hurley

When the level of significance of the Mao–Chiang talks decreased, Zhou went to see Hurley on 18 September, before the latter departed for Washington. Zhou told Hurley that if he was leaving, Mao would like to leave before him. Hurley went to Chiang and swiftly secured Chiang's reassurance regarding Mao's safety in Chongqing.[79] Although Mao was considering walk-away alternatives, the leverage had just tilted in the CCP's favour. The CCP's intelligence agents had obtained information that Chiang's negotiators had, among other concessions, been prepared to accept a CCP army of sixteen infantry divisions.[80]

Although Zhou was informed of his opponents' next move, he needed to manoeuvre tactfully in order to gain more from the bargain. Zhou made his move on 19 September. He offered to cut five more army divisions and reduce the CCP's demands on local governments. He also pledged to cede eight minor Liberated Areas, mostly in southern and eastern China where their positions were vulnerable to Nationalist attack. According to Zhou, the Communist forces from these areas would be redeployed northward from their present positions in roughly two phases. In geographical terms, the CCP would allow the GMD to take control of the territories stretching south from the Lanzhou–Lianyungang railway in the north, in exchange for

---

76   *Chiang Diary*, 17 September 1945, Folder 10, Box 44.
77   Yang Tianshi, *Jiang Jieshi zhenxiang* [The truth about Chiang Kai-shek] (Taipei: Fengyun shidai, 2009), 3: 261–7.
78   *Shilüe*, 62: 588, 63: 80–1, 86, 112–13.
79   Hurley to Mao, 19 September 1945, *FRUS*, 1945, 7: 466.
80   Hu Qiaomu, *Hu Qiaomu*, 403.

Chiang's cooperation in letting the CCP establish a stranglehold on North China.[81] Zhou's concession complied with a well-conceived negotiation trade-off plan developed by Mao before the negotiations began.[82]

To make the deal more attractive to the Nationalists, Zhou promised that when the phased redeployment was completed, the CCP armed forces would withdraw from some of the major base areas, including the one in northern Jiangsu Province.[83] The Communist base in Jiangsu had been an important base area for the CCP since 1941. In the autumn of 1945, the CCP forces took most of the country towns in that region after the Japanese surrender. The CCP's northern Jiangsu base controlled a vast rice production region situated in the Yellow River – Huai River plain of that coastal East China province. Importantly, it was geographically connected with the other two major CCP base areas in the provinces of Shandong and Anhui and posed a direct threat to the Nationalists' political and economic centre at the Nanjing–Shanghai–Hangzhou triangle. In other words, northern Jiangsu was situated in a strategically significant position that the two belligerent sides wanted to get their hands on.[84]

Zhou did not offer any clue as to when the proposed two-phase withdrawal would begin and be complete. If the relationship between two parties continued to improve, the Nationalists could take Zhou's proposal as nothing but conciliatory gestures. However, the Yan'an leadership instructed its armies—only one week after Zhou delivered his proposal—to maintain a preclusive control of territories north of the Yangtze River in both Jiangsu and Anhui provinces.[85]

The Nationalists were compelled to reciprocate Zhou's concessions. During the meeting on 21 September, Zhang Zhizhong conceded begrudgingly that a CCP army of sixteen divisions was acceptable. Simultaneously, Zhang also proposed to negotiate a final deal on the actual number of the CCP

---

81 *Zhonghua Minguo*, 7, book 2: 86; *Chongqing tanpan*, 212–13.
82 Mao, 'Fu Chongqing tanpan qian zai Zhengzhiju huiyi shang de jianghua' [Speech delivered at the Politburo meeting before departing for Chongqing], 26 August 1945, in *Mao Zedong wenji* [Collected works of Mao Zedong], ed. Zhonggong zhongyang wenxian yanjiushi (Beijing: Renmin chubanshe, 1993–99), 4: 15–17.
83 *Zhonghua Minguo*, 7, book 2: 87.
84 Wang Chaoguang, *1945–1949: Guogong zhengzheng yu Zhongguo mingyun* [The GMD–CCP political struggle and the fate of China, 1945–1949], overseas rev. edn (Hong Kong: Hong Kong Open Page, 2011), 209–11.
85 CMC to Central China Bureau, 26 September 1945, *Zhonggong*, 15: 298.

troops, sending a message to Zhou that the GMD was open to bargaining. Zhang's reciprocal concessions indicated that the give-and-take process was finally underway for both parties.[86]

Just when Zhou had the situation well in hand, Wang Roufei lost his temper at this key moment. On one occasion, he described the GMD regime as a 'Mussolinian government' and a 'Hitlerian government'. On another occasion, he simply issued an invitation to war, yelling: 'In that case, it would be better for the central [government] to annihilate all the armies of our party!'[87] The timing of Wang's hot-tempered outburst could not possibly have been worse as it occurred when the peace talks had just swung in the CCP's favour. The negotiations were adjourned after Wang's indiscreet remarks.[88] Recounting these events in a public report made in 1946, Shao did not mention Wang's role in the meeting, but stated that the situation was so tense that the entire negotiation almost broke down.[89]

The tactical use of aggressive behaviour is deemed unacceptable by some scholars for ethical reasons, as it may backfire on the aggressor;[90] ratcheted-up calls for war in peace talks are perceived similarly. In Wang's case, he would have preferred to maintain the momentum rather than forcing an adjournment, because his party had already detected the concession pattern of their rivals. In general, if the adversary's concession patterns are detectable, negotiators will normally prolong proceedings to gain an advantage.[91] Wang, however, chose to let his emotions run wild, and the negotiations teetered on the edge of breakdown.

Zhou had no choice but to take the fight to the GMD. He began to spread news about the negotiation deadlock to various interested parties, including the media,[92] but such an approach ('even the bystanders don't agree with you') ran the risk of further annoying his already angry opponents.[93] In Yan'an, the CCP leaders, believing that Chiang would use his armies

---

86 *Zhonghua Minguo*, 7, book 2: 89–97; *Chongqing tanpan*, 213–18.
87 Tong Xiaopeng, *Fengyu sishi nian* [A forty-year tribulation] (Beijing: Zhongyang wenxian chubanshe, 1994), 374–6; *Zhonghua Minguo*, 7, book 2: 91, 95; Shao Lizi, 'Zhengfu yu Zhonggong daibiao huitan jingguo' [An account of the meetings between the government and the representatives of the CCP], 12 January 1946, in *Chongqing tanpan*, 357–62.
88 *Zhonghua Minguo*, 7, book 2: 89–97; Shao, 'Zhengfu yu Zhonggong'.
89 Shao, 'Zhengfu yu Zhonggong'.
90 Lewicki, Barry and Saunders, *Negotiation*, 33, 61–9.
91 Donald W. Hendon, Matthew H. Roy and Zafar U. Ahmed, 'Negotiation concession patterns: A multi-country, multiperiod study', *American Business Review* 21, no. 1 (2003): 75–83.
92 *Zhou nianpu*, 620–1.
93 Zhou's approach would be a variant of the 'your own friends don't agree with you' tactic. See Herman Kahn, *Thinking about the Unthinkable* (New York: Avon Books, 1968), 190–1.

to intimidate them into capitulation, prepared to fight fire with fire. They telegraphed Mao on 26 September, requesting him to stop the negotiations and return.[94] Mao decided to stay, but the negotiations were in a shambles.[95]

The use of military force was more direct than peace talks. From Chongqing, Mao sent a message to his generals, who were at that time battling the GMD forces under Yan Xishan in south-eastern Shanxi over the previously Japanese-occupied territories. The localised civil war had started in late August when the leaders of both parties were ready to enter peace talks. In mid-September, the CCP forces gained the upper hand in the combat and placed a large group of GMD troops under siege.[96] Mao's message stated: 'The more battles you win, the safer we are here and the more initiative we have in negotiations.'[97] Mao's generals did as he instructed, and the fighting continued unabated. Nowadays, this 'whipsaw' approach is dubbed 'Fight, Talk, Fight, Talk'.[98]

As military confrontations gained momentum and the atmosphere of conciliation could no longer be sheltered by the peace talks, Hurley could not continue as a passive peacemaker. He decided to intervene and bring the negotiations back on track. He went to see Chiang on the night of 21 September, before his departure for Washington. In a negotiation situation, when a party considers making a larger concession, a mediator biased in its favour has the credibility to convince it that the compromise is necessary and all its losses will be compensated in a favourable final settlement.[99] As the United States was a key supporter of Chiang's government, Hurley succeeded in persuading Chiang to accept a compromise: extending the upper limit of the CCP armed forces to twenty army divisions in exchange for the CCP withdrawing its bid for provincial governments in North China. When Hurley brought Chiang's plan to the Chinese Communists, Zhang Qun waited for the outcome in a room next to the meeting venue. It turned out to be a long night for Zhang, as Hurley's meeting with the CCP representatives did not end until the next morning.[100]

---

94 *Liu nianpu*, 1: 502–3.
95 *Tanpan shi*, 324.
96 Guofangbu shizhengju ed., *Kanluan*, 2: 15–16.
97 Nie Rongzhen, *Inside the Red Star: The Memoirs of Marshal Nie Rongzhen*, trans. Zhong Renyi (Beijing: New World Press, 1988), 518.
98 Wilhelm, *The Chinese at the Negotiating Table*, 131.
99 Andrew Kydd, 'Which side are you on? Bias, credibility, and mediation', *American Journal of Political Science* 47, no. 2 (2003): 607; Svensson, 'Who brings which peace?', 463–4.
100 Hurley to Byrnes, 23 September, *FRUS*, 1945, 7: 466–8; *Shilüe*, 62: 626; Hu Qiaomu, *Hu Qiaomu*, 406.

2. RETHINKING THE CHONGQING NEGOTIATIONS

Chiang's overwhelming response sent clear messages to both Mao and Hurley. First, while he agreed to make concessions, he did not change his anti-Communist stance, and the CCP could not regard his final offer as a weakness to be exploited. Second, Chiang's trust in his American ally would not be sustained unless Hurley delivered a deal to his satisfaction.

Hurley ventured into a very different bargaining environment in his meeting with the Chinese Communists. He did not have the same leverage to influence Mao as he did with his ally Chiang. Besides, biased mediators may be unable to communicate effectively with the less 'friendly' disputant, thereby affecting their mediation approach.[101] As discussed, a partial peace broker can be a reliable third party for the least favoured disputant on some occasions. However, biased mediators can also provide less critical information to the disputant they are prejudiced against simply because they are allied with the other disputant.[102] In the CCP's case, Mao might have trusted Hurley to look after his safety in Chongqing, knowing that Chiang was constrained by the United States. However, he may not have trusted Hurley to provide reliable information about the negotiation (e.g. Chiang's bottom line), knowing that the American was motivated to secure a favourable deal for Chiang. While the coexistence of trust and mistrust is not uncommon in negotiations,[103] both Hurley and Mao needed to manage this paradox when they met.

During his meeting with the Chinese Communists, Hurley acknowledged that military and governance arrangements were the two key issues that had not yet been agreed upon; the reason was that both parties were 'attempting to settle too many details'.[104] According to Hurley's own account, he did not do anything that other mediators would not have done under the circumstances. First, he managed the exchange of offers for both parties but let their leaders have the final say. Second, he tried to shift the bargaining situation by urging the two disputants to secure an interim deal on 'basic over-all principles' and work out 'the details' in the next stage of the negotiations.[105] Hurley claimed that Mao accepted his advice: Mao assured

---

101   Corbetta and Melin, 'Exploring the threshold between conflict management and joining', 2212.
102   Kydd, 'Which side are you on?', 607.
103   Lewicki, Barry and Saunders, *Negotiation*, 310.
104   Hurley to Byrnes, 23 September, *FRUS*, 1945, 7: 468.
105   Ibid., 468.

him that the peace talks would not break down and that he would not reject Chiang's offer, although his party would like to consider it thoroughly before deciding.[106]

Nevertheless, Mao and his associates were completely dissatisfied with Hurley's approach. A PRC source claims that Hurley put a great deal of pressure on the CCP negotiators during the meeting.[107] Hurley is also criticised for ignoring that the core of the disagreements actually originated from those matters he regarded as 'the details'.[108] Mao was irritated. 'The American government, Wedemeyer and Hurley treated us very badly', said Mao, venting his frustrations after he returned to Yan'an.[109]

Mao's comment inflamed a deep-set antipathy towards Hurley in some quarters. While Mao's secretary Hu Qiaomu remembered Hurley's act as 'despicable' (*beilie* 卑劣),[110] a recent study describes the American's attitude as 'truculent and unreasonable' (*manheng* 蠻橫) and claims that he 'flew into a rage' (*shengse juli* 聲色俱厲) when he attempted to intimidate Mao into submission.[111] Admittedly, Hurley did not develop a good reputation for being well behaved. He was reportedly short-tempered and rough in his language when he had heated exchanges with a disobedient subordinate, John Paton Davies, a second secretary of the US Embassy, in January 1945.[112] The report seems to support the critics, who offer a damning case against Hurley: the American was desperate to report to the president about the peace talks' progress in a way that looked positive, to obscure the failure of his mission in China.[113]

Criticism of Hurley at the time (from Hu's memoirs) included a hard-hitting broadside against him for ignoring the obvious and arguing the reverse. Knowing that both parties had already come close to issuing a joint communiqué, he threatened that as long as no agreement was reached on the Liberated Areas, no official announcement would be made. According to Hu, Mao talked to Hurley with great forbearance and defended his party's core interests without anger. Consequently, Mao succeeded in

---

106 Ibid., 466–8; Hu Qiaomu, *Hu Qiaomu*, 405–6.
107 Hu Qiaomu, *Hu Qiaomu*, 405.
108 Hsü, *Modern China*, 623.
109 Hu Qiaomu, *Hu Qiaomu*, 406.
110 Ibid., 406.
111 *Tanpan shi*, 323–4.
112 Yu, *OSS in China*, 190.
113 *Tanpan shi*, 323–4; Hu Qiaomu, *Hu Qiaomu*, 405–6.

stopping Hurley from sabotaging the negotiations.[114] In the end, however, Mao agreed—under duress—to reduce his troop numbers to twenty army divisions.[115] Hurley was severely criticised for his unfair bias against the CCP.

After a long adjournment, the negotiations resumed on 27 September 1945, in the wake of Hurley's intervention. Both parties started the discussion with some very positive dialogue, but Wang Ruofei was conspicuously quiet throughout the meeting. The two parties quickly moved on to discuss the technicalities of army reorganisation and unresolved issues about the CCP's Liberated Areas.[116] This progress indicates that both parties were ready to settle most of their differences regarding the armed forces numbers, and an agreement was not too far away.

The two parties also made strides towards agreement on political issues. Zhou had proposed a multiparty political consultation peace forum (later the Political Consultative Conference [PCC]) in early September to discuss issues of political structural reform, including the re-election of all delegates to the GMD-manipulated state legislative body: the National Assembly (*Guomin dahui* 國民大會).[117] The matter had been discussed for almost a month, and both parties had come very close to striking a deal. While the Nationalists believed that the existing delegates to the National Assembly should be considered valid, with no comprehensive re-election necessary, they agreed to expand the number of delegates in addition to those already elected. After several rounds of negotiations, Zhou showed empathy for the Nationalists' position on these issues.[118] In late September, the two parties were able to reach an agreement in principle that the Nationalists would take the necessary steps to convene the PCC. Leaders of the minor parties and non-partisan politicians were also invited to contribute.[119]

The negotiation had an intriguing twist on 5 October. The GMD acknowledged and engaged with the CCP's territorial claims for the first time since the negotiations had begun. As a compromise, Zhang Zhizhong offered to endorse a CCP-nominated administrative inspector (*xingzheng ducha* 行政督察) to govern a cluster of adjacent, CCP-held, counties.

---

114 Hu Qiaomu, *Hu Qiaomu*, 406.
115 *Tanpan shi*, 324.
116 Zhang Jiuru, *Hetan fuzhe*, 134–7; *Chongqing tanpan*, 219–22.
117 *Zhonghua Minguo*, 7, book 2: 60–7; *Chongqing tanpan*, 201.
118 'Chinese Ministry of Information to the American Embassy', 3 September, *FRUS*, 1945, 7: 459–62; *Zhonghua Minguo*, 7, book 2: 73–8.
119 Wu to Robertson, 23 September, *FRUS*, 1945, 7: 468–9; Zhang Jiuru, *Hetan fuzhe*, 138–45.

The 'inspector' would be sent as a civilian commissioner to the area.[120] Zhang's proposal shared some key similarities with the one Zhou had proposed in 1939.[121] The conceptual clarity both parties achieved on the subject from previous negotiations in 1939 prompted Zhou's instant, albeit partial, approval. Zhou stated that the idea would be useful in northern Jiangsu and Anhui, but was not viable in those provinces already under the CCP's tight control. However, the two parties did not seek practical ways to make Zhang's plan work, particularly in those two provinces Zhou deemed most amenable to resolution.[122] From the CCP's perspective, Zhou could not accept Zhang's plan because it would place limits on the CCP local authorities below the provincial level.[123] At the end of the meeting, Zhou promised to convey Zhang's plan to Mao.[124] Zhou's statement seemingly indicated to the Nationalists that he did not have the authority to make agreements. This 'calculated incompetence' approach would have made negotiations more difficult and therefore lengthier.[125] At the negotiating table, however, things often take longer than participants expect.

Although the meeting did not resolve the territorial dispute instantly, the Zhang–Zhou exchange of ideas suggests that local solutions to a nationwide problem were possible. The challenge for the two belligerents was that they must find the courage to pick up where they had left off during their anti-Japanese alliance and activate the 'fractioning' approach to manage their prolonged and intractable disputes. Conversely, if the two parties were not ready to accept creative options to resolve their dispute, Zhang's plan would only represent fractured ideas.

Just when the interlocutors of both parties started to consider partial solutions to a series of broad and complicated issues, their political leaders urgently needed a result. On 8 October 1945, the two disputants reached consensus on a CCP-drafted summary of the negotiations and consented to a signed agreement.[126] Zhang Zhizhong's talk with Mao pithily expressed the state of mind of both party leaders. Soon after the agreement was finalised, he told Mao: 'We can't afford not to publicize this [agreement],

---

120 *Chongqing tanpan*, 224–7.
121 *Tanpan shi*, 204–6.
122 Tong, *Fengyu shishi nian*, 377; *Chongqing tanpan*, 224–7.
123 Deng, 'Lun Guogong', 58.
124 *Chongqing tanpan*, 227.
125 Lewicki, Barry and Saunders, *Negotiation*, 44–5.
126 *Tanpan shi*, 327.

since you came here with great honour, [we] have to produce something.'[127] The agreement would be signed on 10 October, the National Day of the ROC.

Tragedy at the eleventh hour

While the two belligerent parties tried their best to foster a conciliatory atmosphere before the agreement was signed, an unexpected incident almost derailed their efforts. On 8 October, a high-speed hit-and-run traffic incident and subsequent shooting involving a GMD army officer in north-west Chongqing resulted in the death of Zhou's staffer Li Shaoshi. The suspect vehicle was Zhou's official car, but Zhou was not in the car when the fatal incident occurred. The vehicle was fired upon when its driver, who was allegedly a 'new' employee of the Eighteenth Group Army office (the CCP's liaison office in Chongqing), failed to stop after it inflicted grave injury on a GMD soldier who was on the side of the road. Li was a passenger in the vehicle, and succumbed to gunshot wounds inflicted by one of the 'warning' shots from a GMD army officer trying to stop the rampaging car. The driver mysteriously went missing after the incident.[128]

Adding to the seriousness of the incident was the identity of the shooting victim. Li was the son-in-law of senior GMD left-wing leader Liao Zhongkai. Liao had been assassinated by suspected inner-party rivals in 1925. Li's death therefore sent immediate shock waves across Chongqing, and speculation increased that it was an assassination.[129] This was a serious and complicated criminal case because it involved multiple felony offences in addition to the celebrity status of one of the victims' family. To the great chagrin of conspiracy theorists, both parties colluded to minimise the incident. They quickly accepted the result of a rapid investigation to ensure that Li's tragic

---

127 Hu Qiaomu, *Hu Qiaomu*, 411.
128 Zheng Hong, 'Chongqing tanpan jilüe' [A summary of the Chongqing negotiations] and Li Jiexin, 'Guomindang xianbing silingbu pai zhu Guiyuan jingwei ban de huiyi' [My recollections as a member of the security squad of the GMD military police command at the Cinnamon Garden], in *Chongqing wenshi ziliao xuanji* [A selection of literary–historical source materials of Chongqing], ed. Zhongguo renmin zhengzhi xieshang huiyi Sichuan Sheng Chongqing Shi weiyuanhui wenshi ziliao yanjiu weiyuanhui [The literary–historical source materials study committee of the Chongqing city committee of the Sichuan Province of the Chinese People's Political Consultative Conference] (Chongqing: n.p., 1987), 1: 46–7, 92–6.
129 Zheng Hong, 'Chongqing tanpan jilüe', 46–7; Li Jiexin, 'Guomindang xianbing silingbu', 92–6.

passing would not hinder successful signing of the agreement.[130] Although the key person of interest—Zhou's driver—remained at large, a CCP representative swiftly crushed all rumours on 11 October, stating that Li's death was a sad accident.[131] As Hu Qiaomu recalled, the two parties were most concerned about a fiery last-minute breakdown of the negotiations.[132]

On 10 October, the two parties signed the 'Summary of the conversations between representatives of the [National] Government and of the Chinese Communist Party'—more commonly known as the 'Double Tenth Agreement'. It did not provide a comprehensive agreement to resolve all disputes between the two parties. Rather, it was an interim accord proposing mechanisms for further negotiations. First, it confirmed that the PCC would be convened as a peace forum. The PCC would be a multiparty political conference, made up of representatives from the two major parties, minor parties and non-partisans. It would meet as a consultative body to discuss issues concerning democratisation of the government and the nation's military problems. The agreement stated that unresolved issues regarding the convocation of the National Assembly also would be brought before the PCC for settlement.[133] In other words, the PCC would discuss the unresolved issues where the Chongqing negotiations had left off. The problem was that the GMD had already announced at its Sixth National Congress in May 1945 that the National Assembly would be convened on 12 November 1945 to pass the constitution.[134] This issue will receive further attention in chapter 4.

Another critical component of the Double Tenth Agreement was that the CCP would cut its forces to between twenty-four and twenty divisions, pending adoption of a future army nationalisation and reorganisation program. It also stated that the CCP troops deployed in eight scattered areas would be either demobilised or redeployed to other areas, such as the territory located to the north of the Lanzhou–Lianyungang railway line. The show of readiness to reduce the size of its military and concede territories constituted the most significant CCP concessions in the treaty. A key clause in the agreement tried to cultivate an open-ended environment

---

130 Zheng Hong, 'Chongqing tanpan jilüe', 46–7; Li Jiexin, 'Guomindang xianbing silingbu', 92–6; Hu Qiaomu, *Hu Qiaomu*, 412.
131 Zheng Hong, 'Chongqing tanpan jilüe', 46–7.
132 Hu Qiaomu, *Hu Qiaomu*, 407–8.
133 *China White Paper*, 2: 577–81.
134 See GMD's official website at www.kmt.org.tw/p/blog-page_36.html; retrieved 7 August 2020.

for resolving the territorial power-sharing issues, with a declaration that negotiations on the unsettled issues surrounding the Liberated Areas would be continued.[135]

Notably, the agreement made no mention of the CCP's proposal regarding provincial governments in North China and the Zhou-proposed CCP troop withdrawal from northern Jiangsu. As will be discussed later in the book, when the relationship between the two parties went from bad to worse in 1946, the question of northern Jiangsu and the dispute over the redeployment of the CCP forces in Hubei sucked the two parties into the cauldron of a full-blown civil war.

The agreement was signed just after the frenzied fighting in Shanxi ended on 8 October with a CCP victory, which inflicted heavy casualties on the GMD troops.[136] To counteract the poor impression conveyed by the spectacle of the two belligerent parties fighting in one place while signing a peace deal in another, Nationalist officials alleged that the battle was the result of Yan Xishan's own decision and had nothing to do with the negotiations.[137] Mao left immediately after the agreement was signed, but Zhou and Wang Ruofei continued the negotiations with their GMD counterparts.

'Thank God, amen'

China's modern history would be barren without the GMD and CCP's waging of war and quest for peace. The two deadly enemies might have had 'long-term plans'[138] to eliminate each other, but at the precipice, they cooperated. They formed an alliance against Japanese invasion, although bloody skirmishes continued unabated. The two parties therefore cut their intractable conflicts into smaller segments, to gain short-term or alternative solutions and sustain their weak alliance, thwarting a full-blown civil war. After World War II, the Chongqing negotiations set the stage for interlocutors and mediators to negotiate peaceful cooperation at a time when China was edging towards a more fateful round of infighting.

---

135 *China White Paper*, 2: 577–81.
136 Guofangbu shizhengju ed., *Kanluan*, 2: 15–16. For the CCP's combat report of the battle, see *Zhonggong*, 15: 342–3.
137 Lü Guangguang, 'Mao zhuxi tong Zhang Lan de huimian' [Chairman Mao's meetings with Zhang Lan], in *Chongqing tanpan*, 438–45.
138 Kan, 'Irreconcilable Chinese', 100.

The reality around the negotiating table in post-war Chongqing was that there were no quick fixes for entrenched disagreements between the two antagonists. It is, then, not surprising that Chiang and Mao started the negotiations with a hard-nosed approach. But once the two paramount leaders played a role in the negotiations, if they did not want to abandon the talks altogether, they had few options except to strive for incremental progress. 'No concession indicates a deadlock',[139] and neither man wanted to risk his reputation being besmirched through a stalemate, regardless of their initial intent to enter discussions.

The case of the Chongqing negotiations supports the observation that political actors' 'true intention' is a matter of uncertainty. Many factors may influence actors' decision-making, and decision-makers can always change their minds.[140] This chapter shows that the interaction dynamics in the negotiations pushed the two belligerent participants to make concessions, even though these were likely to be small pieces of a bigger puzzle and did not guarantee a comprehensive agreement.

Chiang's anti-Communist mindset did not stop him from allowing his negotiators to find interim compromises, notwithstanding his initial refusal to engage with the CCP over its territorial power-sharing demands. Mao's talk with Chiang led to a watering down of the proposed division numbers of the CCP army. Mao's twenty-eight-division proposal would have been a game changer in the negotiations not only because the actual impact on his forces would be negligible but also because of the advantage it would gain by propelling Chiang into reciprocating without pushing him to the extreme. In this sense, Mao's revocation of his concession makes an interesting case in history. From a theoretical perspective, Mao must have overvalued the concession he once offered and severely undervalued what he could gain in return, because he recanted his commitment to cut the CCP armies down to twenty-eight divisions even before Chiang could reciprocate.[141] Mao remains a forerunner of the 'pre-emptive concession' approach employed by the PRC negotiators decades later, which gained recognition from Kissinger.

---

139 Hendon, Roy and Ahmed, 'Negotiation concession patterns', 80.
140 Alexander Wendt, *Social Theory of International Politics* (Cambridge: Cambridge University Press, 1999), 107.
141 Jack S. Levy, 'Loss aversion, framing and bargaining: The implications of prospect theory for international conflict', *International Political Science Review* 17, no. 2 (1996): 187.

Kissinger was one of the great American negotiators in the 1970s. His sound appreciation of the idea Mao had once advocated back in 1945 is just one example showing that the legacy of the Chongqing negotiations is more significant than previously thought. Mao botched his withdrawal of commitments in his high-level talks with Chiang, but he and Kissinger would have agreed that it is often the failed person who is the pioneer in new undertakings.

Many famous negotiators in history have been controversial, and Hurley was perhaps a leader of this class. The major interest of this chapter, however, is his approach to negotiation, not his personality. During the Chongqing peace talks, Hurley intervened when the negotiations veered off track. As a third-party mediator, he encouraged both parties to stay on, accept an interim deal and strive for breakthroughs via multiple negotiations in the hope that an all-out war could be avoided. That was basically the approach that Mao meekly agreed to in a media interview.[142] Hurley was criticised by some for being too passive[143] and by others for being too opportunist.[144] These assessments seem to encapsulate Hurley's problems. The American was aware from the beginning that although he had the power to induce his ally Chiang to make concessions, a hardline anti-Communist like Chiang would make concessions only out of expediency. As he could only persuade Chiang of the expediency of a peace deal with the CCP, Chiang's trust in him was highly conditional. To broker a deal, Hurley also needed to exert strong and consistent pressure on his CCP clients, but the US government did not have the necessary means to apply such pressure effectively.[145] When Hurley did that, his use of high-pressure tactics ran the risk of infuriating Mao, notwithstanding that mediator pressure on disputants has been recognised as a useful way to resolve conflicts.[146] Hurley's predicament explains the reason mediators often prefer incremental progress,[147] and seek to identify opportunity in every difficulty.

---

142 Mao's interview with reporters from *Dagong bao* (*Ta Kung Pao*, Impartial Daily), 6 September 1945, *Chongqing tanpan*, 105.
143 Hsü, *Modern China*, 622–3.
144 Niu Jun, *Neizhan qianxi: Meiguo tiaochu Guogong maodun shimo* [At the eve of the civil war: An account of the United States' role in mediating the GMD–CCP conflicts] (Taipei: Babilun chubanshe, 1993), 143.
145 Vincent to Hurley, 2 April, *FRUS*, 1945, 7: 323–5.
146 Frank C. Zagare and D. Marc Kilgour, 'Alignment patterns, crisis bargaining, and extended deterrence: A game-theoretic analysis', *International Studies Quarterly* 47, no. 4 (2003): 587–615.
147 Wise, 'Territorial power-sharing', 4, 32.

Hurley has been scrutinised, particularly for his meeting with Mao. On the basis of existing historical evidence, Hurley exerted third-party coercion when he talked to Mao. Whether Hurley overstepped his authority as a mediator will continue to be controversial. While Hurley, Mao and even Chiang struggled to manage the trust/distrust paradox in their relationships, the reality was that Mao relied on Hurley for his personal security in attending the peace conference. When the negotiations hit a deadlock, he reaped the benefits of the powerful but biased American mediator in forcing Chiang to make a concession—a daunting task he was unlikely to accomplish alone.

Mao, like Chiang, was compelled by Hurley to agree on a preliminary resolution of reducing the CCP armed forces to twenty army divisions, willingly or unwillingly. This figure was certainly lower than the twenty-eight-division plan Mao initially proposed and ultimately chose to retract, but it allowed Mao to put a positive spin on his peace efforts. 'Kuomintang propaganda has been saying that the Communist Party is just scrambling for guns. But we have said we are ready to make concessions', Mao declared, on a high note.[148] According to a CCP account, the leaders of the minor parties shifted their support to the Chinese Communists only when Mao accepted the twenty-division proposal.[149]

When the negotiations approached closure and leaders of both parties were pursuing military solutions, negotiators sought partial solutions to their unresolved territorial conflicts. Zhang Zhizhong's 'administrative inspector' solution was a thoughtful move in the way that it acknowledged the territorial claims of his opponent via a creative repurposing of his opponent's old idea. Zhou did not give Zhang's plan his full support, but their exchange of ideas confirmed the availability of peaceful alternatives. Wang's emotional outburst and Zhou's use of calculated incompetence, however, show that the emotional toll was probably too high for the parties to put their bloody past behind them and consider creative peaceful alternatives. To paraphrase Geoffrey Blainey, if the two parties rejected these alternatives, one can only assume that they preferred war.[150]

The Double Tenth Agreement merely promoted an open-ended environment for further negotiations on territorial power-sharing disputes. Some scholars have clearly been disappointed by this. For example, Pepper characterises

---

148 Mao, 'On the Chungking negotiations', 57.
149 *Tanpan shi*, 325.
150 Geoffrey Blainey, *The Causes of War* (New York: Free Press, 1973), 159.

the treatment of the Communist Liberated Areas question in the agreement as 'a key issue on which not even superficial agreement could be reached'.[151] Negotiations could not remain open-ended forever; nevertheless, territorial disputes are often too messy to be resolved immediately. Elements of open-endedness in agreements give disputants and mediators breathing space to manage their competing interests cumulatively.[152] Given that Chiang's and Mao's troops were still engaged in battle when the agreement was about to be signed, formalising the unsettled Liberated Areas problem in the accord seems to have been more practical than pursuing an early settlement.

The peace talks stumbled into their second phase on 20 October 1945, further complicated by the rapidly deteriorating military situation in North China. War is commonly launched by politicians in order to serve their political goals; however, once a war has commenced, the nature of war serves itself, and its initiators must struggle to manage it.[153] China's military situation in late 1945 seems to confirm this view. Although urgent military issues were at the forefront and centre of the negotiations, both parties reached a consensus only on the proportional representation in the PCC. The multiparty peace forum subsequently held in 1946 would be attended by thirty-eight representatives from five different groups. They were the ruling GMD, the CCP, the anti-Communist Youth Party, the Democratic League (a coalition of major elements of the left-wing minor parties later formed an alliance with the CCP) and independent politicians.[154]

The two parties failed to break the deadlock over military issues through negotiation. The Nationalists insisted on government troop movements into Japanese-occupied territories, but the Chinese Communists saw this as an invasion of their territories. The GMD called for an immediate withdrawal of all CCP troops from the lines of communication, but CCP representatives

---

151 Suzanne Pepper, 'The KMT–CCP conflict 1945–1949', in *The Cambridge History of China*, ed. John K. Fairbank and Albert Feuerwerker (Cambridge: Cambridge University Press, 1986), 13, pt 2: 724.
152 Wise, 'Territorial power-sharing', 25, 34, 37.
153 Colin S. Gray, *Defining and Achieving Decisive Victory* (Carlisle, PA: Strategic Studies Institute, US Army War College, 2002), 15.
154 Tong, *Fengyu sishi nian*, 387; *Zhonghua Minguo*, 7, book 2: 111–23.

bluntly rejected this.¹⁵⁵ The two parties soon reached stalemate in their negotiations.¹⁵⁶ Zhou flew back to Yan'an on 25 November,¹⁵⁷ but he told the Americans that he would be back when the PCC was convened.¹⁵⁸

Chiang sent out urgent requests to Hurley for his early return,¹⁵⁹ but as chapter 4 shows, when Hurley departed for the United States on 23 September, his career in China also ended. The US diplomats soon discovered that things would not improve unless they sent someone with authority from Washington to China who could force the leaders of the two parties to agree on a cessation of hostilities.

Back in Yan'an, Mao delivered a report about the negotiations to the cadres. His private talks with Chiang were not mentioned. Rather, Mao emphasised their recent military victory in Shanxi, the combat readiness of the Liberated Areas, and communism's rise in a global context. Mao noted the concessions they had made in the final agreement, but for him, these were designed to 'frustrate the Kuomintang's plot for civil war'.¹⁶⁰ Mao spared no effort to ramp up the war-like rhetoric. 'If they [the GMD] attack and we wipe them out, they will have that satisfaction; wipe out some, some satisfaction; wipe out more, more satisfaction; wipe out the whole lot, complete satisfaction', he asserted.¹⁶¹ The blood-drenched battlefield soon proved that Mao's patter was no joke. Chiang, on the other hand, had maintained his personal antipathy towards Mao at a peak since the negotiations began. He could not hide his joy after learning that Mao had received an angry lecture from Wedemeyer over the involvement of CCP troops in the murder of the US intelligence officer John Birch.¹⁶² 'Thank God, amen', Chiang noted.¹⁶³

---

155 *Tingzhan tanpan ziliao* [Source materials on cease-fire negotiations] (Chengdu: Sichuan renmin chubanshe, 1981), 454–5; *Shilüe*, 63: 358–9; cf. *Tanpan shi*, 337–8.
156 Robertson to Byrnes, 4 November, *FRUS*, 1945, 7: 601–2.
157 *Zhou nianpu*, 627.
158 Memorandum of conversation by Melby, 13 November 1945, *FRUS*, 1945, 7: 624–5.
159 Robertson to Byrnes, 13 November 1945—1 p.m., *FRUS*, 1945, 7: 619.
160 Mao, 'On the Chungking Negotiations', 56.
161 Ibid., 56.
162 Yu, *OSS in China*, 235–41.
163 *Shilüe*, 62: 407–8. The current photocopied edition of *Shilüe* clearly shows that there were manual blackouts against the six traditional Chinese characters of 'thank God, amen' (*ganxie shangdi amen* 感謝上帝阿門), but the blackout was still very readable. For further reference, see *Chiang Diary*, 31 August 1945, Folder 9, Box 44.

3

Civil war in the north-east

The rhetorical use of 'decisive war' and the Manchurian gamble

In the wake of the Chongqing peace talks, a directive from Yan'an urged its regional commanders to expand their armed forces.[1] In this context, Manchuria, with its political, strategic, economic and geographical importance, became a venue for the CCP's expansion.[2] While Mao and his negotiators were engaging the Nationalists at the negotiating table in Chongqing, the Yan'an leadership had already shifted the focus to Manchuria, a key area that was not part of the discussion in the negotiations.[3]

When the CCP forces penetrated the former Japanese puppet state of Manchukuo in late 1945, they did not have an indigenous base area to launch their traditional rural-based insurgency. This was because the CCP guerrillas and party organisations in Manchuria were basically decimated in the early 1940s after suffering years of Japanese extermination campaigns. The CCP's guerrilla teams either fled into exile in the Soviet Union or operated within enclaves at the provincial border between Hebei and Manchuria. Some of these guerrilla forces returned when Soviet invasion of Manchuria began, but they could only play supportive roles.[4] Hence

---

1   Directive, CC to regional bureaux, 12 October 1945, *Zhonggong*, 15: 324–5.
2   Cheng, 'China's Madrid', 77.
3   Zhonggong zhongyang wenxian yanjiushi ed., *Zhu De nianpu*, 1212–13.
4   Chong-sik Lee, *Revolutionary Struggle in Manchuria: Chinese Communism and Soviet Interest, 1922–1945* (Berkeley, CA: University of California Press, 1983), 268–321; Robertson to Byrnes, 28 February, *FRUS*, 1946, 9: 448–9; Wang Yizhi, 'Bayiwu qianhou de Dongbei kangri lianjun' [The North-east Anti-Japanese United Army before and after the V-J Day], *Liaoshen*, 1: 156–66; cf. Tanner, *Battle for Manchuria*, 33.

Yan'an had a pressing need for a rapid increase of its military presence there. As mentioned, the influx of the CCP soldiers from Shandong into Manchuria via the Bohai Sea had already posed a threat to the Nationalist forces, but Mao still urged his generals to send more troops to counter the arriving enemies from Qinhuangdao in late August.[5] As an outcome, the two opposing armies clashed fiercely along the key gateway to the heartland of Manchuria in mid-November 1945. This chapter is about the two parties' race for Manchuria against the backdrop of the peace negotiations.

Expand in the north

The CCP openly announced on 12 August 1945 that it was sending four strong combat units to Manchuria and its neighbouring provinces of Rehe and Chahar. However, the mobilisation of the CCP forces did not live up to the party's propaganda as, almost at the same time, a classified cable from Yan'an to the regional forces clarified the propaganda purpose of the announcement and stated that only Li Yunchang's men from the Hebei–Rehe–Liaoning Military Region was to redeploy; all other units only received a standby order.[6] Yan'an decided to dispatch around a thousand non-military cadres into Manchuria owing to the uncertainty of securing Soviet support for a CCP military presence in Manchuria. Its armed forces would stop advancing at the Rehe border, pending further instructions.[7] Notwithstanding that the CCP forces in China proper were overwhelmed by military engagements against the Nationalists, the commanders of these forces had to manage the ad-hoc requests of generating rank-and-file support for the Manchurian mission and the massive task of getting the conscripted fishing boats ready to enter the north-east.[8]

Yan'an therefore calculatingly set the bar low, making the CCP's policy towards Manchuria in the immediate aftermath of the Japanese surrender rather conservative. Mao was among the strongest supporters of this 'under-promise and over-delivery' approach. He admitted that Manchuria

---

5   CMC to regional bureaux, 20 August 1945, *Junshi*, 3: 45–6.
6   Cheng, 'China's Madrid', 77–8.
7   Cheng, 'Escalation of hostilities in Manchuria', 142; *Liaoshen*, 2: 590. Tang Kai, 'Wei jiefang Dongbei juxing dianjili' [Strengthening the foundation for the liberation of the north-east], in *Shanhaiguan zhi zhan* [The battle of Shanhaiguan], ed. Yuan Wei (Beijing: Junshi kexue chubanshe, 1989), 40–53.
8   Lü Zhengcao, *Lü Zhengcao huiyilu* [The memoirs of Lü Zhengcao] (Beijing: Jiefangjun chubanshe, 1988), 516–23; Wan Yi, *Wan Yi jiangjun huiyilu* [The recollections of General Wan Yi] (Beijing: Zhonggong dangshi chubanshe, 1998), 131, 141–7.

was covered by the Sino-Soviet treaty so that the Nationalist government possessed authority over the region. Meanwhile, Mao expected his generals to secure Rehe, the neighbouring province of Manchuria, and waited until the stance of the fickle Soviets became clearer.[9]

Thus, the first CCP army to depart for Manchuria was Li's forces. With Mao's Rehe plan in mind, Li divided his 13,000-strong forces into three detachments, advancing the first two towards Rehe's provincial capital of Chengde and the strategic town of Chifeng, respectively; only the third contingent, totalling 4,000 men, was to form the vanguard of the CCP forces sent to Manchuria.[10] On 29 August, a directive was telegraphed from Yan'an to regulate the activities of all units preparing to enter Manchuria or the adjacent areas. All units were banned from making formal contact with the Soviets or doing anything that could be seen as causing the Soviets diplomatic embarrassment. Such activities as entering the large cities by train were strictly prohibited.[11]

The direct instruction from Yan'an was shattered by a telecommunication breakdown. Li's scouting team en route to Manchuria did not receive the important final briefing because of inadequate army radio equipment.[12] On 25 August, Li's men departed from their base in eastern Hebei, where Manchuria was within striking distance. The destination was the environs of Shenyang, the largest city in Manchuria.[13]

The gateway to Manchuria was Shanhaiguan. The legendary fortress of the Great Wall is situated at a narrow mountain bypass to the land corridor of Liaoxi, which connected North China and Manchuria. At the end of August, the fortified town was still under the control of Manchukuo troops, who indicated clearly that they would surrender only to the Nationalists. Zeng Kelin, the commander of Li's scouting team, not informed of Yan'an's instruction, led his men to stage a grand rendezvous with the Soviet forces at a small Manchurian town, some 20 kilometres to the north of Shanhaiguan.[14]

---

9   Cheng, 'China's Madrid', 77–9; Cheng, 'Escalation of hostilities in Manchuria', 141–3.
10 Cheng, 'China's Madrid', 78–9; cf. Harold M. Tanner, 'Guerrilla, mobile and base warfare in Communist military operations in Manchuria, 1945–1947', *Journal of Military History* 67 (2003): 1188–9.
11 Cheng, 'China's Madrid', 78–9.
12 Ibid., 78–9.
13 Zeng Kelin, 'Jinjun Dongbei de zuichu shike' [Marching into the north-east: The initial stage], in *Xueye xiongfeng*, Li Yunchang, 8–15; Zeng Kelin, 'Huoyue zhanlüe quanju: Yi gongke Shanhaiguan zhi zhan' [A critical turning point: Recollections of the battle of Shanhaiguan], in *Shanhaiguan zhi zhan*, ed. Yuan Wei, 31–9.
14 Cheng, 'China's Madrid', 79; Cheng, 'Escalation of hostilities in Manchuria', 147.

In an attempt to exploit the goodwill built in the name of Communist internationalism, Zeng proposed to the Soviet commanders a joint CCP–Soviet military operation to capture Shanhaiguan. The Soviets rejected Zeng's plan, stating that the fortified town on the Great Wall line was not within Moscow's mandate for military action. This indicates that individual Soviet Army officers might be sympathetic towards the CCP's course in Manchuria, but as long as the goalposts kept moving, the Soviets' attitude was unpredictable. Zeng in turn initiated hours of negotiations with the Soviets. Both parties finally struck a deal whereby the Soviet forces would be playing only a supportive role in the CCP's offensive against Shanhaiguan. Zeng's troops captured the town on 30 August, thanks to Soviet artillery support.[15]

After taking Shanhaiguan, Zeng's men moved swiftly towards the major cities, leaving only a small force behind to defend the garrison town. With rail transportation and firepower support offered by the Soviet forces, they swept through cities along the main railway line at ease, including the industrial hub of Jinzhou.[16] On 5 September, Zeng disembarked his troops from a fully loaded train and prepared to enter Shenyang. The attitude of the Soviet garrison force was rather hostile to them initially. In the end, Zeng's unorthodox negotiation tactics of insistence and their troops' ability to maintain a high level of discipline stunned the Soviets. With the permission of the Soviets, Zeng's highly disciplined men proudly encamped inside the Shenyang city.[17]

Soon after Zeng secured his troops' deployment into Shenyang, he and his men received a rousing reception from the Soviets.[18] When Zeng's superior Li arrived at Shanhaiguan, he was soon ushered into a Soviet open-top vehicle to lead a prearranged military parade into the town centre. Meanwhile, the Soviet Army officers even allowed the CCP troops to take over a large Japanese armoury located on the outskirts of Shenyang. The quantity of the weaponry was such that Zeng's men had to work hard for three whole

---

15   Zeng Kelin, *Zeng Kelin jiangjun zishu* [An autobiography of General Zeng Kelin] (Shenyang: Liaoning renmin chubanshe, 1997), 83–7; Cheng, 'China's Madrid', 79.
16   Cheng, 'Escalation of hostilities in Manchuria', 147; Dong Zhanlin, 'Gongda Shanhaiguan qianhou' [The battle of Shanhaiguan and its aftermath], in *Shanhaiguan zhi zhan*, ed. Yuan Wei, 73–84; Wu Xiuquan, 'Peihe Sujun jiefang dongbei' [Liberating the north-east in coordination with the Soviet Army], *Liaoshen*, 1: 145–55.
17   Zeng, *Zeng Kelin jiangjun*, 87–98; cf. Lew, *Chinese Revolutionary Civil War*, 26.
18   Yang Kuisong, *Zhongjian didai de geming: Guoji da beijing xia kan Zhonggong chenggong zhi dao* [Revolution in the intermediate zone: The Chinese Communist victory in an international context] (Taiyuan: Shanxi renmin chubanshe, 2010), 472.

days to move them out.[19] However, the CCP cadres in Manchuria reported on 23 September that the Soviet forces were friendly in general but did not show a high level of trust towards their troops.[20] Although done in violation of orders, the capture of Shenyang marked the culmination of the CCP's early success in Manchuria. Using weapons taken from the Japanese armouries, Zeng's troops swiftly added to their numbers.[21] Zeng, now the 'commanding officer of Shenyang garrison command', boarded a Soviet plane back to Yan'an to make his report on 14 September, accompanied by a representative of the Soviet Army.[22]

The Yan'an leadership immediately held a meeting with its Soviet guest. According to PRC records, the Soviet representative requested that the CCP forces vacate the big cities, stating that any troop entry to Manchuria before the complete withdrawal of Soviet forces would be prohibited and that such an injunction was applicable to both the GMD and the CCP armies. The CCP leaders, staying attuned to the verbal cues of their Soviet guest, agreed to an immediate withdrawal of their troops from areas currently occupied by the Red Army on condition that certain units presently stationed in Rehe and the southernmost Manchurian province of Liaoning be allowed to stay where they were.[23] As the CCP leaders chose to comply with the contentious requests of their Soviet visitor, such as that the time frame of China's troop movement into Manchuria had to be set by the Soviets, they made a gesture of goodwill that the CCP would not be an obstacle for the USSR's treaty compliance.

The Soviet representative returned the favour by encouraging the CCP to appoint senior cadres to establish and maintain liaison with the Soviet forces in Manchuria.[24] Perhaps because of this, it is perceived in some quarters that both sides had reached some undisclosed understanding, and the CCP was permitted to send troops into Manchuria without revealing their real

---

19 Zeng, *Zeng Kelin jiangjun*, 101–4.
20 Yang Kuisong, *Zhongjian didai*, 472–3.
21 Cheng, 'Escalation of hostilities in Manchuria', 149; Cheng, 'China's Madrid', 79; Tanner, *Battle for Manchuria*, 43.
22 Zeng, *Zeng Kelin jiangjun*, 98, 105–6.
23 Zhonggong zhongyang wenxian yanjiushi ed., *Zhu De nianpu*, 1208–9.
24 Wu Xiuquan, *Wo de lichen* [A look back over my career] (Beijing: Jiefangjun chubanshe, 1984), 167.

identity.²⁵ At any rate, the achievements of Zeng's vanguard forces went far beyond the expectations of the decision-makers in Yan'an, who began to sense that they could be serious contenders in Manchuria.

Mao's deputy Liu Shaoqi, who played a leading role in decision-making while Mao was in Chongqing, put forward a proposal to establish the North-East Bureau (NEB) of the Central Committee, the CCP's high command in Manchuria. His plan quickly gained consensus in a Politburo meeting on 14 September 1945.²⁶ The new organisation was filled by a large contingent of upper-level cadres who constituted the Manchurian Party leadership. On 18 September, Peng Zhen, a leading member of the powerful CCP Central Committee, set up the NEB headquarters in Shenyang. Under Soviet protection, the NEB effectively accelerated the Communist challenge to the GMD's legitimacy in Manchuria.²⁷ Taking full advantage of this development, Yan'an committed itself to a new civil war strategy summed up in Liu's succinct expression: 'Expand in the north.'²⁸

In a directive to his forces delivered on 19 September, Liu ordered the dispatch of 30,000 troops from Shandong to Manchuria by sea, who would proceed according to schedule, while field forces in eastern China numbering 80,000 were to move northward to fill the vacuum left by the Shandong troops.²⁹ The strategy was in accord with the concession that Zhou made in the Chongqing peace talks of withdrawing from the Liberated Areas in the south. Various army units, notably the elite 1st and 3rd Divisions of the New Fourth Army, began their Manchurian expedition soon after. The redeployment continued on a large scale for the remainder of 1945 and into 1946. The total army redeployment reached a staggering 100,000 troops, representing one-sixth of the regular forces of the CCP.³⁰

At the operational level, Liu endeavoured to undertake two different kinds of army deployment. On the one hand, he attempted to adopt a strategy that would actively seek out major battles as a means to block the GMD's

---

25   Sheng, *Battling Western Imperialism*, 107; Yang Kuisong, *Zhonggong yu Mosike de guanxi, 1920–1960* [The Chinese Communist Party's relations with Moscow, 1920–1960] (Taipei: Dongda tushu gongsi, 1997), 532–3; cf. Niu Jun, 'The origins of the Sino-Soviet Alliance', in *Brothers in Arms: The Rise and Fall of the Sino-Soviet Alliance, 1945–1963*, ed. Odd Arne Westad (Washington, DC: Woodrow Wilson Center Press, 1998), 55.
26   *Liu nianpu*, 1: 490–1.
27   Cheng, 'China's Madrid', 79–80.
28   CC to Chongqing delegation, 17 September 1945, *Zhonggong*, 15: 278–80; Cheng, 'China's Madrid', 79–80.
29   Cheng, 'China's Madrid', 80.
30   Ibid., 79–80; Levine, *Anvil of Victory*, 103.

influx into Manchuria. As Liu's approach required preclusive defence of the entire north-east to the exclusion of other parties, a massive concentration of regular forces was needed to deny Chiang the chance even to set foot in the region.[31]

Liu, who had meanwhile called for a forward defence formation of his armies, proposed to the NEB in late September that they disperse combat units into the most uninhabitable areas of Manchuria to avoid battle in the interim.[32] A directive from Yan'an to the NEB revealed the reason for putting the two diametrically different strategies in place: the leadership was not confident about waging a major battle. Its decentralisation scheme was based on worst-case assumptions: if their field forces could not counter the more modernised GMD armies in the imminent battles, they could still revert to their rural base-area strategy.[33] Although Liu's approach supported Mao's vision of using both guerrilla and regular forces in war, the army found it difficult to prosecute two distinct military strategies.[34]

In practical terms, Liu's redeployment schedule was under pressure from the very beginning. In October, Liu found out that the landing operation was running well behind schedule,[35] although the situation at sea was overwhelmingly in the CCP's favour by the end of 1945. The GMD navy, managing to get only one inland river gunboat (CNS *Changzhi*) ready for operation, was unable to stop the CCP enjoying unfettered sea access.[36] Given that the CCP flotillas recorded just one ship lost in two months because of bad weather, the campaign was undoubtedly underperformed.[37] 'If immediate remedial measures are not taken, [you] will be condemned by history', wrote Liu, venting his frustration to Peng.[38] Mao's intervention, however, soon circumvented Liu's blunt and disparaging criticisms.

---

31 Cheng, 'China's Madrid', 80–1.
32 Cheng, 'Escalation of hostilities in Manchuria', 188–9; Liu to NEB, 24 September, 9 October 1945, *Liu nianpu*, 1: 502, 510; CMC to NEB, 28 September 1945, *Zhonggong*, 15: 299–301.
33 CMC to NEB, 28 September 1945, *Zhonggong*, 15: 299–301; Cheng, 'China's Madrid', 81; cf. Tanner, 'Guerrilla, mobile, and base warfare', 1192.
34 Cheng, 'China's Madrid', 80–1.
35 Ibid., 80–1.
36 Chen Shaokuan to Chiang Kai-shek, 30 November 1945, *Shilüe*, 63: 679.
37 Xiao Hua, 'Hengkua Bohai, jinjun Dongbei' [Cross the Baohai Sea and march towards the north-east], *Liaoshen* 1: 206–16; Li Bingling, 'Hengdu Bohai, jinjun Liaodong' [Cross the Bohai Sea and march towards Liaodong], in *Xueye xiongfeng*, Li Yunchang, 41–5.
38 Liu to Peng, 1 October 1945, *Liu nianpu*, 1: 505.

Mao: Political leader and military planner

Mao overruled Liu's decentralisation policy after he returned from Chongqing. His new ambition was to defeat the Nationalists at the metropolitan centres of Manchuria and to occupy the entire region. He instructed his generals to concentrate the main forces inside the industrialised Jinzhou–Yingkou–Shenyang triangle and prevent the Nationalists from having a quick and easy entry. The strategy would have gained more time for the NEB to establish stable base areas for the total control of the region.[39]

Mao's force concentration strategy was first developed against the backdrop of the Soviet–GMD dispute over Manchuria, which forced Chiang to push his troops into the north-east via an overland route and staked everything on the hope that his armies could capture the Shanhaiguan–Jinzhou land transport corridor. The CCP's bold and successful military actions since mid-October in North China also offered Mao grounds for optimism. In the Henan–Hebei border, for instance, the CCP's operational successes had motivated the defection of a senior GMD commander and his 10,000 followers. Further north, Fu's Nationalist cavalry units were besieged by Mao's armies in the strategic towns of Baotou and Guisui along the section of Beiping–Guisui railway located in the province of Suiyuan.[40] For the CCP, there would not be a more opportune time than this to strike Chiang's isolated expeditionary forces at the gate of Manchuria. Stepping up preparations for war, Mao reorganised his Manchurian forces, establishing the North-East People's Autonomous Army (NEPAA); at the end of October, Lin Biao, one of Mao's best generals, was appointed its commander.[41]

In early November, the advanced detachments of the GMD 13A had started the assault on the CCP-occupied Shanhaiguan but were easily repulsed by the NEPAA. The CCP commanders soon discovered that the more modernised enemy forces were not as strong as they originally thought. The 13A was a US-armed army, meaning that it was an elite force equipped with a full suite of army equipment supplied by the Americans under the US wartime commitment of refitting thirty-nine GMD army divisions with advanced US weapons. However, the 39 Division Program was only

---

39 CC to NEB, 19 October 1945, *Zhonggong*, 15: 364–6.
40 CC to regional bureaux, 9 November 1945, *Zhonggong*, 15: 417–18; Geng Routian, *Zhongguo jiaofei kanluan*, 2: 31–2.
41 Cheng, 'China's Madrid', 82.

about 43 per cent complete by September 1945.⁴² The US military advisers refitted the infantrymen of the 13A with US carbines as standard rifles but did not supply the bayonets and provided bullets for military exercises only. Rifles without bayonets retained only half their value to the Nationalist infantrymen, who still relied heavily on the bayonet charge as a major infantry tactic. The logistical challenge affected the combat readiness of the 13A, particularly in close-range engagement against the enemy's bayonet charges, although it still enjoyed enormous superiority in artillery firepower over the NEPAA.⁴³

With great confidence, Mao envisaged large-scale battles in Jinzhou. He requested the NEPAA units charged with garrisoning Shanhaiguan to hold the first line of defence for at least three weeks and to inflict great losses on the enemy. His plan was that while the Nationalists procrastinated, the NEPAA's main forces of around 70,000 men in the Jinzhou area would mount pre-emptive attacks when the GMD armies, weakened by the Shanhaiguan defenders, arrived. Mao's war plan had quickly become a widespread article of faith among the army's high command. Li Yunchang, now the deputy commander of the NEPAA, put forward a fairly aggressive proposal to Lin requesting a geographical expansion of the battlefield into Hebei that sought to sever the GMD's supply line between North China and Manchuria.⁴⁴

Mao's plan received overwhelming inner-party support for practical reasons: it was almost impossible for the CCP to launch the Maoist guerrilla-warfare-influenced protracted war at that stage in Manchuria. Manchuria, like some of the formerly Japanese-held territories in China proper, had been occupied only recently by the CCP combatants, who did not enjoy the local support they were accustomed to in their home bases. The CCP's preferred guerrilla tactic of sabotaging railroad lines, for instance, was now facing possible local resistance. The GMD hailed the restoration of commuter rail services as a priority policy⁴⁵ and vehemently criticised the CCP's guerrilla-style railway sabotage operations, which deprived locals of their right to return to their

---

42   Patterson to Byrnes, 18 February 1946, *FRUS*, 1946, 10: 728–35.
43   Cheng, 'Modern war', 42–4; Du Yuming, 'Guomindang pohuai heping', 524–8; Zheng Dongguo, *Wo de rongma shengyai* [My army life] (Beijing: Tuanjie chubanshe, 1992), 290, 298.
44   Cheng, 'China's Madrid', 82–3.
45   Du Yuming to Chiang, 25 November 1945, *Shilüe*, 63: 645–6.

pre-war homes.⁴⁶ Mao subsequently urged his commanders to give away the dismantled railway timber sleepers and metal parts to the locals, hoping that this tactic would reduce the public backlash against his troops.⁴⁷

Operating in Manchuria, the CCP forces were disconnected from the self-sufficient economy of the Liberated Areas, meaning that these forces would be facing logistics problems almost immediately.⁴⁸ This had been a widespread problem for many other CCP army units operating away from their guerrilla headquarters after the Japanese surrender. In late 1945, Mao was always in an unpleasant mood when he was asked to offer supply and financial assistance to his frontline commanders.⁴⁹ For Mao and his generals, the most direct way to fix the problem was ousting Chiang's two isolated US-armed armies from Manchuria by means of a number of force-concentrated military operations in quick succession and establishing self-sufficient permanent bases after the military success.⁵⁰ After he returned from Chongqing, Mao pitched his expectations to his armies' force-concentrated offensives against the enemy in both Manchuria and China proper, and he sent a flurry of directives to his field commanders promoting the principle of force concentration. According to Mao, the highly concentrated CCP forces should not attempt to win the campaign with one decisive attack. Rather, the strategic goal of destroying the enemy forces should be achieved by several successive military operations within a relatively short period.⁵¹

Mao, as a military planner, could not guarantee quick operational successes at bearable cost; but as a political leader, he tried to create aura of optimism in order to persuade his generals that the war was something worth fighting for. The deliberate use of strong emotive phrases was therefore required in Mao's directives for shoring up support. Mao's persuasive tactics employed a variety of morale-boosting political language, which alluded to the *decisiveness* of the imminent battles. For example, in his exhortatory and mandatory directives to his generals, Mao regularly applied rhetorical devices, describing his forces' combat assignments as 'sacred' (shensheng 神聖), of 'great significance'

46   Fu Zuoyi to Mao Zedong, *Zhongyang ribao* [Central Daily News], 26 October 1945, Shanghai.
47   Mao to Chen Yi and Li Yu, cc. Central China Bureau, 30 October 1945, Mao to Xiao Ke and Luo Ruiqing, 10 November 1945; Mao to Li Yunchang and Sa Ke, 14 November 1945, *Junshi*, 3: 97–8, 128–9, 139–40.
48   Wang Chaoguang, 'Guogong neizhan chuqi', 531.
49   See, for example, Mao to Zheng Weisan and Li Xiannian, 22 October 1945, *Junshi*, 3: 69–70.
50   Mao to Shanxi–Hebei–Shandong–Henan Bureau, 17 October 1945; Mao to Peng Zhen, 2 November 1945, *Junshi*, 3: 60–1, 117–18.
51   Mao to Luo Ronghuan, Li Zuopeng, Chen Yi and Li Yu, cc Central China Bureau, 19 October 1945; Mao to Liu Bocheng and Deng Xiaoping, 30 October 1945, *Junshi*, 3: 65–6, 93–4.

(weida yiyi 偉大意義) and as having 'important bearing' (guanxi zhongda 關係重大), and the battles themselves as 'shifting the balance of the situation' (zhuanbian jushi 轉變局勢).⁵² Since Mao's political rhetoric frequently mingled with the actual combat instructions in his telegrams, these military telegrams sometimes pose a challenge for contemporary scholars who study them. Meanwhile, Mao was not worried about which components in his war plans were more Maoist than others. He was waiting in suspense for his frontline commanders to carry out his orders.

The insurgents and the counterinsurgents

The difficulty lay not so much in whether the CCP army high command would support Mao's plan but whether Mao was demanding his troops do more than they were capable of. A military report revealed that the CCP defenders in Shanhaiguan had no more than 13,000 men—a force substantially outnumbered by some 70,000 incoming enemy troops. The troops were also hampered by a lack of arms. It was true that the Soviets had transferred a certain amount of Japanese weaponry to the CCP forces, but they were initially unable to bring most of the newly acquired weapons to the front lines. The reason for the delay was, among other causes, the CCP's inferior logistic capability.⁵³ In short, the CCP army units in Shanhaiguan were equivalent only to an ill-armed militia in late 1945.

Mao's main striking force, the 3rd and 1st Divisions, were in no way better equipped than their understrength comrades. The two army divisions had just arrived at eastern Hebei en route to Manchuria. In order to fulfil Mao's requirements, they needed to reach Jinzhou well before the Nationalists so that they could fortify positions and fight the incoming enemies as defenders. Unfortunately, the 3rd Division suffered from non-combat casualties, and troop numbers dropped from 35,000 to 32,000 after arriving from northern Jiangsu. The surviving combatants were seriously underfed. Also, the army was deliberately not equipped with winter outfits suitable for the pitiless cold in Manchuria so that it could move rapidly; the strategy succeeded, but at great cost.⁵⁴

---

52 See, for example, Mao to Shanxi–Chahar–Hebei Bureau and Shanxi–Suiyuan Bureau, 16 October 1945; Mao to Liu Bocheng, Deng Xiaoping, Bo Yibo, Zhang Jichun and Li Da, 27 October and 3 November 1945; Mao to Liu Bocheng and Deng Xiaoping, 29 October 1945, *Junshi*, 3: 57–9, 84–6, 91–2, 119–20.
53 Cheng, 'China's Madrid', 83; *Liu nianpu*, 1: 502.
54 Cheng, 'China's Madrid', 83–4.

Mao showed little sympathy for his distressed troops. He required his main forces to act as combat-capable regular armies, but at the same time he advocated the guerrilla warfare principle of self-sufficiency. When Huang Kecheng, the head of the 3rd Division, telegraphed his grievances to Mao, the chairman sulked over Huang's complaint. In his reply, Mao asked Huang to organise logistic supplies by himself. As a field commander, Lin Biao apparently did not want to do anything to ruffle Mao, but he nevertheless overruled Li's 9 November proposal to expand operations into Hebei. In a dispatch to Mao on 13 November, Lin refined Li's plan into a smaller-scale offensive scheme and planned a hit-and-run attack against the enemy that would employ guerrilla tactics. Although Lin Biao pandered to Mao's opinions by endorsing the latter's emphasis on the enemy's weakness, his plan was entirely incompatible with Mao's ambitious war plan.[55]

Mao's battle plan was severely challenged when the Nationalists launched the final assault on 15 November. The 13A began to storm Shanhaiguan after a light infantry unit from the 52A was dispatched to manoeuvre around the NEPAA's north-west flank.[56] In contrast to the 13A, the 52A was a lightly armed army, half of which was armed with US weapons.[57] This meant that the infantrymen of the 52A were armed with locally made rifles, but the army was also equipped with a small number of US arms (e.g. US-made submachine guns and anti-tank guns). It is notable that the troop numbers of GMD army units were in constant fluctuation and the quantity of the weaponry in each army varied accordingly; but in general, the quantity of the US weapons in a GMD 'half American-armed' army was around a third to a sixth less than its 'full' American-armed contemporary during the Chinese Civil War. For example, the 52A was equipped with US 60mm mortars as company-level fire support but each infantry company only possessed two pieces, whereas a similar company in the Nationalist US-armed New First Army (N1A), which operated in Manchuria in 1946, had six.[58]

---

55   Ibid., 84; Cheng, 'Escalation of hostilities in Manchuria', 202–4.
56   Cheng, 'China's Madrid', 84; Cheng, 'Escalation of hostilities in Manchuria', 203–4.
57   Du Yuming, 'Guomindang pohuai heping', 525.
58   Wang Chuying (commissioner, Nanjing City Branch Committee, the People's Consultative Conference, formerly head of the Operational Department, 14th Division, the New 6th Army, National Army), interviewed by Victor Cheng, Nanjing, 14 November 1996; Liao Yaoxiang and Du Jianshi, 'Guanyu Meijiang goujie de neimu' [A behind-the-scenes report of the Americans' collaboration with Chiang Kai-shek], in *Wenshi ziliao jingxuan* [A selection of literary–historical source materials], ed. Wenshi ziliao xuanji bianji bu [Editorial group of the literary–historical source materials collections] (Zhongguo wenshi ziliao chubanshe, 1990), 12: 1–64.

The infiltration capacity of the light infantry of the 52A was superb as long as it was put under the command of competent officers with discretionary powers. A recent study shows that the GMD's speedy light infantry units were the only real threat to the CCP guerrillas in the initial stage of the fighting in Manchuria. These units were capable of adopting forced night marches and employing unorthodox artillery tactics effectively against the enemy.[59] Nevertheless, the main fighting machine of the 52A, the three combat-capable infantry divisions, had been stretched thin. One division was withdrawn from the main battlefield at the beginning of the campaign under Du's order and redeployed to eastern Hebei near Du's command centre in Qinhuangdao.[60] The deployment was a reaction to increased CCP guerrilla activities in the south of the Great Wall line, which threatened the rear of the entire GMD Manchurian expeditionary force. At times, the 52A had to spare as much as one division to protect its supply battalions and field hospitals attached to the army's headquarters. In short, the 52A could have been left with just one division to engage the enemies at the point of contact.[61] Furthermore, both the 52A and 13A not only were scrupulous in protecting the impediments from enemy attacks but also were meticulous about following the pre-planned combat arrays in pushing the armies forward. Disordered marches of some combat units at the beginning of the campaign were quickly rectified.[62] The conservatism poses the question of whether the Nationalists intended to win the war on its defence power alone or just aimed to repel the insurgents from the main communication line.

The Nationalists also were punctilious about confidentiality, but this was achieved at the expense of the efficiency of army staff and communication between units. During the critical stage of the battles in the Shanhaiguan–Jinzhou zone from 14 to 25 November 1945, it took about ten hours on average for a combat instruction to be passed from Du's headquarters to the headquarters of the 52A before it moved through the chain of command down to the divisional heads. The slowest and the fastest times recorded for

---

59 Cheng, 'Modern war', 44–5.
60 Du Yuming to Zhao Gongwu, 16 November 1945, in *Kangri zhanzheng shiqi Guomindang jun jimi zuozhan riji* [Confidential field diaries of the GMD armies during the War of Resistance against Japan], ed. Zhongguo dier lishi dang'anguan [The second historical archives of China] (Beijing: Zhongguo dang'an chubanshe, 1995), 2015 (hereafter *Zuozhan riji*).
61 Zhao Gongwu to all unit heads of the 52A, 17 November 1945, *Zuozhan riji*, 2018–19.
62 Chen and Chang eds, *Shi Jue xiansheng*, 213–14; Du Yuming to Zhao Gongwu, 19 November 1945, *Zuozhan riji*, 2020–21.

these orders to be sent from Du's headquarters to the divisional heads of the 52A were, respectively, twenty-two hours on 14–15 November and three hours on 19 November.[63]

Of the two Nationalist main forces operating in Manchuria in November, the 13A was normally sent to carry out frontal assaults, whereas the 52A was responsible for flanking attacks. Zhao Gongwu, the commander of the 52A, had to tread carefully to ensure that his troops would not complete the flanking movement too quickly and, in particular, not occupy the positions that were originally supposed to be for the 13A, as this would cause embarrassment for Shi Jue, his fellow army commander of the 13A. On one occasion, Zhao halted the pursuit in order to avoid overtaking the 13A instead of continuing the circle movement towards an NEPAA-held town.[64]

As their superiors were overwhelmed by bureaucracy and politics, individual officers of the 52A had to ignore orders and perform unauthorised and audacious actions for combat success.[65] Individual acts of heroism were rare, however. The GMD elite corps could be a lethal fighting force given that their commanding officers allowed them to be. Cases like this were also rare in the history of the National Army during the Chinese Civil War. On 15 November 1945 in Shanhaiguan, however, it happened.

'Build stable base areas in the north-east'

On 15 November in Shanhaiguan, a contingent of the 52A made an oblique thrust across the NEPAA's unfortified flank. The Communist defenders realised that the garrison town would soon become a cut-off bastion. They received orders to retreat on 16 November.[66] The Nationalist deep-penetration corps pushed forward to overtake the withdrawing NEPAA, but their poor coordination allowed the CCP troops to slip through.[67]

Also, on 15 November, Mao cabled a long epistle to Lin and Peng, enunciating a fairly ambitious war plan. At the beginning of the telegram, Mao acknowledged that there were no combat-ready units in his main forces

---

63 Zhao Gongwu's field diaries, entries 14–25 November 1945, *Zuozhan riji*, 2011–35.
64 Zhao Gongwu to 2nd Division commander Liu, 20 November 1945, *Zuozhan riji*, 2023.
65 Yang Jingbin ed., *Wushierjun*, 17–18.
66 Zhang Heming, 'Guanyu Shanhaiguan baoweizhan de zongjie baogao' [A report on the battle of defence of Shanhaiguan], c. 1946, in *Shanhaiguan zhi zhan*, ed. Yuan Wei, 172–6.
67 Yang Jingbin ed., *Wushierjun*, 5–10; Cheng, 'China's Madrid', 84.

3. CIVIL WAR IN THE NORTH-EAST

at present as a number of combat units were still en route to Manchuria and besieged by severe fatigue. Before moving on to tactical issues, Mao tried to boost the morale of his commanders and exhausted armies. Mao, as most political leaders would have done in the same situation, expressed hope to his men that the hardships they endured in the short term would be rewarded by a decisive victory *in the future*.[68] In this regard, Mao's rhetorical style in the telegram was consistent with those he sent to the frontline commanders in China proper since he had returned from Chongqing.

Mao told Lin and Peng to take prudent measures to ensure that these main forces would be sent to fight only when they were combat-ready and 'in the hope that the problems will be solved in a decisive battle in the future'.[69] Although Mao did use the phrase 'decisive battle' (*jue zhan* 決戰) twice in his ambitious war plan, his explication was so clear that Lin and Peng could not be under any misapprehension that they were being pushed to accomplish one final, decisive victory over the GMD in Manchuria. Put simply, Mao's rhetorical use of 'decisive battle' was nothing but one of the magic terms from his political language intended to create an atmosphere of war-eve optimism.[70] As Mao's subordinates, Lin and Peng certainly knew that it was not up to them to make judgements on the *decisiveness* of a military victory because it was a political issue to be determined by politicians. As Colin Gray puts it, such a judgement was 'above their pay grade'.[71] What really mattered was what Mao would order Lin to do under the circumstances.

Mao delivered his combat instruction to Lin in the second half of the telegram, calling for force-concentrated counter-attacks against the Nationalists at the time and place of Lin's choosing: 'to split the offensive into a number of combats, eliminate two to three enemy divisions one at a time and finally accomplish the annihilation of the enemy's *three armies* [emphasis added]'.[72] Mao envisaged that when Lin's main force conducted the *decisive* future war, it would be bolstered by two new brigades, albeit these anticipated reinforcement units were still deployed in eastern Hebei at that time.[73] In short, Mao overruled Lin's guerrilla-minded hit-and-run and Liu's decentralisation plans, but his ambitious war plan was in line with the

---

68   Mao to Lin Biao and Peng Zhen, 15 November 1945, *Junshi*, 3: 143.
69   Ibid., 143.
70   For further discussion, see Blainey, *The Causes of War*, 35–56.
71   Gray, *Defining and Achieving Decisive Victory*, 12.
72   Mao to Lin Biao and Peng Zhen, 15 November 1945, *Junshi*, 3: 143–4.
73   Ibid., 144.

instructions he had sent to other forces fighting in China proper: achieving operational successes via several force-concentrated offensives, securing self-sufficient Communist bases in the aftermath of the battles and embracing a decisive victory in the future.

Notably, Mao stated at the opening of the telegram that Chiang was currently sending two armies (i.e. the 13A and the 52A) to the north-east, but he speculated that there would be at least one more enemy army to come, and the timing of its arrival remained uncertain.[74] Even if Lin won the current battles against the existing two enemy armies, Chiang would send another one to fight them. In other words, Mao had predicted that the war would drag on. Mao micromanaged Lin's battle plans, but he considered military victory from a strategic perspective even though it might affect Lin's tactical decision-making. In the strategic level of war, victory is not likely to be achieved before a series of attritional battles have been waged. Gray has argued that a strategically decisive victory does not need to be 'a single climactic clash of arms, but may rather be the outcome of an attritional struggle' for policy-makers.[75]

Mao's ambitious plan wilted quickly as the GMD armies surged forward in force along the main railway before Lin could concentrate his forces. With only token resistance, they allowed the GMD to seize towns between Shanghaiguan and Jinzhou on 22 November.[76] In the environs of Huludao, several retreating NEPAA detachments were outpaced by a contingent of the 2nd Division of the 52A waiting for its enemies to arrive after completing an unauthorised pursuit with crushing momentum the night before. More than 150 NEPAA combatants were taken prisoner by the Nationalists when they fronted the machine-gun formations of the 2nd Division.[77]

While the CCP war machine was thrown out of gear, its supreme leader also endured an enforced layoff. Mao was hospitalised from mid-November for neurasthenia. Liu took charge again. Guerrilla tactics (e.g. hit-and-run attacks and night-time raids) and in-depth defence were once again the priority of the Yan'an leadership. The CCP's misfortunes were exacerbated when the Nationalists launched a diplomatic offensive. In mid-November, the GMD ordered the withdrawal of its delegation from Changchun in protest against Moscow's uncooperative attitude—a major event that is discussed further in

---

74 Ibid., 143.
75 Gray, *Defining and Achieving Decisive Victory*, 11.
76 Cheng, 'China's Madrid', 85.
77 Yang Jingbin ed., *Wushierjun*, 13–30; Du Yuming, 'Guomindang pohuai heping', 532–4.

chapter 5. The Soviets, caught in a barrage of diplomatic criticism, resorted to sacrificing the CCP. The Red Army therefore informed the NEPAA that it would hand over the cities along the Chinese Changchun Railway to the Nationalists, and the NEPAA would be required to retreat. Liu immediately instructed the NEPAA to evacuate the big cities, apparently trying to avoid ruffling the Soviets.[78]

Lin was acutely aware that the change in the political status quo would inevitably entail modifications to the CCP military strategy. On 21 November, he dispatched a telegram from the front line to both Yan'an and the NEB requesting permission to withdraw his forces northward away from Jinzhou in order to avoid being crushed by the enemy. An unpalatable subtext of Lin's idea was that unless the enemy's units stretched out in a battle line and made themselves vulnerable, an offensive would be pointless.[79] While acknowledging Lin's tactics, Liu was slowly but steadily moving towards reinstating his policy of force decentralisation and gradually abandoning Mao's more ambitious war plan. This trend was evident in an oft-quoted precept delivered on 22 November: 'Leave the high road alone and seize the land on both sides.'[80]

The NEB was evacuated from Shenyang on 23 November under pressure from the Soviets and moved to Benxi, a town in the south-east of Shenyang.[81] The Nationalists continued to orchestrate the proceedings on the battlefield. On 26 November, the GMD armies took Jinzhou after subduing the NEPAA's token resistance. When Jinzhou fell to the Nationalists, Huang's division was still lumbering through the periphery of the city. The fall of Jinzhou dashed Mao's hopes for the chance of an early operational success. Huang's troops finally retreated from the outskirts of Jinzhou after gaining Lin's permission.[82]

The occupation of Jinzhou kick-started the Nationalists' campaign to recover the vast territory of the north-east, but it also began to show in this early stage that the increasing logistics and communication difficulties had already stretched Du's armies to the limit. The logistics simply failed to keep

---

78 Cheng, 'China's Madrid', 85.
79 Cheng, 'China's Madrid', 85, 105, fn. 15; Cheng, 'Escalation of hostilities in Manchuria', 181–223; cf. Tanner, 'Guerrilla, mobile, and base warfare', 1204.
80 CC to Chongqing delegation, 22 November 1945, *Liu nianpu*, 530–1; Cheng, 'China's Madrid', 85–6.
81 *Liaoshen*, 2: 597.
82 Cheng, 'China's Madrid', 86.

up with the needs of the armies, and Du was forced to halt the pursuit in order to recuperate.[83] The Americans agreed to provide immediate relief for ammunition shortage, but even modern US military transport aircraft struggled to deal with the poor conditions of the Jinzhou airfield.[84] The GMD's US-equipped armies, like their CCP enemies, were faced with communication problems. When his command centre headed north, Du was unable to maintain direct radio communication with Chongqing because of poor radio reception. Chiang Kai-shek was left in disbelief after receiving a three-day delayed telegram from Du.[85]

The inadequacy of radio equipment might take Chiang by surprise, but he was well informed that his expeditionary force had been stretched thin and that its left flank was vulnerable to enemy attack across provincial borders from Rehe.[86] In early December, Chiang sent two consecutive instructions to Du, prohibiting the latter from pushing the armies north-east towards Shenyang.[87] On 6 December, Du was summoned back to Chongqing to receive confidential briefings from Chiang.[88] As it turned out, the GMD armies were tied at the first line of defence in Jinzhou for a month, providing the NEPAA with a long lull in which to consolidate its newly occupied territories.

Liu tried to turn disappointment into success by shifting the focus from Manchuria to North China.[89] The military picture there, however, led to further disappointment. Successful Nationalist counter-attacks started in mid-November brought the CCP campaign in Suiyuan Province to a sorry end in early December.[90] The developing situation in North China strengthened Liu's determination to restore his force decentralisation scheme in Manchuria. He dispatched a deluge of telegrams to both the NEB and the NEPAA pressing for decentralisation and strategies focused on small towns from late November onward.[91]

---

83 Du Yuming, 'Guomindang pohuai heping', 535.
84 Geng Routian, *Zhongguo jiaofei kanluan*, 2: 40–2.
85 Wang Shuming to Chiang, 29 November 1945, *Shilüe*, 63: 700–1; Chiang to Du, 3 December 1945, *Shilüe*, 64: 14.
86 This was the advice that Chiang received from his aide Yu Jishi on 22 November 1945. See *Shilüe*, 63: 622.
87 Chiang to Du, 3 and 6 December 1945, *Shilüe*, 64: 14, 43.
88 Chiang to Du, c/o Wang Shuming, 6 December 1945, *JZZW*, 002-020400-00001-114, AH.
89 Liu to Nie Rongzhen, Geng Biao, He Long, Li Jingquan and Zhang Jingwu, 22 November 1945, *Liu nianpu*, 1: 532–3.
90 Geng Routian, *Zhongguo jiaofei kanluan*, 2: 31–3.
91 Liu to NEB, 20 November to 8 December 1945, *Zhonggong*, 15: 431–75.

While Liu was making decisions in a fluid and fluctuating environment, he kept imposing minor changes on his plans, although he and the leadership did not back away from the idea of building permanent rural bases. For example, Liu instructed the NEB to gain the initiative in the big cities on 19 November but revised it a day later by asking for the NEB to control the secondary cities after evacuating from the metropolis.[92] Liu's decision-making style was not unusual for leaders in modern Chinese history, who kept changing their mind on decisions they had made. It nonetheless provides a niche for a claim that the Yan'an leadership 'rejected a strategy of building countryside bases' and adopted the so-called three large cities strategy (i.e. capturing Shenyang, Changchun and Harbin) allegedly proposed by Peng, the NEB boss.[93]

Such a claim is made primarily on the basis of a speech that Peng delivered on 26 October 1945.[94] In that policy speech to the cadres, Peng unveiled a variety of policies, including the rural base areas development and a northward decentralisation scheme. The urban area was only one of many focuses in Peng's speech. He asserted that his bureau was committed to taking over all the provinces, cities and counties in Manchuria.[95] Contrary to the aforementioned argument, Peng did not advocate a 'city first' or the 'Three Large Cities Strategy' to the extent that it 'represented a radical departure from the party line'.[96] Notably, Peng did not even mention the names of the three biggest Manchurian cities during his speech. The full text shows that Peng, the NEB's top bureaucrat, did not want to go rogue in relation to Yan'an's policies. Rather, he followed them *all* in a broad sense—trying to motivate his forces to overrun the *whole* north-east.[97]

In his recollections, Peng insisted that he merely followed instructions from Yan'an together with the party's campaigning zeal at that stage. Peng also remembered that the orders he received from Yan'an between late

---

92   Liu to the NEB, 19–20 November 1945, *Zhonggong*, 15: 429–32.
93   Lew, *Chinese Revolutionary Civil War*, 29.
94   Ibid., 28–30, 160–1, fn. 56.
95   Peng Zhen, 'Wo men de renwu shi zhengqu quan dongbei' [Our responsibilities for dominating the whole north-east], 26 October 1945, in *Peng Zhen wenxuan* [Selected works of Peng Zhen], ed. Zhonggong zhongyang wenxian bianji weiyuanhui [Historical source materials compliance committee of the Central Committee of the CCP] (Beijing: Renmin chubanshe, 1991), 103–5.
96   Lew, *Chinese Revolutionary Civil War*, 28–30, 160–1, fn. 56, esp. 28, 30; Tanner, *Battle for Manchuria*, 89.
97   Peng Zhen, 'Wo men de renwu'.

September and mid-October 1945 were plans for both decentralisation and force concentration. Peng maintained that he did not in any way act against orders from the top.[98]

As well as a lack of consistent advice from Yan'an on operational priorities, the tactical difficulties caused an added burden to Peng in executing Liu's decentralisation plan. In Manchuria, most of the population and industrial infrastructure were concentrated in a few industrial belts along the main railways. Away from these urban centres were areas of primitive wilderness and inaccessible mountainous terrain.

A Japanese military analyst of the 1930s, Shinsake Hirata, once used the phrase 'uncivilised war zone' to describe conducting military operation in the Manchurian backcountry. This was a mission to be feared even by the best-equipped corps.[99] The harsh conditions of the bandit-plagued rural areas made it all but impossible for the ill-equipped CCP forces to live off the country without establishing strong ties with the local population. However, the territories that Liu required the NEB to penetrate in September were the remote and sparsely inhabited parts of southern and northern Manchuria.[100]

Most importantly, as Liu's initial plan was to occupy the entire north-east, which required control of the cities, the NEB had developed certain affiliates to further that purpose; these organisations could survive only in urban areas. The North-East Bank, for example, was established as an agency to expand the CCP fiscal–military state to Manchuria. It issued currency by using the industrial plants in Shenyang as fixed assets, but it was now facing bankruptcy after evacuating from the city. Once they abandoned all they had already done, the NEB headquarters argued, they would find themselves holding only a few enclaves in the mountainous regions and would be reduced from a position of superiority to being in dire straits.[101] Peng was therefore in agreement with Liu that, while it was important to develop rural bases through the decentralisation of forces,

---

98 Peng Zhen, 'Dongbei jiefang zhanzhen de tou jiugeyue' [The first nine months of the Liberation War in the North-east], November 1988, in *Liaoshen juezhan xuji* [The Liaoshen Campaign, a supplementary volume], ed. Liaoshen zhanyi jinianguan guanli weiyuanhui [The Committee Board of the Museum of Liaoshen Campaign] and Liaoshen juezhan xuji bianshen xiaozu [The editorial group of 'Liaoshen Campaign, a supplementary volume'] (Beijing: Renmin chubanshe, 1992), 3–19.
99 Quoted in Waijiao yanjuhui [The association for the study of diplomacy] ed., *Dongbei zhanlüe tieluwang* [Strategic railway network in Manchuria] (n.p.: 1936), 70–1; available at Ministry of Justice Investigation Bureau, Taipei; call no. Diao (調) 527.254.7445.
100 CC to NEB, 28 September 1945, *Zhonggong*, 15: 299–301.
101 Cheng, 'China's Madrid', 86–7. For the significance of financial power to the CCP rule, see Lai, *Springboard to Victory*.

3. CIVIL WAR IN THE NORTH-EAST

it was equally important that enough troops remained in the small towns and minor communication lines and that they stayed close enough to ramp up pressure on the big cities, which the enemies would occupy.[102] The resulting ambiguity and obscurity of Liu's approach nonetheless gave rise to an internal debate between Liu and his NEB comrades over the most appropriate level of force decentralisation.

Amid his unceasing worries, Liu sent exhortative telegrams to the NEB in late December pressing for the development of rural bases in the most remote areas near the border. The gist of the telegrams was basically identical to that which Liu and the leadership delivered in late September, only the tone was much stronger. In one occasion, Liu badgered Peng to give up hopes of seizing the major cities, criticising Peng's move as 'risky' and advising him to take precautionary measures to avoid being attacked by both the Nationalists and the bandits in the event of real war.[103] The debate abruptly ended when Mao broke his silence and made the final ruling from his hospital bed. On 28 December, he sent a lengthy telegram to the NEB to rehabilitate the *old* base-area strategy as his *new* plan. 'Our party's present task in the north-east is to build base areas ... The regions in which to build stable bases are the cities and vast rural areas comparatively remote from the centres of Kuomintang occupation', Mao wrote.[104] Mao's expectations for force-concentrated operational successes seemed at that moment to be no more than a distant memory.

'Wipe out the enemy forces one by one'

During the battles of Shanhaiguan–Jinzhou zone, Mao and Liu were fighting their own battle against competitive military priorities. As political leaders, Mao and Liu needed their frontline commanders to realise combat successes in order to force Chiang to pull his troops out of Manchuria and concede at the negotiating table. Nevertheless, as Lawrence Freedman notes, war's political character attracts politicians who wish to run it themselves,[105] and Mao and Liu were not immune to the behaviour of micromanaging the military, which is commonly seen among political leaders in war. In the

---

102 NEB directives, 8 and 15 December 1945, *Zhonggong*, 15: 505–11.
103 CC to NEB, 21 December 1945, *Zhonggong*, 15: 504–5; Cheng, 'China's Madrid', 87.
104 Mao Zedong, 'Build stable base areas in the north-east', 28 December 1945, in *Selected Works, Mao*, 4: 81–3.
105 Lawrence D. Freedman, 'Calling the Shots: Should politicians or generals run our wars?', *Foreign Affairs* 81, no. 5 (2002): 188–94.

critical stage of battles, Mao had a proclivity for meddling in key operational matters, ranging from force deployments and the duration of maintaining an area defence to the scale of the offensive. In other words, Mao and Liu, in addition to their roles as political leaders, had to find a way to connect the political objective and military power through the 'highly imprecise art' of strategy.[106]

Lin and Peng, the CCP's top leaders in the north-east, were labouring under pressure from Liu and Mao. While Peng tried in vain to follow the party line, Lin attempted to advise Mao as to what the armies could and could not achieve by imposing major revisions on Li's ambitious battle plan instead of testing Mao's tolerance to his recalcitrance. As a soldier, it was hard for Lin to deny reality: the enemy suffered from political and diplomatic difficulties at the top and military incompetence on the field. In addition, his fellow commanders in China proper had enjoyed a recent successful experience in annihilating the GMD's US-armed armies.[107] These occurrences provided more justification for quick and large-scale military actions than risk-averse measures. This is because the lesser the aggressiveness of the battle plan, the more modest the political objective, thus allowing the enemy more leeway to manoeuvre.[108] As a field commander, Lin's position was even more awkward, particularly when he could not find a unified view among his subordinates about the conduct of battles. Freedman has argued that 'war management is political through and through' and that civilian leaders should accept the responsibilities of making crucial decisions in war.[109] When their generals disagreed among themselves, Mao and Liu's political guidance seemed not a violation of common sense.

Yet political interference with military affairs is a daunting task for politicians, and the quality and consequences of such meddling cannot be guaranteed.[110] As shown, Mao and Liu had to come to terms with the error-prone human calculation of logistical supplies of their armies and cope with the usually conservative, sometimes vulnerable and yet potentially dangerous US-armed enemies. The exhortatory telegrams from Mao and Liu to their generals vividly demonstrate the contradictory role of both men as political leaders and military planners. Mao's discourse on force-concentrated operations in quick succession was constructed as part of the

---

106 Gray, *Defining and Achieving Decisive Victory*, 15.
107 Mao to Chongqing delegation, 2 November 1945, *Junshi*, 3: 115–16.
108 Gray, *Defining and Achieving Decisive Victory*, 15.
109 Freedman, 'Calling the shots', 191.
110 Ibid., 191.

war atmosphere rather than an act of sheer folly. As a military planner, Mao surely was not a perfect man who was able to design an ideal war plan ahead of time. Helmuth Graf von Moltke once asserted: 'No plan of operations reaches with any certainty beyond the first encounter with the enemy's main force.'[111] The ability to adjust and adapt seems to be more important to military planning.[112] This perhaps explains why the party historians of the CCP have been extolling Mao's virtues for his change of heart over the party's Manchurian strategy.[113]

Mao never would have thought his rhetorical use of the term 'decisive war' would prompt later generations to assume that he asked his generals to deliver victory via a single, decisive and climactic battle against the Nationalist elite corps at Jinzhou in November 1945. However, Mao would have agreed that, in a sense, the decisive battle characterisation of his military thoughts acknowledges his courage in making tough decisions. One of Mao's military treatises written in 1946 nevertheless seems to provide a good summary of his directives delivered at the end of 1945: he asserted that the attacking CCP combat units should not attempt to annihilate 'all the encircled enemy simultaneously at one swoop'. Rather, they should 'wipe out the enemy forces one by one', as this 'has been a fine tradition of our army ever since its founding more than a decade ago'.[114]

China without tears?

While his armies halted at the first line of defence at Jinzhou, Du hurriedly flew to Chongqing to meet Chiang on 8 December. Chiang ordered Du to push his armies to the environs of Shenyang, where he would be liaising with the Soviet forces for the takeover of the city. Du would also wage a northward offensive, at Chiang's behest, to secure the Manchuria–Rehe–Hebei cross-border transport links.[115] Meanwhile, the Soviets dropped heavy hints that the Nationalists would be requested to negotiate an agreement with the Soviet forces before advancing troops to cities still

---

111 Trevor Royle ed., *A Dictionary of Military Quotations* (New York: Simon & Schuster, 1989), 94.
112 Gray, *Defining and Achieving Decisive Victory*, 21.
113 Mao, 'Build stable base areas', 82, fn.
114 Mao, 'Concentrate a superior force to destroy the enemy forces one by one', 16 September 1946, in *Selected Works*, Mao, 4: 103–5.
115 Du Yuming, 'Guomindang pohuai heping', 536.

under Soviet occupation.¹¹⁶ The Soviets' attitude forced Chiang to review his troop deployment planning. He began to consider temporarily delaying the deployment of extra troops to Manchuria in mid-December.¹¹⁷

Chiang's decision leads to a view that he adopted a temporary do-nothing policy on Manchuria, but the plan fell flat and a serious opportunity to defeat the CCP forces in the north-east was lost.¹¹⁸ This assumption is linked to a 'what-if' discussion that has emerged in recent years regarding whether Chiang should sent his best troops to Manchuria. The most prominent popular belief is that the Nationalist Manchurian troop surge was Chiang's fatal decision. Arthur Waldron, in particular, speculates that the better trained and equipped Nationalist armies could have won the civil war in China proper without Chiang's Manchurian gamble. Had this occurred, Waldron argues, Chiang's rule in China might have been extended and the subsequent Korean War would never have been fought.¹¹⁹

However, others have suggested that Chiang would have been better off had he committed his troops to Manchuria without delay, as the Nationalists' armies were unlikely to achieve anything in China proper. One concludes that Chiang's order to halt the advance of his force after the occupation of Jinzhou was a case of missed opportunity.¹²⁰ In sum, there are disagreements among scholars about what would have been the best civil war strategy for the Nationalists. On one side are those who believe that GMD forces should not have been deployed to Manchuria before China proper was secured. Against this are those who argue that if Chiang had taken early and decisive military action, the GMD could at least have cut its losses in Manchuria.

---

116 Xu Yongchang's diary, 13 December 1945, *Xu Yongchang riji* [The diary of Xu Yongchang], Xu Yongchang (Taipei: Institute of Modern History, Academia Sinica, 1991), 8: 199.
117 *Chiang Diary*, 13 December 1945, Folder 13, Box 44.
118 Wang Chaoguang, 'Guogong neizhan chuqi', 530–2.
119 Waldron, 'China without tears'. Also, Diana Lary, *China's Civil War: A Social History, 1945–1949* (Cambridge: Cambridge University Press, 2015), 59; Jiang Yongjing and Liu Weikai, 'Yi zhu shi quanpan bai: Zhanhou Jiang Jieshi chuli Dongbei wenti de yipan daiqi' [One bad move is all it takes to lose a chess game: A chess blunder in Jiang Jieshi's handling of the Manchurian problem during the post-war period], *Zhuanji wenxue* (Taipei) 97, no. 3 (2010): 25–38.
120 Wang Chaoguang, 'Guogong neizhan chuqi', 528–32.

3. CIVIL WAR IN THE NORTH-EAST

As surviving historical records attest, the Nationalists and their American advisers had already considered the above two scenarios in the winter of 1945. The opinions from Chiang's generals and his American facilitators at the time unanimously supported the first view. The US Army Liaison Group based in Chongqing claimed that Chiang's government was totally unprepared for occupation of Manchuria against the CCP's opposition. The recommendation from this group was that Chiang should consolidate China proper first before moving the bulk of his forces into the north-east. According to the Americans, the Nationalist elite corps was more than capable of securing North China, if they did not disperse to Manchuria.[121] Wedemeyer was quick to support his subordinates' China proper first strategy. As the US chief of staff to the generalissimo, he reminded Chiang that the size of the forces sent into Manchuria and North China should not exceed the combined US and Nationalist logistical capabilities. In his memorandum, Wedemeyer noted clearly that the Americans could only maintain 'a steady flow of ammunition and other equipment' supplies to five more armies in North China and another army (i.e. in addition to the 13A and the 52A) in Manchuria.[122]

Although Wedemeyer's recommendations looked like a deliberate diminution of Du's earlier call for an urgent increase in the number of GMD troops in Manchuria to ten armies in order to battle Lin Biao's forces,[123] Chiang's deputy chief of general staff, Bai Chongxi, unexpectedly echoed the Americans' opinion. Bai, who was believed by some to be the GMD's best strategist, recommended that the order of priorities in the Nationalist counterinsurgency operations against the CCP should be the Rehe–Chahar areas, the Beiping–Tianjin region and Manchuria.[124] After discussions with the Americans, the Nationalists came to a conclusion in favour of Bai's plan: the control of the major rail lines in Rehe–Chahar and the rest of North China should come first and, even if China proper was secured, the GMD could support no more than five infantry armies operating in Manchuria at the same time.[125]

---

121 HQ, Army Liaison Group, Chungking, China to War Department, 14 November 1945; 'China–India–Burma (1945)'; Chairman; Leahy; 11–13; Box 3; JCS; RG 218, NACP.
122 Wedemeyer to Chiang Kai-shek, 5 December 1945, *Zhonghua Minguo*, 7, book 1: 162–5.
123 Xu Yongchang to Chiang Kai-shek, 16 December 1945, *Shilüe*, 64: 154–6.
124 Bai to Chiang Kai-shek, 12 December 1945, *Shilüe*, 64: 122.
125 Xu Yongchang to Chiang Kai-shek, 16 December 1945, *Shilüe*, 64: 154–6.

The question is, had Chiang taken heed of his advisers and sent more troops to North China instead of Manchuria, would that have made his armies' mission improbable a little bit more possible? Available archival materials demonstrate that even Wedemeyer, who lobbied hard for the GMD forces to stay in China proper, did not believe that was possible. In a situation report to Washington, the American stated:

> The Generalissimo has asked the United States to move five more armies to North China. I feel that this would not give him sufficient strength to cope with the Communists ... I question the ability of the Chinese Central Government to support logistically an additional five armies in that area.[126]

According to Nationalist documents, the situation was much worse than Wedemeyer reported. The CCP combatants had moved to choke off supply lines into Beiping since late October, leaving the Nationalists in a grinding struggle for subsistence. While Huludao and Qinhuangdao were the centres of Nationalist sea-based logistics to the north-east, Beiping became the GMD military's North China headquarters by the end of 1945 and later the Nationalist Air Force base for airlifting supplies to its forces in Manchuria.[127] The devastating impact of the blockade spread across the entire Beiping–Tianjin region in December, and the authorities began to ration food to policemen, school teachers and students and were forced to adopt a food price control policy.[128] The situation in Beiping questioned the wisdom of using resources in China proper to support the GMD's war efforts in Manchuria simply because its military headquarters and rear logistical base was itself in dire need of food rations and virtually under siege by the CCP. This perhaps explains Wedemeyer's lukewarm attitude in helping Chiang to increase the GMD troop numbers in North China: he was even less inclined to send additional Nationalist armies to Manchuria and cart supplies to the battlefield.

Chiang's generals and American advisers were free to make their own comments, but it was Chiang who put words into action. The critics might be right: sending troops to either Manchuria or North China was

---

126 Commanding General, HQCT to War Department, 23 November 1945; 'China–India–Burma (1945)'; Chairman; Leahy; 11–13; Box 3; JCS; RG 218; NACP.
127 Sun Lianzhong to Chiang Kai-shek, 26 October 1945, *Shilüe*, 63: 300–1; Zhou Zhirou to Chiang Kai-shek and Chiang's remarks on Zhou's report, 6 May 1946, *Shilüe*, 65: 487–8; Chen Cheng to Chiang Kai-shek, 7 February 1946, *Shilüe*, 64: 568–9.
128 Chiang Kai-shek to Li Zongren, Sun Lianzhong, Xiong Bin and Zhang Er, 17 December 1945; Song Ziwen to Chiang Kai-shek, 20 December 1945, *Shilüe*, 64: 182–3, 205.

logistically untenable for the GMD. However, Chiang's success might be contingent upon how fast Du's troops could secure the key Manchurian railway lines and big cities. If Du's forces could enter the major cities soon enough, the Central Bank of China could set up its branch offices there to enhance the circulation of Circulating Currency for the Nine Provinces of the North-East (CCNE)—a local currency specially issued for the north-east. Notably, the GMD government issued CCNE at the end of 1945 as the official regional currency of Manchuria. The currency was to circulate only within the north-eastern provinces under GMD government legislation.[129] The advice that Chiang received from his bankers was that the value of the GMD-issued currency would be stabilised given that an inter-city commodity money system could be established quickly.[130] This meant that Du's armies could use bank notes to purchase food supplies locally and the logistical problems could be at least partially solved. In sum, the control of big cities and major communication lines in Manchuria was important to the war economies of both the CCP and the GMD.

On the other hand, the Nationalist armies were riddled with poor morale and discipline. Many of those who had been previously deployed in Vietnam (where the 52A was before Manchuria) were involved in illegal opium and gold trading.[131] Chiang could either put these combat units through an army reorganisation program or dispatch them straight to Manchuria, where he could gamble them for the highest payoffs on operational success. Chiang chose the latter. He would rather stick to his beating-a-dead-horse approach while he still thought he had an outside chance. Chiang rued that he could not give up the attempt to recover Manchuria, even though he knew that sending the troops in was unlikely to stem the Communist movement in the region.[132] If Chiang knew anything, it was that the Nationalists were trapped in a passive political position in which they could only halt the troop advance for logistics and diplomatic reasons but by no means could they call off the military campaign in the north-east altogether.

---

129 'Zhongyang yinhang Dongbei Jiusheng Liutongjuan faxing banfa' [Regulations about the issuance of circulating currency for the nine provinces of the north-east by the Central Bank of China] and 'Dongbei jiusheng huidui guanli banfa' [Remittance regulations for the nine provinces of the north-east], 2 November 1945, *Zhonghua Minguo*, 7, book 1: 44–5.
130 Zhang Jia'ao to Chiang Kai-shek, 15 December 1945, *Shilüe*, 64: 140.
131 *Wang riji*, 30 November 1945, 5: 223.
132 *Chiang Diary*, retrospection log, 9 December 1945, Folder 13, Box 44.

After a month-long recuperation in Jinzhou, Du launched a multipronged offensive on 23 December against the areas where the Soviet forces had already withdrawn. Du ordered a troop contingent to advance in the direction to Shenyang.[133] To the north, Du's armies advanced towards key Rehe towns.[134] The third contingent of Du's troops attacked south-eastward towards Yingkou and occupied the port city on 10 January.[135]

While the Nationalist offensive continued apace, Du struck an agreement with the Soviets for a non-hostile takeover of Shenyang scheduled for 15 January; however, as the fighting stretched further, Du did not have enough troops to occupy the city.[136] Much to Du's chagrin, although the Nationalists were fighting some poorly trained CCP troops, the enemy resistance was getting stronger all the time. In some combat situations, the Nationalists needed to employ improvised and risky measures, such as using burning sorghum straws, to overcome stiff enemy resistance.[137] The following chapters will show that the escalation of military confrontation in Manchuria became a threat multiplier to the US-sponsored peace negotiation. Du might have had no idea how to protect his overstretched armies, but the Americans were about to help him with a ceasefire proposal.

---

133 Du Yuming, 'Guomindang pohuai heping', 537–8.
134 Chen and Chang eds, *Shi Jue xiansheng*, 223–5; Yang Jingbin ed., *Wushierjun*, 47–8.
135 Yang Jingbin ed., *Wushierjun*, 52–6.
136 Du Yuming, 'Guomindang pohuai heping', 538.
137 Yang Jingbin ed., *Wushierjun*, 41–3.

4

A shattered peace

Ambiguous provisions in agreements for ceasefire, the Political Consultative Conference and army nationalisation

On 26 November 1945, Chiang sent letters of appointment to all delegates of the multiparty peace forum of the Political Consultative Conference (PCC) from the five different groups (as discussed in chapter 2), making it an eventful day in Chinese politics. Zhou Enlai was among the seven Chinese Communist appointees.[1] These appointments could not have come at a worse time. It was announced one day after Zhou returned to Yan'an and on the day Hurley resigned as the US ambassador to China. Hurley's resignation sent a shockwave across the Pacific from the United States to China. In his resignation letter, Hurley fired a broadside at some employees of the US State Department, accusing them of siding with the CCP.[2] Truman reacted quickly. On 27 November, he appointed George C. Marshall, the retired army chief of staff, as his special envoy to China with ambassadorial rank.[3] Truman hinted that he needed to send someone to China on a difficult mission to prevent civil war. Marshall was the best choice for the assignment owing to his personal qualities and unique experiences in high-level international negotiations during World War II.[4]

---

1 *Zhonghua Minguo*, 7, book 2: 111–23.
2 Hurley to Truman, 26 November 1945, *China White Paper*, 2: 581–4.
3 *New York Times*, 28 November 1945.
4 Mark A. Stoler, 'Why George Marshall? A biographical assessment', in *George C. Marshall's Mediation Mission to China, December 1945–January 1947*, ed. Larry I. Bland (Lexington, VA: George C. Marshall Foundation, 1998), 3–14.

The instructions Marshall received from the State Department and Truman before the mission clearly demonstrate that both the Washington leadership and Marshall were aware that pushing for a representative democracy in China was a difficult and long-term challenge.[5] Although Truman still raised the banner of promoting democracy in his China policy statement at the beginning of Marshall's mission (which could have been construed as indirect intervention in China's internal affairs),[6] the two major tasks he asked his special envoy to accomplish in China were more conservative. Politically, Truman requested Marshall to persuade Chiang to call a national conference involving all major political elements. As discussed (see chapter 2), the Double Tenth Agreement provided for the convocation of the PCC. Despite the date of the PCC remaining undecided, representatives of both parties categorically reassured the US Embassy in Chongqing of their commitment to participate the conference.[7] If the PCC was held successfully, it could settle outstanding issues about the convocation of the National Assembly and ultimately 'bring about the unification of China', as Truman wished.[8]

If the two parties reached a compromise and allowed the PCC to go ahead, Marshall would not need to intervene. Hence, mediating a cessation of hostilities for the two belligerent parties was the most urgent task at the onset of Marshall's mission. As the Truman administration had specifically requested, a ceasefire in North China should be brokered before any other.[9] John F. Melby was a US diplomat in Chongqing in 1945. He remembered that the US government at the time considered 'a cessation of hostilities as the only condition in which the Chinese could work out their own problems'.[10] The following sections will show that Marshall was determined to push a truce deal over the line first. This chapter studies the high politics of negotiation at the beginning of Marshall's mission.

---

5   Truman to Marshall, 15 December 1945; 'Memorandum for the War Department', 9 December 1945, *Marshall's Mission to China, December 1945–January 1947: The Report and Appended Documents*, George C. Marshall (Arlington, VA: University Publications of America, 1976), 2: 1–2, 3–4; notes of meeting between Marshall, Truman, Byrnes and Leahy, 11 December 1945, *FRUS*, 1945, 7: 767–9.
6   John F. Melby, *The Mandate of Heaven: Record of Civil War, China 1945–49* (New York: Anchor Books, 1971), 61.
7   *China White Paper*, 1: 110–12.
8   Truman to Marshall, 15 December 1945, *Marshall's Mission to China*, Marshall, 2: 1–2.
9   Ibid., 1–2.
10 Melby, *Mandate of Heaven*, 60.

Marshall's new dam

Marshall was sent to China to mediate the end of the Chinese Civil War, but direct dialogue between the two parties had actually resumed weeks before his arrival.[11] The parties had struck a deal to reopen negotiations in early December and had started to exchange views on a range of issues, including their commitment to a ceasefire.[12]

On 5 December in Yan'an, Zhou submitted a report to the party leadership on the progress of the negotiations. In the most revealing part of the report, Zhou admitted that it was anti-war sentiment, rather than the Communist revolution, that had gained most public support. He acknowledged that the CCP's continued military campaigns were so unpopular that even the CCP's sympathisers found them difficult to justify. The report also questioned the wisdom of CCP guerrilla attacks that had severed the Tangshan–Qinhuangdao coal train route, stopping coal shipments to Shanghai. The coal shortage had affected Shanghai's expatriate communities.[13] Zhou's report suggests that the CCP shared the same degree of urgency as the GMD in relation to securing a ceasefire, regardless of Marshall's presence. This conflicts with two popular arguments advanced by previous studies. First, it has been argued that the reopening of negotiations resulted from a false hope for creating peace through Marshall's mission.[14] Second, it is believed that the CCP's short-term tactical manoeuvres in handling Marshall's third-party intervention in the GMD–CCP conflicts were central to the history of this period.[15]

Marshall departed for China on 15 December,[16] the day Truman delivered a statement on US policy towards China. While Truman reconfirmed US support for the GMD government, he asserted that US interests would be

---

11 *Manchuria*, 30 November 1945, 140–1.
12 Dong Biwu nianpu bianji zu [The editorial group of the chronological biography of Dong Biwu] ed., *Dong Biwu nianpu* [The chronological biography of Dong Biwu] (Beijing: Zhongyang wenxian chubanshe, 1991), 232–3; Deng Ye, *Lianhe zhengfu yu yi dang xunzheng: 1944–1946 nian jian Guogong zhengzheng* [Coalition government and one party political tutelage: The GMD–CCP political struggle 1944–46] (Beijing: Shehui kexue wenxian chubanshe, 2003), 261–2.
13 Zhonggong zhongyang wenxian yanjiushi and Zhonggong Nanjing Shi weiyuanhui [The CCP Nanjing branch committee] eds, *Zhou Enlai yijiusiliu nian tanpan wenxuan* [Selected essays of Zhou Enlai in the peace negotiations of 1946] (Beijing: Zhongyang wenxian chubanshe, 1996), 3–4, 9 (hereafter *Zhou 1946*).
14 Tsou, *America's Failure in China*, 404.
15 Sheng, *Battling Western Imperialism*, 120.
16 *Shilüe*, 64: 145.

best served if the two opposing Chinese parties could resolve their differences via negotiation.[17] On the same day, a Nationalist plane departed for Yan'an to collect the Chinese Communist PCC delegates.[18] After returning to Chongqing, Zhou was conciliatory, stating that the CCP would seek a ceasefire deal with the government before the opening of the PCC.[19]

Marshall conferred with Chiang on 21 December. He had resolved to carry out Truman's mandate. This authorised him to be blunt with Chiang and state that the US was likely to reduce its aid to the GMD government if it refused to forgo the pursuit of military solutions to internal strife.[20] On the other hand, Chiang attended the meeting with an intelligence report detailing confidential dialogue between Marshall and Truman. This noted that the United States was committed to back his government even if he refused to make reasonable concessions in the peace talks.[21] Although the record of the conversation also demonstrates Truman's position on non-involvement in China's civil strife,[22] it has become an often-quoted exposition of Chiang's tough stance.[23]

During the meeting, Marshall pleaded with Chiang to take a conciliatory approach. He maintained that the American people wanted the two Chinese factions to make major concessions and terminate military conflict. However, Chiang told Marshall that the only way to force the CCP to settle the situation via peaceful means was to send the bulk of his forces to secure North China. This would make it possible for him to accomplish China's unification. The subtext of Chiang's statement was that Marshall's calls for peace would ring hollow unless US military assistance to the GMD was increased to a level that enabled Chiang's forces to quash the Communist rebellion.[24]

Marshall held his first conference with Zhou on 23 December. Zhou presented a string of demands, which he claimed would 'guarantee' the CCP's support for a truce. These included the CCP's participation in accepting the Japanese surrender, a ban on the GMD's use of puppet and

---

17 *China White Paper*, 2: 607–9.
18 *Tanpan shi*, 345; *Wang riji*, 15 December 1945, 5: 230.
19 *Zhou 1946*, 17–21.
20 Truman to Marshall, 15 December 1945, *Marshall's Mission to China*, Marshall, 2: 1–2.
21 Wei Daoming to Chiang, 15 December 1945, *Shilüe*, 64: 151–3.
22 Notes of meeting between Marshall, Truman, Byrnes and Leahy, 11 December 1945, *FRUS*, 1945, 7: 767–9.
23 Taylor, *Generalissimo*, 328–9; Tanner, *Battle for Manchuria*, 82–3.
24 *FRUS*, 1945, 7: 794–9; *Chiang Diary*, 21 December 1945, Folder 13, Box 44.

Japanese forces in civil strife, and the establishment of a power-sharing coalition government 'right now'. Although Zhou presented his conditions for peace to Marshall with a heavy dose of euphemism, he hinted that these conditions must be fulfilled to avoid 'a resumption of the fighting'.[25]

Chiang and Zhou's tough bargaining stance certainly constituted an obstacle to a ceasefire, but the negotiations were still moving towards a resumption. On 27 December, the two parties began to negotiate a truce proposal, but the meetings did not go well.[26] Marshall started to exert his influence on the negotiations. He held talks with Chiang and pledged to attend the GMD–CCP peace talks in person, rendering the negotiations tripartite.[27] Both parties struck a preliminary consensus after Marshall's intervention. The accord declared a nationwide ceasefire, but essentially assigned the task of negotiation to the representatives of the two parties and 'General Marshall'.[28] As events developed, Marshall went on to chair a special Committee of Three on the ceasefire agreement and its implementation in which the two opposing sides were equally represented. On 31 December, the GMD government officially approved the PCC being held on 10 January 1946.[29]

Marshall prepared a US version of the ceasefire plan despite the two parties having reached a preliminary agreement.[30] The most outstanding feature of the Marshall truce was that it would grant the GMD the right to undertake troop movement in Manchuria. Marshall showed his draft to Zhou and stressed that the US government was committed to the movement of GMD troops into Manchuria.[31] While Zhou expressed his complete understanding of Marshall's position, he indicated that he wanted to think it over. In other words, Zhou agreed to let Marshall mediate his party's conflict against the GMD, notwithstanding the American's biased mediation position in favour of his Nationalist opponents. Marshall admitted to Zhou that the agreements reached by both parties were all 'water over the dam' now. He nevertheless insisted that the Americans had found a better plan. 'I have a new dam', Marshall intoned.[32]

25 *FRUS*, 1945, 7: 800–4.
26 Sprouse for the US Embassy in China, 29 December, *FRUS*, 1945, 7: 826–7; *Tanpan shi*, 347–8.
27 *Wang riji*, 30 December 1945, 5: 237–8.
28 Draft proposal of the GMD, 4 January 1946, *FRUS*, 1946, 9: 18–19; *Tanpan shi*, 349–50.
29 Guo Tingyi, *Zhonghua Minguo shishi rizhi*, 4: 444.
30 Byroade to Marshall, 5 January 1946, *FRUS*, 1946, 9: 25–6.
31 Notes of meeting between Marshall and Zhou, 3 January 1946, *FRUS*, 1946, 9: 11–17.
32 Ibid., 17.

Marshall's truce

Marshall embarked on small-scale 'shuttle diplomacy' on 5 January. He presented his truce plan to Chiang. Although Chiang had reservations about certain conditions in the proposal, he found the execution of the truce in general, and the terms about troop movement in Manchuria in particular, rather persuasive.[33] From the GMD's perspective, Marshall had demonstrated commitment to strive for a satisfactory deal for his ally; he was clearly more supportive of sending GMD armies to Manchuria than Wedemeyer.

After presenting a plan with creative new settlement options to Chiang, Marshall conferred with Zhou. The meeting centred on the Nationalists' freedom of troop movement in Manchuria after the ceasefire deal was in effect. Zhou had received a directive from Yan'an on 2 January that all troop movements after the ceasefire should be undertaken through consultation because the CCP forces needed freedom for military movements.[34] Zhou nevertheless knew that he had to wait for the right moment to raise this. He told Marshall the CCP did not reject GMD troop movement in Manchuria but that it was unnecessary to include words to this effect in the ceasefire declaration. However, Marshall was insistent, arguing that if there was a joint declaration, it needed to be 'businesslike and exact' and that the announcement must address the movement of troops into Manchuria. 'I am not the negotiator ... I am the demander', he stated.[35]

Given that Marshall was working to secure a ceasefire deal before the inaugural session of the PCC commenced on 10 January, the savagely tight deadline seemed to warrant his get-tough approach. It forced the two belligerent parties to accept a given solution to avoid prolonged disputes. Nevertheless, while Marshall assumed control of the negotiations, his involvement inevitably shifted from negotiation and mediation, becoming something closer to arbitration. This meant that the two parties would let Marshall take greater control of the negotiations. The main drawback of abdicating control over the negotiation process to a third party is that it is likely to prompt the disputants to believe that they have also lost control

---

33 *Chiang Diary*, 5 January 1946, Folder 2, Box 45.
34 Sheng, *Battling Western Imperialism*, 128; Yang Kuisong, *Shiqu de jihui*, 232–3.
35 Notes of meeting between Marshall and Zhou, 5 January 1946, *FRUS*, 1946, 9: 20–5, citation from 23.

of the negotiation outcome, making them increasingly fearful of losing.[36] When disputants are trapped between the hope of winning and the fear of losing, they are more likely to adopt hard-line positions. The unfolding of events around the negotiation shows that while the two disputed parties ostensibly allowed Marshall to control the discussion, pace and flow at the conference table,[37] they did not let the American manipulate them into accepting a less ambitious negotiation stance.

Meanwhile, Chiang was preparing to impose more conditions on the agreement and take an unyielding stand on matters. If Chiang had instead decided to compromise on some points and the situation went badly afterwards, he could always lay the blame on Marshall. He sent Zhang Qun to see Marshall on 6 January with a number of new requests. The most controversial demand was that the province of Rehe be considered part of Manchuria in the ceasefire accord and that the Nationalist forces had the right to take over the entire province from the withdrawing Soviet forces. In particular, Marshall was informed that the GMD had reached an agreement with the Soviets for the takeover of the two strategic towns, Chifeng and Duolun, in the provinces of Rehe and Chahar, respectively. Marshall urged Zhang to compromise. He made it abundantly clear that he would not discuss Chiang's new demands with Zhou because the CCP would definitely oppose it.[38]

Marshall's pleas went unheard. Zhang and Zhou held six Committee of Three meetings between 7 and 10 January. Marshall attended all the meetings as a mediator, only to discover that the two parties had turned his mediation sessions, aimed at finalising a ceasefire order, into a political tug of war. Zhou rejected Zhang's position on Chifeng and Duolun. Zhou supported freedom of movement for the Nationalist armies in Manchuria, but insisted that this should be written in the meeting minutes rather than the official ceasefire announcement. In turn, Zhang proposed a horse trade: if Zhou accepted the GMD's package, including the occupation of Chifeng and Duolun, he would accept Zhou's view that certain exceptions should be recorded in the minutes. Zhang, however, added that the meeting minutes on these specific areas should also be published.[39]

---

36 Christopher W. Moore, *The Mediation Process: Practical Strategies for Resolving Conflict*, 2nd edn (San Francisco: Jossey-Bass, 1996), 6–14.
37 Kurtz-Phelan, *China Mission*, 94–6.
38 Notes of meeting, *FRUS*, 1946, 9: 26–39.
39 Committee of Three meeting records, no. 1, 7 January and no. 2, 10 a.m., 8 January 1946, *FRUS*, 1946, 9: 43–59, 59–75.

Given that Chiang had repeatedly instructed Zhang that the takeover of Chifeng and Duolun was a high military priority for the GMD,[40] Zhang was presenting his concession as a small package, tailor-made for the Nationalists. Here, Zhang had employed a packaging concessions tactic: proposing a trade-off settlement via offering concessions on low-priority issues for major gains on issues of higher priority. In general, the key to making this tactic successful is that its users must create win–win options for their opponents. In particular, its users must ensure that the item offered as a quid pro quo is high on the other party's agenda.[41] In the GMD's case, a caveat of Zhang's approach was that if Zhou considered the proposed package in a negative light, a positive joint outcome would not be achievable.

Zhou was not interested in the offer at all. He steadfastly denied Zhang's demand over Chifeng and Duolun. His argument was supported by two important claims. First, Zhou declared that the two towns had been overtaken by CCP forces. As the sovereignty of these towns had already ceded to Chinese forces, the presence of GMD armies was unnecessary. According to Zhou, the movement of non-Communist troops into these places would only make the ceasefire order difficult to implement. Second, Zhou challenged his GMD opponents to prove the existence of the alleged GMD–Soviet accord that authorised the takeover of these towns.[42] If the Nationalists wished to prove that their claim was true, Zhou suggested, Soviet representatives should be invited to attend the negotiations.[43] To Zhang's dismay, he proposed that GMD military movements in Manchuria would be allowed only after consultation with the CCP.[44]

Marshall tried almost everything, including suspending meetings and cutting off Zhou's tirade,[45] to prevent the negotiations from descending into political slanging matches, but he soon exhausted his repertoire. Negotiations had made little headway when they approached a desperate

---

40 *Chiang Diary*, 7 and 9 January 1946, Folder 2, Box 45.
41 Lewicki, Barry and Saunders, *Negotiation*, 53, 85–6.
42 Committee of Three meeting records, no. 1, 7 January 1946; no. 2, 10 a.m., 8 January 1946; no. 4, 9 January 1946, *FRUS*, 1946, 9: 43–59, 59–75, 98–104, esp. 47–50, 61–73; *Zhou 1946*, 35–40, 50–2.
43 Committee of Three meeting records, no. 1, 7 January 1946, *FRUS*, 1946, 9: 46.
44 Committee of Three meeting records, no. 3, 4:30 p.m., 8 January 1946, *FRUS*, 1946, 9: 76–98, esp. 78–80; *Zhou 1946*, 43–6.
45 Committee of Three meeting records, no. 2, 10 a.m., 8 January 1946, no. 3, 4:30 p.m., 8 January 1946, no. 4, 9 January 1946, *FRUS*, 1946, 9: 65, 78–80, 97–8.

late stage on 9 January. While Zhang still refused to change his stance over questions concerning the GMD's takeover of Chifeng and Duolun, Zhou derided Zhang's demand as 'in principle unreasonable'.[46]

Marshall was left with no choice but to see Chiang in person. He pleaded with Chiang to prioritise the ceasefire and noted that it would be better to drop the demand regarding Chifeng and Duolun.[47] Chiang did not have the authority to tough it out as he was addressing the inaugural ceremony of the PCC the following morning. It would have been a political setback for Chiang if he were unable to announce the agreement to cease hostilities in his speech. Chiang therefore grudgingly agreed to drop his demands in relation to the provinces of Rehe and Chahar.[48] Almost simultaneously, the CCP interlocutors made last-minute appeals to the Soviet ambassador for Moscow's direct intervention in the negotiations, but their request was snubbed.[49] As Zhou told Marshall, 'There are some similarities in theoretical aspects between the Chinese Communist Party and the Soviet Union, but these two are definitely of two nations.'[50]

The trio held an urgent meeting on the morning of 10 January, only a few hours before the PCC started. The concession Chiang had made the night before gave Zhou an advantage in the arduous negotiations. After receiving confirmation about Chiang's concession, Zhou told Marshall and Zhang that he accepted the Nationalist military movements 'into or within' Manchuria, provided that the movements were reported daily to the truce monitoring headquarters. In the case that the GMD forces wished to move troops to Manchuria through Communist-occupied areas, Zhou proposed an understanding from both parties. This did not need to be written into the official agreement, and he noted that such movements would be discussed with the CCP beforehand. As his time was limited, Zhang immediately accepted Zhou's proposal. With two of the most contentious issues resolved, the trio agreed to release the order for the cessation of hostilities to the press and return for another meeting in the afternoon.[51]

---

46 Committee of Three meeting records, no. 4, 9 January 1946, *FRUS*, 1946, 9: 99.
47 *Chiang Diary*, 9 January 1946, Folder 2, Box 45.
48 Marshall to Truman, 10 January 1946, *FRUS*, 1946, 9: 129–30; *Chiang Diary*, 9 January 1946, Folder 2, Box 45.
49 Yang Kuisong, *Zhonggong yu Mosike*, 554–5.
50 *FRUS*, 1946, 9: 537.
51 Committee of Three meeting records, no. 5, 8:15 a.m., 10 January 1946, *FRUS*, 1946, 9: 104–16. For the press release, see *China White Paper*, 2: 609–10.

During the afternoon meeting, the trio reached an agreement on issues related to the establishment of a small Executive Headquarters in Beiping to implement the ceasefire order under the leadership of the Committee of Three. Three commissioners of the headquarters representing the GMD, the CCP and the United States would be appointed to take charge of the headquarters with authority to vote and negotiate among themselves. However, unanimous agreement by the three commissioners was required for all actions of the headquarters. The headquarters' personnel comprised an equal number of GMD and CCP members, along with a similar number of American staff. Contingents of the headquarters (known as field teams) would be sent to supervise the ceasefire at conflict hot spots. The team delegates, who were also equally represented and accompanied by interpreters and communication officers, would conduct investigations on the ceasefire status and report to the headquarters; before making reports, the team had to reach a unanimous agreement.[52]

Later, the headquarters was assigned to supervise matters concerning the reopening of transportation lines and railway reconstruction, as part of the Restoration of Communications Agreement signed by the Committee of Three on 9 February.[53] This was a difficult task, as the agreement's enforceability was limited by several ambiguous terms. The headquarters commissioners needed to contemplate further negotiations to resolve the problems. One outstanding example was that the agreement provided for the removal of structures (e.g. fortifications) that obstructed the transportation lines, but this begged the question of whether certain structures actually provided safe passage over the railways and roads.[54]

As a result of private talks between Zhang and Zhou, both parties agreed to a grace period of three days, allowing the opposing armies to receive the ceasefire order. In other words, all military action would be terminated by 14 January.[55] As the following discussion reveals, this arrangement provided the two belligerent parties with a reason to continue fighting for a few more days after the ceasefire order had been issued.

In summary, the GMD and the CCP agreed upon an order for the cessation of hostilities in a joint declaration on 10 January. This provided a nationwide ceasefire, but it was also the result of an inescapable trade-

---

52 Marshall, *Marshall's Mission to China*, 2: 126–34.
53 *FRUS*, 1946, 9: 398–425.
54 Marshall, *Marshall's Mission to China*, 1: 34.
55 Committee of Three meeting records, no. 6, 10 January 1946, *FRUS*, 1946, 9: 119–25, esp. 123.

off between the two parties in Manchuria and its neighbouring provinces. The declaration granted an exception permitting the GMD to undertake military movements in certain areas, especially Manchuria. In return, the advance of the Nationalist troops in Rehe and Chahar was halted. As on 9 January, the Yan'an leadership had expected that the GMD forces would reach the town of Chifeng within days; this was a success that the CCP could not have achieved by military means alone.[56]

On the Manchurian question, the two parties had reached an understanding before the signing of the truce that the GMD would not send a large number of troops into Manchuria.[57] The understanding was hardly enough to compensate for the ambiguous provisions of the ceasefire agreement. The newly appointed three commissioners—Ye Jianying, the chief of staff of the CCP 18th Group Army; Zheng Jiemin, a prominent intelligence chief of the GMD; and Walter S. Robertson, the US chargé d'affaires—were forced to admit at a joint press conference on 18 January that they had no jurisdiction over Manchuria. Marshall was furious. He questioned Robertson, asking: 'Who do the Commissioners assume will act to settle any sporadic or serious fighting or differences between Chinese factions in Manchuria?'[58] Marshall should perhaps have asked himself this question, because he had brokered a ceasefire deal for the two sides that almost invited them to keep pursuing a military resolution in Manchuria.

Jockeying for final position

The ceasefire was designed to create a peaceful ambience for the PCC's inauguration on 10 January. In a directive, Mao described the truce period as a 'new stage of democratic construction'.[59] In reality, however, both parties pushed their armed forces ahead nationwide before the ceasefire came into effect, leading to fierce fighting. As the newly appointed US director of operations of the Executive Headquarters, Henry A. Byroade, reported, both parties were 'jockeying for final positions'.[60]

---

56 Cheng, 'China's Madrid', 88, 106, fn. 19.
57 Zhou to Gillem, 31 March 1946, *Zhou 1946*, 182–3.
58 Marshall to Robertson and reply, 21–22 January 1946, *FRUS*, 1946, 9: 371–2.
59 Circular of the CC to all levels of party organisations, 10 January 1946, *Zhonggong*, 16: 15.
60 *FRUS*, 1946, 9: 361.

On 10 January, Chiang Kai-shek instructed Du to secure positions within striking distance of Chifeng, stating that the ceasefire would not come into effect until 'three or five days' after its official announcement. In other words, Chiang was granting latitude for Du to attack beyond the legal limit of midnight on 13 January.[61] Nevertheless, Du's forces aborted the assault near Chifeng on 13 January.[62] In general, however, eyewitness reports have confirmed that the Nationalists were the habitual offenders in violating the ceasefire order,[63] although the 13A commander, Shi, insisted that the CCP violated the truce agreement much more than they did.[64]

On 14 January, Zhou filed a complaint to Marshall about alleged Nationalist ceasefire violations in various contested areas, but it was the GMD troop advancement in the province of Rehe that was the focus of Zhou's angst. He insisted that if the Nationalists took Chifeng, his party would not consider it a minor incident. Zhou then called for an urgent deployment of ceasefire field teams and reconnaissance planes to the troubled province.[65] The Americans acted as Zhou requested. A US Marine Corps plane was sent to Chifeng between 14 and 15 January. The aircraft landed safely on the town's airfield, but the pilot was temporarily interned by Soviet troops for an identification check. In subsequent contacts, the Russians gave assurances that the field team's plane was welcome to land there.[66]

As the incident was a result of Soviet military presence at Chifeng, it debunked Zhou's claim that the CCP forces had restored sovereignty there, although it was reported that a group of CCP-aligned militia had entered the town in mid-August and remained active.[67] From a pro-Nationalist perspective, the GMD government had the right to take the town from the Soviets.[68] Nevertheless, the Sino-Soviet Treaty did not consider Rehe as a Manchurian province,[69] and therefore the town was covered by the

---

61 Chiang to Du, 10 January 1946, *Shilüe*, 64: 366–7.
62 Du to Chiang, 13 January 1946, *Shilüe*, 64: 367.
63 The GMD battalion commander Yang Jia Ming's diary, 11 January 1946, *Guomindang xiaji junguan de riji: Cong Jiangnan dao Dongbei 1946–1948* [Diaries of the GMD's junior officers: From the south of the lower reaches of the Yangtze River to Manchuria 1946–1948], Li Disheng (Beijing: Huawen chubanshe, 2012), 34.
64 Chen and Chang eds, *Shi Jue xiansheng*, 229.
65 Minutes of meeting between Marshall and Zhou, 14 January 1946; Robertson to Byrnes, 18 January 1946, *FRUS*, 1946, 9: 347–9, 365–6.
66 *FRUS*, 1946, 9: 350–1, 353–61.
67 Robertson to Marshall, 30 January 1946, *FRUS*, 1946, 9: 389–91.
68 Liang Jingchun, *Maxie'er shihua baogao shu jianzhu* [Marshall's mission to China: A commentary on the report] (Taipei: Institute of Modern History, Academia Sinica, 1994), 84–5.
69 *Sino-Soviet Treaty*, 206–7.

4. A SHATTERED PEACE

ceasefire agreement. If Du advanced his forces to occupy the town, Zhou would surely have lodged a complaint against the Nationalists for ceasefire violation.[70]

While the controversy lingered in Chongqing, the pro-CCP local militiamen had no qualms about challenging the Nationalists' authority. They took control of Chifeng after the Soviet withdrawal finally occurred on 23 January and refused to leave.[71] Commissioner Ye of the CCP began to back away from Zhou's initial proposal of sending a team to Chifeng after Soviet military presence in the town was confirmed. Ye insisted that the team for Chifeng postpone its departure until his own qualified men arrived from Zhangjiakou (formally Kalgan, the CCP's North China headquarters). When these men arrived, they turned out to be bodyguards and technicians.[72] Ultimately, Marshall had to plead with Zhou to press Ye to allow field teams to enter conflict areas.[73]

After existing in a state of uncertainty, the Chifeng field team was among the first to finally receive approval to depart for conflict spots from 17 January.[74] It managed to bring the volatile military situation under control after some effort,[75] but this was achieved at the expense of the unanimity principle. As the CCP militiamen were already stationed in the town, the field team reached a unanimous agreement for GMD troops to move into the suburbs.[76] The CCP militiamen were to withdraw from the security cordon on high ground outside the town.[77] This was a concession that Zhou would have liked to retract because it would allow Du's troops to besiege the CCP militia at Chifeng. His attempt to recant the agreement was unorthodox: the CCP member of the Chifeng team began to absent himself and refused responsibility.[78]

---

70 *Zhou 1946*, 53–5.
71 The Three Commissioners to the Committee of Three and Robertson to Marshall, 26 January 1946, *FRUS*, 1946, vol. 9, 381–2.
72 Notes of meeting of Executive Headquarters, 16 January, attached in Memorandum by Sprouse for US Embassy in China, 18 January 1946; Byroade to Marshall, 16 January 1946; Robertson and Byroade to Marshall, 17 January 1946, *FRUS*, 1946, 9: 353–9, 359–61, 362–4.
73 Marshall to Robertson, 17 January 1946, *FRUS*, 1946, 9: 364–5.
74 *FRUS*, 1946, 9: 455.
75 Robertson to Marshall, 30 January 1946, *FRUS*, 1946, 9: 389–91.
76 Minutes of meeting between Marshall and Zhang Qun, 24 January 1946, *FRUS*, 1946, 9: 374–5 (1st section), 196–8 (2nd section).
77 Jin Cha Ji ribao ziliao ke [The documentation section of the Shanxi–Chahar–Hebei Border Region Daily] ed., *Junshi tiaochu zhixing qingkuang huibian* [Executive Headquarters information publication] (n.p.: c. 1946), 60–2.
78 Robertson to Marshall, 26 and 30 January 1946, *FRUS*, 1946, 9: 381–2, 389–91.

On the other hand, Zhou quickly re-established the vertical decision-making hierarchy within his team. In his telegram to Ye, Zhou issued a sobering reminder of the importance of reporting problems in the negotiations to a higher level. Despite this, he acknowledged his men's efforts to avoid negotiation breakdowns at the lower level.[79] The CCP representatives soon understood how to use their veto power over team decisions. The right of veto enabled them to delay sending field teams, refuse responsibility and retract agreements simply by replacing team representatives.[80] When uncooperative and inappropriate behaviour began to spread, the first casualty was the field team morale.[81] The memoirs of the Executive Headquarters veterans recorded cases of the US and CCP field team members' prostitution scandals and indecent behaviour towards female civilians.[82]

While ceasefire implementation remained unconvincing at some contested areas in China proper, a 'powder keg' exploded in Manchuria during the truce period. After receiving intelligence reports of a possible GMD troop advance in Rehe, Liu instructed Lin to wage an immediate one-week offensive (starting 13 January) to reopen the communication line between Manchuria and Rehe. Liu's directive was apparently founded in a belief that a civil war in Manchuria was inevitable and that the option Liu gave Lin Biao was not a choice between war and peace but between waiting for the attack and pre-empting it.[83]

On 4 January, the NEPAA had been renamed the North-East Democratic United Army (NEDUA), showing the party's determination to achieve military control over Manchuria. On the day the ceasefire agreement was implemented, a strong NEDUA contingent attacked the isolated GMD battalion at the port of Yingkou and eliminated the entire battalion. According to the CCP's account, the assault did not end until 15 January, beyond the ceasefire date, although the city was captured on the evening

---

79 Zhou to Ye and Luo Ruiqing, 28 January 1946, *Zhou 1946*, 91.
80 Li Jukui, 'Zai Beiping juntiao bu' [My days in the Executive Headquarters in Beiping], *Dangshi ziliao zhengji tongxun* [Newsletters for compiling materials on party history], ed. Zhonggong zhongyang dangshi ziliao zhengji weiyuanhui (Beijing: Zhonggong dangshi chubanshe, 1985), 6: 26–31.
81 Robertson to Marshall, 30 January 1946, *FRUS*, 1946, 9: 389–91.
82 Li Jukui, 'Zai Beiping'; Fang Zhongfu, 'Huiyi sanren xiaozu zai Shandong de huodong qingkuang' [A recollection of the field team in Shandong], in *Shandong dangshi ziliao*, ed. Zhonggong Shandong shengwei dangshi ziliao zengji weiyuanhui [Committee for compiling materials on party history of the Shandong provincial committee of the CCP] (Jinan: Zhonggong Shandong shengwei dangshi ziliao zengji weiyuanhui, 1985), 4: 58–77.
83 Cheng, 'China's Madrid', 88–9.

of the 13th.⁸⁴ In the wake of this incident, Marshall called for a team to be sent immediately to Yingkou. Chiang baulked at the idea, citing potential conflicts with the Soviets as an excuse.⁸⁵

The CCP seemed to believe that a peace settlement would soon materialise, but the question was how much power it could obtain from a coalition government-in-waiting. A large-scale military offensive in Manchuria was therefore deemed necessary to achieve the CCP's ambition. Liu knew that waging war while talking peace was against the people's wishes.⁸⁶ However, he expected that the war in Manchuria would be short-lived, because once fighting broke out, Marshall would immediately plead for a truce. The peace settlement to follow would end any chance for military action. Liu coined his call for war 'the final battle in this historical new stage'⁸⁷ and stated that this would still be a positive result even if the battle ended in a draw.⁸⁸

Lin faced a significant task in answering Liu's call for war. Boosted by the arrival of the elite New Sixth Army (N6A) in early February, the Nationalists continued their advance in Manchuria. Most of Lin's divisions retreated after presenting a weak resistance.⁸⁹ While the GMD armies kept pushing forward without submitting reports of troop movements to the Executive Headquarters (as the ceasefire agreement specifically provided), a vicious spiral ensued.⁹⁰ On 13 February, NEDUA's fast-moving foot soldiers encircled an isolated regiment of the 13A at a village north of Shenyang. As the Nationalists' US long-range artillery was ineffective in close-range engagement against the NEDUA, Lin's men annihilated the entire GMD regiment.⁹¹ The GMD officers learnt this lesson (about NEDUA's soft siege warfare tactics) from their defeat. On 15 February, a superior NEDUA force ambushed a regiment of the N6A at another village south of Shenyang. The GMD's lightly armed relief column was able to sneak behind the NEDUA line and launch a surprise attack, inflicting heavy casualties on Lin's troops.⁹² As both parties received a drubbing in the fierce fighting, this was deemed a draw, as Liu had wished.

---

84   Ibid., 88–9.
85   Marshall to Zhang Qun; minutes of meeting between Zhang Qun and Caughey, 24 and 28 January 1946, *FRUS*, 1946, 9: 375–6, 386–7.
86   CC to NEB, Lin Biao and Huang Kecheng, 26 January 1946, *Zhonggong*, 16: 57–60; CC to Chongqing delegation, 26 January 1946, *Liu nianpu*, 2: 12.
87   CC to NEB, Lin Biao and Huang Kecheng, 27 January 1946, *Liu nianpu*, 2: 14.
88   CC to Peng Zhen, Lin Biao and Huang Kecheng, 5 February 1946, *Liu nianpu*, 2: 18.
89   Cheng, 'Imagining China's Madrid', 90.
90   Marshall to Zhang Zhizhong, 20 February 1946, *FRUS*, 1946, 9: 437.
91   Cheng, 'China's Madrid', 90–1; Cheng, 'Modern war', 44.
92   Cheng, 'Modern military technology', 4; Cheng, 'China's Madrid', 91.

The PCC resolutions: A Machiavellian manipulative device?

Thus the multiparty forum of the PCC was convened concurrently with a shaky truce. Chiang was worried about whether the PCC could make satisfactory progress. He requested Marshall's comments regarding the PCC on 21 January. In his reply, Marshall hinted that he was mainly concerned with military issues but not the political debate at the PCC.[93] Nevertheless, Marshall drafted a brief paper to Chiang, outlining his personal opinion concerning the organisation of a multiparty interim Chinese government.[94] Chiang considered Marshall's plan outrageous because, if all went according to Marshall's plan, the GMD government's authority to promulgate acts in relation to the CCP-controlled territories would be greatly limited.[95]

However, a recent study claims that Marshall should be credited for his contributions to the subsequent political resolutions at the PCC because Chiang repackaged Marshall's ideas and introduced them for debate at the PCC.[96] Participant parties' proposals recorded in the existing PCC documents, and Marshall's original paper handed to Chiang on 22 January, nonetheless suggest that this claim ignores three important facts.

First, the key components of one of Marshall's two ideas in his paper—what he coined the 'Interim National Council'—did not include any major differences from what the participants had already discussed and agreed to at the PCC meetings held well before Marshall submitted his proposal to Chiang. Second, the most innovative idea in Marshall's paper—limiting the central government's power to enact laws affecting the administration of local governments—was too radical even for the Chinese Communists, who had been advocating that provincial governments have their own constitution.[97]

Existing PCC meeting documents do not show any proposal from all participant parties regarding the power of local governments that can be related to Marshall's original idea. It is not surprising then that the final PCC agreement on central–local government relations endorsed

---

93 Meeting records between Marshall and Shang Zheng, 21 January 1946, *FRUS*, 1946, 9: 138.
94 'Charter for the Interim Government of the Republic of China', *FRUS*, 1946, 9: 139–41.
95 *Chiang Diary*, 22 January 1946, Folder 2, Box 45.
96 Kurtz-Phelan, *The China Mission*, 111, 117.
97 *FRUS*, 1946, 9: 139–41; *Zhonghua Minguo*, 7: book 2, 146–8, 165–73, 218, esp. 167, 173.

4. A SHATTERED PEACE

by all participant parties was the exact opposite of Marshall's idea: local government-enacted regulations must not contravene the laws and decrees of the central government.[98] In addition, a letter from Marshall to Truman shows that Marshall had been ignorant about the PCC debates. This was partly because he was busy getting the Executive Headquarters to work, but mostly it was because he maintained a calculated silence when the PCC took centre stage, in order to avoid accusations of political meddling.[99]

While Marshall considered his next move carefully, the PCC delegates had needed to find resolutions without the mediator's participation since the opening of the PCC on 10 January. The multiparty conference, which Chiang chaired, was convened in both public and closed sessions. The public sessions discussed five fundamental themes that had emerged from the Chongqing negotiations, including reorganisation of the government and armies, the National Assembly and the Draft Constitution. The views and recommendations presented at the public sessions upon each of the five subjects would be referred to five specialised subcommittees, which met in closed sessions, for the drafting of specific resolutions. Among these five subcommittees, the Government Organisation, Draft Constitution (later taken over by the Committee for the Reviewing of the Draft Constitution, CRDC, or *xiancao shenyi weiyuanhui* 憲草審議委員會) and Military Affairs Subcommittees are most relevant to the following discussion. A Steering Subcommittee was established to oversee the work of the five subcommittees.[100] These subcommittees played a crucial role during the PCC, and some continued meeting to discuss unresolved problems after the conference had ended.

At its closing session on 31 January, the PCC adopted resolutions as the result of agreement on the topics established by the conference.[101] In essence, the PCC resolutions strove to set an agenda for a power-sharing government that would be legitimised by a constitution accepted by all parties. To put the resolutions into historical context, they were a set of guidelines for post-conflict management vis-à-vis the two civil war rivals: the GMD and the CCP. For the CCP, there could be only one acceptable interpretation of these guidelines, which stipulated that the resolutions must be implemented in two discernible stages. In the first stage, the one-party-

---

98 *China White Paper*, 2: 613.
99 Marshall to Truman, 24 January 1946, *FRUS*, 1946, 9: 142–3, 193, 373–4, esp. 193.
100 Marshall, *Marshall's Mission to China*, 1: 24–5; *FRUS*, 1946, 9: 196–8.
101 *China White Paper*, 2: 610–21.

ruled GMD regime must be reorganised into a power-sharing government and the CRDC would reach a consensus on the Draft Constitution. The new government would then summon a session of the National Assembly to adopt the constitution.[102] As these two phases were not negotiable from the CCP's perspective, any attempt to defy the two-phase procedure constituted a violation of the resolutions.

Nevertheless, the PCC resolutions, like many other peace treaties in history, were written ambiguously, emerging from a series of compromises over the conflicting interests of the disputed parties. The ambiguities lay in one open-ended provision concerning the all-important State Council (*Guomin zhengfu weiyuanhui* 國民政府委員會), the deadline for the completion of the final draft of the constitution and the date for the official opening of the National Assembly. These three elements constituted a 'cross-textual ambiguity' that could be open to incompatible interpretations of the resolutions.[103]

The PCC resolutions enabled the establishment of the State Council as the highest level of government, with both legislative and administrative power preparatory to the inauguration of constitutional rule. To place the State Council's authority in perspective, it would be a multiparty organisation that potentially had the power to settle matters that remained unresolved in the Double Tenth Agreement between the two major parties and make important decisions to reform the existing government.[104] Conversely, it would be more difficult for the two major parties to justify their use of force to settle disputes once the State Council was fully functioning. In short, the State Council was a significant first step towards government reorganisation.

The relevant provision of the resolutions stated that half of the forty state councillors would be Nationalists. Members of other parties and non-partisan candidates would comprise the other half. However, the provision did not stipulate how non-Nationalist state councillor positions (i.e. twenty seats) would be allocated, particularly the exact number of seats the CCP could obtain. Rather, the provision was written with an open-ended structure, whereby the twenty undecided seats would be 'the subject of separate

---

102 Wang Chaoguang, *Zhonghua Minguo Shi* [A history of republican China], ser. ed. Zhongguo shehui kexue yuan jindaishi yanjiusuo Zhonghua Minguo shi yanjiushi [Department of Research in Republican Chinese History, Institute of Modern History, Chinese Academy of Social Sciences] (Beijing: Zhonghua shuju, 2011), 11: 181–2.
103 For a conceptual discussion, see Pehar, 'Use of ambiguities', 179.
104 *China White Paper*, 2: 610–11.

discussion'.[105] While the provision concerning the State Council specified that the seat allocation was still unsettled, the resolutions also stated that the CRDC would have only two months to revise the Draft Constitution—initially promulgated by the Nationalist government in 1936—so it could be passed in the National Assembly, which the resolutions had scheduled to open officially on 5 May 1946.[106]

The ambiguities increased the likelihood of the worst-case scenario: revision of the Draft Constitution would be completed before 5 May, but the governmental reorganisation would be delayed because the undecided State Council seats remained unsettled. The Chinese Communists could then insist on their two-stage theory, arguing that the reorganisation of the existing government must precede the passing of the constitution. Therefore the opening of the National Assembly would be postponed until disputes over the State Council were resolved.[107]

The Nationalists, who preferred to maintain the status quo, could argue otherwise. This was because the resolutions had expressly stipulated the time frame for completing the revision of the constitution and the exact date of the National Assembly inauguration to approve the constitution. From the GMD's perspective, these two provisions were to be considered retroactively specified, meaning that all parties involved must agree on the representation of the State Council before 5 May. Even if this deadline was extended owing to unforeseen circumstances, the terms and spirit of the resolutions had ruled out the possibility of the matter remaining unresolved indefinitely. If the parties involved failed to strike a deal over the membership of councillors, the GMD government could argue for calling the National Assembly ahead of government reorganisation in order to break the deadlock; in this way, all unresolved disputes could be settled via the constitutional assembly.[108]

If the GMD acted unilaterally, the CCP and its ally, the Democratic League, would be likely to protest and refuse to attend the National Assembly. The ramifications would then go far beyond the issue of treaty compliance. The frightening reality was that the Nationalists could still have the constitution passed in the absence of a significant number of delegates in the National Assembly. The resolutions stipulated that the Assembly could

---

105 Ibid., 610–11.
106 Ibid., 619–21.
107 Mao to the CCP delegation, 23 April 1946, *Mao nianpu*, 3: 73.
108 Chiang Kai-shek, *Soviet Russia in China: A Summing-up at Seventy* (London: George G. Harrap, 1957), 172–4.

convene with at least more than half of its delegates (i.e. 1,026 out of 2,050) and could make decisions with three-quarters of those present. Given that the resolutions provided for the GMD to retain 1,200 old delegates, the Nationalists had the power to convene the Assembly.[109] The adoption of the constitution without the CCP's support would inevitably be developed into a national split.

Notwithstanding the ambiguous provisions, the PCC resolutions were not an agreement that Dražen Pehar would have considered a 'Machiavellian manipulative device'—a treaty that brought nothing but false hope, generating misunderstandings and worsening the already bad relationship between disputants.[110] The parties who adopted the resolutions seemed to find that managing the ambiguities at their core was key to understanding one of the provisions about forcing bills involving changes in 'administrative policy' (i.e. important policy changes) through the State Council, which was more conflict prone than others. The provision in question required a two-thirds supermajority vote by the councillors present to be passed.[111] This created potential points of contention. The CCP and the Democratic League insisted upon having fourteen or more votes (i.e. more than one-third of seats) in the council to secure veto power. The GMD, on the other hand, would try to prevent other parties from reaching that threshold number.

However, most PCC delegates preferred to leave the distribution of the State Council seats open to future negotiations, citing constraints over the discussion deadlines dictated by the adjournment of the PCC.[112] Instead, they devised a few provisions, which were written into the resolutions, to make the potential dispute over the State Councillor seats a non-issue. One of these specified whether a given act involving changes in 'administrative policy' was to be determined by a simple majority vote of the state councillors present.[113] Given that the Nationalists had already obtained twenty votes, they were likely to win over at least one more vote from the anti-Communist Youth Party and override vetoes consistently. Put simply,

---

109 *China White Paper*, 2: 619. For regulations concerning the convocation of the Assembly, see *Zhonghua Minguo*, 7, book 2: 557–65.
110 Pehar, 'Use of ambiguities', 172.
111 *China White Paper*, 2: 610–11.
112 Wang Yunwu, 'Su e zai Zhongguo du hou gan' [Impression after reading *Soviet Russia in China*], in *Xiulu lun zheng* [Writing political commentary at my mountain abode], Wang Yunwu (Taipei: Faling yuekan she, 1964), 455; Liang Shuming, 'Wo canjia Guogong hetan de jingguo' [An account of my participation of the GMD–CCP peace talks], in *Liang Shuming quanji* [Collected works of Liang Shuming], Liang Shuming (Jinan: Shandong renmin chubanshe, 2005), 6: 944–5.
113 *China White Paper*, 2: 611.

a symbolic veto power was all the CCP could achieve, even if it could secure fourteen votes.[114] Conversely, if the Nationalists intended to pass a bill that even their political ally deemed unacceptable, all of the twenty non-GMD councillors could combine to vote it down. In other words, the veto power would not be the prerogative of the CCP–Democratic League bloc,[115] but the GMD would still hold a dominant position even if it agreed to let the CCP enjoy a nominal veto power. Thus the provision would have substantially reduced the competitive dynamics of the distribution of seats to the council, unless more than one signatory party intended to exploit the ambiguities of the resolutions for partisan purposes.

On the other hand, the provisions stipulated that the president of the National government had the power to nominate any non-partisan politicians as state councillors, but if the nomination was opposed by one-third of the other nominees, the president must make a different nomination.[116] Given that the Nationalists later accepted the formula of eight (CCP), four (Democratic League), four (the Youth Party), four (independent) regarding the twenty non-GMD state councillors,[117] the stipulation gave the CCP–Democratic League coalition enough votes (i.e. twelve out of thirty-six) to ensure that the four non-partisan councillors would be likely to vote with them rather than the Nationalists. This meant that even if the CCP–Democratic League bloc was two seats short of the required fourteen needed for veto-wielding power, the bloc could still easily gain support from at least two non-partisan councillors and obtain the votes it demanded.[118] The 'inconvenient truth' here would be that the CCP would have the added complication of needing to negotiate not only with the Democratic League but also with the four independent politicians who might have a wide variety of policy platforms.

In summary, the resolutions concocted by the PCC showed signs of a compromise deal written as a rather rudimentary outline. Simultaneously, the resolutions also included terms and conditions that could minimise the competitive dynamics over certain ambiguous provisions. The only caveat was that the treaty parties must continue to expand interparty cooperation in the post-treaty stage, as the resolutions would not have any genuine value otherwise.

---

114 Liang Shuming, 'Tan guofu weiyuan ming'e fenpei wenti' [On the distribution of seats in the State Council], in *Liang Shuming quanji*, Liang Shuming, 6: 686–9.
115 Wang Yunwu, 'Su e zai Zhongguo'.
116 *China White Paper*, 2: 611.
117 *FRUS*, 1946, 9: 173–5.
118 Notes on meeting between Marshall and Stuart, 5 October 1946, *FRUS*, 1946, 10: 295–6.

The resolutions adopted by the PCC were good enough to fuel hopes for a permanent peace in China. On 1 February, the Yan'an leadership instructed its forces to terminate military action, declaring a sharp turn from armed insurgency to non-violent popular and parliamentary-based resistance.[119] This was perhaps the first time since the signing of the truce that negotiators and mediators from all parties started to believe they were close to achieving their objectives.

A deal is better than no deal: The army reorganisation agreement

By the end of February, the two belligerent parties struck an agreement to reorganise all Chinese armies and integrate the CCP forces into the National Army.[120] This was an agreement that both parties were obliged to negotiate as the PCC resolutions stipulated. For the CCP, entering into a negotiation with the GMD on equal terms in relation to army reorganisation as a legitimate Chinese armed force might be considered an initial success.[121] The increasing appearance of 'legitimacy' could be used to intimidate opponents in negotiations.[122] The Yan'an leadership saw the army integration negotiation as a worthy experiment, as long as its armed forces were still firmly under the party's control and the reorganisation timetable was consonant with the CCP's interests.[123]

The Nationalists entered the negotiation with an entirely different state of mind. Although the PCC resolutions provided for the GMD army to conduct its existing reorganisation program without scrutiny,[124] the GMD interlocutors were forced to admit that a joint reorganisation program for all Chinese armed forces was a superior plan.[125] The Nationalists needed to transform themselves into genuine reformists in the eyes of the Americans, ensuring their appeal in relation to receiving US military aid. More importantly, the GMD urgently needed an army nationalisation deal with the Chinese Communists if they were to have any chance to integrate

---

119 *Zhonggong*, 16: 62–7.
120 *China White Paper*, 2: 622–6.
121 *Tanpan shi*, 375.
122 Lewicki, Barry and Saunders, *Negotiation*, 67.
123 *Tanpan shi*, 371–2.
124 *China White Paper*, 2: 617–19.
125 *FRUS*, 1946, 9: 212.

the opposing armies into a single military system.[126] Wedemeyer's planning staff, who had been involved in the army reorganisation negotiations, had pointed out nonetheless that the army integration program required good faith and cooperation from both parties. If either side withheld armed forces to perpetuate its own interests, the plan was doomed to fail.[127]

The United States could not avoid becoming involved in the negotiations for China's army nationalisation, given the strong military ties between the two nations. However, Marshall did not sit on the PCC Subcommittee of Military Affairs. In mid-January, the GMD and the CCP reached a consensus, inviting Marshall to act as an 'adviser' in an exclusive tripartite, three-member Military Subcommittee to develop a plan for army nationalisation with Zhou, Zhang Qun or Zhang Zhizhong.[128]

Marshall entered the negotiation with a new plan to motivate the CCP. He offered an American-sponsored training program for selected CCP army officers from those forces to be integrated.[129] This transitional program would start with basic training with the prospect of establishing special schools for infantry, artillery and armour in Zhangjiakou. The Americans would provide instructors and equipment enough to train ten CCP army divisions.[130] The CCP quickly accepted the offer.[131] The military assistance to the CCP gave Marshall the opportunity to gain the leverage to influence the Chinese Communists in the negotiation.

From late January to early February, Marshall talked to the two parties separately on several occasions. Zhou and the two Zhangs also held meetings for an exchange of ideas without Marshall.[132] These get-togethers, and the multiparty talks in the Military Affairs Subcommittee of the PCC,[133] helped the two major parties understand each other's stance. Marshall arranged seven formal, three-party meetings in quick succession from 14 February.[134]

---

126 Minutes of meeting between Marshall and Zhang Qun, 24 January 1946, *FRUS*, 1946, 9: 196–8.
127 Ibid., 187.
128 Ibid., 188–9, 191, 193–4.
129 Ibid., 258–9.
130 Ibid., 327–9.
131 Ibid., 263–4.
132 Ibid., 194–206, 209–11.
133 *Zhonghua Minguo*, 7, book 2: 223–4.
134 Marshall, *Marshall's Mission to China*, 2: 205–90.

On 25 February, the negotiations concluded with an agreement. The Executive Headquarters acted as an agency to implement the agreement. The essence of the agreement (titled 'Basis for Military Reorganisation and for the Integration of the Communist Forces into the National Army') shows that it was consistent with the CCP's interests in a number of critical areas. First, the agreement overwhelmingly allowed the CCP to retain control of its combat units. A CCP army consisting of three infantry divisions would be under the full control of a CCP army commander in the first twelve months after promulgation of the agreement. The only major difference was that this army unit would be assigned into an 'army group' together with a GMD army.[135]

Although further integration of the two opposing forces would be carried out in the six months after the end of the first year, all CCP infantry divisions, except those being demobilised, would still be separated from their GMD counterparts at the end of the program. The only notable change was that a CCP division and its GMD equivalent would find themselves in the same chain of command under a designated army unit commander of either a CCP or a GMD officer. In other words, the CCP combat units maintained a quasi-independent status up to the divisional level at the end of the integration program. This was despite the fact that it would appear they had merged with the GMD forces in the organisational chart.[136] A Nationalists' proposal to mix both parties' troops in the same infantry division, termed 'fusion', received no support and was quickly shelved before the agreement was finalised.[137] The agreement stipulated that the CCP could retain ten all-Communist divisions alongside fifty all-Nationalist divisions (each consisting of no more than 14,000 men) in the eighteen months after promulgation of the reorganisation. No provision was made for further integration.[138] This meant that the CCP would possess a strong, streamlined and concentrated combat force capable of rejecting peace treaties unilaterally and fighting again, even if the agreement was fully implemented.

The time frame of the army integration program also coincided with the interests of the CCP. The initial stage of the integration would not commence until the seventh month after the accord was signed. It was agreed that the

---

135 *China White Paper*, 2: 622–6.
136 Ibid., 622–6.
137 Marshall, *Marshall's Mission to China*, 2: 217–21.
138 *China White Paper*, 2: 623–4; cf. Kurtz-Phelan, *The China Mission*, 124.

overall force-to-force ratio of the GMD armies and CCP forces would be maintained at a ratio of 5:1 nationally. In North China, where the majority of CCP troops were based, the troop ratio between the opposing forces was much closer. The agreement allocated a seven-division quota to the CCP against eleven GMD divisions in that strategically important region eighteen months after the signing of the agreement.[139]

CCP leaders in Yan'an concluded that the US-proposed army reorganisation plan would damage the structure of powerful military factions within the GMD, making the agreement more valuable to the CCP.[140] Perhaps the only drawback for the CCP in accepting the agreement was that it agreed to kick-start the reorganisation program by providing vital information about its forces. This included, among other things, a full list of all combat units currently under its control, including detailed information (e.g. strength, unit locations and designations), within three weeks of the agreement being signed.[141] Clearly, this commitment could have led the CCP leaders to undertake actions they would rather not. They decided, even before the agreement was signed, to re-designate half of their regular forces as local militia units and concealed the whereabouts of one-third of the military cadre personnel in order to avoid the army reorganisation program.[142] As Zhou later admitted, the CCP was confronting its ultimate fear of losing military power.[143]

Previous studies of the 1946 military reorganisation negotiation consider the GMD an outright loser. According to one study, Chiang was compelled to accept the agreement mainly because the CCP had decided to endorse it. He was quoted as stating, '[This deal was] the biggest loss of our government.'[144] However, Chiang also noted that obtaining a deal was preferable to the status quo.[145] In other words, Chiang considered that the army reorganisation agreement did not go beyond his resistance point, even though the deal was not optimal. The problem was whether the agreement was effective enough for the CCP to partially uphold its end of the bargain.

---

139 *China White Paper*, 2: 624–5.
140 CC to Zhou, 6 February 1946, in *Mao Zedong junshi nianpu 1927–1958* [The chronological military biography of Mao Zedong, 1927–1958] (Nanning: Guangxi renmin chubanshe, 1994), 473.
141 *China White Paper*, 2: 623.
142 Liu Shaoqi to regional bureaux, 24 February 1946, *Liu ninapu*, 2: 23; Cheng, 'Escalation of hostilities', 287.
143 Minutes of meeting between Marshall and Zhou, 26 June 1946, *FRUS*, 1946, 9: 1211–12.
144 Quote in Qing, *From Allies to Enemies*, 80.
145 *Chiang Diary*, the point-form list of scheduled events of the month following the diary's retrospection log of February 1946, Folder 3, Box 45.

Chiang, meanwhile, received the US aid he wanted. Marshall began to arrange a loan worth US$50 million to the GMD government after the signing of the army reorganisation deal.[146]

How much is too much?

The situation took another odd turn in mid-March. The PCC met as a consultative body, but it had no legal authority. Although all the parties represented were morally obliged to accept the PCC resolutions, the legal status of the resolutions was subject to recognition from the respective leaderships of the signatory parties.[147] Right-wing elements within the GMD resorted to activism as means of expressing resentment against the PCC.[148] The Second Plenary Session of the GMD's Sixth Central Executive Committee (CEC) met at Chongqing from 1 to 17 March to endorse the PCC resolutions. The congress was convened in an extremely anti-Communist atmosphere.[149] Strident condemnations pointed directly to some of the political reforms adopted in the PCC resolutions, such as limiting the power of the GMD-controlled National Assembly, enhancing executive responsibility of the legislature, and increasing the autonomy of provincial governments.[150]

The PCC members involved were left to handle the dispute by themselves. Their most recognisable mediator, Marshall, returned to Washington on 11 March to report to Truman.[151] The PCC Steering Subcommittee and the CRDC convened a joint conference to counteract the CEC's virulent attack on the PCC resolutions. Meetings held on 14–15 March resulted in a three-point compromise agreement initially proposed by Zhou on some of the resolution's most controversial components. The compromise deal included allowing the National Assembly to exist as a substantive entity.

---

146 Tsou, *America's Failure in China*, 410–11.
147 Smyth to Byrnes, 21 March 1946, *FRUS*, 1946, 9: 158.
148 *China White Paper*, 1: 143–4.
149 Cheng, 'China's Madrid', 91.
150 Smyth to Byrnes, 9 April 1946, *FRUS*, 1946, 9: 163–6.
151 John Hart Caughey's diary, 11 March 1946, *The Marshall Mission to China, 1945–1947: The Letters and Diary of Colonel John Hart Caughey*, ed. Roger B. Jeans (Lanham, MD: Rowman & Littlefield, 2011), 244.

This abandoned the provision that ensured the accountability of the executive government to the legislature and limited provincial autonomy, as proposed in the original resolution.[152]

It is always difficult for negotiators to decide how much of a concession is too much. In the Chinese negotiations, even the minor party leaders believed that Zhou was giving away too much too early.[153] However, the PCC resolutions had generally made it difficult to perpetuate the Nationalist's monopoly of government. 'The door towards democracy is now pushed open, regardless of how narrow the opening still is', an elated Zhou told Marshall after the PCC.[154] If the Nationalists reneged on the resolutions, that small window of opportunity would not be open for long. Hence, Zhou needed to address—at least nominally—the interests of the Nationalists' right-wing groups so that the GMD's reformists could maintain their roles and pass PCC resolutions at the CEC. Zhou therefore agreed to drop the provision for provinces to draw up provincial constitutions, changing this to a provision that gave provinces the right to self-government.[155] This change would not compromise his party's autonomy in the Liberated Areas. Neither was Zhou's compromise on the National Assembly a bad idea. A strong legislature could impose constraints on executive power. It was true that the Nationalists would hold the majority in the assembly, but not all of them supported a Chiang–Song family empire.

Although Zhou was working hard to achieve integrated results at the negotiating table, the CCP leadership in Yan'an decided to pursue its political goals by other means in the face of the Nationalists' anti-Communist activism. It therefore intensified the war in Manchuria. Liu believed that the GMD could not spare more than about 150,000 troops for Manchuria. If Lin's troops could eliminate some of the existing GMD Manchurian forces, the Nationalists would soon find themselves fighting a losing battle. While the CCP was toughening its stance, the GMD–Soviet

---

152 *Zhou nianpu*, 651; Zhou Enlai, 'Statement on the Second Plenary Session of the Sixth Central Executive Committee of the Kuomintang', in *Selected Works of Zhou Enlai*, Zhou Enlai (Beijing: Foreign Language Press, 1980), 1: 252, 460, fn. 351.
153 Luo Longji, 'Canjia jiu Zhengxie de yixie huiyi' [Some of my recollections of the old PCC]; Liang Shuming, 'Canjia jiu Zhengxie de jingguo' [An account of my work in the old PCC], in *Zhengzhi xieshang huiyi jishi* [True history of the PCC], ed. Chongqing Shi zhengxie wenshi ziliao yanjiu weiyuanhui [The Literary-Historical Source Materials Research Committee of the PCC Chongqing City Branch] and Zhonggong Chongqing shiwei dangxiao [Chongqing Party School of the CCP] (Chongqing: Chongqing chubanshe, 1989), 1: 723, 735.
154 Marshall to Truman and Byrnes, 1 February 1946, *FRUS*, 1946, 9: 151–2.
155 Zhou, 'Statement on the Second Plenary Session', 252, 460, fn. 351.

relationship turned from bad to worse. Both governments were deadlocked in negotiations over the proposed economic cooperation in Manchuria (a topic that receives further attention in chapter 5). From mid-March, most cities and prefectures situated to Shenyang's north, including the transportation hub of Sipingjie, fell into CCP hands as the result of Soviet non-cooperation.[156] On 18 March, Liu telegraphed Zhou, telling him to renege on all concessions that had recently been made to the GMD.[157]

The Nationalists' CEC ratified the PCC resolutions in total on 16 March,[158] but a five-point revision was proposed for the PCC resolutions vis-à-vis the Draft Constitution. Two main areas for revision not only went beyond the scope of Zhou's three-point compromise agreement of 15 March but also stirred up most of the controversies. The first recommended revision in question was a demand that 'in drawing up the constitution, the Programme of National Reconstruction shall be taken as the fundamental basis'.[159] The Program of National Reconstruction (*Jianguo dagang* 建國大綱) refers to a twenty-five-point set of concise guiding principles for the National government originally drafted by its founding father Sun Yat-sen in 1924. Notably, the document only provided general rules for governing and was not custom-made for one-party dictatorship. If the GMD intended to use it to nullify the PCC constitutional principles, the CCP could use the Sun dogma stated in the same document, such as the right of direct suffrage and self-governing local authorities, to argue for the legitimacy of the PCC constitutional agreement.[160]

The second proposed revision in contention was that 'the Control *Yuan* shall not have the right to ask for dissolution of the Legislative *Yuan*'.[161] The Control *Yuan* (*Jiancha Yuan* 監察院) and the Legislative *Yuan* (*Lifa Yuan* 立法院) were two of the five branches of the GMD government, of which the former functioned as an agency to monitor the government. The proposed amendments were clearly an attempt to push beyond the boundaries of Zhou's three-point compromise and create a political environment of

---

156 Cheng, 'China's Madrid', 91–2.
157 Liu to Chongqing delegation, 18 March 1946, *Liu nianpu*, 2: 29.
158 *China White Paper*, 2: 634–9.
159 Zhou, 'Statement on the Second Plenary Session', 460, fn. 352; *Zhonghua minguo*, 7, book 2: 58.
160 Qin Xiaoyi ed., *Guofu Quanji* [The complete works of the father of the country] (Taipei: Jindai Zhongguo chubanshe, 1989), 1: 623–5; *China White Paper*, 2: 619–21.
161 Zhou, 'Statement on the Second Plenary Session', 460, fn. 352.

weak checks and balances in which the president reigned supreme. For the Nationalists who proposed the amendments, however, the revisions might create more problems than they solved.

Moreover, the CEC's five-point revision could only be considered a summary of opinions because the Nationalists did not have the authority to revise a multiparty resolution unilaterally. PRC writer Xiao Jiansheng has argued that the CCP leaders should not have used the revision as an excuse for 'breaking up' and 'civil war'. Xiao's book has been banned in China since 2007.[162] To date, mainstream studies in China contend that the GMD blatantly tore up the PCC resolutions during the CEC and that the CCP was forced to resist it.[163]

The controversy over the GMD's 'proposed revision' against the PCC resolutions was that it allowed 'irreconcilable elements' within the party to show their belligerent stance towards the PCC.[164] Even if the Yan'an leadership did not directly mimic such a radical stance, it was unlikely to respond in a cooperative manner. In a hard-line bargaining situation, negotiators tend to match the other party's tactics with their own.[165] As it turned out, the CCP leaders chose to meet belligerence with belligerence. Using the GMD-proposed revision as a pretext, Zhou triggered the falling-out with the Nationalists at a press conference in Chongqing on 18 March. The CCP thereafter stopped using the expression 'new stage of democratic construction' and dropped policies couched in those terms.[166]

A shattered peace

In an address at the Bureau of Personnel Administration in 1925, Mary Parker Follett, an early proponent of win–win dispute resolution, elaborated her visionary fear of resolving conflict by merely making compromises. 'If we get only compromise, the conflict will come up again and again in some other form', she warned.[167] Follett's premise was progressive for the

---

162 Xiao Jiansheng, *Zhongguo wenming de fansi* [Chinese history revisited] (Hong Kong: New Century Press, 2009), 361.
163 See, for example, *Tanpan shi*, 367–8.
164 *China White Paper*, 1: 144.
165 Lewicki, Barry and Saunders, *Negotiation*, 50.
166 Zhou, 'Statement on the Second Plenary Session', 250–7; Cheng, 'China's Madrid', 92.
167 Mary Parker Follett, 'Constructive conflict', in *Dynamic Administration: The Collected Papers of Mary Parker Follett*, ed. Henry C. Metcalf and L. Urwick (Bath: Management Publications Trust, 1941), 35.

time. Although not many took her ideas seriously in the 1920s, the history of the Chinese Civil War does not seem to contradict her. As the discussion in this chapter shows, both the Nationalists and Chinese Communists continued to find reasons for compromise—on the basis of the Double Tenth Agreement—over conflict-prone issues in relation to ceasefire, restoration of transportation, the PCC resolutions and army nationalisation—and they did this both with or without their American mediator. There was no shortage of compromise along the way.

Zhou's report to the Yan'an leadership shows that the CCP's ambitious military strategies were unpopular with the Chinese public and the international community, if not politically absurd. A peace deal was needed for the CCP as much (as demonstrated in chapter 2) as for the GMD. Hence, it was the necessity to secure an immediate ceasefire, and not just Marshall's personal clout, that prompted both parties to engage in a series of compromises and let the multiparty PCC forum proceed. When the US-brokered ceasefire negotiation pushed ahead rapidly, however, both parties bargained hard for an agreement in which they could take more and give less.

The bargaining game played out in an extraordinary way. Marshall took over the negotiation process for ceasefire and tried to exert influence through the US government's inherently biased stance. Unlike his predecessor Hurley, Marshall intervened at an early stage of the ceasefire negotiation instead of waiting until talks teetered. He enforced an ambiguous agreement exception for the GMD's troop movement in Manchuria and used it to entice Chiang to accept the truce. Given the new negotiation space that the ambiguous provision about Manchuria opened up for both parties, this might have been a worthwhile endeavour for Marshall. In this sense, Marshall could have considered his mediation a success because he accomplished the task as Truman had requested: brokering a ceasefire in China proper, including North China, in a short time frame.

Importantly, Marshall received a grateful letter from Mao, thanking him particularly for his 'fair attitude and approach in handling the ceasefire'.[168] Mao was in no way suggesting that Marshall was an unbiased mediator here. Rather, the letter can be understood as an acknowledgement of Marshall's apt use of peaceful mediation techniques in the context of the United States' biased stance towards Chiang's government.

---

168 Quotation translated from an extract of meeting between Marshall and Zhou. See *Zhou 1946*, 92.

Yet, while Marshall enforced an ambiguous ceasefire agreement, he must have accepted the risk. The Chinese Communists acceded to Marshall's demands regarding the GMD troop movement in Manchuria, but they were determined to benefit from fighting to counter the losses experienced in negotiations. A previous study has considered Liu's short-war expectation and the notion of fighting a 'final battle' during the ceasefire period as exemplifying the CCP policy-makers' high-risk decision-making in the Chinese Civil War.[169] As discussed, both Chiang and Zhou reacted to Marshall's pressure with more stringent demands. Marshall's plan to trade Manchuria for a truce in China proper also made compatibility between the ceasefire agreement and its execution a major concern. The Executive Headquarters was initially 'a short term, shoestring organisation',[170] but it was tasked with a number of highly challenging assignments of ceasefire implementation, disarmament and the repatriation of Japanese soldiers, restoration of transportation, and army reorganisation.[171] Chapter 6 shows that the headquarters was soon overwhelmed by the large volume of difficult tasks to the extent that the entire organisation's effectiveness was jeopardised.

Nobody could have expected Marshall to get everything right the first time in such a high-stakes negotiation, but the following chapters show that his handling of the Manchurian and Rehe issues soon returned to haunt him. Most importantly, Marshall would have been dealing with the side effects of pushing the two parties too hard in the ceasefire negotiations. All too often, unnecessary intervention would only make the situation worse. Marshall's shift from high-pressure tactics to moderation after the commencement of the PCC was nothing but common sense.

Admittedly, the reaction from both parties to Marshall's intervention in the ceasefire negotiation almost pushed it towards collapse. Zhang Qun had been hailed as the wise man of the GMD, but the package deal he offered to Zhou was unattractive at best. The difficulty of proposing a package in negotiations is that the initiating party must ensure that the deal offered is a low priority for itself and simultaneously greatly beneficial to the other party. Recent research has shown that trade-off deals are often accomplished by trial and error and a meaningful exchange of information between disputants.[172] In other words, Zhang needed to find a mutually

---

169 Cheng, 'China's Madrid', 100–1.
170 *FRUS*, 1946, 9: 910.
171 Marshall, *Marshall's Mission to China*, 2: 126–34.
172 Lewicki, Barry and Saunders, *Negotiation*, 85–6, 88, table 3.1.

acceptable solution with Zhou. However, as long as Chiang drew the line between winning and losing the negotiation on the occupation of Duolun and Chifeng, Zhang's bargaining range was perhaps too restricted to make any meaningful offer.

In her recollections of Marshall's mission, Zhang Zhizhong's daughter Suchu suggests that the Chinese were less prone to compromise.[173] However, the Nationalists and the Chinese Communists seemed quite susceptible to give and take when negotiating the agreements discussed in this chapter. Perhaps Zhang Suchu has identified the risk that could have potentially aggravated relations between the disputed parties in accepting ambiguous agreements but not the culture of making compromise itself. The experiences of Wedemeyer's analytically minded planning staff may have provided the basis for an observation with which Follett would have agreed: in a high-stakes negotiation, acting in good faith towards the other party to achieve integrative solutions is more important than simply accepting compromises.

Nevertheless, relations founded on good faith, cross-party cooperation and unanimity were hard to come by, if not totally out of reach, in the GMD–CCP post-ceasefire relations. Hence, the participating parties of the PCC added ambiguous provisions to the resolutions, using them to bridge the gap between the disputed parties. The PCC case shows that the ambiguous provisions paradoxically made the post-treaty conflict predictable. The participant parties of the PCC established different terms and conditions in an attempt to reduce the risks of post-treaty conflicts caused by ambiguities within the resolutions. In this sense, the ambiguous and somewhat confusing provisions in the PCC resolutions support the view that ambiguity was the reality in treaty negotiations; there was no need to negotiate an all-embracing agreement to achieve the negotiation objectives. An ambiguously worded settlement, however, requires all parties involved to face a bitter truth: a bumpy road exists on the way towards long-lasting peace, as significant challenges remain. The post-treaty relationship between the erstwhile enemies, as Pehar has observed, involves a long process of conflict transformation, which can only take root slowly.[174]

---

173 Zhang Suchu, 'Why Marshall's mission failed', 62.
174 Pehar, 'Use of ambiguities', 190–6.

The regrettable turn of events that unfolded after Zhou's 18 March press conference, however, indicates that both the GMD and the CCP found it difficult to cope with their differences. On 21 April, the CRDC convened its final meeting. Some of the attendees believed that a compromise agreement had been struck and the assistant clerk was instructed to read out the revised Draft Constitution. The CCP representative, Li Weihan, unexpectedly filed an oral declaration at the very last minute: the CCP had substantial reservations about vital articles in the revised Draft Constitution. Li further asserted that the constitution draft prepared by the committee could only be considered as meeting minutes because the committee did not have settlement authority. He later explained that the reservations were made because the discussion draft was outrageously doctored by GMD representatives. A GMD representative, Wu Tiecheng, replied that the work completed by the committee could be considered meeting minutes until it passed the National Assembly.[175]

The exchanges between Li and Wu created another serious dispute between the two parties. The GMD insisted that the PCC resolutions had set a two-month deadline for the review of the Draft Constitution. If the Chinese Communists were unhappy about the review after the deadline was due, they would have to take their case to the National Assembly.[176] The CCP, on the other hand, asserted that the reviewing process had not been completed. The GMD's request for the CCP to produce the list of delegates to the National Assembly before completion of the constitutional review was therefore not in accordance with its 'two-stage' interpretation of the resolutions.[177]

In a statement also issued on 21 April, the CCP declared its refusal to tender the list of nominees for the National Assembly, after accusing the GMD government of failing to deliver on its promised democratic reforms. The statement was particularly critical of the GMD's disagreement with the CCP's demand for ten Communist members to sit on the State Council, hinting at a Nationalist plot to deprive the CCP of veto power at the highest decision-making level of the multiparty interim government.[178] The statement added to the increasingly heated rhetoric over the CCP's claim

---

175 Jiang Yuntian, *Zhongguo jindaishi*, 63; Li Weihan, 'Renmin wu quan, dufu jiquan—wei xianfa de jia mianmu' [The people are powerless, but the dictators maintain their grip on power: The false front of the bogus constitution], *Qunzhong* [People] 14, no. 3 (1947): 10–14.
176 This view was implicitly expressed in Chiang's public statement published in *Shenbao* [Shanghai News], 9 November 1946.
177 Minutes of meeting between Marshall and Zhou, 9 October 1946, *FRUS*, 1946, 10: 332–41.
178 Guo Tingyi, *Zhonghua Minguo shishi*, 4: 511–12.

regarding violations of the PCC resolutions regarding the GMD. Notably, the CCP had already announced (on 30 March) that it would not submit the list of nominees for state councillors under the present circumstances.[179] A CCP Central Committee meeting originally scheduled for 31 March in Yan'an to pass PCC resolutions was also postponed indefinitely.[180]

Meanwhile, the CCP failed to meet the deadlines for mandatory submission of the lists of its military units in accordance with the army reorganisation agreement, although the GMD had submitted the relevant lists in March and April 1946, respectively.[181] The CCP had also stopped the reconstruction of main railways in the provinces of Hebei and Shandong since late March, using unresolved disputes over the removal of fortifications on and along the railways and the GMD's large troop movements to justify its unilateral decision.[182]

The GMD then opposed Marshall's plan to supply equipment for the proposed CCP military training school at Zhangjiakou before the CCP force's completion of the army reorganisation.[183] Ultimately, Chiang's opposition forced Marshall to shelve his plan to supply and train the CCP armies. Marshall's unsuccessful attempt to provide military assistance to the CCP gave Zhou an additional justification to accuse the Americans of helping the Nationalists to wage war against them.[184]

On 24 April, Chiang decided that the National Assembly scheduled for 5 May should be rescheduled after consulting leaders of his own party and the PCC members of other parties.[185] The much-anticipated 1946 legislative session was therefore postponed, and no party could propose a new date for it.

In replying to the CCP's accusations against them, the Nationalists contended that these were not true, and affirmed their disinterest in refuting the charges.[186] Rather, they preferred to answer all allegations in a

---

179 Li Yong and Zhang Zhongtian eds, *Jiefang zhanzhen shiqi tongyi zhanxian dashiji* [A chronology of the united front in the period of the Liberation War] (Beijing: Zhongguo jinji chubanshe, 1988), 139.
180 Smyth to Byrnes, 31 March, *FRUS*, 1946, 9: 159–62.
181 Memoranda by Gillem to Zhou, 31 March and 22 April 1946, *FRUS*, 1946, 9: 331, 337.
182 Robertson to Gillem, 26 March 1946, *FRUS*, 1946, 9: 601–2.
183 Xu Yong Chang and Chen Cheng to Chiang Kai-shek, 2 May 1946, *Shilüe*, 65: 387–9; Memorandum by Marshall to Chiang Kai-shek, 20 April 1946, *FRUS*, 1946, 9: 335–6.
184 Minutes of meeting between Marshall and Zhou, 9 August 1946, *FRUS*, 1946, 9: 1484.
185 *Shilüe*, 65: 411, 413–14.
186 Zhang Qun, Shao Lizi and Zhang Lisheng to Zhou Enlai, 22 April 1946, published in *Shenbao*, 23 April 1946.

lengthy memorandum to Marshall. This declared that the GMD's proposed amendments to the constitutional agreement adopted by the PCC were merely a display of opinions. The revision was proposed in accordance with the understanding reached in the PCC that all involved parties were obliged to propose more effective approaches pertaining to the constitution for consultation and agreement. Regarding the dispute over the quota of state councillors, the memorandum states that the GMD had already proposed a new plan—that only twelve votes would suffice to block a vital decision—while the CCP would hold eight seats and the Democratic League would have four members on the State Council. As the memorandum concludes, 'But even this the Communists would not accept.'[187]

The Nationalists could argue that the CCP had already accepted the eight-seat quota back in early February, when it had prepared an internal list of eight nominees for state councillors.[188] Arguably, the proponents of such an argument overlooked that the polarised interparty relations had worsened since early March. On 17 March, Mao had decided that all plans—including joining the government and the participation of National Assembly—had to return to the drawing board if Chiang conspired to renege on the PCC resolutions. Therefore, Zhou was under orders not to submit any list of names to the GMD.[189] Hence, if the Nationalists' new plan on exercising a veto was as attractive as they described, they should perhaps have clarified their position to the CCP: they had no intention of exploiting ambiguities in the resolutions.

The actions and reactions of both parties created more uncertainty. On 23 April, Zhou ridiculed the GMD's passive response to criticism.[190] Disputes after the Nationalist CEC, the subsequent reaction of the CCP, and the further CCP–Soviet alignment in Manchuria together buried the short-lived but celebrated period of negotiated peace. The unfolding conflagration in Manchuria would make the death of the peace efforts apparent to all.

---

187 Memorandum by the Chinese Ministry of Information to Marshall, 21 April 1946, *FRUS*, 1946, 9: 173–5.
188 Tong, *Fengyu sishi nian*, 419.
189 Mao to CCP delegation, 17 March 1946, printed in entry 6 February 1946, *Mao nianpu*, 3: 56.
190 *Zhou nianpu*, 660.

5

Planting radishes in the desert

The Nationalists' handling of the negotiations for Sino-Soviet economic cooperation in Manchuria

While the dispute over Dalian continued to cause stand-offs in the GMD–Soviet negotiation, disagreements over the ownership of the Japanese–Manchukuo industrial assets sparked yet another round of fierce wrangling. The withdrawing Soviet forces confiscated stockpiles of supplies, machinery and industrial installations as war trophies. The Soviets' unilateral action infuriated the Americans. In June 1946, after full Soviet military withdrawal from Manchuria, Washington dispatched a reparations mission to China to investigate the condition of Japanese industries. The ensuing report held the Soviet government responsible for the severe damage to Manchurian industrial complex during its military occupation.[1]

This official US view set the tone for the subsequent report and analysis. Studies have emphasised the systematic Soviet pillage in China's northeast.[2] With righteous overtones, recent studies contend that the Soviet claims to substantial parts of the Japanese industrial complex as war booty and requests for the GMD's cooperation in the post-war Manchurian economy were gross violations of international law. These studies claim that the Soviet leadership had deliberately occupied and monopolised the Japanese assets in Manchuria. Given such offensive manifestations of

---
1   Edwin W. Pauley, *Report on Japanese Assets in Manchuria to the President of the United States*, July 1946 (Washington, DC: n.p., 1946), 7–15.
2   Lary, *China's Civil War*, 46–7; Tanner, *Battle for Manchuria*, 31; Westad, *Decisive Encounters*, 83; Levine, *Anvil of Victory*, 68–9, 182.

Soviet hegemony, these studies argue that the GMD leadership's refusal to cooperate with Soviet demands was entirely justifiable; hence the failure of the GMD–Soviet economic negotiations was inevitable.³ The Soviet Union's economic despoliation of Manchuria certainly did take place. Nevertheless, recent disclosure of Britain's role in the organised dismantling of Italian industrial installations as spoils of war in post-war Eritrea demonstrates the complexities and competing interests involved in wartime and post-war looting by the Allied powers.⁴

There was once a dissenting view from Dong Yanping, NEHQ deputy chief of staff and head of the GMD military mission in Manchuria. Despite being an anti-Communist diehard,⁵ Dong regarded diplomacy, not military power, as a *sine qua non* for long-term stability in the north-east. Assessing the impasse with the Soviets, he warned his superiors that the ever-deepening trust deficit could push worsening Sino-Soviet relations out of control and defeat the purpose of the Sino-Soviet Treaty. The Soviets, he pointed out, might not have intended to simply monopolise the Manchurian economy. Soviet efforts to capture various monopoly privileges in Manchuria stemmed, according to Dong, from a misguided sense of insecurity and sensitivity. In the original version of his mission report written in 1946, Dong recommended that the Nationalist government revitalised the negotiation with a reciprocal proposal of economic cooperation with the Soviets in order to alleviate the Soviet Union's heightening suspicions of the GMD.⁶

In the 1980s, a heavily abridged version of Dong's original report was published by the Nationalist authorities with an appendix that contains an article written by Dong shifting towards anti-Soviet sentiment. In that article, he categorically rejected any possibility of reaching a settlement with the Soviets via diplomacy. He asserted that the Soviet request for a share of

---

3 Wang Chaoguang, 'Zhanhou Zhongsu Dongbei jingji hezuo jiaoshe yanjiu' [A study of the post-war Sino-Soviet economic cooperation negotiation in Manchuria], *Jindaishi yanjiu* 6 (2002): 63–4, 86–8; Wang Chaoguang, *1945–1949*, 99, 128–9, 143; Xue Xiantian, 'Sulian chaiyun Dongbei jiqi shebei shuping' [Critical comments on Soviet removal of industrial equipment in the north-east], in *Dier jie jindai Zhongguo yu shijie guoji xueshu yantao hui lunwen ji* [Proceedings of the second international symposium on modern China and the world], ed. Dier jie jindai Zhongguo yu shijie guoji xueshu yantao hui [The second international symposium on modern China and the world] (Beijing: Zhongguo shixue hui, 2000), 640, 648.
4 Astier M. Almedom, 'Re-reading the short and long-rigged history of Eritrea 1941–1952: Back to the future?', *Nordic Journal of African Studies* 15, no. 2 (2006): 129–30; Nene Mburu, 'Patriots or bandits? Britain's strategy for policing Eritrea 1941–1952', *Nordic Journal of African Studies* 9, no. 2 (2000): 88–9.
5 As is evident in his memoirs, published in 1965; see Dong Yanping, *Su e ju dongbei*.
6 Dong Yanping, 'Report', 7.

Manchurian industrial enterprises was merely part of a massive conspiracy to subjugate China. Even with a joint venture deal, the Soviet Union would still have propped up the CCP.[7] The following discussion presents a new look at the history of the Nationalists' handling of negotiating a Soviet-proposed economic cooperation scheme in Manchuria with their powerful Soviet opponents that was more chequered than Dong's conflicting recollections.

Generalissimo Chiang's defiance

Soon after the signing of the Sino-Soviet Treaty, the GMD authorities had already tried to pre-empt the Soviets by sending memoranda to both the United States and the Soviet Union declaring that all Japanese properties and enterprises on Chinese soil should be regarded as Japan's war reparations to China.[8] On 17 October in Changchun, Xiong expressed China's intention to take over the Japanese industries in Manchuria. Malinovsky responded unequivocally that all Japanese factories and Sino-Japanese industrial joint ventures in the region were spoils of war for the Soviet Army.[9] The focus at that particular juncture of the negotiations was Dalian, however, and both parties agreed that Zhang Jia'ao would discuss economic issues further with the economic counsellor of the Soviet Army Command in Manchuria, M.I. Sladkovsky.[10]

In his report to Chiang Kai-shek, Zhang Jia'ao speculated darkly that even if the Soviet Union were to withdraw its preposterous demand of 'war booty' and agree to run Manchurian industrial enterprises as joint ventures, China would still lose its 'economic autonomy'.[11] In other words, Zhang considered China's economic independence as a key national interest and did not consider such options as negotiating cooperation or accepting an asymmetrical Sino-Soviet economic interdependence, even if they had strategic and economic appeal. In reality, however, China and the Soviet Union had already developed asymmetrical economic ties since the war years. China was still repaying Soviet wartime loans via Wolfram trades,

---

7   *Zhonghua Minguo*, 7, book 1: 218–40.
8   Smyth to Byrnes, 26 February 1946, *FRUS*, 1946, 10: 1109–11.
9   *Manchuria*, 17 October 1945, 78–83.
10 Dong Yanping, 'Report', 11.
11 *Manchuria*, 20 October 1945, 85–6.

and a new contract for the 1945–46 payment year had just been signed on 12 December 1945.[12] The Nationalists simply could not exclude the Soviets from China's post-war economy.

Zhang's concern might actually be justified. In a decision-making process, options within the realm of the political dimension that are considered politically unacceptable may be discarded outright even though these options appear to have a cost-benefit attraction in other dimensions.[13] However, Chiang's own intelligence sources warned his inner circle that remaining on bad terms with the Soviet Union was not an option: to be able to fend off a militarily superior and disgruntled neighbour, the GMD would need to deploy 120 US-armed, heavy-armoured infantry divisions along the Sino-Soviet border—something deemed impossible for the war-depleted Nationalist government.[14]

Chiang was indecisive initially. He asked Zhang to do whatever was possible to adapt to the changing circumstances.[15] Chiang's hesitation amplified the GMD's problems by allowing the Soviets more latitude. On 29 October, Sladkovsky successfully forced the Japanese management of the key Manchurian industries to relinquish control to the Soviets, prompting Zhang's bitter recognition that the dispute over the GMD takeover of Manchuria must be solved together with the disputes over economic issues.[16]

Chiang then decided to pursue the tactic of passivity to the extreme. In early November 1945, still fuming over being forced to send GMD troops overland to the Shanhaiguan area, where they encountered strong CCP resistance, Chiang decided to protest by means of a walkout from the negotiations in Changchun. He explained to his cabinet that the withdrawal would expose the truth of Soviet lack of cooperation to the world.[17] Chiang's plan resembles the negotiation tactics of 'withholding', whereby less powerful

---

12 See the copy of contract in both Chinese and English languages presented to Chiang Kai-shek by Weng Wenhao and Qian Changzhao on 5 January 1946: 'Contract between the Nation Resources Commission of the Ministry of Economic Affairs of the Republic of China and the Trade Representation of the USSR in China', 12 December 1945, *JZZW*, 002-020400-00048-022, AH.
13 Jonathan W. Keller and Yi Edward Yang, 'Leadership style, decision context, and the poliheuristic theory of decision-making', *Journal of Conflict Resolution* 52, no. 5 (2008): 687–712.
14 Tang Zong, *Zai Jiang Jieshi shenbian banian: Shicongshi gaoji muliao Tang Zong riji* [Diaries: My eight years as Jiang Jieshi's confidential secretary], ed. Gonganbu dang'an guan [Archives of the Public Security Bureau] (Beijing: Qunzhong chubanshe, 1991), 551–4.
15 Chiang to Zhang, 25 October 1945, *Manchuria*, 90.
16 *Manchuria*, 13 November 1945, 111–16.
17 *Wang riji*, 8 November 1945, 5: 209–11.

parties attempt to exercise counter-control over their stronger opponents.[18] With calculated passivity (e.g. withdrawal), a negotiator can disrupt the opponent's course because it is tantamount to an appeal. It also establishes an image of the weak as a victim of injustice, which discredits the stronger rival. As a negotiation technique, however, accusing the other of an injustice does not change the nature of the conflict but only sustains or even escalates it, and in the longer term creates more opportunities for the stronger party to discount or belittle its weaker opponent.[19]

The NEHQ was ordered to withdraw from Changchun on 15 November. All NEHQ personnel were to be evacuated except those in the Military Mission. The mission, headed by Dong, was to keep liaising with the Soviet forces and would be attached to the Soviet headquarters. As it turned out, the NEHQ was first relocated to Beiping in December 1945 and then moved to Jinzhou in March 1946 before relocating to Shenyang in April 1946.[20] After Chiang made the decision to suspend his government's participation in the negotiation with the Soviets, Sladkovsky unexpectedly told Zhang that the Soviets intended to use the 'confiscated enemy property' (i.e. the industrial plants) for a joint venture project with the Nationalists. This was the first time the Soviets had raised the prospect of Soviet–GMD collaboration in Manchuria since the talks began in mid-October.[21] However, the change of tack by the Soviets did not stop the Nationalists from going ahead with their plan to withdraw from the negotiations, amid the intensified hostilities in Shanhaiguan, where their troops had begun to triumph.

The Soviets responded to the GMD's announced withdrawal with a carrot-and-stick approach. In Changchun, the GMD officials in the NEHQ were subjected to intimidation. On 16 November, those in the NEHQ compound found themselves without running water or electricity, as well as besieged by non-Soviet police armed with heavy machine guns. A GMD plane sent on 17 November to rescue staff managed to evacuate only 160 personnel; the remainder scrambled to get out, amid scenes of chaos.[22] Simultaneously, the Soviets softened their negotiating stance. Sladkovsky now expressed interest in allowing China to play a major role in running a

---

18 Kritek, *Negotiating at an Uneven Table*, 104–7.
19 Ibid., 104–7; Deutsch, 'Justice and conflict', 56.
20 Xiong to Chiang Ching-kuo, received on 15 November 1945, *Manchuria*, 118; Xiong, *Haisangji*, 500–4, 508, 512–13, 520.
21 *Manchuria*, 14 November 1945, 116–17; Wang Chaoguang, *1945–1949*, 131.
22 *Manchuria*, 17 November 1945, 126–7.

number of Manchurian industries.[23] The Soviet troops also quickly stepped in to defend the NEHQ compound and chased away the armed men.[24] In a communiqué from the Soviet Embassy in Chongqing to the GMD Foreign Ministry, the Soviets pledged to ensure preferential treatments for the GMD airlifted troops arriving in Shenyang and Changchun, and announced that the Soviet forces would be able to stay in Manchuria for one to two more months if the Chinese government so wished.[25]

The Soviets were keen to reopen negotiations with the Nationalists in the wake of this series of damage control exercises. On 20 November, Sladkovsky met Zhang and told him that while regarding all Manchurian industrial plants that had supplied the Japanese army as war booty, the Soviet government was willing to split the ownership of these industries equally with China and operate them as joint ventures.[26] Zhang departed for Chongqing on 24 November with the last contingent of NEHQ evacuees. He reported to Chiang positively about the entry of GMD troops into Manchuria, if there was a consensus by both parties on economic cooperation.[27]

Chiang, riding high after the GMD's occupation of Shanhaiguan, was in no mood to negotiate a plan that was congenial to the Soviets.[28] Many GMD leaders, including the moderate Wang Shijie, expressed their support for Chiang's strategy of non-engagement until the GMD had completed its takeover.[29] Both Wang and Premier Song mistrusted the Soviets and viewed their war booty claim as a breach of the Sino-Soviet Treaty. Continuing negotiations would lead only to a poor outcome.[30] Wang personally regarded Soviet 'power politics' as the biggest impediment to reconciliatory negotiation.[31] To borrow Cohen's example of Japanese–American negotiations, the Soviets seemed unaware that their heavy-handed attempts at bludgeoning the Nationalists into submission could create difficulties for the GMD in terms of obtaining a 'domestic consensus'.[32] In this sense, Song

---

23 Record of conversation between Zhang Jia'ao and Sladkovsky, *Manchuria*, 16 November 1945, 121–5.
24 Dong Yanping, 'Report', 23–4.
25 Chinese Foreign Ministry to the Soviet Embassy in China, 19 November 1945, *Zhonghua minguo*, 7, book 1: 153; *Wang riji*, 17 November 1945, 5: 216.
26 Record of conversation between Zhang Jia'ao and Sladkovsky, *Manchuria*, 20 November 1945, 128–31.
27 *Manchuria*, 24–25 November 1945, 135–6.
28 Chiang Kai-shek to Chiang Ching-kuo, 14 November 1945, *Shilüe*, 63: 533–6.
29 *Wang riji*, 27–28 November 1945, 5: 220–2.
30 *Manchuria*, 28 November 1945, 137–40.
31 *Wang riji*, 23 November 1945, 5: 218–19.
32 Cohen, *Negotiating across Cultures*, 70–1.

and Wang's approach might not have been a bad idea: they could minimise their dependence on a party they did not fully trust. But the GMD leaders had not fully assessed the possible ramifications of withdrawal.[33]

Chiang and his associates seemed to believe that they could have their cake and eat it too. First, they sought to secure the Soviets' full cooperation for their troop-airlifted campaign and accepted the Soviets' offer of a month's extension for Soviet troop withdrawal.[34] In pursuit of the first goal, they decided to send Zhang Jia'ao and Chiang Ching-kuo back to the negotiating table.[35] As it turned out, the Soviet forces were granted an extension of their withdrawal to 1 February 1946 following an understanding reached by the two governments on 9 December 1945.[36]

Concurrently, however, they attempted to cut the Soviets out of Manchuria's economy by hatching a plan that included more posturing, along with a harsh stipulation that the negotiations on economic issues would be reopened only after the GMD took control of Manchuria. The plan the GMD authorities prepared for Zhang was not attractive to the Soviets at all. The key elements of the plan were that economic cooperation would be based on barter and that China encouraged Soviet investment in Manchuria.[37]

Zhang flew back to Changchun on 4 December. In Xiong's absence, Zhang bore the brunt of the negotiations, without much latitude to work with. Sladkovsky ridiculed the GMD's proposal as 'lacking in coherence' and demonstrating that China had no intention of entering into joint ventures of industries already in Soviet hands. The Soviet confronted his Chinese counterpart with a fait accompli that the war booty was in Soviet hands. China had only two options. One was to form a joint venture with the Soviets. The other was to let everything deteriorate.[38] This was effectively a threat because the alternative would be the total destruction of industrial infrastructure in Manchuria.

---

33 For the tactical use of negotiation avoidance and the danger of using it, see Lewicki, Barry and Saunders, *Negotiation*, 7, 113, 310–12.
34 Xiong Shihui's diary, 17 November 1945, *Xiong Papers*, Box 13, portfolio 2.
35 *Manchuria*, 26 November 1945, 136–7.
36 Xiong, *Haisangji*, 503.
37 *Manchuria*, 1 December 1945, 144–5.
38 Record of conversation between Zhang Jia'ao and Sladkovsky, 7 December 1945, *Manchuria*, 153, 155.

The Soviet position was further clarified by Malinovsky on 9 December. The Soviet marshal told Zhang Jia'ao and Chiang Ching-kuo that his party called for economic cooperation with China on the grounds of security concerns, as Moscow was seeking assurance that Manchuria would never become an anti-Soviet base. Malinovsky hinted that his party was seeking to resolve the problem in a time-efficient way and that if China wished to own certain industries and mines independently, it was negotiable.[39]

The Soviets had revealed their hand, and Zhang and Chiang Ching-kuo quickly advised Chiang Kai-shek that regardless of the war booty issue, China would be better off making economic concessions to obtain, in exchange, an unhindered political position in Manchuria. They advised Chiang Kai-shek to consider seriously the factories and mines the Soviets wished included in the joint ventures, while ensuring that the structure of each venture, such as equity contribution and the ownership of the resources underground, were congenial to Chinese interests.[40]

Sladkovsky sent an inventory of proposed enterprises to Zhang on 13 December as requested.[41] Tsou has estimated that the Soviet list included 80 per cent of Manchuria's heavy industries,[42] such as the Manchurian Heavy Industries Company and Manchurian Electric Company. Malinovsky followed up on 17 December by telling Zhang that they were committed to allowing a certain number of heavy industries to operate as wholly Chinese-owned enterprises.[43] The Soviets did not concede their stance on the 'war booty' issue, but skilfully presented it only in the attached memorandum of the inventory.[44]

On 19 December, Zhang Jia'ao and Chiang Ching-kuo arrived at Nanjing to join Chiang Kai-shek, who was there to meet Marshall, and they talked for many hours. Chiang Kai-shek was still unhappy about the Soviet claim of war trophies, but he told Zhang that he could offer the Soviets a one-off

---

39 *Manchuria*, 9 December 1945, 159–61; Chiang Ching-kuo to Chiang Kai-shek, 9 December 1945, *Zhonghua Minguo*, 7, book 1: 395–6; Dong Yanping, 'Report', 34–5.
40 Zhang Jia'ao and Chiang Ching-kuo to Chiang Kai-shek, 8–9 December 1945, *Zhonghua Minguo*, 7, book 1: 394–7; *Manchuria*, 8 December 1945, 158–9.
41 *Manchuria*, 167–71.
42 Tsou, *America's Failure in China*, 335–6.
43 *Manchuria*, 17 December 1945, 175.
44 *Manchuria*, 169.

payment of 10 billion Circulating Currency for the Nine Provinces of the North-east (CCNE) as compensation 'for expenses incurred by them as a result of postponing the date for withdrawing their troops'.[45]

This meant, on the one hand, that Chiang Kai-shek preferred to reimburse the Soviets via a GMD-initiated payment in the name of 'military expenses' rather than acknowledging that the Manchurian industries were 'war booty' to the Soviet forces, despite the fact that a substantial number of the crucial industrial plants had already been removed and possessed by the Soviet forces. On the other hand, Chiang Kai-shek's move also conveyed a clear message to the Soviet negotiators that their 'war booty' claim had breached the bounds of the GMD's tolerance. More importantly, the payment was offered to the Soviets as a GMD initiative and was not directly connected to the Soviet demands. Chiang Kai-shek's 'free concession' therefore entailed no loss of face for him. In addition, Chiang Kai-shek's unilateral gesture also effectively exonerated him from being accused domestically of succumbing to foreign pressure and making abject compromises.[46]

Chiang Kai-shek told Zhang Jia'ao during the meeting that the Ministry of Economic Affairs would thoroughly consider the Soviet plan before dispatching officials to Changchun to take over the negotiations. The decision virtually downgraded Zhang's role from being a negotiator to that of messenger.[47] Unfolding events would soon demonstrate that the Nationalist top officials were increasingly unhappy about Zhang's performance, believing that he was too soft on the Soviets.

Zhang returned to Changchun and held talks with Sladkovsky on 24 December. Zhang presented the payout plan and proposed that the Soviets treat the money offered as the capital for the joint venture in exchange for Soviet cooperation on the 'war booty' issues.[48] In other words, the proposal that the GMD put on the table did not require the Soviets to actually accept payment in a currency that had little credibility. Rather, the plan effectively acknowledged the Soviet shares in the joint venture while avoiding the term 'war booty'. Given that the Soviets had been haggling

---

45 *Manchuria*, 19–20 December 1945, 176–7.
46 For an interesting discussion on the use of unilateral gestures in negotiation, see Cohen, *Negotiating across Cultures*, 99.
47 *Manchuria*, 19–20 December 1945, 176–7.
48 Record of conversation between Zhang Jia'ao and Sladkovsky, 24 December 1945, *Manchuria*, 179–82.

extensively with the Americans and the British since Yalta to secure their war reparations payment in kind, the GMD proposal had considered Soviet needs.[49]

The estimated market value of the cooperative joint venture was only about 38 billion Chinese Currency (*Fabi* 法幣),[50] whereas 10 billion CCNE was worth more than 100 billion *Fabi*. The market rate of CCNE to *Fabi* was around 1:13 when the CCNE was first launched by the Changchun branch of Central Bank of China in late December 1945.[51] Hence the GMD's proposal was by no means a bad deal for the Soviets to kick-start a stalled negotiation.

Sladkovsky was reticent on the GMD's payout plan. He regarded the move to send new negotiators as a retrograde step and dismissed it as unnecessary.[52] The GMD's decision to change its team was tantamount to signalling to the Soviets that the GMD was changing the negotiating setting, and this also meant that its substance could be changed accordingly. The most important item in the agenda—Chiang Kai-shek's payout plan—was not discussed at all. Zhang Jia'ao, relegated to the position of messenger, was understandably rather disinclined to persuade Sladkovsky, repeatedly hinting that he would like to leave the problem to the new negotiators.[53] The meeting ended without making any headway.

Meanwhile in Chongqing, Chiang Kai-shek and his top aides were making every effort to improve ties with Moscow, and Chiang decided that his son Chiang Ching-kuo should go to Moscow as his personal envoy and meet Stalin. Chiang Ching-kuo had strict instructions to avoid negotiating any specific issue with the Soviets.[54] The GMD leaders apparently wanted nothing more than showing friendship, assuaging Soviet suspicions of the GMD and explaining GMD's policy direction towards the CCP. Chiang Kai-shek had consulted Marshall about the matter, and the advice he received was that nothing constructive would be achieved unless the

---

49 Harbutt, *Yalta 1945*, 293.
50 *Manchuria*, 169.
51 Dong Xin and Mao Shuai, 'Dongbei jiu sheng liutongquan pingshu' [Observations on the circulating currency of the nine provinces of the north-east], *Zhongguo qianbi* [Chinese coinage] 1 (2018): 45.
52 Record of conversation between Zhang Jia'ao and Sladkovsky, 24 December 1945, *Manchuria*, 179–82.
53 Record of conversation between Zhang Jia'ao and Sladkovsky, 24 December 1945, *Manchuria*, 179, 181. A change of scene can lead to negotiating impasses. See Lewicki, Barry and Saunders, *Negotiation*, 481–2.
54 *Wang riji*, 23–24 December 1945, 5: 234.

individual selected for the task was an eminent person who had the power to deal directly with Stalin.⁵⁵ The problem for the Nationalists was that if Chiang Ching-kuo negotiated the major disagreements unsuccessfully with Stalin, it would make the situation even worse. They therefore preferred Chiang Ching-kuo to pay a friendship visit to Stalin.⁵⁶

Chiang Ching-kuo conferred with Stalin on 30 December 1945 and 3 January 1946 in Moscow. Under strict instructions not to get into specifics, Chiang Ching-kuo could not provide more convincing details of Chiang Kai-shek's payout plan. Not surprisingly, Stalin rejected Chiang Ching-kuo's proposal, citing his generals' objection to the plan as an excuse. On the war booty dispute, Stalin maintained that the Soviets were entitled to a share of the Japanese industries in Manchuria and that further delay in signing the joint venture deal could incur more losses of industrial assets. He used the case of Poland as a precedent, pointing out that the Red Army had done the same with the German industries there.⁵⁷ The Soviets had sought to legitimise the Soviet claim over the defeated Axis powers' war matériel and industrial infrastructure in Europe as war booty and reparations. The United States showed a détente posture by recognising the Soviet-controlled Polish government in July 1945.⁵⁸ By invoking Poland, Stalin left Chiang Ching-kuo with no room to make any powerful counter-argument regarding Manchuria. The meeting ended without any easing of the tensions between the two nations.

In a second major attempt to improve relations with the Soviets, Chiang Kai-shek sent his wife, Madame Chiang, to visit the Soviet soldiers in Changchun. Madame Chiang arrived at Changchun on 22 January 1946 on her three-day official ceremonial visit, but she received perhaps the coldest reception of her otherwise lustrous diplomatic career. Malinovsky apologetically absented himself for the duration of her visit—to exercise his right to vote in a domestic election in the Soviet Union, he said. In his place, the Soviet marshal sent one of his subordinates to meet Madame Chiang—

---

55 Notes of meeting between Marshall, Chiang Kai-shek and Madame Chiang, 26 December 1945, *FRUS*, 1945, 7: 814–15; Robertson to Byrnes, 3 January, *FRUS*, 1946, 9: 17.
56 Zhang Jia'ao to Chiang Kai-shek, 11 November 1945, *JZZW*, 002-020400-00001-070, AH.
57 Chen Chunhua trans., 'Sidalin yu Jiang Jieshi siren daibiao Jiang Jing'guo de huitan jilu (yi)' [Record of conversation between Stalin and Chiang Ching-kuo, the personal representative of Chiang Kai-shek, series 1], 30 December 1945; 'Sidalin yu Jiang Jieshi siren daibiao Jiang Jingguo de huitan jilu (er)' [Record of conversation between Stalin and Chiang Ching-kuo, the personal representative of Chiang Kai-shek, series 2], 3 January 1946, *Ming Pao Monthly* 32, no. 2: 47–56, no. 3: 44–51.
58 Geoffrey Roberts, *Stalin's Wars: From World War to Cold War, 1939–1953* (New Haven, CT: Yale University Press, 2006), 264–77, 268–70; Miscamble, *From Roosevelt to Truman*, 163–5.

a gesture just short of insulting China's First Lady.[59] In return, Madame Chiang delivered something that may have had the effect of thwarting the GMD's efforts to use her visit to further engage the Soviets. In her speech addressing the Soviet Army officers during the banquet held in her honour at their headquarters, Madame Chiang told her audience that the format of cooperation for the two nations should not follow the precedent set by the Japanese, who had forced their will on the Chinese people. 'But this kind of cooperation would not last', she warned.[60]

Planting radishes in the desert

While successive diplomatic setbacks and stalemates were bad enough for the GMD leaders, the situation on the ground remained volatile. Perhaps the most potentially explosive incident was a GMD air strike that resulted in Soviet casualties at the post-conflict hot spot of Chifeng. On 8 January, two GMD fighter planes pounded targets on the barracks precinct of the Soviet forces at the town. The attack inflicted Soviet casualties and damaged Soviet military equipment.[61] The attack may have been a case of mistaken identity, but the operation was directed from the top: Wang Shuming, one of Chiang Kai-shek's most trusted air force commanders, gave Xiong a first-hand report of the air strike in Beiping in the immediate aftermath of the raid.[62]

Malinovsky called on Dong on 10 January to launch a broadside against the attack, describing the belligerent actions as in contravention of the Sino-Soviet Treaty. The fallout from the incident was limited, however. Moscow did not join its army headquarters in Changchun in condemning the attack and let the GMD leadership exonerate itself by sending Dong to offer an apology to Malinovsky on 13 January, attributing the 'mistaken fire' to intelligence failure.[63]

Failing to revive their spirit of cooperation, both the GMD and Soviet frontline officers in Manchuria were in a bad fix. The Soviet Army commanders, on the one hand, were struggling to maintain the appearance that they had adhered to the treaty and done their best to assist the GMD

---

59   *Manchuria*, 22 January 1946, 214–15.
60   Dong Yanping, 'Report', 72.
61   Ibid., 55.
62   Xiong's diary, 8 January 1946, *Xiong Papers*, Box 13, portfolio 2.
63   Dong Yanping, 'Report', 55, 57.

takeover. On the other hand, the GMD officials were finding it difficult to demonstrate that their government was capable of assuming full control over Manchuria. After pulling his NEHQ team out of Changchun, Chiang Kai-shek began to press his senior civilian officials to get ready for the takeover.[64] On 11 December 1945, a deal was struck between Dong and the Soviet chief of staff Trotsynko that the Soviets would dispatch armed liaison officers as escorts for GMD civilian officials en route to assume takeover duties in major Manchurian cities.[65]

Chiang Kai-shek considered it an opportunity and told Zhang Jia'ao on 19 December that the takeover of the largest Manchurian cities had to be accomplished by the end of 1945 before taking over the various provincial governments in 1946. Hence, from the end of 1945, GMD bureaucrats were sent in groups to establish municipal and provincial governments in the major cities in Manchuria without the protection of the GMD regular forces.[66]

The dangers were clearly present. On 6 January, Zhang Jia'ao sent Zhang Xinfu, a special envoy from the GMD Ministry of Economic Affairs, to take over the Fushun Coal Mines north-east of Shenyang, the largest coal-producing area in Manchuria and an important source of fuel for the Chinese Changchun Railway. The decision was made after reaching an agreement with the Soviet board of directors of the Chinese Changchun Railway Bureau.[67] The arrangement was made in accordance with the provisions of the Sino-Soviet Treaty. The treaty stipulated that the Chinese government supplied coal to operate the railway.[68] The attempted takeover was thwarted by Soviet Army officers in Fushun. On 16 January, on their return trip on train guarded by Soviet troops, Zhang Xinfu and his entourage of seven were murdered by unidentified gunmen. Nationalist authorities sought to blame the Soviets and the CCP for the deaths of the officials, but the Soviet forces refused to accept responsibility.[69] A CCP account of the incident identifies GMD secret agents as the perpetrators.[70] In the end, the Nationalists and

---

64   Xiong's diary, 17 December 1945, *Xiong Papers*, Box 13, portfolio 2.
65   Dong Yanping, 'Report', 37, 43–4.
66   *Manchuria*, 19 December 1945, 176–7; Tian Yushi, 'Dongbei jieshou', 36, no. 2: 80–3.
67   *Manchuria*, 25 December 1945 and 6 January 1946, 182, 195.
68   *Sino-Soviet Treaty*.
69   *Manchuria*, 25 January 1946, 217–18; record of conversation between Dong Yanping and Trotsynko, 'Report', Dong Yanping, 74–6, 92–3; Trotsynko to Dong Yanping, 27 February 1946, in *Su e ju Dongbei*, Dong Yanping, 128. For a Nationalist's report of the incident, see *Zhonghua Minguo*, 7, book 1: 315–16.
70   *Zhonggong*, 16: 85, fn 3.

the Soviets had to move forward despite the rancour. A CCP soldier was captured by the GMD military in July 1946 as the murder suspect and later court-martialled. He was sentenced to death in late 1948.[71]

While Chiang Kai-shek was willing to risk dispatching civilian officials to take over Manchuria, he was wary about sending in his elite troops. In early January 1946, the Nationalists suspended the original plan to airlift a US-armed army division to Changchun. Instead, they decided to airlift the paramilitary security maintenance corps of 4,000 men to the city.[72] The difficult and costly airlift began on 5 January. On 9 January, thirty-six lives were lost in a collision between two GMD troop carrier planes over Changchun's suburbs. After struggling with fuel supplies for nearly a month, the GMD air force only managed to send a negligible 3,000 second-rate troops into Changchun, expecting that these units would be split up and sent to various provincial cities. The commanders of the Soviet garrison forces in Changchun were quick to question the wisdom of the plan, as they felt that these troops were not up to the task of taking over the defence of the outskirts.[73] Given the presence of the CCP forces in the nearby rural areas, the Soviets had a point.

As discussed, the January truce granted the GMD the exclusive right to troop movement in Manchuria. The new development soon prompted Chiang Kai-shek to abort the airlift campaign at the end of January because he expected his elite armies to reach Changchun overland by that time.[74] The remaining paramilitary forces soon got into trouble. In some unpleasant encounters in January and February, the Soviet forces disarmed and detained contingents of the GMD's 'security maintenance police' in Changchun and other Manchurian cities.[75] Disillusioned with his superiors' handling of the Sino-Soviet negotiations, Zhang Jia'ao speculated pessimistically that the GMD's last chance for a peaceful takeover of Manchuria might have been just lost.[76]

On 16 January, the GMD authorities finally sent Special Envoy Sun Yueqi from the Ministry of the Economic Affairs to meet Zhang Jia'ao in Changchun, bringing with him a joint venture proposal. The proposal left little room to bargain. It reiterated the GMD's initial position that all

---

71 *Zhonghua Minguo*, 7, book 1: 339–42.
72 Zhang Jia'ao's diary, 3 January 1946, in *Zhang Gongquan*, ed. Yao Songling, 1: 615.
73 *Manchuria*, 9 January 1946, 197–8; Dong Yanping, 'Report', 45–8, 78.
74 Chiang Kai-shek to Xiong and Du, 26 January 1946, *Shilüe*, 64: 457–8.
75 *Manchuria*, 16 January 1946, 206–7; Dong Yanping, 'Report', 63, 66, 70, 90.
76 *Manchuria*, 16 January and 7 February 1945, 206–7, 243–4.

industries and mines in Manchuria were the property of the Chinese people. Most of the important coal mines (e.g. Fushun and Hegang) and major industrial plants were not on the list.[77] Clearly, the plan underlined the GMD's preferred solutions rather than indicating a willingness to bargain.

Zhang Jia'ao bore the brunt again. In a letter to Chiang Kai-shek, he warned that a lack of flexibility at the negotiating table would only encourage the Soviets to be adversarial and undercut the GMD's bid to establish authority over Manchuria.[78] Chiang told Zhang in his reply that he had no alternative but to reduce the Soviets' joint venture demands. Taking an anti-colonial stance, Chiang was worried about whether the joint venture would set a bad precedent for other foreign powers.[79] Privately, however, Chiang admitted that a more practical option for him at that particular juncture of decision-making was to make the best possible concessions to cater to the Soviets' pleasure in exchange for the GMD's recovery of Manchuria.[80]

While Chiang Kai-shek's concerns over China's sovereign rights dominated his decision-making, both Zhang and Sun were calling for a quick agreement with the Soviets on the joint ventures. Both felt that an early settlement would minimise the GMD's losses. Taking the Yalu River Hydroelectric Power Plant near the Sino-Korean border as an example, they pointed out that the Soviets had already demonstrated their intention to occupy it permanently. The GMD authorities would be better off seizing the opportunity when the Soviets were actively seeking a settlement before their withdrawal, and cut China's losses by writing the power station into the joint venture inventory, even if certain concessions would have to be made in order to secure a cooperative settlement.[81]

Both Zhang and Sun urged Chiang to make his proposal more attractive to the Soviets. Notably, the Zhang–Sun plan did not vigorously seek to negotiate a settlement based on mutual concessions because reciprocal

---

77 Yao Songling ed., *Zhang Gongquan*, 1: 625–8. For the coal-producing conditions and production quality of Fushun and Hegang in the 1940s, see *Dongbei jingji xiao congshu: Meitan* [A concise compendium on the economy of the north-east: Coal industry], ed. Dongbei wuzi tiaojie weiyuanhui yanjiu zu [The study group of the north-east goods and materials regulated committee] (Shenyang: Dongbei wuzi tiaojie weiyuanhui, 1948), 8: 160–1; Shi Liang, *Dongbei de kuangye* [The mining industries in the north-east], in *Dongbei jingji congshu* [The north-eastern economy series], ser. ed. Dongfang jingji yanjiusuo [The eastern institute of economic research] (Shanghai: Dongfang shudian, 1946), 3: 87–9.
78 *Manchuria*, 16 January 1946, 206–8.
79 Ibid., 16 January 1946, 208.
80 *Chiang Diary*, 19 January 1946, Folder 2, Box 45.
81 Zhang Jia'ao and Sun Yueqi to Weng Wenhao, cc. Chiang Kai-shek, 19 January 1946, *Manchuria*, 209–11.

concessions were bound to incur obligations and would have affected China's sovereignty and legal status—the issues that Chiang Kai-shek were most concerned about. Zhang and Sun intended to let the Soviets gain in order to create a less belligerent environment for the GMD negotiators over the long term.[82] Accommodating strategists might settle for a suboptimal deal and let the other party win for the sake of a good relationship but seek to balance the books in the long run.[83]

The problem with the Zhang–Sun plan was, however, that it did not take into account how much responsibility the GMD leaders were willing to bear for allowing the Soviets to hold large shares of prominent mines and key industries in Manchuria. In a private letter to Zhang Jia'ao on 20 January, Chiang Kai-shek implicitly told Zhang that it would be better to conduct such negotiations in an informal way, and it would have been even more inconvenient if the Ministry of Economic Affairs was directly involved in this matter. This meant that Chiang Kai-shek now did not want Special Envoy Sun to take over the negotiations. Zhang assured Chiang that he would negotiate with the Soviets in the way Chiang wished.[84]

Sun presented the GMD's joint venture proposal to the Soviets in a meeting, but it ended badly.[85] Sun was not sent to the forthcoming meetings between Zhang, Sladkovsky and Malinovsky. Sladkovsky held talks with Zhang on 26 and 28 January, and the GMD's plan was criticised at both meetings. Sladkovsky was unhappy about the omission of important coal mines, iron mines and electricity power plants in the GMD proposal. He demanded inclusion via joint ventures in China's largest iron ore mines at Anshan, high-quality engineering/steaming coal producer Hegang and the Fengman Hydroelectric Power Plant. Sladkovsky mocked the lack of commercial value in the GMD proposal as akin to 'planting radishes in the desert' and considered the GMD plan unacceptable.[86]

---

82   Ibid., 209–11.
83   Lewicki, Barry and Saunders, *Negotiation*, 113–15.
84   Chiang Kai-shek to Zhang Jia'ao, 20 January 1946, *Manchuria*, 216, and Zhang's reply, 23 January 1946, *Zhonghua Minguo*, 7, book 1: 420–1.
85   Sun Yueqi, 'Huiyi wo yu Jiang Jieshi jiechu er shan shi' [Remembering a few things in dealing with Chiang Kai-shek], in *Wenshi ziliao xuanji* [A selection of literary–historical source materials], ed. Zhongguo renmin zhengzhi xieshang huiyi quanguo weiyuanhui wenshi ziliao yanjiu weiyuanhui, 84 (1982): 113–34.
86   Record of conversation between Zhang and Sladkovsky, 26 and 28 January 1946, *Manchuria*, 218–22, 225–7, esp. 220, 226.

5. PLANTING RADISHES IN THE DESERT

Reports from the field: Hegang and Anshan

While the negotiators were arguing about the details, there were struggles for control of the important mines—Hegang and Anshan—between groups associated with the CCP and GMD as well as the Soviet forces, with different outcomes in each case. The Hegang Coal Mines were situated in what is today eastern Heilongjiang Province close to the Soviet border, strategically located to supply coal to the Soviet Union. In mid-August 1945, the mine sites and its township were occupied by a Soviet Army company after the Japanese surrender.[87] Directed to maintain coal supplies to the Soviet forces,[88] Soviet troops in Hegang made possible the urgent repair of the local power station. It took only three weeks for the plant to resume full operation.[89] This suggests that although the Soviets removed some of the deployed large machines from the mine site, they did not take the generators away from the plant so that they could supply electricity to the mine, which had suffered war damage.[90] This was in stark contrast to the Soviet dismantling of key mining machinery and power generators in coal mines in southern Manchuria that made these mines virtually inoperable. The official US investigation by Edwin W. Pauley later speculated on the long-term strategic goals behind the Soviet removals and destruction of industrial plant in Manchuria.[91] In the Hegang case, however, the Soviets seemed to have had a reason to maintain it intact.

The local Soviet forces allowed the pro-GMD elements and former Manchukuo officials to maintain peace preservation forces and mine site security officers.[92] Although the Soviets also allowed the pro-CCP elements to set up their local militias and later supported a CCP candidate taking

---

87   Tian Liang, 'Xingshan Shi jiefang chuqi de wuzhuang jianjun gongzuo' [Establishing armed forces in the city of Xingshan during the early years of liberation] in *Hegang dangshi ziliao* [Source materials for party history of the city of Hegang], ed. Zhonggong Hegang shiwei dangshi gongzuo weiyuanhui [Committee for party history compilation of the Hegang City branch committee of the CCP] (Internal circulation materials, 1986), 2: 140–2.
88   Du Tao, 'Huiyi dang diyi ren shizhang de qingkuang' [As the first mayor for the city of Hegang: My recollections], in *Hegang dangshi ziliao*, ed. Zhonggong Hegang shiwei dangshi gongzuo weiyuanhui, 2: 53–5.
89   Entry 3 September 1945, timeline of events in the history of Hegang, September 1945 to September 1949, in *Hegang dangshi ziliao*, ed. Zhonggong Hegang shiwei dangshi yanjiushi [Research office for history of the CCP Hegang City branch committee] (Internal circulation materials, 1990), 11: 12.
90   Zhang Zengjie ed., 'Huifu he fazhan meikuang shengchan zhiyuan jiefang zhanzheng' [Supporting the war of liberation: Resuming and developing coal production], in *Hegang dangshi ziliao*, ed. Zhonggong Hegang shiwei dangshi gongzuo weiyuanhui, 2: 188.
91   Pauley, *Report on Japanese Assets*, 12, 66, 78.
92   Du Tao, 'Huiyi dang diyi ren shizhang', 54.

charge of the mine site,[93] the Communist cadres did not at first enjoy the same kind of latitude to expand their local influence as Steven Levine has found in other Manchurian cities and counties during the same period.[94] On the contrary, Soviet officials in Hegang made the CCP cadres join a group of people who now worked for them, including the ex-Manchukuo mine chief and the head mine engineer, who had a strong GMD background.[95] The Soviets reminded the CCP head cadre in Hegang that revolutionary radicalism had no place under their rule, and on one occasion Soviet Army officers seized his handgun.[96]

The Hegang case suggests that despite their deliberate removal of key industrial equipment, the Soviets needed to maintain certain industrial sites in reasonable shape. In Hegang, the Soviets were keen to keep up coal production to supply their forces in Manchuria and perhaps for future Soviet needs. The pro-GMD mine executives had the technical skills necessary to step up production, so the Soviets had good reason to get the Nationalists on board in a joint venture for mutual gain.

However, the situation in Hegang remained fluid: as the economic negotiations were at a stalemate, the balance did not shift to the GMD's favour. The CCP gradually expanded its influence in the town.[97] A battle-seasoned regular CCP army company from Shandong arrived and established a militia unit, recruiting all kinds of people, including local bandits.[98] Between December 1945 and January 1946, the strengthened pro-CCP militia succeeded in disarming the pro-GMD mine site security guards.[99] This incited a counter-attack from pro-GMD elements in the nearby township. The assault occurred about the same time as Sladkovsky

---

93 Wang Qiqing, 'Dui jieshou Hegang meikuang de huiyi' [My recollections on the takeover of the Hegang coal mines]; Chen Mingde, 'Liu Yinxi he shouqiang dui' [Liu Yinxi and the handgun squad], in *Hegang dangshi ziliao*, ed. Zhonggong Hegang shiwei dangshi gongzuo weiyuanhui, 2: 50–2, 135.
94 Levine, *Anvil of Victory*, 114–21.
95 Wang Qiqing, 'Dui jieshou Hegang', 50–2.
96 Luo Shiquan, 'Huiyi zai Hegang gongzuo de rizi li' [Remembering my days at Hegang], in *Hegang dangshi ziliao*, ed. Zhonggong Hegang shiwei dangshi gongzuo weiyuanhui, 2: 63.
97 'Xingshan Shi jiuge yue de zongjie baogao 1945.12.20–1946.9.25' [A summary report for the nine months in the city of Xingshan from 20 December 1945 to the period ending 25 September 1946], in *Hegang dangshi ziliao*, ed. Zhonggong Hegang shiwei dangshi gongzuo weiyuanhui, 2: 20–2, 24, 26–7.
98 Chen Mingde, 'Liu Yinxi', 135; Luo Shiquan, 'Huiyi zai Hegang', 65; Fang Qiang, Wu Liangping, Liu Ying and Chen Bocun, 'Hejiang renmin de juexing: Yi Hejiang Sheng tugai yundong he genjudi jianshe' [Mass awakening in Hejiang: Remembering the land reform movement and the establishment of base areas], *Liaoshen* 2: 50–67.
99 Wang Qiqing, 'Dui jieshou Hegang', 52–3; entry 'early December' 1945, timeline of events in the history of Hegang, September 1945 to September 1949, in *Hegang dangshi ziliao*, ed. Zhonggong Hegang shiwei dangshi yanjiushi, 11: 13.

talked up the possibility of writing the Hegang Coal Mines into the joint venture proposal. The Soviet troops were forced to join the pro-CCP militia to repel the pro-GMD raiders in order to protect the coal mines.[100] In the wake of the attack, the CCP cadres executed the ex-Manchukuo mine chief, but the execution drew limited mass support and the pro-GMD head mine engineer was able to flee to safety.[101] The CCP asserted total control over the Hegang Coal Mines and the adjacent area only after the withdrawal of Soviet forces in early April 1946.[102]

In contrast, the city of Anshan, a key source of iron and steel at the centre of the Liaodong Peninsula, was experiencing a different kind of struggle. As discussed, the GMD–CCP race for Manchuria was blown wide open by the arrival of a substantial number of CCP troops at the southern tip of the peninsular via sea transport. The CCP forces established a quasi-permanent base at Anshan and established a municipal government in mid-November. A few pro-GMD paramilitaries active in the area attempted to fan resistance. However, their uncoordinated attacks inflicted casualties on the Soviet forces instead. The Soviets in turn assisted the CCP forces to fight off these paramilitary units.[103] The Nationalist authorities later limited the scope of their military operations, recruitment and funding, but these changes came too late as the attacks against the Soviets had further fuelled GMD–Soviet tensions.[104]

Meanwhile, Soviet removal of the major industrial plants in Anshan was extensive. The GMD armies took Anshan in April 1946 after Soviet withdrawal. Eyewitness reports estimated that more than two-thirds of the essential equipment in complete sets from the Japanese Shōwa Steel Works had been systematically removed by the Soviet forces, reducing production to a negligible level.[105] In iron mines in the city's north-east, all surface

---

100 Zhonggong Hegang shiwei dangshi yanjiushi ed., *Hegang dangshi ziliao*, 11: 13.
101 'Xingshan Shi', 20–1, 24; Wang Qiqing, 'Dui jieshou Hegang', 52.
102 Zhonggong Hegang shiwei dangshi yanjiushi ed., *Hegang dangshi ziliao*, 11: 14–16.
103 Xu Jie, 'Si jin gang cheng' [Our four campaigns for the steel city], in *Anshan wenshi ziliao xuanji* [A collection of selected literary–historical source materials of Anshan], ed. Zhongguo renmin zhengzhi xieshang huiyi Anshan Shi weiyuanhui wenshi ziliao yanjiu weiyuanhui [The literary–historical source materials study committee of the Anshan City committee of the Chinese People's Political Consultative Conference] (Internal circulation materials, 1986), 1: 6, 10, 13–23.
104 Xiong Shihui's diary, 15 October, 28 December 1945, 4 April and 4 November 1946, *Xiong Papers*, Box 13, portfolio 2.
105 Jin Dejun (posthumous), 'Jieshou Anshan Zhaohe zhigangsuo de huiyi' [Remembering the takeover of the Shōwa Steel Works], ed. Jiang Yanshi; Zhang Keliang, 'Guomindang jieshou Angang mianmianguan' [The GMD takeover of the Anshan Iron and Steel Company in perspectives], in *Anshan wenshi ziliao xuanji*, ed. Zhongguo renmin zhengzhi xieshang huiyi Anshan Shi weiyuanhui wenshi ziliao yanjiu weiyuanhui, 1: 140–9, 157–62; Pauley, *Report on Japanese Assets*, 106–25.

equipment had been completely stripped.[106] The removal of generators, including two turbo-generators from the steel mill's power plant, paralysed the plant for more than a year. The power plant remained inoperable until it went through a GMD-sponsored repair program in September 1946.[107]

The contrasting cases of Hegang and Anshan demonstrate that GMD–Soviet economic relations in Manchuria were wide-ranging and complex. Nevertheless, the conflicts that the two parties needed to resolve in certain areas were clearly less intractable than others. The challenge for both parties was whether they were able to divide an overall economic cooperation proposal into smaller projects and seek breakthrough in those areas deemed more amenable to resolution. Sladkovsky's demand for selective mine sites and power plants, in a sense, gave the GMD negotiators a good opportunity to seek partial agreement on selected subject matters—a more effective way than pursuing an all-or-nothing-deal with their more powerful Soviet opponents. This is because negotiating a make-or-break deal with a stronger party is likely to narrow the room for manoeuvre for the less powerful party and consequently leaves the latter extremely vulnerable.[108]

An overdue 'yesable' proposal

The GMD authorities were not ready to rethink their approach, however, and allowed Soviets to continue dominating the negotiations. In a meeting held on 1 February 1946, Malinovsky told Zhang that they could temporarily set the war booty dispute aside in order to facilitate a speedy settlement. He requested specifically that the Hegang Coal Mines and the Anshan iron works be included in the final deal. The Soviet marshal insinuated the spectre of US aggression, saying: 'I am deeply aware that China and the Soviet Union will never go to war. But I fear that a foreign power, a wolf in sheep's clothing, may encroach on Manchuria.'[109]

---

106 Pauley, *Report on Japanese Assets*, 91.
107 Zhang Keliang, 'Guomindang jieshou Angang', 157–62, 166; Jin Dejun, 'Jieshou Anshan'; Pauley, *Report on Japanese Assets*, 91, 106–25 and 'Anshan Steel Works' in subsection titled 'Power Plants of Liaoning Province' under 'Individual Electric Power Plant Summary Reports', Appendix 3 (no pagination).
108 Lewicki, Barry and Saunders, *Negotiation*, 217.
109 Record of conversation between Malinovsky, Zhang and Sladkovsky, 1 February 1946, *Manchuria*, 235–41, quotations from 238.

Malinovsky was sending his first unambiguous signal that forcing the GMD to accept the Soviet position on the 'war booty' was less important than reaching a settlement on the basis of economic interests, regardless of his anti-American rhetoric. His concession could be seen as a 'de-escalating gesture' towards resolving Sino-Soviet conflicts.[110] Zhang immediately travelled to Chongqing to report to his leader. Although some GMD top officials found fault with Zhang,[111] they agreed to respond positively to Malinovsky's initiative. After rounds of internal consultation, Chiang finally agreed on 10 February to include the Hegang Coal Mines and the iron and steel enterprises in Anshan in the joint venture proposal. In addition, the oil refinery plant in Dalian, the salt fields on the Liaodong Peninsula and the civil aviation industry in Manchuria were all on the table. The entire package would constitute GMD's final concessions.[112] Given that there were only limited differences between the GMD's final proposal and that of the Soviets, both parties had effectively arrived at the emerging point of an agreement.

But just as the GMD and the Soviet negotiators finally had a glimmer of hope, the Americans dashed it by asserting their position over the Japanese assets. On 11 February, the Yalta Agreement was released simultaneously by the British, Soviet and US governments[113] amid increased mistrust between the Soviet Union and its Western allies, which underlined a list of unpleasant events from the end of 1945. Most of these events were related to the conflicts between the Soviet Union and the West in the Near East and over the minor Axis states.[114]

As its embarrassing concessions to the Soviets at Yalta reached the public domain, the US government sought to toughen its Soviet policy. On the same day that the Yalta Agreement was publicised, the United States sent communiqués to the Soviet Union and China, respectively, declaring that a Sino-Soviet agreement for 'exclusive' control over industrial enterprises

---

110 Louis Kriesberg, 'De-escalating gestures', September 2003, *Beyond Intractability*, ed. Guy Burgess and Heidi Burgess, Conflict Research Consortium, University of Colorado, retrieved 28 May 2022; www.beyondintractability.org/essay/disarming_behavior.
111 *Wang riji*, 5 February 1946, 5: 264.
112 *Manchuria*, 4, 7 and 10 February 1946, 242–6.
113 'Yalta Agreement on the Kuriles'.
114 Harbutt, *Yalta 1945*, 372–9, esp. 383; Miscamble, *From Roosevelt to Truman*, 262–306; Roberts, *Stalin's Wars*, 296–305; Bruce Robellet Kuniholm, *The Origins of the Cold War in the Near East: Great Power Conflict and Diplomacy in Iran, Turkey, and Greece* (Princeton, NJ: Princeton University Press, 1980), 244–342.

in Manchuria would be contrary to US interests from the perspective of its Open Door policy; therefore, any removal of Japanese external assets in Manchuria as war booty was considered inappropriate.[115]

Trying to accommodate his American ally, Chiang Kai-shek reneged on his commitment to support the Zhang Jia'ao-led negotiation[116] by instructing Foreign Minister Wang Shijie to put the negotiations on hold.[117] Instigated by GMD hawks, Manchurians in Chongqing began to stage rallies against Soviet atrocities in the north-east on 16 February.[118] The demonstrations provoked the Soviets into verbally remonstrating with Wang Shijie via Ambassador Petrov on 19 February. Petrov reiterated the war booty issue, asserting that it was the nub of the problem and that nothing would be settled without resolving it first. Chiang Kai-shek reacted by instructing Zhang Jia'ao and Chiang Ching-kuo to cancel their scheduled return trip to Changchun. This decision effectively suspended the entire negotiations, with Dong now left as the most senior GMD official to liaise with the Soviets in Changchun.[119]

Anti-Soviet and anti-Communist movements continued to surge in China's wartime capital. One large-scale demonstration on 22 February involved more than 30,000 students and a few Americans. Nationalist right-wingers were again suspected of aiding and abetting the rally organisers. The Soviets in turn escalated the diplomatic spat by not attending a GMD-sponsored banquet to commemorate Red Army Day before lodging a formal diplomatic protest over the anti-Soviet activities on 26 February.[120] Sino-Soviet relations plummeted to a new low.

Meanwhile, the disposition of Japanese industrial assets in Manchuria had become the focus of a diplomatic tussle between the United States and the Soviet Union. On 5 March, the day Winston Churchill delivered his famous 'Iron Curtain' speech, Byrnes instructed the US chargé d'affaires in Moscow to inform the Soviets that the Sino-Soviet negotiation on economic

---

115 Byrnes to Kennan, 9 February; Kennan to Byrnes, 5 March, *FRUS*, 1946, 10: 1104–5, 1112–13; *Zhonghua Minguo*, 7, book 1: 453–4.
116 Chiang to Zhang Jia'ao, 17 Feburary 1946, *Manchuria*, 252.
117 *Shilüe*, 64: 632.
118 *Wang riji*, 19 February 1946, 5: 271–2.
119 *Manchuria*, 19–20 February 1946, 253–5.
120 *Manchuria*, 22 February 1946, 255–6; *Wang riji*, 22 and 26 February 1946, 5: 273–4, 277.

cooperation in Manchuria should take place only after the Chinese government resumed control over Manchuria and other Allied nations were also in a position to discuss Manchuria's economy with the Chinese.[121]

In this less-than-benign environment of Great Power politics, Chiang Kai-shek resorted to some double-dealing to manoeuvre between the United States and Soviet Union. Chiang neither put a halt to the anti-Soviet movement nor embedded himself in the GMD's ultra-right turn. As Donald Gillin and Ramon Myers point out, the anti-Soviet and anti-CCP sentiment helped the GMD to improve its public image—if Chiang had agreed to the Soviet demands, he would have faced a backlash against his regime.[122] Not unexpectedly, the wave of protests rapidly spread nationwide.[123]

A statement by Chiang Kai-shek nevertheless reflected the need to prevent a rupture in Sino-Soviet relations. In a public speech delivered on 25 February, he warned against overreaction in Manchurian affairs.[124] Chiang also reprimanded the GMD right-wing leader Chen Lifu for his role in the anti-Soviet demonstrations.[125] Yet Chiang was equally keen to persuade the Americans, at the Soviets' expense, that the GMD–US alliance was unbreakable. In his talk with Marshall on 10 March, Chiang raised the issue of a potential Soviet conspiracy to undermine China's partnership with the United States.[126]

Chiang Kai-shek and his associates quickly found it difficult to maintain the right balance between Great Power diplomacy and domestic politics that was pushing the GMD's Soviet policy in a more hard-line direction. During the GMD's CEC held in March, Central Committee members took turns to berate senior government officials for their incompetent handling of Manchurian affairs and Sino-Soviet relations.[127] After being broadsided by his party rival over the GMD's Soviet policy on 5 March, Wang Shijie aligned the GMD foreign policy with that of the United States by telling Petrov that his government would be ready for negotiations only after the withdrawal of Soviet forces from Manchuria.[128] A recent study

---

121 Kennan to Byrnes and reply, 5 March, *FRUS*, 1946, 10: 1112–13, 1113–14.
122 *Manchuria*, 17.
123 *Wang riji*, 3 March 1946, 5: 280.
124 Speech synopsis, Chiang Kai-shek delivered at the Sun Zhongshan Memorial Week service, 25 February 1946, *Shilüe*, 64: 666–8.
125 *Manchuria*, 25 February 1946, 258–9.
126 *Chiang Diary*, 10 March 1946, Folder 4, Box 45.
127 Wang Chaoguang, *1945–1949*, 97–108.
128 *Wang riji*, 5 and 7 March 1946, 5: 281–3.

argues that the basis for negotiation ceased to exist after March 1946,[129] but Chiang Kai-shek's attitude towards the anti-Soviet demonstrations still gave Zhang Jia'ao a small ray of hope. On 11 March, the tireless Zhang invited Sladkovsky to move the negotiations to Chongqing.[130]

Both the Soviet and Nationalist armies in Manchuria engaged in hostilities against each other. In the city of Shenyang and adjacent areas, both sides had clashed since the GMD forces arrived at the outskirts of the city in mid-January. The Soviet military command was unable to restrain its forces from violent acts, including beating and humiliating GMD army officers.[131] GMD troops and unspecified anti-Soviet elements, for their part, were implicated in detentions, robberies and even assassinations against the Soviets.[132] While anti-Soviet protests spread across China proper in February, the Soviet forces in Shenyang conducted provocative military exercises in late February and there was a deadly exchange of fire in early March.[133]

The Soviet forces decamped northward from Shenyang on 12 March with no takeover arrangements with the Nationalists. The GMD forces were able to sweep through the entire city the next day, but encountered CCP forces on the outskirts.[134] Stalin admitted that some of his troops were 'far from being angels',[135] but the Nationalist armies were no angels either. The GMD commanders seemed to believe that they had *carte blanche* over Soviet interests as the city was now in their hands: the Soviet forces' coal supply northbound from Shenyang was intentionally cut off after their withdrawal; Soviet railway staff at Shenyang station were shot at, subject to summary arrests and verbally abused; and Soviet expatriates in the city were forced to wear identifying armbands, resembling Nazi practice in wartime Europe. In Changchun, the Soviet military command protested to the GMD representative Dong, but did little to control their own rampaging troops from retaliating against Chinese civilians in the city.[136]

---

129 Wang Chaoguang, *1945–1949*, 140–1.
130 *Manchuria*, 25 March 1946, 296–7.
131 Dong Yanping, 'Report', 61, 67–8, 78, 80.
132 Ibid., 67–8; Xiong Shihui's diary, 7 May 1946, *Xiong Papers*, Box 13, Portfolio 2.
133 Chiang Kai-shek to Xiong Shihui, Du Yuming, Zheng Dongguo, Liang Huasheng and Zhao Jiaxiang, cc. all unit heads of combat, training, security and general staff to the battalion level, 5 March 1946, *Shilüe*, 65: 33–4; Dong Yanping to Trotsynko and a summary of Trotsynko's verbal reply, 7 March 1946, Dong Yanping, 'Report', 111–14.
134 *Shilüe*, 65: 90; Dong, 'Report', 121–2.
135 Roberts, *Stalin's Wars*, 263–4.
136 Dong, 'Report', 129–30, 134, 140–1; Wang Shijie to Xiong Shihui, 3 April 1946, in *Zhang Gongquan*, ed. Yao Songling, 1: 706–8.

5. PLANTING RADISHES IN THE DESERT

As atrocities on both sides spiralled, the Soviet forces kept retreating north. Without coordinating with the Nationalist forces, the withdrawing Soviets created a security vacuum between Shenyang and Changchun. On 26 March, a week after the fall of Sipingjie to the CCP, the Soviet military command in Changchun informed the Nationalist authorities that it could not stop the scheduled withdrawal and wait for the Nationalist forces to take over defence, and hence would transfer responsibility for security to 'whatever armed force currently exists'.[137]

Despite the Soviet forces' disinterest in supporting the GMD forces, Moscow had the incentive to return to the negotiating table for international political reasons. Soviet activities abroad had been under increasing international scrutiny since 1946, particularly over the presence of Soviet troops in Iran. A series of events concerning the Soviet Union's refusal to withdraw its armies from Iran developed into a crisis involving the United States and the Soviet Union in late March 1946.[138]

Notwithstanding its refusal to yield to the pressure exerted by the United States, Moscow was seeking a breakthrough with the GMD. In late March, Ambassador Petrov personally delivered a pragmatic joint venture proposal to Wang Shijie. Petrov's package was almost identical to the GMD's February proposal, except for the Fushun Coal Mines. The proposal was clear and straightforward, omitting the term 'war booty'.[139] As Zhang Jia'ao observed, the Soviet proposal was devised on the basis of an expectation that the GMD leadership would agree upon,[140] a 'yesable' proposition. From an impasse-breaking perspective, a proposal devised to meet the needs of the other party rather than emphasising one's own interests is acknowledged as a 'yesable' proposal because the expected answer would only be 'Yes, it is acceptable'.[141]

The military picture in Manchuria had distinctly worsened for the GMD since February. As Sipingjie had fallen into the CCP's hands, and as the city was located in the main rail hub, the Nationalist armies had to reassert control over it before they could catch up with the withdrawing Soviet forces in northern Manchuria in order to accomplish a joint takeover of

---

137 Dong Yanping to Zhang Jia'ao, cc. Chiang Kai-shek, 26 March 1946, in *Zhang Gongquan*, ed. Yao Songling, 1: 698–9.
138 Harbutt, *Yalta 1945*, 388–90; Kuniholm, *The Origins of the Cold War*, 338–9; Roberts, *Stalin's Wars*, 308–9.
139 *Wang riji*, 26–27 March 1946, 5: 291–3.
140 *Manchuria*, 27 March 1946, 298–300.
141 Lewicki, Barry and Saunders, *Negotiation*, 500.

the defence of Changchun. The Soviets, however, informed the Nationalists on 23 March that the deadline for a complete Soviet troop withdrawal was scheduled for the end of April 1946.[142] Zhang Jia'ao was aware that even though a formal takeover of defences from the Soviet forces was quite unlikely, the GMD was still capable of reclaiming Manchuria by force in the future. Hence, it was in the GMD's interest to foster ties with its powerful northern neighbour. Zhang speculated that this was something Moscow was predicting.[143]

Zhang's views seemed to have had little influence on his government's decision-making. Chiang Kai-shek saw Petrov's concession as evidence of the tactical efficacy of his negotiation disruption.[144] A meeting with Wang Shijie on 13 April soon moved Petrov to protest. Petrov was appalled that the GMD had reinstated its initial position regarding all Japanese properties in Manchuria as war reparations to China. Wang concluded the meeting by telling Petrov that what had happened in Sipingjie must not be repeated in Changchun. The GMD leadership's response to Petrov's proposal certainly did not help improve relations; on 18 April, Changchun too fell into the hands of the CCP. Meanwhile, Petrov continued to show great disposition to compromise, most notably by expressing the Soviet intention to take the Fushun Coal Mines off the agenda on 17 April. But the Nationalist leaders, fuming over Changchun, insisted that the Soviets had to assist the Nationalist forces in taking over the defence of Manchuria before they would consider restarting the negotiations.[145]

After the fall of Changchun, the GMD maintained its fierce military campaign against the CCP in Manchuria and succeeded in recovering major cities along the main railway at the end of May, including Changchun—a subject that is discussed further in chapter 6.[146] Meanwhile, the Soviet troop withdrawal continued, and the last Soviet combat forces pulled out of Manchuria at the end of April.[147] Formal diplomatic ties between Chongqing and Moscow did not end, but the negotiations on economic cooperation came to a complete halt with the spread of the Chinese Civil War.

---

142 Wang Shijie to Petrov, 27 March 1946, in *Zhang Gongquan*, ed. Yao Songling, 1: 701; *Wang riji*, 19 and 23 March 1946, 5: 288, 290.
143 *Manchuria*, 27 March 1946, 298–300.
144 *Chiang Diary*, 25 March 1946, Folder 4, Box 45.
145 *Manchuria*, 13 and 17–18 April 1946, 327, 331–5; *Wang riji*, 13 April 1946, 5: 302–3.
146 Ding Xiaochun, Ge Fulu and Wang Shiying eds, *Dongbei jiefang zhanzhen dashiji* [The chronology of the Manchurian Liberation War] (Beijing: Zhonggong dangshi ziliao chubanshe, 1987), 57–8.
147 Dong Yanping, 'Report', 189–90.

5. PLANTING RADISHES IN THE DESERT

The GMD had also been dealing with ongoing US interference in Manchurian affairs. As mentioned, in June 1946, the Truman administration had sent a reparations mission under Edwin W. Pauley to inspect the Japanese assets. After a month-long investigation in Manchuria, Pauley's mission delivered a damning report in July detailing the removal and destruction of Japanese industrial equipment during the Soviet occupation.[148] Pauley's report further intensified the post-war reparations row between the Soviet Union, China and the West.[149]

When the GMD's offensive against the CCP in Manchuria reached its height in 1946, Chiang Kai-shek was simultaneously brainstorming ideas to return to the negotiating table with the Soviets, but his inner circle opposed the idea and the military conflicts dissuaded him from doing it.[150] Chiang confided to Zhang Jia'ao that he felt 'the Soviets did not show favouritism to the CCP. If they wanted to practice partiality towards the CCP, how was it possible that the Nationalist armies could conquer Changchun?'[151] Chiang asked the right question.

Last chance in Manchuria

In March 1945, when the Nationalist diplomats were trying to get to the bottom of the Anglo-American–Soviet secret deal in Yalta, Chiang Kai-shek had noted that he must have the courage to take risks in dealing with the Soviets.[152] Indeed, Chiang's foreign policy decisions towards the end of World War II show a strong element of risk-taking, as his government was constantly being forced into crisis management mode. The prime example of this was when Chiang staged a walkout from the negotiations when the Soviets started to press hard for economic privileges in Manchuria. Chiang's risky tactic did achieve some short-term effects. The Soviets were forced to slow down their takeover of Japanese enterprises and forge a more negotiable joint venture scheme. Although Chiang's ploy put substantial pressure on his frontline negotiators, his 10 billion CCNE payout plan was an attractive transitional arrangement that could have turned the tables and resolved the war booty disagreement.

---

148 Pauley, *Report on Japanese Assets*, pp. vi–x, 9–15.
149 Roberts, *Stalin's Wars*, 352.
150 *Wang riji*, 25 May 1946, 5: 326.
151 Zhang Jia'ao's diary, 4 November 1946, in *Zhang Gongquan*, ed. Yao Songling, 1: 761.
152 *Chiang Diary*, 4 March 1945, Folder 4, Box 44.

However, Chiang Kai-shek's own decision to change the negotiation venue and replace his lead negotiator in midstream was counterproductive, as the decision robbed his negotiators of authority, albeit Special Envoy Sun played a limited role in the negotiations. When the downgraded Zhang Jia'ao put forth Chiang's proposal, it was received coldly. In the same vein, although Chiang Kai-shek sent his son to meet Stalin personally, Chiang Ching-kuo could not promote his father's plan as the GMD leadership limited his authority to negotiate. And while Madame Chiang might have had sufficient prestige for ceremonial purposes, her official visit to the Soviet forces did little to patch up relations with the Soviets.

Meanwhile, the Soviet Union was wielding and trying to extend its supremacy globally over weaker states. The Soviets used Poland as a precedent to try to press the Turkish government to submit to a range of Soviet demands, including territorial cession, in June 1946.[153] Stalin also drew on the Polish case to press Chiang Ching-kuo to accept the Soviet claim of war booty, but the Soviets' tepid protest against the Nationalists' air attack demonstrates that they were unwilling to go beyond a certain point. Evidently, Moscow was less interested in risking a war with the West and its allies. Succumbing to Anglo-American pressure, the Soviets agreed not to send armies to Hokkaido, abandoned their claim to Turkey and withdrew their forces from Iran.[154] As Marshall told Chiang Kai-shek, the tactic that the Soviets were using in dealing with the GMD was also used in dealing with other countries.[155] Moscow did not pressure the GMD any harder than it did other smaller powers.

As discussed in chapter 1, Chiang Kai-shek once thought that a policy of appeasement on the Soviet Union was his best option. The Zhang–Sun plan was a negotiator's answer to Chiang's vision because it was not only a plan designed to make the best of a bad situation but also a far-sighted approach to creating a manageable relationship: 'If the other side has big guns, you do not want to turn a negotiation into a gunfight.'[156]

---

153 Kuniholm, *The Origins of the Cold War*, 258–9.
154 E.J. Hobsbawm, *The Age of Extremes: The Short Twentieth Century, 1914–1991* (London: Michael Joseph, 1994), 71, 232; David Holloway, *Stalin and the Bomb: The Soviet Union and Atomic Energy 1939–1956* (New Haven, CT: Yale University Press, 1994), 168.
155 Notes of meeting between Marshall, Chiang Kai-shek and Madame Chiang, 26 December, *FRUS*, 1945, 7: 814–15.
156 Fisher, Ury and Patton, *Getting to Yes*, 110.

5. PLANTING RADISHES IN THE DESERT

Looking for ways to tackle a stronger adversary, Chiang Kai-shek acknowledged the necessity to broaden his bargaining range in order to induce the desired behaviour on the part of the Soviets. From a negotiation point of view, Chiang was correct. Arguably, the toughest bargainers do not usually finish first, and the deficit incurred by settling for a suboptimal deal can be overturned via multiple negotiations down the track.

Realistically, however, Chiang did not have many options. After he played his two trump cards (i.e. the walkout tactic and the one-off payout), with unconvincing results, Chiang was forced, for the most part, to wait for his stronger opponents to make the next move. Besides, Chiang had to be sensitive to his American allies, who had been pushing the GMD to toughen its Soviet policy—this further complicated his decision-making.

Then again, the Nationalists came to the economic negotiations against the backdrop of rising discontent with the Soviets' stance on Dalian and their war reparations claim. Also, Chiang Kai-shek and his inner circle would have to further risk weathering domestic opposition if they offered more concessions. As Wang Shijie told Marshall, the GMD had already made huge concessions in the Sino-Soviet Treaty and could not afford to pay extra for Manchuria under threat.[157] In other words, Chiang Kai-shek's decision to reduce the scope of economic cooperation with the Soviets provided an easy but dangerous way out for the GMD.

Soviet negotiator Sladkovsky had described the process of seeking an economic accord with the GMD as akin to 'planting radishes in the desert'. In reality, growing radishes in the desert is difficult, but it is not impossible. Tsou has argued that the USSR was fundamentally hostile towards the GMD.[158] If so, the GMD–Soviet negotiation for economic cooperation in Manchuria would be notable because despite the high level of mutual mistrust and conflict, the Nationalists still shared considerable common interests with the Soviets. In early February 1946, both parties actually came tantalisingly close to an accord; hence Zhang Jia'ao's concern that the GMD had its last chance for a peaceful takeover of Manchuria.[159]

The cases of Hegang and Anshan demonstrate the full complexity of issues confronting the Nationalist–Soviet economic negotiations. Soviet actions in Hegang prove that ideology does not always prevail over material needs and

---

157 Marshall to Truman, 9 February, *FRUS*, 1946, 9: 426–9.
158 Tsou, *America's Failure in China*, 338.
159 Donald G. Gillin and Ramon H. Myers, 'Introduction'; *Manchuria*, 16 January 1946, 48–9, 206–7.

that common interests shared by both parties do have the potential to make a difference. Although common interests were available, they unfortunately did not facilitate an agreement between the Nationalists and the Soviets in the end. As Roger Fisher, William Ury and Bruce Patton observed, 'Conflict lies not in objective reality, but in people's heads.'[160] In the GMD's case, its decision-makers could not break out of their straitjacket of legality and moral righteousness and simultaneously influence the perception of their strong international opponents and allies. This was probably one of the missing links between Chiang Kai-shek's vision and his execution of it.

Malinovsky's rhetorical comment on US aggression justifies Dong's initial claim that the origins of Soviet recalcitrance came from Moscow's insecurity complex and that it was something the GMD authorities needed urgently to deal with. However, the Nationalist negotiators were unable to secure an acceptable deal with their Soviet counterparts before the domestic and international political environment deteriorated into a perpetual logjam of negotiation. In particular, the Nationalists' proposal in February and the two proposed by the Soviets in March and April demonstrate that both sides did not have irreconcilable disagreements on specific economic issues. The crux of the matter was the domestic anti-Soviet atmosphere in China, the strong CCP presence in Manchuria and the venom of post-Yalta and pre–Cold War international politics, which were responsible for the erosion of the bilateral relationship. This perhaps justifies Dong's final and arguably most pessimistic observation: that an agreement on economic cooperation alone would not be enough to reverse the downward spiral of Nationalist–Soviet relations.

Force replaced negotiation in Manchuria after the Soviet troop withdrawal was completed in April 1946. The GMD–CCP rivalry escalated into a full-scale war. Zhang Jia'ao had no further role to play in the Sino-Soviet negotiations because both Premier Song and Wang Shijie believed that Zhang was not tough enough to be a negotiator.[161] Moscow evacuated the Soviet employees of the Chinese Changchun Railway in July. In October 1946, the Soviet Union began to evacuate hundreds of Soviet citizens from Manchuria, indicating that a GMD–Soviet split was in the making.[162]

---

160 Fisher, Ury and Patton, *Getting to Yes*, 23.
161 Song Ziwen to Chiang Kai-shek, 27 May 1946, *Shilüe*, 65: 609–10.
162 Zhang Jia'ao's diary, 1 July, 3 October and 9 December 1946, in *Zhang Gongquan*, ed. Yao Songling, 1: 745, 757–8, 772–3.

6

'China's Madrid'

The synonym of civil war

In mid-March 1946, after a series of setbacks in the Nationalists' bid to take over Manchuria, the GMD armies deployed in Shenyang and its environs launched sweeping operations to take selected Communist positions. The prime target of the GMD assault was Sipingjie.[1] The city, which lay about half way between Shenyang and Changchun, was now used by NEDUA as a stronghold to stop the northern advance of the Nationalists. This should have given the US-armed GMD armies the best chance to eliminate the CCP forces in positional warfare. The GMD Manchurian force's military capability, however, was hampered by a lack of logistic support.

The GMD's main striking force, N1A, was shipped to Manchuria by US Navy vessels, but logistics difficulties hindered the transportation of some of the most lethal artillery capable of piercing the CCP's defences.[2] The problem for the GMD army officers in Manchuria was that they had to reconcile the backwardness of their traditional logistics system with the relatively sudden arrival of military equipment from the United States. In early 1946, the N1A commander Sun Liren pleaded with Wedemeyer to supply cold weather clothing to his army, which operated in the north.[3] In February, the Americans supplied 43,000 sets of US military Arctic-type

---

1 Guofangbu shizhengju ed., *Kanluan*, 4: 72–8.
2 Cheng, 'Modern war', 45–6.
3 Sun Liren to Wedemeyer, 14 January 1946; 'New 1st Army'; Record of the China Theater of Operations, US Army; SS, Transportation, Headquarters, Reports and bulletins, Shipping reports—Water transportation bulletins, THRU, New 1st Army—Commanding Gen. Sun Li Jen, Box 687; CBIT; RG 493; NACP.

clothing, blankets and sleeping bags to the GMD's forces in Manchuria with a promise of more to come.[4] The GMD armies were forced to carry the US winter gear with hired carrying coolies, commandeered pack animals and conscripted mule carts. Some of the soldiers were forced to wear oversized US rubber snow boots on the march in mild weather conditions. The troops' speed and the security of the armies were therefore compromised.[5] The GMD's frontline logistic units at the port of Huludao were stretched out when shipments of US military winter gear continued to reach Manchuria until the summer months of 1946.[6]

The officers of the N1A could rely on the army's pack animals to transport their US military equipment. However, to their chagrin, thousands of military animals were left in the South China city of Guangzhou, owing to the difficulty of obtaining US logistical support. Logistical assistance for the GMD government was only the fourth priority of the US Army.[7] US Army logistics officers informed their Nationalist counterparts that only six properly converted LSTs would be allowed to move the livestock for all GMD armies departing for Manchuria. As only six vessels were available for a massive sea transport operation, it could take many months to complete. This meant that the troops and weaponry could reach Manchuria well before the horses and mules. The Americans advised the Nationalists to make use of US Army trucks as an alternative means of transportation but took no account of the difficulty of supplying fuel to truck columns.[8]

As the pack animals were unlikely to arrive any time soon, the officers of the New 38th Division of the N1A had to purchase fodder from the front line and ship the provisions back to Guangzhou to keep the livestock fed. Also included was immediate relief to a contingent of about 2,000

---

4   'Notes on the movement of the New First Army from Kowloon to Chinwangtao', no. 9, 29 January 1946; 'New 1st Army'; Record of the China Theater of Operations, US Army; SS, Transportation, Headquarters, Reports and bulletins, Shipping reports—Water transportation bulletins, THRU, New 1st Army—Commanding Gen. Sun Li Jen, Box 687; CBIT; RG 493; NACP.
5   Cheng, 'Modern war', 45–6.
6   John Liu to W.M. Brown, 16 May 1946; CAM; Record of the China Theater of Operations, US Army; SS, Transportation, Headquarters, Reports and bulletins, Shipping reports—Water transportation bulletins, THRU, New 1st Army—Commanding Gen. Sun Li Jen, Box 687; CBIT; RG 493; NACP.
7   Cheng, 'Modern war', 46, 58, fn. 5.
8   Paul W. Caraway to Yu Ta-wei, subject: 'Additional Chinese Army moves', 27 January 1946; CAM; SS; CT; Box 687; CBIT; RG 493; NACP. Also, 'Notes on the movement of the New First Army from Kowloon to Chinwangtao', no. 9, 29 January 1946; 'New 1st Army'; Record of the China Theater of Operations, US Army; SS, Transportation, Headquarters, Reports and bulletins, Shipping reports—Water transportation bulletins, THRU, New 1st Army—Commanding Gen. Sun Li Jen, Box 687; CBIT; RG 493; NACP.

men who had stayed behind with the division's livestock and were living in abominable conditions. The rescue campaign managed to save only 380 animals, and 62 per cent of the division's transport capacity was lost.[9] The loss of manpower and animal power was not unique to the New 38th Division. The US Army records show that the N1A needed to assign a whopping 11 per cent of its total strength (i.e. 4,781 men) to stay behind in order to take care of the army's horses and mules.[10] The commander of the 93rd Army, by contrast, gave the order to use captured enemy weapons to barter for pack animals with the civilian inhabitants.[11] The improvisation was intended to provide a quick fix for the army's logistical problem, albeit it would not mitigate the risk of army corruption.

The US forces preferred to move the GMD armies to the north sooner than later. This was because the Nationalists needed the Americans' help to ship almost everything, including green vegetables, to supply those Nationalist forces waiting to board the US ships.[12] But when the Chinese soldiers encountered the American sailors on the American vessels, both parties experienced culture shock. Some American liaison and naval personnel made disparaging remarks about the sanitary habits of the Chinese soldiers without considering that those aboard their ships were the GMD's best troops and that many of them were English-speaking. Recalcitrant elements of the American personnel considered that the US arms and equipment in the hands of the Nationalist servicemen should be subject to confiscation and looting.[13] A Nationalist eyewitness report paints the American servicemen accompanying Chinese soldiers aboard the US ships as pirates, who committed theft and vandalism, initiated unprovoked assaults on Chinese officers and accepted bribes.[14] Diaries of the Nationalist

---

9 'Lujun xinbian shi zhenzhong riji (Xin sanshiba shi)' [Field diaries of the New Organised Army Division—New 38th Army], 1946–47, entry 15 December 1946, Quanzong: 'Guofangbu shizheng bianyiju' [Bureau of Historical Compilation and Translation, Ministry of National Defence], file no.: B5018230601/0035/540.4/7421.5C, National Archives Administration, National Development Council, Taipei (hereafter NAA); Cheng, 'Modern war', 46.
10 'Strength and locations of all New First Army units', 27 January 1946; 'New First Army'; SS; CT; Box 687; CBIT; RG 493; NACP.
11 Li Daren, *Dongbei kanluan huiyi* [Remembering the war of bandit suppression in the north-east] (Taipei: Boxue chubanshe, 1979), 79–80.
12 'Colonel Brown—G-3 troop mover deluxe', 4 April 1946; CAM; SS; CT; Box 687; CBIT; RG 493; NACP.
13 W.M. Brown to Hayman, subject: 'Indoctrination of US personnel', 10 February 1946; 'New First Army'; SS; CT; Box 687; CBIT; RG 493; NACP.
14 Diary of GMD staff officer Yang, 87th Division of the Nationalist 71st Army, 16–17 and 22 March 1946, in *Guomindang xiaji junguan*, Li Disheng, 25–7.

junior officers have demonstrated that the GMD forces en route to the north-east were plagued by discipline problems and growing war-weariness among the soldiers.[15]

The GMD's elite corps, not unexpectedly, did not start their Manchurian campaign auspiciously, even though many of them had brilliant fighting records against the Japanese. The stiff resistance of the CCP forces exacted a significant toll on the Nationalists during the intense and gruelling skirmishes in the lead-up to the GMD's main offensive. After the occupation of a railway town within 60 kilometres to the south of Sipingjie on 3 April, the N1A was ready to launch a major offensive on the CCP's stronghold.[16] This chapter is about these military operations amid the collapse of the US-backed ceasefire mechanism.

'Debating societies'

In Chongqing, Marshall's deputy Alvan Gillem took up the facilitator's role in the absence of the former and made every effort to broker a deal between the two warring factions for the entry of truce teams into Manchuria. Zhou, however, rejected a Chiang-approved settlement outright, particularly over the provisions allowing the Nationalists to exclusively occupy key localities along a strip 30 kilometres wide on either side of the main railways in the name of national sovereignty.[17] As Marshall had drafted the original proposal, a PRC source considers it the beginning of Marshall's betrayal of his impartiality, despite the fact that he had explained to both parties before he departed for Washington that he merely wanted to help them to find the simplest way of getting the truce teams into Manchuria immediately.[18] Given that Zhou was well aware of Marshall's biased stance in favour of the GMD, such a claim literally questioned the purpose of the American's proposal: rather than resolve the conflict via peaceful mediation, Marshall, under conditions of bias, only wanted to create conditions for the GMD's troops to advance.

---

15 See a collection of diaries of three junior officers from later December 1945 to early April 1946: clerical assistant Li Disheng, 2nd Company, 66th Regiment, 22nd Division, New 6th Army; platoon leader Lu Zhongjie, 9th Company, 64th Regiment, 22nd Division, New 6th Army; staff officer Yang, 87th Division, 71st Army, in *Guomindang xiaji junguan*, Li Disheng, 3–28.
16 Guofangbu shizhengju ed., *Kanluan*, 4: 74–88.
17 'Document prepared by General Marshall', 9 March 1946, *FRUS*, 1946, 9: 542.
18 Minutes of meeting of the Committee of Three, 11 March 1946, *FRUS*, 1946, 9: 543–53; *Tanpan shi*, 388–9.

Chiang Kai-shek, in turn, rejected Zhou's counter-proposal and found the stipulation that the GMD troops could only move into the localities 'now' being evacuated by the Soviet forces most irritating. Consequently, both parties quickly deadlocked at the word 'now'.[19]

Given that resentment ran high on both sides after the Nationalist CEC and the ease of NEDUA's occupation of territory to Shenyang's north following the Soviets' withdrawal since mid-March, Zhou was in no mood to compromise. When Gillem began to speculate whether Zhou was using delaying tactics, Zhou simply returned to Yan'an on 21 March, citing communication difficulties with Yan'an as the reason for his departure.[20] Chiang felt the time pressure more acutely than Zhou, as the military picture in Manchuria was not looking up for the GMD. He succumbed to pressure on 22 March, informing Gillem that he would make concession.[21]

Zhou flew back to Chongqing on 25 March. Both parties quickly agreed to eliminate all controversial points and signed an instruction regarding the entry of field teams into Manchuria. It authorised the truce teams 'to bring about a cessation of fighting and to make the necessary and fair readjustments'.[22] The instruction certainly was general enough for both parties to subscribe to it, but it did not produce a mechanism for its practical implementation. Previous studies have found the instruction useless because it did not even pick a ceasefire date.[23]

From the perspective of the mediator, it should be the goal of the mediator to secure an entirely efficient deal for the disputants, not merely an agreement that is acceptable to both.[24] Instructions on detailed matters could have been easier on the members of the truce teams. The problem was that the instruction also went to hundreds of army officers of both opposing factions who might have a different understanding of the local situation. As Marshall elucidated later, an inflexible instruction would have been less

---

19 'Draft prepared by General Chou En-lai', 17 March 1946; notes of meeting between Gillem and Chiang Kai-shek, 21 March 1946, *FRUS*, 1946, 9: 564–5, 588–90.
20 Gillem to Marshall, 18 March 1946; Zhou to Gillem, 20 March 1946, *FRUS*, 1946, 9: 583–4, 586–7.
21 Gillem to Marshall, 23 March 1946, *FRUS*, 1946, 9: 593–4.
22 Committee of Three to the Three Commissioners, 26 March 1946; Gillem to Marshall, 27 March 1946, *FRUS*, 1946, 9: 603, 605.
23 Chuande Tu, 'The 1945–1946 GMD–CCP peace talks and the origins of the Chinese Civil War' (PhD diss., University of Wisconsin—Madison, 2000), 227.
24 Kevin Gibson, Leigh Thompson and Max H. Bazerman, 'Shortcomings of neutrality in mediation: Solutions based on rationality', *Negotiation Journal* 12, no. 1 (1996): 69–80.

adaptive to changes in circumstances.[25] The January truce agreement had a clear-cut ceasefire date on which both parties should cease fighting, but it was not as efficient as expected. In high-stakes negotiation scenarios, how a party should behave and how other parties might behave can be entirely asymmetric.[26]

Byroade soon discovered that the instruction did not provide enough details for his Executive Headquarters to turn it into an action plan.[27] The truce teams to Manchuria were either helplessly immobilised or could only accomplish little more than a fact-finding tour.[28] When Manchuria became a synonym for civil war in May, individual field team members of the two belligerent parties soon engaged in activities that defeated the entire purpose of sending truce teams. A CCP veteran admitted that the CCP delegates had used their privilege to radio intelligence on GMD troop dispositions to the NEDUA's headquarters.[29] US documents recorded a GMD delegate suspected of being engaged in espionage inside the NEDUA occupied area.[30] This pattern of behaviour soon spread to China proper.[31]

These regrettable incidents also exacerbated the diminishing prestige of the Committee of Three, the Executive Headquarters and its field teams. The Executive Headquarters and its field teams had been put under pressure to resolve alleged ceasefire breaches, which made them particularly vulnerable. A report in May 1946 shows that a staggering 1,800 complaints of alleged truce violations had been lodged with the Executive Headquarters since January, and a great number of cases remained unresolved. When agreements on complaints over ceasefire violations could not be reached at the field-team level, the cases in dispute would be referred to the Executive Headquarters. The members of the Executive Headquarters reviewed the

---

25 Minutes of meeting of Committee of Three, 22 June 1946, *FRUS*, 1946, 9: 1139–51, esp. 1149.
26 Howard Raiffa, *The Art and Science of Negotiation* (Cambridge, MA: Belknap Press, 1998), 20–2.
27 Smyth to Byrnes, 6 April 1946; Byroade to Marshall, 28 May 1946, *FRUS*, 1946, 9: 736, 908–11.
28 Robertson to Gillem, 3 April 1946, *FRUS*, 1946, 9: 728–9; Pei HQS GRP to all field teams except Manchuria, 15 April 1946; 'Outgoing messages, "secret"', 8 April–14 November 1946'; 'Outgoing messages, "confidential"', 'Outgoing (26 July 1946) thru "dragon" outgoing (19 November 1946)'; Box 17; Records of the Office of the Commanding General, Chief of Administration and Personnel, Adjutant General; Records of the Peiping Headquarters Group 1946–47; CBIT; RG 493; NACP.
29 Geng Biao, *Geng Biao huiyilu* [The memoirs of Geng Biao] (Beijing: Jiefangjun chubanshe, 1991), 391–92.
30 Team 36 to Pei HQS GRP for Three Commissioners, 25 April 1946, 'Incoming messages team #36, 4–15 November 1946'; 'Messages received from field teams, messages—team 22 thru messages—team 36'; Records of the Executive Headquarters, Peiping, China; Records of the Office of the Commanding General, Chief of Administration and Personnel (G-1), Adjutant General; Box 26; CBIT, RG 493, NACP.
31 Marshall to Zhou, 2 May; Robertson to Marshall, 3–4 May, *FRUS*, 1946, 9: 807–10.

cases to no avail owing to the lack of facts. The failure to make decisions distressed all parties of the Executive Headquarters as some behaved like members of 'debating societies', as Byroade put it. The Executive Headquarters ended up passing the buck to the Committee of Three, but as matters often could not be decided merely by meetings at the top, the dispute became a merry-go-round that no party could get off.[32]

Sipingjie: China's Madrid

On the Manchurian battlefield, the NEDUA dragged the Nationalists into a two-front battle: amassing forces in Sipingjie and Benxi for a strong defence. While a big battle loomed at Sipingjie, the leaders of the two belligerents had different concerns about the use of force. Towards the end of March, Mao, having recovered from his illness, directed his armed forces with the aim of holding Sipingjie with large-scale positional warfare. He ordered Lin to defend Sipingjie at all costs. Both Lin and Zhou doubted their military capability for conducting trench warfare. They suggested that it was more appropriate to reduce the physical strength of the enemy rather than defending the city and, in the long run, force a peace deal. This strategy received Mao's support, which concurred completely with the paradigm of offensive accommodation.[33]

Chiang, unlike Mao, was less sanguine about the prospects of a military victory. He was more concerned about his armies' rear area security than a swift and decisive victory over the elusive enemy, despite the fact that he asked about the possibility of taking Sipingjie by 20 April.[34] He was aware that his main striking forces in Manchuria, the N1A and the N6A, were inexperienced in fighting the NEDUA,[35] although they had been battle hardened in the China–Burma–India theatre during World War II. Chiang's generals shared his view. The N1A was under orders to stay close to the 71st Army (71A; arriving at combat positions in late March 1946), and the two armies would push forward towards Sipingjie together in a trapezoid shape.[36]

---

32 Minutes of meeting between Byroade and Zhou, 12 May 1946; Byroade to Marshall, 28 May 1946, *FRUS*, 1946, 9: 834–9, 908–11, citation from 908.
33 Cheng, 'China's Madrid', 93–4.
34 Chiang to Xiong and reply, 6 and 13 April 1946, *Shilüe*, 65: 279–80, 338.
35 Chiang to Xiong, 26 March 1946, *Shilüe*, 65: 170–1.
36 Xiong to Chiang, 8 April 1946, *Shilüe*, 65: 288; Guofangbu shizhengju ed., *Kanluan*, 4: 81.

The caveat was that if the two large friendly combat units stayed too close, it would make it even easier for the CCP troops to break up their formation and start a dogfight: launching attacks to push the Nationalist flank guard units into their already overcrowded main body and causing enormous congestion. While the Nationalists' formation was split up, the stampeding Nationalist troops became manoeuvring targets of the CCP's close-range assaults. The CCP forces adopted this tactic in the final phase of the Laiwu campaign of February 1947 in the province of Shandong. An entire GMD army corps of roughly 40,000 men was annihilated in no more than two hours fighting in that battle.[37]

Therefore, when the 71A approached an area on the outskirts of Sipingjie on 16 April, it maintained a distance of more than 20 kilometres from the N1A. Considering that the 71A was only about 35 kilometres southwest of an enemy-held city, a 20-kilometre lateral distance between the two US-armed friendly forces was a matter of necessity rather than choice if the 71A intended to synchronise the N1A's frontal attack with a left-hook manoeuvre around and through the enemy positions to the west of Sipingjie. However, the NEDUA was still able to exploit that small gap between the two Nationalist forces and successfully ambushed and paralysed a division of the 71A. At Benxi, the NEDUA successfully immobilised the Nationalists, including a division of the elite N6A.[38]

Chiang called for a perfectly safe plan for troops to advance in the northeast after repeated military setbacks. He outlined a foolproof plan for his generals: they should shorten their front and avoid the rash advance of troops, thereby enabling them more easily to defend their supply lines even if it would relegate the conquest of Changchun to a lower priority.[39]

Chiang also scrupulously limited the use of aerial warfare tactics, such as strafing, bombardments and even reconnaissance over the Sipingjie line, for fear of provoking the Soviets.[40] As a crucial portion of the NEDUA's defences were constructed inside the closely built buildings at downtown

---

37 Guofangbu shizhengju ed., *Kanluan*, 7: 129–30; Geng Routian, *Zhongguo jiaofei kanluan*, 3: 14–15.
38 *Zhongguo remin jiefangjun zhanyi zhanli xuanbian* [Selected case studies of the operational history of the PLA], ed. Zhongguo renmin jiefang jun zhengzhi xueyuan diyi junshi yanjiaoshi [The first unit for teaching and research on military affairs, PLA institute of politics] (Beijing: Zhongguo renmin jiefangjun zhengzhi xueyuan chubanshe, 1984), 2: 40–1; Cheng, 'China's Madrid', 94; cf. Tanner, *Battle for Manchuria*, 121.
39 Chiang to Xiong, 18 April 1946, *Shilüe*, 65: 370–2.
40 Chiang to Xiong and Wang Shuming, 7 April 1946, *Shilüe*, 65: 296–7.

Sipingjie,⁴¹ air bombardment could have easily brought the city to its knees. The American military personnel who visited the front line were perplexed by the Nationalists' insufficient use of aerial bombardment against the NEDUA positions in Sipingjie.⁴² The following paragraphs will show that Chiang's generals were overly conservative and cautious during the Sipingjie campaign, which they undertook to observe Chiang's precept of 'seeking security first, employing tactical change-up second' (*xianqiu wendang, ciqiu bianhua* 先求穩當, 次求變化).⁴³

By contrast, the operational successes buoyed the warlike mentality of the CCP leaders. Mao changed his stance after being informed that Marshall was returning from Washington. As Mao expected that Marshall would immediately step in to halt the fighting, he was more interested in seizing more territory before the fighting stopped than seeking an equitable peace deal. He therefore pressed Lin to capture Changchun and Harbin, the capital of Heilongjiang Province, before Marshall intervened. The NEDUA took Changchun on 18 April. The capture of the old capital of Manchukuo symbolised the Communists' control of Manchuria, and Mao now considered the city their last line of defence. 'Turn Changchun into China's Madrid if necessary', Mao exhorted Lin.⁴⁴

Perhaps because Mao felt that he needed further military successes to support his Madrid plan, he ordered his commanders to eliminate the N1A. But the enemy was not a paper tiger. After a cautious three-pronged operation, the GMD armies captured some crucial positions on the outskirts of Sipingjie, and the city now came within range of direct Nationalist fire. On 20 April, the N1A began to storm the city, but the NEDUA was able to put up staunch resistance thanks to the overly cautious approach of the attackers. Until the end of April, the Nationalists had Sipingjie essentially under siege, and the NEDUA was entirely on the defensive.⁴⁵

Marshall returned to China on 18 April amid the rapid deterioration of the situation in Manchuria. He was unable to stop the fighting as Mao wished, instead receiving complaints from the two warring parties on

---

41 Guofangbu shizhengju ed., *Kanluan*, 4: 91–2.
42 Zheng Dongguo, *Wo de rongma shengyai* [My army life] (Beijing: Tuanjie chubanshe, 1992), 410.
43 Zheng Dongguo, 'Cong daju jingong dao zhongdian fangyu' [From massive attack to the defence of key points], in *Liaoshen zhanyi qinliji*, ed. Zhongguo renmin zhengzhi xieshang huiyi quanguo weiyuanhui wenshi ziliao yanjiu weiyuanhui Liaoshen zhanyi qinliji shenbianzu, 570.
44 Cheng, 'China's Madrid', 94; *Mao nianpu*, 3: 70–1.
45 Cheng, 'China's Madrid', 94–5.

ceasefire violations against each other.[46] Chiang contended that the CCP had not upheld its end of the deal, as evidenced by its capture of major Manchurian cities and its failure to comply with the army reorganisation agreement.[47] Chiang might have felt that negotiating with the Communists was useless; he could not rule out a ceasefire in Manchuria, as it remained a political and military quagmire for him. Politically, Chiang refused to settle for anything less than his armies' occupation of Changchun and the large cities to its north, which he regarded as the symbolic recognition of the power of his government.[48] Such a goal could only be achieved by the destruction of the NEDUA in a major battle to reclaim Sipingjie.[49] Militarily, however, Chiang showed his willingness to recognise—in light of the military realities in Manchuria—that his armies were vulnerable, if not in danger of annihilation.[50]

In the face of the GMD's Manchurian dilemma, Chiang's dependence on Marshall increased, although he knew that the American would bring him nothing but a temporary truce.[51] As discussed, one immediate consequence of dependence on third-party intervention is that the disputants are more inclined to adopt hard-line positions during negotiation. In Chiang's case, he allowed Marshall to assume control of the proceedings in the January truce, yet the outcome was not what he expected. He therefore outlined a truce proposal that was replete with tough conditions and, if there were an agreement, he requested Marshall's 'guarantee' of CCP compliance.[52]

One of Chiang's preconditions for peace was that the CCP would not obstruct his government in taking over the sovereignty of Manchuria, which implied the CCP military withdrawal from all Manchurian cities currently occupied. On the other hand, Chiang insisted that the CCP must earnestly carry out the cessation of hostilities agreement of 10 January and the army reorganisation agreement of 25 February they had previously signed. Chiang also supported the most controversial US-initiated proposal that the American officers of the Executive Headquarters and ceasefire teams

---

46 Xu Yongchang to Marshall, 6 May 1946; Zhou to Marshall, 19 May 1946, *FRUS*, 1946, 9: 819, 862–3.
47 Marshall, *Marshall's Mission to China*, 1: 101.
48 Minutes of meeting between Marshall and Yu Dawei, 11 May 1946, *FRUS*, 1946, 9: 830–3.
49 Chiang to Xiong and Du, 21 April 1946, *Shilüe*, 65: 383–4.
50 Marshall, *Marshall's Mission to China*, 1: 101.
51 *Chiang Diary*, 20 April 1946, Folder 5, Box 45.
52 Chiang to Marshall, 28 May 1946, *FRUS*, 1946, 9: 907–8.

should have the final say in the event of a disagreement between the CCP and GMD delegates.[53] Chiang would not consider a ceasefire in Manchuria without the fulfilment of all these preconditions.

The CCP leadership, in contrast, insisted that peace talks would not be successful without an immediate and unconditional ceasefire.[54] In other words, the CCP was seeking a truce deal that was entirely congenial to the consolidation of its newly acquired territories in Manchuria. Zhou also put forward a new demand: the deployment of five CCP army divisions along the major Manchurian cities now under its control, making it a five-times increase against the army reorganisation agreement of February.[55] On the question of the authority to make a final decision, Zhou advised Marshall that even one small attempt to throw the issue into open discussion would press the Chinese Communists to the wall, and that could be a hindrance to the ceasefire.[56]

Marshall was aware that the civil war in Manchuria had dealt a serious blow to his credibility as a mediator.[57] One of the warning signs was that Marshall could not find a favourable juncture to call the Committee of Three meetings since he returned from Washington simply because there was no point of mutual agreement between both parties. Instead, Marshall could only settle issues verbally via meeting individually with one party and then the other.[58] The Committee of Three was in a state of flux since the falling out between the two parties in March and the deterioration of the military situation in April in Manchuria. The committee changed four GMD members in only a month. It began with Chiang's decision to send his military protégé Chen Cheng to replace Zhang Zhizhong regardless of protests from Gillem. Chen was quickly succeeded by Yu Dawei, the minister of communication, and then Xu Yongchang, the director of military operation. Some of these officials were just there to make up the numbers. Yu told Gillem openly that he had no desire to sit on the committee.[59]

---

53   'Draft of directive regarding the movement of field teams, prepared by Brigadier General Henry A. Byroade', 11 May 1946; Madame Chiang to Marshall, 24 May 1946; Chiang to Marshall, 28 May 1946; *FRUS*, 1946, 9: 833–4, 891–2, 907–8.
54   Minutes of meeting between Marshall and Zhou, 23 April 1946, *FRUS*, 1946, 9: 790–2.
55   Minutes of meeting between Marshall and Zhou, 21 May 1946, *FRUS*, 1946, 9: 868–79.
56   Minutes of meeting between Marshall and Zhou, 3 June 1946, *FRUS*, 1946, 9: 971.
57   Minutes of meeting between Marshall and Zhou, 30 May 1946, *FRUS*, 1946, 9: 915–26.
58   Marshall to Robertson, 7 June 1946, *FRUS*, 1946, 9: 993.
59   Gillem to Marshall, 6 April 1946; minutes of meeting between Marshall and Zhou, 23 April 1946, *FRUS*, 1946, 9: 737, 790–2.

Marshall nonetheless focused on what he could do, not what he had lost. Marshall told Chiang that the Nationalists were militarily powerless to achieve the total destruction of the NEDUA in Manchuria. If Du's troops continued to push northward, they would be in imminent danger of being defeated. A military fiasco would seriously compromise Chiang's position. The GMD should, according to Marshall, concentrate its best troops in between Shenyang and Huludao rather than pushing them northward into a calamitous civil war.[60] Marshall then made representations to Zhou, telling him that the Chinese Communists' occupation of Changchun 'would boomerang to their great disadvantage',[61] as the fall of Changchun aggravated Chiang's thirst for revenge. The CCP might be entirely unfazed by Chiang's crack troops, but Marshall acquainted Zhou with the fact that further escalation of the military conflict would only be to the detriment of China.[62]

Marshall spared no effort to urge both Zhou and Chiang to endorse the petition submitted by the Democratic League in late April to settle the Manchurian problem.[63] The petition sought to sanction all GMD troop movements on the railways in Manchuria. The CCP forces would pull out from the rail lines (i.e. the big cities) in support of the sanction, and the Nationalists would be allowed to send representatives into key cities in northern Manchuria, meaning that Lin Biao needed to withdraw his forces from Changchun. It was also averred in the petition that the Nationalist bureaucrats sacked from the chairmanship of the Political Council of the NEHQ were to be replaced by three non-partisan members.[64]

The two belligerent parties failed to appreciate the bipartisan interests of the proposal from a minor party. Zhou suggested that he agreed to send a joint commission to Manchuria after a general ceasefire, but made no mention of the CCP withdrawal from the big cities. Chiang was less diplomatic and rejected the proposal outright.[65] Struggling against the odds to keep the hope of peace alive, Marshall envisaged a major embarrassment for Washington if he continued to be involved in China's internal strife without finding

---

60 Marshall to Chiang, 10 May 1946, *FRUS*, 1946, 9: 824–8; Tanner, *Battle for Manchuria*, 155.
61 Minutes of meeting between Marshall and Zhou, 25 May 1946, *FRUS*, 1946, 9: 894.
62 Minutes of meeting between Marshall and Zhou, 21 May 1946, *FRUS*, 1946, 9: 868–79.
63 Notes of meeting between Marshall and Zhou, 27 April 1946, *FRUS*, 1946, 9: 797–800.
64 Marshall, *Marshall's Mission to China*, 1: 105.
65 Notes of meeting between Marshall and Zhou, 27 April; minutes of meeting between Marshall and Zhou, 29 April 1946, *FRUS*, 1946, 9: 797–800, 802–5; cf. Tu, 'The 1945–1946 GMD–CCP peace talks', 234–6.

a circuit breaker to stop the military conflict.[66] He revealed to Zhou later on that he would not be placed in the position of a mediator when there was almost certainty that a stalemate would develop.[67]

Mao's offensive accommodation plan was thus effectively thwarted: first, hopes for a workable peace agreement in the foreseeable future were dashed, and second, it was unprofitable to continue a war of attrition, as Sipingjie was under siege by the enemy's elite. The military picture was grim on the southern front, too. The gradually improved logistics made it possible for the Nationalists to bring more troops and artillery pieces to the front in their second-phase assault against Benxi. On 22 April, the NEDUA's captains from Benxi reported that it looked unlikely that they could defend their positions should the Nationalists launch a large-scale offensive.[68]

But Mao was unmoved and insisted that they press ahead. He ordered the commanders in Benxi to fight tenaciously at least to delay the enemy until there was finally a peace agreement. The consequence of Mao's order was effectively to turn the CCP's operations in Manchuria into a defensive accommodation mode of warfare, which aimed to use the war of attrition to compel a favourable peace. There was no favourable intelligence to support Mao's plan, but he conjured a justification from thin air for his alteration of the CCP's military strategy, which was in line with his Madrid motto. On 27 April, Mao asked Lin Biao to augment the numbers of the defence forces in Sipingjie, and their last line of defence was therefore shifted from Changchun to the besieged city. 'For peace and democracy … turn Sipingjie into China's Madrid', he wrote, demanding that his officers conjure up a military miracle.[69]

Meanwhile, the GMD's victorious offensive on 3 May finally forced the NEDUA to retreat from Benxi. The fall of Benxi radically compromised Mao's strategic position, allowing the enemy a freer hand to strike Sipingjie and making it all but impossible for the NEDUA to maintain numerical superiority. Mao was well informed about the change in the force-to-force ratio, but he preferred that Lin Biao conduct one more strike before seeking to terminate the operation, in case his Sipingjie defenders were able to

---

66 Marshall to Truman, 6 May 1946, *FRUS*, 1946, 9: 815–18.
67 Minutes of meeting between Zhou and Marshall, 17 May 1946, *FRUS*, 1946, 9: 849–61.
68 Cheng, 'China's Madrid', 95; Guofangbu shizhengju ed., *Kanluan*, 4: 99–107.
69 Cheng, 'China's Madrid', 95–6.

prevail against the attackers and turn the tide. Lin gave Mao a simple and direct reply: it was not possible to dislodge—much less rout—the battle-hardened enemy within such a short time.[70]

Mao ignored Lin's report, as he decided to stake his armed forces on maintaining the status quo in the major cities of northern Manchuria. Hopes for peace vanished on 29 April. Chiang bluntly rejected a proposal to settle the Manchurian problem that was endorsed by both Marshall and Zhou. Mao, however, remained adamant on the unyielding defence of Sipingjie. He urged Lin to defend the city for the longest possible time and to avert enemy breakthroughs. As peace was unimaginable at that stage, Mao's decision in effect shifted the strategy of defence accommodation into a plan for defending the status quo that relied on gradually diluting the enemy's strength without realistic hope for a peace settlement.[71]

The defenders at Sipingjie came under greater threat when the GMD's N6A arrived, fresh from its victory in Benxi. The enemy's reinforcements robbed Lin's defenders, 70,000 to 100,000 in number, of their clear numerical superiority, because they were now facing more than ten GMD divisions (more than 120,000 men). The Communists at Sipingjie were left with only two options: either to heed Mao—that is, continue their courageous positional battle—or to disengage in a planned retreat at a moment of their choosing. Although Mao's recalcitrant general Huang Kecheng had urged him to call off the defence of Sipingjie and shift the troops to consolidate their rural rear, he asserted that the longer the defence was maintained, the greater the chance of achieving a peace settlement and thus averting an open general war. Mao therefore directed Lin to retain Sipingjie, to ensure that he had enough bargaining power in hand when in due course he played the trump card (Changchun) to revitalise the negotiations.[72]

Mao's contingency plan was soon shattered by the N6A, which on 14 May launched an assault from the east flank of Sipingjie and gained ascendancy. From NEDUA defenders' views, the N6A's use of fast-moving mechanised infantry was like a German Blitzkrieg operation of World War II. Testimonies of the NEDUA veterans and a study based on these accounts emphasised the rapidity and intensity of the Nationalists' motorised infantry—particularly an account detailing the swiftness of 600 GMD

---

70 Ibid., 96.
71 Ibid., 97.
72 Ibid., 97–8; Cheng, 'The escalation of hostilities', 310–14; cf. Tanner, *Battle for Manchuria*, 157–8.

trucks pushing through the NEDUA line in a late stage of the campaign.[73] However, recollections of the N6A commander Liao Yaoxiang have revealed that the Nationalists' advance in the final stage of the campaign was not at all similar to a lightening war. Liao remembered that one of the N6A's so-called acts of gallantry was the sending of a small number of troops at night scouting ahead to the location they intended to occupy. These troops were under order to attain one linear objective only: making sure the NEDUA combatants were not there. The army then halted for its commander's fresh instruction until the next day, before advancing large groups of troop-laden trucks to the same spot their reconnaissance squads had already declared a safety zone the previous night.[74]

Nevertheless, conservative tactics had the advantage of secrecy. While the NEDUA defenders were caught unaware, elements of the N6A bypassed the enemy line from a few undefended spots further east to Sipingjie. When the N6A was in a strong position to curl into the enemy's rear and cut the NEDUA off from retreat, the rest of the GMD armies conducted further large-scale operations on 16 May, making their offensive multipronged. On 18 May, detachments of the N1A, supported by armoured vehicles, occupied the position of most advantage immediately to the east of the city. A total collapse of the NEDUA defence seemed imminent, and Lin Biao and his forces fled the city at night.[75]

The fifteen-day truce

When the battle of Sipingjie was nearing its end and an NEDUA defeat seemed inevitable, Chiang sent Defence Minister-in-waiting Bai Chongxi to Shenyang on 17 May, ordering Du to halt troop advance with the capture of Sipingjie. The Bai–Du meeting, however, reached a consensus that Chiang should be advised otherwise.[76] When his forces had advanced

---

73 Chen Yi, 'Siping baoweizhan' [The battle of defence of Sipingjie], *Liaoshen*, 1: 219–28; Tanner, *Battle for Manchuria*, 160–1.
74 Liao Yaoxiang, 'Jiangjun xin liu jun yuhui Sipingjie de jingguo' [An account of the flanking maneuver of Chiang Kai-shek's New Sixth Army toward Sipingjie], in *Wenshi ziliao xuanji*, ed. Zhongguo renmin zhengzhi xieshang huiyi quanguo weiyuanhui wenshi ziliao yanjiu weiyuanhui, 42 (1980): 77. The GMD records confirm that Liao's army conducted night-time missions in small groups at that particular stage of the battle. See Guofangbu shizhengju ed., *Kanluan*, 4: 119.
75 Chen Yi, 'Siping baoweizhan'; Cheng, 'China's Madrid', 98.
76 Du Yuming, 'Guomindang pohuai heping', 555–6; Guo Tingyi, Chia Ting-Shih, Ma Tien-kang, Chen San-Ching and Chen Tsun-Kung eds, *Bai Chongxi xiansheng fangwen jilu* [The reminiscences of General Pai Chung-Hsi] (Taipei: Institute of Modern History, Academia Sinica, 1984), 2: 815.

to within 70 kilometres of Changchun on 22 May,⁷⁷ Du received a telegram from Chiang instructing him to stall the chase immediately.⁷⁸ Du defied the order in the belief that Bai would persuade Chiang to change his mind in no time.⁷⁹

After he was briefed by Bai, Chiang flew to Shenyang on 23 May.⁸⁰ Marshall was told that Chiang had to be there for fear that his generals might do 'the wrong thing' and launched an assault on Changchun. In other words, Chiang was in agreement with Marshall that the GMD's occupation of Changchun before a peace settlement with the CCP was inadvisable.⁸¹

It is harder to end a war than start one. When Chiang's plane touched down at Shenyang, Du's forces had already defeated the NEDUA defenders in Changchun and regained control of the city.⁸² The Nationalists' military victory was achieved amid the leaders of the Democratic League's last-minute peace call to Mao and Chiang on 22 May, briefly reiterating their petition of April to settle the Manchurian issues peacefully. Mao accepted the petition in a telegram on 23 May, the day his forces fled Changchun.⁸³ Democratic League leader Liang Shuming rued the day that their pleas were not acted upon soon enough.⁸⁴

While Mao won the propaganda war, Chiang's generals wanted to exploit the enemy's military vulnerabilities. Chiang therefore ordered Du to continue the northern troop advance at a quicker pace towards Harbin at the northern branch of the Sungari River, although he indicated that he was searching for a peaceful solution to end the conflict.⁸⁵ Chiang invited his victorious generals to banquets in Shenyang before heading to Changchun for an official review and inspection of the troops. Chiang ended his inspection tour to Manchuria on 30 May and departed for Beiping without returning

---

77 Guofangbu shizhengju ed., *Kanluan*, 4: 128–9.
78 Chiang to Du, 22 May 1946, *Shilüe*, 65: 565–6.
79 Du to Chiang, 22 May 1946, *Shilüe*, 65: 566; Zheng Dongguo, 'Cong daju jingong', 573.
80 *Shilüe*, 65: 567–8.
81 Marshall to Truman, 22 May 1946; notes of meeting between Wang Shijie and Marshall, 23 May 1946, *FRUS*, 1946, 9: 880–3, citation from 883.
82 *Shilüe*, 65: 568–9.
83 Zhang Junmai, Huang Yanpei, Shen Junru, Zhang Bojun and Liang Shuming to Chiang and Mao, 22 May 1946, and Mao's reply on the 23rd, *Zhongguo minzhu tongmeng lishi wenxian* [Historical materials of the Chinese Democratic League], ed. Zhongguo minzhu tongmeng zhongyang wenshi ziliao weiyuanhui [The literary–historical source materials committee of the Central Committee of the Chinese Democratic League] (Beijing: Wenshi ziliao chubanshe, 1983), 170–1.
84 Liang Shuming, 'Wo canjia guogong hetan', 926.
85 *Chiang Diary*, 25 May 1946, Folder 6, Box 45; 'Siping baowei zhanyi an' [Records of the Sipingjie defense], 1946–47, Quanzong: 'Guofangbu shizheng bianyiju', B5018230601/0035/543.6/6021.2, NAA.

to the pre-war capital Nanjing, where his government had relocated earlier. He stayed in Beiping for another three days, doing almost the same things as he did in Shenyang, particularly in holding military meetings with his senior commanders in the North China theatre.[86] Chiang sent a short note to Marshall from Beiping on 1 June to explain the delay in his return to duty in Nanjing, refusing the latter's call for an immediate ceasefire.[87]

Nevertheless, Chiang's thoughts on Manchurian issues during this period were a strange mixture of hopes of a comprehensive military victory, fears of full diplomatic fallout with the Americans and the Russians,[88] and angst about the economic consequences of the civil war on the day-to-day life of the people.[89] Chiang's rhetoric was also a mixed bag. While he acknowledged Marshall's advice that reclaiming Changchun by force was imprudent, he was simultaneously spreading the news, via unofficial contacts, to American semi-official personnel that his armies would not stop until they captured Harbin. Chiang's intentions were therefore open to interpretation. A recent study concludes that Chiang would not announce a ceasefire until he had exploited his military gains against the enemy as much as he could.[90]

The problem was that Chiang went to Shenyang followed by a prolonged sojourn in the war zone while his troops sped up the advance in Manchuria. Given that Chiang's inspection tour had virtually suspended the peace talks, it might be argued that the CCP leaders would naturally consider his intentions on the basis of worst-case assumptions.

Zhou was among the first to condemn Chiang's tour to the front line, suggesting that his real intention was to settle the conflict by force.[91] Nonetheless, the recollections of Chiang's Manchurian field commander Du seemed to suggest otherwise. As discussed, Chiang gave the order for his troops to continue the pursuit of the fleeing enemy after the occupation of Changchun, but his order did not match his actions. While the GMD's elite corps attacked further north, a large contingent of the NEDUA's surviving force after its recent defeat in Benxi launched a major offensive against the Nationalists' weak garrison force in the Anshan–Haicheng zone

---

86 *Shilüe*, 65: 594, 640–4, 66: 12–13, 16–18.
87 Robertson to Marshall, 1 June 1946, *FRUS*, 1946, 9: 930.
88 *Shilüe*, 65: 588–9.
89 *Chiang Diary*, retrospection log for May 1946, Folder 6, Box 45.
90 Tanner, *Battle for Manchuria*, 170, 175.
91 Minutes of meeting between Marshall and Zhou, 23 May 1946, *FRUS*, 1946, 9: 884–90.

on 25 May.⁹² As the attack took place in an area less than 100 kilometres to the south-west of Shenyang, it posted a big threat to the GMD's rear. Chiang and Du hurriedly recalled two attacking divisional units of the N1A from the Changchun front to Shenyang on 25 May to form a task force. Considering that the Nationalists could only deploy three army divisions to spearhead their northward pursuit, the withdrawal of two combat-capable divisions drastically affected the conduct of the operation.⁹³

Just when the task force was expected to be sent at once as a relief column to the besieged garrison, Chiang made a baffling decision that the relief assignment would be put on hold until the task force finished a three-day break. The decision was a disaster to the besieged Nationalists, as it prompted their commander Pan Shuoduan to defect with a substantial number of troops to the CCP on 30 May. When the Nationalists' relief column reached the trouble spot five days later, the NEDUA combatants had already retreated. Chiang's decision left Du dumbfounded because it looked as if Chiang had just rubbed salt into his own wounds. In his memoirs, Du contended that Chiang's judgement was distorted by the insubordinate N1A commanding general Sun.⁹⁴ Du's simplistic conclusion seems plausible. However, Chiang's decision raises the question of whether the GMD's elite corps in Manchuria was more vulnerable than Du might have thought because the only notable achievement of Chiang's dubious decision was that it essentially reduced the tactical combat casualties of his two elite army divisions.

The Nationalists emerged victorious in the battle of Sipingjie. They succeeded in routing the enemy forces but failed to annihilate its main body. The Nationalists claimed that they killed 40,000 enemy fighters, but as the captured NEDUA prisoners of war reportedly numbered around 400, the Nationalists' claim is questionable at best.⁹⁵ If Du's US-armed armies went non-stop in pursuit of the routing enemies for a considerable distance, their far-flung battle lines could be laid completely open to attack by Lin's surviving field forces. The GMD commanders attempted to rout Lin's NEDUA from the battlefield by using their mechanised infantry in

---

92 Junshi kexueyuan junshi lishi yanjiu bu [Military History Research Department of the Military Science Academy of the PLA] ed., *Zhongguo renmin jiefangjun liushi nian dashi ji, 1927–1987* [Major events in the PLA's 60 years, 1927–87] (Beijing: Junshi kexue chubanshe, 1988), 361.
93 Guofangbu shizhengju ed., *Kanluan*, 4: 134–5, 149–50.
94 Du, 'Guomindang pohuai heping', 559–61; Junshi kexueyuan junshi lishi yanjiu bu ed., *Zhongguo renmin jiefangjun*, 361; Tanner, *Battle for Manchuria*, 183–5.
95 Song Ziwen to Chiang, 26 May 1946, *Shilüe*, 65: 597–9.

the pursuit, and managed to concentrate 150 motor vehicles in a critical flank on one occasion.⁹⁶ A CCP source has confirmed that the formation of the NEDUA was broken up but not exterminated by the enemy's motorised infantry.⁹⁷

Using more than a hundred military vehicles in one operation was a lot in China in the 1940s, but it was a drop in the ocean compared to the vast space of northern Manchuria. The heavily loaded GMD foot soldiers lacked the foot speed necessary to outpace the CCP combatants.⁹⁸ In the end, the GMD's northern pursuit forced the enemies to break up into small groups and flee into the adjacent territory of the northern branch of the Sungari River, leaving behind twenty-eight cities for the Nationalists to occupy and defend.⁹⁹

Now the GMD forces in Manchuria had to defend their expanded territories. Their supply lines therefore relied even more on US logistics support. Chiang, who conferred with Marshall on a daily basis before he left for Shenyang,¹⁰⁰ knew better than anybody else within his party about the transport capabilities of the US forces in China. At the beginning of June, the operational logistics capabilities of US Navy forces in China were dwindling. The US Seventh Fleet, which had been playing a crucial role in the Nationalists' troop movement into the north-east, was multitasked with the transport of food for the United Nations Relief and Rehabilitation Administration (UNRRA) in China and the US atomic tests in the central Pacific. The fleet, however, needed to carry out these urgent tasks under force demobilisation.¹⁰¹ Other elements of the US naval units in the Pacific, most of which suffered from depleted crew strengths, were unlikely to reinforce the fleet effectively.¹⁰² The US Navy turned over a number of vessels to the GMD navy in the hope that it could use these ships to improve the GMD's logistical capabilities, but the program was marred by the lack of Nationalist trained crews.¹⁰³

---

96 Guofangbu shizhengju ed., *Kanluan*, 4: 150.
97 NEB to Lin Biao, 2 June 1946, *Peng Zhen nianpu 1902–1997* [Chronological biography of Peng Zhen 1902–1997], ed. Peng Zhen zhuan bianxie zu [Editorial group of the biography of Peng Zhen] (Beijing: Zhongyang wenxian chubanshe, 2002), 1: 429; cf. Tanner, *Battle for Manchuria*, 176–7.
98 Cheng, 'Modern war', 46–7.
99 Guofangbu shizhengju ed., *Suijing diyi nian zhongyao zhanyi tiyao* [A summary of major operations in the first year of the War of Pacification] (n.p.: Guofangbu shizhengju, 1948), 90–3.
100 Notes of meeting between Marshall and Chiang, 22 May 1946, *FRUS*, 1946, 9: 880–1.
101 Marshall to Truman, 6 May 1946, *FRUS*, 1946, 9: 815–18.
102 Enclosure, memorandum by the State–War–Navy Coordinating Committee to Byrnes, 1 June 1946, *FRUS*, 1946, 9: 943.
103 Minutes of meeting between Marshall and Zhou, 3 June 1946, *FRUS*, 1946, 9: 956–7.

In sum, Chiang's elite corps in Manchuria and China proper could be only partially effective without US logistical support.[104] It was therefore not surprising that the CCP remained cocky even after it lost Changchun. Zhou told Marshall on 3 June that they would continue fighting in Manchuria and China proper unless the enemy halted the offensive.[105] Chiang and his advisers knew that Zhou's assertion was not just a game of political brinkmanship.[106] If the fighting in Manchuria showed no sign of abating, it would engulf the entire nation. As Marshall had observed, the Nationalists were incapable of winning a full-scale civil war against the Chinese Communists even with US logistics and the presence of US Marines in North China.[107]

Chiang returned to Nanjing on 3 June, ending his twelve-day tour of inspection. In a meeting with Marshall the very next day, Chiang agreed that his armies in Manchuria would cease all aggressive action for a period of ten days. He stated in the subsequent truce statement that the temporary truce gave the CCP a chance to carry out the agreements they had previously signed in good faith, to negotiate a permanent ceasefire in Manchuria and the restoration of transportation in North China, and to carry out the army reorganisation agreement.[108] Despite his provocative remarks, Chiang's statement effectively abandoned all of the preconditions he previously set for a ceasefire (e.g. Marshall's guarantee) and agreed to a pause of hostilities in Manchuria to allow time for peace talks. Zhou quickly accepted Chiang's offer. He even successfully argued for a change of the truce length from ten to fifteen days.[109] On 6 June, by the time the NEDUA was preparing to give up its northern Manchurian headquarters in Harbin,[110] the two warring parties issued press releases independently to endorse a fifteen-day temporary truce in the north-east.[111] While Lin's troops got the fighting lull they were seeking, Du's overextended armies were under orders to stop and fortify defensive positions near the southern branch of the Sungari River, no more than 130 kilometres away from the enemy they pursued.[112]

---

[104] Enclosure, memorandum by the State–War–Navy Coordinating Committee to Byrnes, 1 June 1946, *FRUS*, 1946, 9: 943.
[105] Minutes of meeting between Marshall and Zhou, 3 June 1946, *FRUS*, 1946, 9: 951.
[106] *Wang riji*, 20 May 1946, 5: 323–4.
[107] Marshall to Truman, 6 May 1946, *FRUS*, 1946, 9: 815–18.
[108] Marshall to Truman, 5 June 1946; press release issued by Chiang, 6 June 1946, *FRUS*, 1946, 9: 977–9, 982.
[109] Marshall to Chiang, 5 June 1946; press release issued by Chiang, 6 June 1946, *FRUS*, 1946, 9: 981, 982.
[110] Mao to NEB, Lin Biao, Huang Kecheng and Li Fuchun, 3 June 1946, *Junshi*, 3: 250–1.
[111] *FRUS*, 1946, 9: 982–3.
[112] Geng Routian, *Zhonggou jiaofei kanluan*, 2: 65–6.

6. 'CHINA'S MADRID'

In Yan'an, Mao and Liu were busy in sending directives to their field commanders not to initiate new offensives in China proper in the hope of appeasing the Nationalists, but they also authorised their generals to launch localised attacks in the hope of recovering lost ground and retaliation. Notably, undertaking localised military actions to prevent enemy reinforcements were also considered as acts of reprisal.[113] Hence, whether the war had moved into a withdrawal appeasement mode or shifted into a state of 'localised fighting' in the interim was just a figure of speech.

Much to Marshall's vexation, the fifteen-day short truce in Manchuria was marred by new truce breaches. If the ceasefire violations during the January truce were committed by both sides to control key positions before a political settlement was reached, clashes within the temporary ceasefire indicated that honouring the ceasefire was optional for the two belligerent parties. On 7 June, the day that the truce came into effect, Lin Biao's surviving field forces attacked the GMD outpost at the village of Lafa, some 200 kilometres east of Changchun.[114] The GMD regiment that undertook garrison duties from 6 June at that newly occupied but isolated spot was trounced and its commander killed in the battle.[115] While Zhou flippantly dismissed the Nationalists' claims of CCP ceasefire breaches in his memorandum to Marshall,[116] Lin's blustering captains made a mockery of their enemy by sending the dead body of the GMD brigadier, which they captured at Lafa, back to the Nationalists in a coffin.[117]

Byroade proposed sending more field teams to Manchuria with the aim of pushing for a pause in fighting. His plan did not receive tripartite approval until towards the end of the truce period, on 15 June.[118] Both the GMD and the CCP members in the Executive Headquarters were verging on defeatism. They advised Byroade not to go to Changchun because they saw no hope for peace. For the Chinese Communists, the truce statement of

---

113 Mao's telegrams to Zhou Enlai, Ye Jianying and field commanders in Manchuria and China proper, 19–21 May 1946, *Junshi*, 3: 228–32; Liu to all local bureaux, Zhou Enlai and Ye Jianying, 21 May 1946, *Liu nianpu*, 2: 46–7.
114 Marshall to Zhou, 9 June 1946, *FRUS*, 1946, 9: 1006.
115 Geng Routian, *Zhonggou jiaofei kanluan*, 2: 65–6; Ling Shaonong, 'Yi Xinzhan, Lafa zhandou' [Remembering the battle of Xinzhan and Lafa], in *Xueye xiongfeng*, Li Yunchang, 122–7; Tanner, *Battle for Manchuria*, 190–1.
116 Zhou to Marshall, 12 June 1946, *FRUS*, 1946, 9: 1034.
117 Du Yuming, 'Guomindang pohuai heping', 561–2.
118 Marshall, *Marshall's Mission to China*, 1: 135–6; 'History of the Conflict Control Group', *History, 2nd quarter 1946 (1 April–30 June), Section IV, Operations C, Conflict Control Group, History, Peiping Executive Headquarters: Forces in China Theater, 1st–4th Quarters, January–December, 1946* (Washington, DC: National Archives of the United States, n.d.), United States Army Forces in China, 1.

the Nationalists looked like an ultimatum; they believed that Chiang's true intention in stopping the troops' advance was to buy time in preparation for a full-scale civil war.[119]

Towards the end of the ceasefire period, the two belligerent parties and their American mediators seemed to accept that sporadic fighting and mutual accusations of truce violations were a new norm in Manchuria.[120] The American peacemakers knew that the temporary truce would not invoke miracles for them. All they could do was to avert a full-scale confrontation, but as Marshall revealed to Zhou, they were getting tired of doing it.[121]

While the brittle truce in Manchuria had been temporarily maintained, the province of Shandong became the post-ceasefire fighting hotspot. The CCP forces launched massive coordinated attacks, once again at the start of the Manchurian truce on 7 June, against the GMD-held cities, towns and garrison points along the two main land transportation corridors of that coastal province in China proper, the Qingdao–Jinan and the Tianjin–Pukou railways. When those week-long devastating post-truce attacks finally ended, the GMD forces in Shandong could defend only a few isolated spots, including the provincial capital of Jinan and the port of Qingdao.[122]

From their position as mediators, the Americans considered the attacks as the CCP's move to counterbalance its defeat in Manchuria.[123] The relative de-escalation on the Manchurian front line against the rapid escalation of conflict in China proper within the truce period could be considered as post-ceasefire conflicts triggered by the 'non-winner' in the ceasefire negotiations.

In early July 1946, an NEB meeting held in Harbin passed a resolution reconfirming the correctness of Mao's rural strategy and mobile warfare principles. According to Mao, the Sipingjie campaign was an exceptional case, not to be invoked when considering future strategy. Rather, he advanced the idea that there were important trade-offs between the defence of big cities and mobile warfare, with the latter providing greater rewards in reducing the enemy's effective strength. In the second half of 1946, approximately 12,000 cadres were dispatched to mobilise the rural

---

119 Minutes of meeting between Marshall and Zhou, 14 June 1946, *FRUS*, 1946, 9: 1047–56.
120 Smyth to Byrnes, 21 June 1946, *FRUS*, 1946, 9: 1123.
121 Minutes of meeting between Marshall and Zhou, 6 June 1946, *FRUS*, 1946, 9: 985–91.
122 *Junshi*, 3: 265, fn. 1; Geng Routian, *Zhonggou jiaofei kanluan*, 2: 165–6.
123 Smyth to Byrnes, 21 June 1946, *FRUS*, 1946, 9: 1123.

population of Manchuria in order to carry out the party's bid for a more aggressive land reform program, bolstered by military operations that eradicated the bandits. The development of Communist base areas in Manchuria later proved to be indispensable for the CCP's ultimate victory on the mainland.[124]

One day

Mao's assessment of the 1946 Sipingjie campaign has become a standard view of the assessment of the NEDUA's debacle in that battle; for decades, studies have given credit to Mao for his ability to make tough decisions in accordance with actual political needs, and have accepted that the defence of cities in Manchuria was dictated by international politics and the negotiations.[125]

Mao's original plan for the defence of Sipingjie was designed to achieve a clear objective: to destroy the GMD's crack troops in mobile warfare and to ensure that a peace deal would be made on Communist terms. But the offensive accommodation mode of combat was short-lived, as the combat conditions made this policy all but impossible to implement. Mao then changed to a defensive accommodation plan, committing his forces to a positional war in the belief that the Nationalists would halt the fighting and reopen negotiations as soon as Marshall returned. This approach miscalculated the revenge-seeking enemy's determination to reclaim Changchun, however, and therefore it too was shelved. Mao refused to withdraw his troops, still confident that his negotiators could bring about a ceasefire. Nevertheless, his attempt to sustain the defence of Sipingjie became less rewarding in the later stages of the battle, as his objective became increasingly difficult to achieve and hence his commitment to prosecuting the battle became ever more difficult to justify.[126]

With hopes for a favourable peace deal dashed and in the face of the enemy's ever-growing military superiority, Mao called on the spirit of his Madrid concept and compelled the NEDUA to realise it through a devastating defence. In this desperate late stage, however, the paramount leader could only imagine that he still had a good grip on what would turn out to be

---

124 Cheng, 'China's Madrid', 99.
125 Ibid., 99–100.
126 Ibid., 101–2.

the optimal strategy. In imagining China's Madrid in Manchuria, Mao had a vision of the defence of Sipingjie that was outside his normal tactical discourse: using mobile warfare rather than a static war of attrition to defeat the enemy.[127]

In their private talk in 1959, Mao was confronted once again by the insubordinate Huang about his decision-making in the defence of Sipingjie. Huang's query pointed exactly to the problem: why did Mao insist on sustaining the defence when all chances of achieving the original goal had evaporated?[128] In conceptual parlance, the 'certainty effect' is likely to reduce policy-makers' tolerance for accepting risk but, as this chapter shows, Mao's act was outside the postulations of modern theories of risk-taking. Huang's disagreement with Mao underscored the latter's style: his timing of a switch from a strategy of risk acceptance to a conservative but cost-effective approach occurred far later than one would have expected in a prudent policy-maker.[129]

Chiang, on the other hand, did not have a general who was courageous enough to remind him that the political and military realities simply did not support his great gamble in Manchuria. Chiang noted his wishes to use the air force in the fight against the NEDUA, but it was difficult for him to turn wishes into reality.[130] As mentioned, Chiang restricted the use of aerial warfare over Sipingjie in an attempt to avoid ruffling Soviet feathers. It deprived the Nationalists of using air raids to eliminate the enemy, although the decision must have inadvertently reduced the scale of civilian casualties. Chiang's generals followed his directive and carried out a war plan that was designed to avoid enemy ambush more than to execute frontal attacks. However, no war plan was foolproof in a war against the CCP's best tacticians. While forces spread out wide were vulnerable to CCP attacks, a close formation was not much safer. The Nationalists' counterinsurgency operation in Manchuria in 1946 was a case of damned if you do, damned if you don't.

Chiang noted, in the immediate aftermath of his armies' recapture of Changchun, that the civil servants and school teachers went on strike in the big cities as a result of continuing food insecurity and severe inflation.

---

127 Ibid., 102–3.
128 For a detailed account of the Mao–Huang talks in 1959, see Cheng, 'China's Madrid', 99; cf. Tanner, *Battle for Manchuria*, 209.
129 Cheng, 'China's Madrid', 103.
130 *Chiang Diary*, 12 May 1946, Folder 6, Box 45.

Although he believed that the recapture of Sipingjie and Changchun had forestalled the escalation of unrest, he acknowledged that his government needed to clamp down on the illegal stockpiling of food.[131] The middle-class professional city dwellers should have been the Nationalists' key support base. No matter how much political capital Chiang could earn from the battlefield, the economic consequences of the war could destroy it quickly. Chiang once used 'crossing a broken bridge on a snowy night' to describe his ambivalent attitude towards a number of destabilising forces, such as talking peace while waging war against the CCP.[132] Chiang used many similes and metaphors in his writings to convey his thoughts so he must have known that most broken bridges are impassable on snowy nights.

Chiang informed Marshall that he wanted to occupy critical areas of the north-east like Changchun only as symbols of the power and authority of his government, but Marshall warned him that it was unwise, even from a symbolic standpoint, to deploy his best troops to defend these areas without a political settlement with the CCP.[133] Chiang stopped the fighting in the end, but his elite corps did not annihilate Lin's forces and none of his preconditions for a ceasefire were fulfilled. If every war is as ironic as Paul Fussell sees it,[134] Chiang's temporary truce ironically added another controversial case of *casus belli* against the GMD for the CCP. It gave one more justification for the Chinese Communists to flout the truce and fanned the fire of the civil war from Manchuria back to China proper, as Chiang's ceasefire statement read like an ultimatum to them. The GMD was incapable of winning a full-blown civil war against the CCP, as Chiang had been advised by the Americans. Chiang surely knew what he wanted, but he might not have known how much he was capable of getting.

Hence the two warring parties virtually collaborated to create a vicious circle of attack and retaliation. The Nationalists launched offensives against the NEDUA in retaliation for the capture of Sipingjie and Changchun. The Chinese Communists then retaliated for the retaliation. A cycle of vengeance and retaliation can only spiral towards calamity. A recent study has raised the importance of setting limits or compensating the other

---

131 *Chiang Diary*, retrospection log of May 1946, Folder 6, Box 45.
132 Citation translated from *Shilüe*, 64: 488. For further reference, see *Chiang Diary*, retrospection log, January 1946, Folder 2, Box 45.
133 Marshall to Chiang, 10 May 1946, *FRUS*, 1946, 9: 824–8.
134 Paul Fussell, *The Great War and Modern Memory* (Oxford: Oxford University Press, 1975), 7.

party's loss before seeking revenge in future negotiations.[135] In the case of the Chinese Civil War, however, retaliatory military actions had become something similar to a crutch that both parties could not walk without.

The escalation of military actions during the truce period furnished considerable scope for the two belligerent parties to toughen their negotiation stance. Both parties began to put forward proposals that not only caused offence to the other party but also removed Marshall's power to influence matters. Disagreements ran particularly high between the two parties on two critical fronts. On the arrangements of a permanent ceasefire in Manchuria, Zhou claimed that the ceasefire of 10 January had lost its effect as there was no need for the GMD forces to restore sovereignty in Manchuria after the Soviets' withdrawal.[136] On carrying out the army reorganisation agreement of 25 February, Chiang maintained that if the CCP desired to amend the existing agreement by increasing its troop quota to Manchuria, the CCP forces must withdraw from the provinces of Rehe and Chahar before September 1946, and evacuate from all localities they occupied after 7 June 1946 in the province of Shandong before 1 July 1946. Chiang also requested that the CCP fulfil extra conditions and terms, according to which the Chinese Communists would be most offended, by demanding that the two CCP-held seaports and logistics centres of Yantai (formerly Chefoo) and Weihaiwei in north-eastern Shandong be turned over to the GMD.[137]

Although the two parties could not find sufficient common grounds for holding a Committee of Three meeting, they kept Marshall busy writing one party's verbal demands or turning general statements into draft proposals, having the draft documents translated into Chinese and returning them for approval before passing them to the other party.[138] This chapter shows that Marshall pushed a course that had little traction. His efforts to send field teams into Manchuria has been regarded with scepticism. Although these efforts seemed fruitless, he continued to pass subtle messages to both

---

135 Andreas Nikolopoulos, *Negotiating Strategically: One Versus All* (New York: Palgrave Macmillan, 2011), 143–6.
136 Minutes of meeting between Marshall and Zhou, 17 June 1946, *FRUS*, 1946, 9: 1065–74.
137 'Draft proposal by the Chinese government', 12 June 1946; annex 1, memorandum by Caughey to Zhou, 17 June 1946, *FRUS*, 1946, 9: 1035–7, 1075–6.
138 Marshall to Truman, 18 June 1946, *FRUS*, 1946, 9: 1099–101.

parties that he was ready to steer them to the best potential solution, akin to salespersons of today starting to fill out the retail invoice before the buyers agree to the purchase.[139]

When the stakes were stacked against him, however, staying in the game was going to be a struggle for Marshall. In a meeting with Yu, Marshall was informed that the two parties did not share any common ground.[140] While the truce deadline appeared likely to slip without any hope of reaching agreement, Marshall asked Yu what might be a proper extension of the fifteen-day ceasefire. Yu's answer was enough to make the most seasoned mediator cringe: '1 day'.[141]

---

139 For the assume-the-sale tactics, see Joe Girard, *How to Close Every Sale* (New York: Warner Books, 1989), 41–53.
140 Minutes of meeting between Marshall and Yu Dawei, 18 June 1946, *FRUS*, 1946, 9: 1082–3.
141 Minutes of meeting between Marshall and Yu Dawei, 20 June 1946, *FRUS*, 1946, 9: 1105.

7

Towards an all-out civil war in China

Short-term solutions, long-term success and the veto players

The Manchurian truce of June 1946 displaced the civil war to China proper, together with the vicious cycle of attack and counter-attack. Marshall therefore needed to deal with the two revenge-seeking parties at the negotiating table. He rejected Yu's stingy offer of extending the ceasefire for just one day, but Chiang had prepared to prolong the truce anyway. On 21 June, the GMD unilaterally announced an eight-day extension of the Manchurian truce to 30 June. As the extension was not the result of an agreement with the CCP, Chiang's statement turned the partial truce into a one-way ceasefire. The extension gave Marshall a little more than a week to negotiate three complex agreements with the two warring parties. The subjects at issue were permanent ceasefire in Manchuria, implementation of the army reorganisation agreement and restoration of transportation.[1] This chapter is about Marshall and the members of Chinese minor parties' last-ditch peace bid.

---

1   Marshall, *Marshall's Mission to China*, vol. 1, 158.

Short-term success versus long-term win

To exacerbate Marshall's agony, the two parties almost simultaneously showed strong disinclination to resolve the disputes one by one or stage by stage. Zhou found it totally unacceptable that while they were being pushed to make concessions on military issues, the Nationalists made no commitment at all on political reforms.[2] Chiang demanded that the three agreements together must be signed at the same time and that there would be no agreement until *all* three agreements were settled.[3] While Zhou's approach can be interpreted as the tactic of evaluating the problem in its entirety, Chiang's prerequisite could not be treated as a common holistic approach.[4] This was because Chiang's approach not only issued an all-or-nothing ultimatum to the CCP but also reduced the effectiveness of the negotiation: the first two agreements reached would never be done deals if there was no agreement on the third. The immediate impact of Chiang's harsh proviso was that it made all involved parties lose a sense of purpose to argue their case. 'I believe there should be no objection … after all, the paper is not being signed right now', Zhou commented.[5]

Paradoxically, the negotiation went relatively smoothly. Marshall was able to call the first Committee of Three meeting since he returned from the United States, on 22 June. The two warring sides soon reached two vital but unsigned agreements on a complete termination of hostilities in Manchuria and the reopening of transportation trunk lines in China proper. An unsigned settlement was also passed on granting the American representatives in the field teams and Executive Headquarters with final decision power in case of disagreement.[6]

---

2   Minutes of meeting between Marshall and Zhou, 21 June, *FRUS*, 1946, vol. 9, 1125–33.
3   Minutes of meeting of Committee of Three, 22 June 1946, *FRUS*, 1946, 9: 1139–51; Xu Yongchang's diary, 22 June 1946, *Xu Yongchang riji* [The diary of Xu Yongchang] (Taipei: Institute of Modern History, Academia Sinica, 1991), 8: 291.
4   For a theoretical discussion, see Joshua N. Weiss and Sarah Rosenberg, 'Sequencing strategies and tactics', September 2003, *Beyond Intractability*, eds. Guy Burgess and Heidi Burgess, Conflict Research Consortium, University of Colorado, retrieved 29 May 2022; www.beyondintractability.org/essay/issue-segmentation.
5   Minutes of meeting of Committee of Three, 22 June 1946, *FRUS*, 1946, 9: 1148.
6   'Directive for the termination of hostilities in Manchuria'; 'Directive for the reopening of lines of communications in North and Central China'; 'Stipulations for the resolution of certain disagreements among the field and communication teams, and Executive Headquarters in Changchun and Peiping', 24 June 1946, not signed, *FRUS*, 1946, 9: 1186–7, 1187–8, 1189.

The final hurdle of the negotiation was far more difficult. Marshall needed to find a mutually agreeable amendment for agreement implementation of the army reorganisation deal of February for the two belligerent parties. The disagreement between the two parties finally boiled down to the redisposition of troops. In other words, it was all about who could station its armed forces in which localities to the exclusion of the other party in implementing the agreement.

Chiang drove a hard bargain. He let CCP troops garrison two large cities that were already in CCP hands—Qiqihar in northern Manchuria and Zhangjiakou—but expected a lot in exchange. His demands included, among other things, the CCP's evacuation from the city of Chengde and all cities in the province of Shandong occupied after 7 June as well as the CCP's complete withdrawal from all base areas in northern Jiangsu Province.[7] Chiang's demands were allegedly out of safety concerns against CCP attack.[8]

Zhou replied with a counter proposal that the CCP could pull its troops out of the main railway in Shandong and reduce its troop numbers in northern Jiangsu on condition that the GMD forces would not enter these areas and take over the CCP-aligned local governments.[9] Given that the CCP had been using the rice supply from Jiangsu to wage economic warfare against the GMD, northern Jiangsu was not the territory that Zhou would concede.[10] The Nationalists, however, believed that Zhou had already pledged the CCP's withdrawal from northern Jiangsu last year, and they felt that the CCP now must be getting ready to withdraw.[11]

Marshall was aware that if they failed to reach an understanding on the amendment of the army reorganisation agreement before 30 June, the other two unsigned agreements would fall victim to the renewal of hostilities. He therefore pinned his hopes on helping the two disputants to reach a settlement on key areas and getting it signed as a preliminary agreement. On 29 June, he successfully won over Zhou's support for a compromise

---

7   Memorandum from Chiang's headquarters, 25 June 1946; minutes of meeting between Marshall and Zhou, 28 June 1946, *FRUS*, 1946, 9: 1193–4, 1231–40.
8   Records of conversation between Chiang and Marshall, 30 June 1946, *Shilüe*, 66: 219–32.
9   Minutes of meeting between Marshall and Zhou, 27 and 28 June 1946, *FRUS*, 1946, 9: 1218–28, 1231–40.
10 Minutes of meeting between Marshall and Xu Yongchang, 9 June 1946, *FRUS*, 1946, 9: 998–1006.
11 Minutes of meeting between Marshall, Wang Shijie, Shao Lizi and Chen Cheng, 9 July 1946, *FRUS*, 1946, 9: 1331–5.

solution, particularly on a deal that the CCP forces in Jiangsu Province would not be garrisoned beyond the latitudinal south of Huai'an city in central Jiangsu.[12]

When Marshall brought Zhou's plan to Chiang, he quickly ran into a stone wall. Chiang bristled at the condition that allowed the CCP to continue its occupation of northern Jiangsu. He was sceptical about the relevance of short-term success (e.g. ceasefire) to a long-term win and had no desire to accept any agreement unless it would ensure that there was no more trouble from the CCP.[13] He insisted on the complete withdrawal of CCP forces from Jiangsu into the north of the Lanzhou–Lianyungang railway near the Jiangsu–Shandong border within a month. Chiang's demand was tantamount to giving the CCP one month's notice to vacate the entire Jiangsu–Anhui base, covering an area of approximately 95,000 square kilometres. In his own defence, Chiang told Marshall that he had let his forgiveness of the Chinese Communists exceed what God might think of as fair.[14]

On 1 July, Chiang issued a directive on the prolongation of restraint from aggressive action by his armies.[15] The directive did not state a deadline as it was intentionally omitted to suit Chiang's thirst for revenge. His wishful thinking was that the deliberate omission of a ceasefire deadline would give his army the freedom to attack at any time, as the line between offence and defence is often blurry.[16] Chiang's ceasefire order made the Committee of Three and the Executive Headquarters a lot less relevant, as it was directly issued by the GMD government. According to Chiang, this would set him free from constraints imposed by the ceasefire supervision organisations.[17] Marshall had little choice but to pass the buck to Zhou and Chiang. Zhou conferred with Chiang and Chiang's associates in early July but made no headway.[18] The minor party and non-partisan PCC delegates weighed in to remind the two warring factions of the catastrophe ahead if they failed to compromise. Their appeals were ignored.[19]

---

12 'Preliminary agreement to govern the amendment and execution of the army reorganization plan of February 25, 1946', 29 June 1946, *FRUS*, 1946, 9: 1246–8.
13 Notes on meeting between Marshall and Chiang, 29 June 1946, *FRUS*, 1946, 9: 1248–9.
14 Records of conversation between Chiang and Marshall, 30 June 1946, *Shilüe*, 66: 219–32.
15 'Radio message by Generalissimo Chiang Kai-shek, July 1, 1946', *China White Paper*, 2: 647–8.
16 *Chiang Diary*, 30 June 1946, Folder 7, Box 45.
17 Chiang to Zheng Jiemin, 5 July 1946, *Shilüe*, 66: 288–9.
18 Records of conversation between Chiang Kai-shek and Zhou, 2 July 1946, *Shilüe*, 66: 265–72; *Wang riji*, 2 and 4 July 1946, 5: 345–6.
19 Liang Shuming, 'Wo canjia Guogong hetan', 936–7.

Mao matched Chiang every step of the way. On 1 July, he issued an order prohibiting the use of force except in self-defence.[20] Despite having a no-first-use of force directive, Mao had already issued an attacking order instructing his main force to sally out and took the war further south into the GMD's heartland.[21] Zhou told Marshall on 26 June that the CCP did not have an aggressive military plan.[22] He had perhaps been misinformed.

'Stripping of the revolution to its military core'

The Nationalists launched a major offensive in late June aimed at pushing the CCP forces away from the trunk rail route in Shandong,[23] but it was battles between the encircled CCP forces and the GMD besiegers at the outskirt of the metropolis of Wuhan in eastern Hubei Province that triggered the full-scale civil war via a massive CCP breakout offensive. The CCP troops in a frantic breakout through the Nationalists' siege lines were a force, 60,000 strong, of well-equipped troops commanded by Li Xiannian.[24] Li's forces were deployed in one of the eight enclaves that the CCP agreed to concede in the Double Tenth Agreement. Mao decided to renege on the promises in early November 1945, citing concerns over the killing of civilians after the withdrawal of the CCP troops. Li's units soon received an instruction to hold out against the enemy siege for another year. Since Li's forces were stationed in places at the core areas of the GMD regime, the Yan'an leadership intended to use their presence to tie down a large number of the GMD troops.[25]

---

20 Mao and Zhu De to all CCP field commanders, 1 July 1946, *Marshall's Mission to China*, Marshall, 2: 379.
21 Mao to Liu Bocheng, Deng Xiaoping, Bo Yibo and Chen Yi, 22 June 1946, *Junshi*, 3: 283–5.
22 Minutes of meeting between Marshall and Zhou, 26 June 1946, *FRUS*, 1946, 9: 1209.
23 Guofangbu shizhengju ed., *Kanluan*, 7: 90–9, 111–14.
24 Zhongguo renmin jiefang jun zhengzhi xueyuan diyi junshi yanjiaoshi ed., *Zhongguo remin jiefangjun zhanyi*, 2: 47–8; minutes of meeting of Military Sub-Committee, 9 March 1946; meeting of the Acting Committee of Three, 8 May 1946, *FRUS*, 1946, 9: 521, 674–5.
25 CC to the CCP delegation to Chongqing, 3 November 1945, *Mao nianpu*, 3: 45; CC to the Central Plain Bureau, 28 November 1945, *Zhonggong*, 15: 453–4; Wang Chaoguang, *Zhonghua Minguo shi*, ser. ed. Zhongguo shehui kexue yuan jindaishi yanjiusuo Zhonghua Minguo shi yanjiushi, 11: 456.

The Nationalists saw Li's army as a threat and had been tightening the ring of encirclement for months. Ceasefire field teams had tried desperately to de-escalate the tension and brokered four local truce agreements from January to June 1946, respectively, including the one signed by the Committee of Three in May.[26]

Without Mao and Chiang's fundamental change of heart on their respective military strategies, however, no local truce could be held up indefinitely. This was due to the fact that these local truces required both parties' troops to remain in situ in order to bring an abrupt end to military engagements. The troop movement restrictions virtually compelled the bulk of the two opposing forces to concentrate in a confined area, even though a demilitarised zone had been implemented in the first place. The American field team members observed in early June that the fighting had been caused by the opposing forces being too close to each other.[27] Hence, the Committee of Three needed to negotiate further approaches to support the local ceasefires implemented by the field teams.

The two belligerent parties had entered into negotiations at the Committee of Three since March for the possibility of transferring the encircled CCP troops to other places. Zhou proposed that two-thirds of the CCP troops should be moved back to the base areas where they came from, while the remaining 20,000 combatants were to be demobilised on the spot. He nominated the city of Anyang and the county of Wuhe in the provinces of Anhui and Henan, respectively, as relocation options. The two places were at a great distance from where Li Xiannan's forces were presently deployed, and there were GMD-controlled areas in between. The Nationalists had to let a corps-sized enemy pass their controlled areas by train or on foot.[28]

Besides, these two places were strategically located in two bitterly contested war zones. The city of Anyang was a frontline headquarters of the GMD forces, and it was only about 60 kilometres south of CCP-held Handan—

---

26 'Meeting at Hankow, March 5, 1946'; 'Presentation by Colonel Briggs to the Acting Committee of Three at Hankow, May 5, 1946, 4 p.m.'; 'Memorandum by the Acting Committee of Three', 10 May 1946, *FRUS*, 1946, 9: 503–10, 654–7, 700–1; entry 20 June 1946, 'Historical record of Field Team No. 32', History, 2nd quarter 1946 (1 April–30 June), Section IV, Folder No. 2, Operations C, Conflict Control Group, *History, Peiping Executive Headquarters*, United States Army Forces in China, 25.
27 Entry, 6 June 1946, 'Historical Record of Field Team No. 32', History, 2nd quarter 1946 (1 April–30 June), Section IV, Folder No. 2, Operations C, Conflict Control Group, *History, Peiping Executive Headquarters*, United States Army Forces in China, 24.
28 Minutes of meeting of Military Sub-Committee, 9 March 1946; Draft of directive by Zhou to the Executive Headquarters and Field Teams, 26 March 1946, *FRUS*, 1946, 9: 516–28, 620–1.

the capital of the CCP's Shanxi–Hebei–Shandong–Henan Liberated Area. Wuhe was a CCP-controlled county, but it was within striking distance to the city of Bengbu—one of the GMD's subheadquarters for its counterinsurgency campaign against the CCP on the Anhui–Jiangsu border. The Nationalists preferred to find a local solution for the problem because Zhou's plan virtually forced them to allow a large group of enemy troops to trespass on their areas before these enemies crossed into the other side of the battlefield and turned the guns against them.[29]

Zhou further claimed that if Li's armies continued to be held up at their present locations, the local population would bear a disproportionate share of burden of providing subsistence for these troops whereas other CCP-controlled areas had 'stores of food'.[30] Nonetheless, Li Xiannian admitted in a meeting with Field Team No. 9 on 22 February 1946 that the CCP did not have sufficient funds to support his 60,000-member army, which consumed around 90,000 catties (i.e. 45,000 kg) of rice every day.[31]

From a ceasefire negotiator's point of view, Zhou's proposal might not have been a bad suggestion.[32] It offered total withdrawal of the CCP forces from the conflict zone as a next step for the *in situ* ceasefires, but the Nationalists rejected it on practical grounds. Zhou, in his turn, issued warnings that if the GMD launched a general offensive against Li's forces, the CCP would deem it to be the start of a full-blown civil war.[33] The negotiations at the Committee of Three dragged on for two months, but were able to reach a truce on 10 May only with a special provision provided for the immediate evacuation of a thousand sick CCP personnel with family members, administrative and medical staff to the city of Anyang.[34]

Zhou paid a visit to Li's besieged army on a fact-finding tour of the Committee of Three just before the signing of the truce. During his visit, Zhou enforced a mandatory order for Li's troops to plan a breakout. At the negotiating

---

29   Minutes of meeting of Military Sub-Committee, 9 March 1946, *FRUS*, 1946, 9: 516–28.
30   Ibid., 516–18.
31   'Historical record of Field Team No. 9', 1st Quarter, 10 January–March 1946, *History, Peiping Executive Headquarters*, United States Army Forces in China, 2: 14–16.
32   A combination of methods of separating the two opposing forces may be utilised in the same ceasefire. See *The Ceasefire Drafter's Handbook*, Public International Law and Policy Group (Washington, DC: PILPG, 2013), 19–30, retrieved 22 May 2022; static1.squarespace.com/static/5900b58e1b631 bffa367167e/t/5b730a224fa51ab1083c22bb/1534265892577/PILPG+Ceasefire+Drafter%27s+Hand book+%28Including%2BTemplate%2BCeasefire%2BAgreement%29-2.pdf.
33   Zhou to Marshall, 29 April 1946; meeting record of the Acting Committee of Three, 5 May 1946, *FRUS*, 1946, 9: 648–9, 657–67.
34   'Memorandum by the Acting Committee of Three', 10 May 1946, *FRUS*, 1946, 9: 700–1.

table, however, the truce was signed and executed, as the evacuation of the sick CCP personnel began on 15 May.[35] The evacuees considered their mass departure a plan to minimise the non-combat personnel and therefore help the main fighting units prepare for the planned breakout.[36]

On 23 June, Mao ordered Li's troops to launch the breakout offensive at once.[37] According to CCP sources, the GMD armies fired the first shot of the all-out civil war by launching a general offensive on the 26th, which resulted in counter-attacks by Li's forces.[38] The American field team members, who witnessed the breakout, reported that both parties were at fault. The GMD besiegers had been sending large reinforcements to stifle the mobility of the enemy, but Li's forces had filtered out a substantial number of men and finally executed a pre-planned breakout.[39]

While the Nationalists threw approximately 200,000 to 300,000 troops at the enemy, Li's armies fought tenaciously with a well-planned, three-pronged breakout into the Nationalists' porous defence. The battle soon devolved into a melee of brutal but disjointed breakouts, pursuits and intercepts that spread over six provinces in China proper for more than three months.[40] Li's combat forces were drastically reduced to some 20,000 men and broke into small groups at the end of the breakout campaign. Some of these contingents fled into several remote and hilly enclaves between the borders of a number of major provinces in China proper, while the other groups returned to their home bases in North and East China.[41] The supply

---

35 Wang Chaoguang, *Zhonghua Minguo shi*, ser. ed. Zhongguo shehui kexue yuan jindaishi yanjiusuo Zhonghua Minguo shi yanjiushi, 11: 458; Zhonggong Henan shengwei dangshi gongzuo weiyuanhui [The party history working committee of the Henan provincial committee of the CCP] ed., *Zhongyuan tuwei qianhou* [The central plain breakout, before and after] (Zhengzhou: Henan renmin chubanshe, 1988), 464.
36 Li Zhengguan and Chen Tongshen, 'Sui shangbing yuan lieche beishang tuwei' [Breakout to the north in the train with the ill and injured personnel], in *Zhongyuan tuwei qianhou*, ed. Zhonggong Henan shengwei dangshi gongzuo weiyuanhui, 252–8.
37 Mao to the Central Plain Bureau, 23 June 1946, *Junshi*, 3: 288–9.
38 Li Xiannian zhuan bianxie zu [Editorial group of the Biography of Li Xiannian] and Er-Yu bianqu geming shi bianji bu [Editorial group of the revolution history of the Hubei–Henan border region] eds., *Li Xiannian nianpu* [The chronological biography of Li Xiannian] (Beijing: Zhongyang wenxian chubanshe, 2011), 1: 563–6.
39 Minutes of meeting between Marshall and Yu Dawei, 11 July 1946, *FRUS*, 1946, 9: 1338–40.
40 Ren Zhibin, 'Zhongyuan tuwei de zhandou lichen jiqi zhanlüe zuoyong' [The empirical process of the battles and the strategic significance of the Central Plain breakout]; Li Xiannian, 'Yao zhengque pingjia zhongyuan tuwei' [Properly evaluate the Central Plain breakout], in *Zhongyuan tuwei qianhou*, ed. Zhonggong Henan shengwei dangshi gongzuo weiyuanhui, 1–18, 19–22; Guofangbu shizhengju ed., *Kanluan*, 9: 22–40.
41 Li Xiannian, 'Yao zhengque pingjia'; Pi Dingjun's diary, 24 June to 9 July 1946, *Pi Dingjun riji*, Pi, 28–35.

problem of Li's forces was now becoming easier to fix, as troop numbers were greatly reduced after ferocious fighting. When a stricken contingent of Li's armies arrived at the Hebei–Henan–Anhui base area in October, the troops received good food and new cotton-padded clothes.[42]

Despite heavy casualties on Li's troops, veterans and historians alike in China nowadays attribute the CCP's ultimate victory in the civil war to the breakout offensive for disrupting the Nationalists' war plan and troop deployment.[43] A veteran CCP negotiator confirmed that Li Xiannian had personally instructed his representatives in mid-June to sustain the peace talks as cover to prepare the breakout operations.[44]

In the conflict-prone province of Jiangsu, the two combatant parties had amassed their best armies on the north bank of the Yangzi River since late June. Chiang's corps of 120,000 men was eager to attack northward with the intention of rooting out the CCP insurgents in the region. The CCP, on the other hand, dispatched a combat-capable field army of 30,000-plus troops down towards the lower reaches of the Yangzi.[45]

The CCP forces initiated a pre-emptive strike against soft spots in the GMD's defence on the north bank of the Yangzi on 13 July. The Yan'an leadership admonished its generals at the onset of the offensive that the battle would not be a hit-and-run operation but rather was a dramatic prelude to a series of all-out offensives. The CCP's logistic systems, which relied heavily on manpower, partially contributed to this military strategy. The CCP armies could not accomplish an operational concentration of forces for a major offensive without massive peasant mobilisation. The peasants,

---

42   Wang Shoudao, *Wang Shoudao huiyilu* [The memoirs of Wang Shoudao] (Beijing: Jiefangjun chubanshe, 1988), 447–9.
43   Wang Shoudao, 'Cong zhanlüe shang renshi Zhongyuan tuwei de zhongyao yiyi' [A strategic perspective on the significance of the Central Plain breakout], in *Zhongyuan tuwei qianhou*, ed. Zhonggong Henan shengwei dangshi gongzuo weiyuanhui, 27–8.
44   Zheng Shaowen, 'Balu Jun Xin Si Jun Zhongyuan Junqu Wuhan banshichu dui Mei-Jiang de douzheng' [The struggle against the Americans and the Nationalists in the Wuhan branch office of the Central Plain Military Region of the Eight Route Army and the New Fourth Army], in *Wuhan wenshi ziliao* [The literary–historical source materials of Wuhan], ed. Zhengxie Huibei Sheng Wuhan Shi weiyuanhui wenshi ziliao yanjiu weiyuanhui (Hankou: Zhongguo renmin zhengzhi xieshang huiyi Wuhan Shi weiyuanhui wenshi ziliao yanjiu weiyuanhui, 1981), 5: 1–10.
45   Li Moan, *Shiji zhi lü: Li Moan huiyilu* [A walk through the 20th century: The memoirs of Li Moan] (Beijing: Zhongguo wenshi chubanshe, 1995), 255–6; Zhongguo renmin jiefangjun zhengzhi xueyuan diyi junshi yanjiaoshi ed., *Zhongguo remin jiefangjun zhanyi*, 2: 59–61; Wang Chaoguang, *1945–1949*, 210–14; Guofangbu shizhengju ed., *Kanluan*, 2: 31.

who had been doing weeks of hard labour in moving military equipment and supplies to the front lines for the CCP, would have been disappointed if the CCP combatants retreated rapidly after a few skirmishes.[46]

Chiang had to decide whether he should order his armies to go toe to toe with the CCP in an all-out offensive that would take place on his doorstep, as Nanjing and Shanghai were alarmingly close on the other side of the Yangzi or whether he should at least consider scaling back his harsh demands and supporting Marshall's quest for more short-term successes at the negotiating table. Chiang claimed that he received a tacit revelation from God on 14 July, which gave the go-ahead for military actions against the CCP forces in Jiangsu.[47] Chiang did not disclose the fullness of the divine intervention he received. It therefore remains a puzzle whether Chiang's divine sources had reminded him that, during a Committee of Three meeting in May, the deputy chief of staff of his Wuhan Field Headquarters, Wang Tianming, had pledged in all sincerity the GMD's commitment to settle all disputes exclusively by peaceful means.[48]

The two opposing forces staged full-scale military confrontations near China's capital for the next two months. Strategically and tactically, the campaign concluded with a CCP victory since, although not giving the CCP forces territorial gains, it inflicted 54,000 Nationalist casualties at the cost of 16,000 men.[49]

According to Mao, his armies' military success in Jiangsu hinged on the principle of striking the vulnerable points of a numerically superior enemy through efficient and rapid concentration of forces. A series of such battles in quick succession could effectively destroy an enemy's combat power.[50] As discussed, Mao later elaborated this principle in a popular treatise, entitled 'Concentrate a superior force to destroy the enemy forces one by one'.[51] It disseminated the idea that the nationwide civil war could be won by annihilating the GMD forces in a piecemeal fashion. Following

---

46 Su Yu to Shandong Field Army headquarters, CMC and Central China Military Region, 27 June 1946; CMC to Zhang Dingcheng, Deng Zihui and Tan Zhenlin, c/o Su Yu, Chen Yi and Song Shilun, 15 July 1946, *Su Yu nianpu* [Chronological biography of Su Yu], ed. Zhonggong Jiangsu shengwei dangshi gongzuo bangongshi [Office for party history of the Jiangsu provincial committee of the CCP] (Beijing: Dangdai zhongguo chubanshe, 2006), 156, 160.
47 *Chiang Diary*, 14 July 1946, Folder 8, Box 45.
48 Meeting record of the Acting Committee of Three, 8 May 1946, *FRUS*, 1946, 9: 682.
49 Wang Chaoguang, *1945–1949*, 217.
50 CMC to all theatre commanders, 28 August 1946, *Junshi*, 3: 438–9.
51 Mao, 'Concentrate a superior force to destroy the enemy forces one by one', 16 September 1946, in *Selected Works*, Mao, 4: 103–7.

Mao's lead, the CCP propaganda further glorified the battles in Jiangsu in 1946 as the 'seven battles and seven victories in central Jiangsu'. It remains a mainstream narrative about the history of the battles today.[52]

Mao's way of warfare required his forces to accomplish successive combat missions with minimal breaks and achieved victory through enormous sacrifices of human lives.[53] When the main body was taking a break, in the case of the CCP army's 'seven victories' in Jiangsu, alternative combat units were brought forward to play a key role in the battle. The Nationalists were deprived of a lull to regroup or withdraw.[54] The strategy was effective in maximising enemy casualties, but it also contributed to the civil war's further perpetuation.

Yan'an had a well-thought-out game plan: while the GMD armies suffered massive casualties in Jiangsu, the CCP combatants in other theatres of war would be surging forward in force from their respective bases and spreading the war to the Nationalists' territory.[55] Such an approach can be considered a radical version of the strategy of taking the fight to the enemy, and it undoubtedly ensured that the cancerous tumour of civil war engulfed China as quickly as possible. In 1947, the two warring factions adopted a similar strategy and rushed their troops towards each other's territories. The strategy was later known by its sarcastic appellation of 'the enemy is coming over to my house, but I am going to the enemy's house, too' (*Di dao wo jia lai, wo dao di jia qu* 敵到我家來, 我到敵家去).[56] To paraphrase Benton's description of the unprecedented level of military activism of the CCP during the 1930s, Mao's strategy was another 'extreme case of this stripping of the revolution to its military core'.[57]

The repeated operational failures drove Chiang to send more troops to the battlefield. For instance, the Nationalists launched diversionary attacks and infiltrated the CCP's rear base in northern Jiangsu in mid-September. The CCP main forces on the north bank of the lower Yangzi were therefore

---

52 Wang Chaoguang, *1945–1949*, 217–18; Lew, *The Third Chinese Revolutionary Civil War*, 45.
53 Cheng, 'Modern war', 50.
54 Zhongguo renmin jiefangjun zhengzhi xueyuan diyi junshi yanjiaoshi ed., *Zhongguo remin jiefangjun zhanyi*, 2: 64–5.
55 CMC to Chen Yi, Zhang Yunyi, Li Yu, Liu Bocheng et al., 13 July 1946, *Zhonggong*, 16: 244–5; CMC to Zhang Dingcheng, Deng Zihui and Tan Zhenlin, c/o Su Yu, Chen Yi and Song Shilun, 15 July 1946, in *Su Yu nianpu*, ed. Zhonggong Jiangsu shengwei dangshi gongzuo bangongshi, 160.
56 Geng Routian, *Zhongguo jiaofei kanluan*, 3: 70.
57 Gregor Benton, *Mountain Fires: The Red Army's Three-Year War in South China, 1934–1938* (Berkeley, CA: University of California Press, 1992), 5.

forced to disengage. The GMD troops also started another round of large-scale offensives in Shandong almost simultaneously.[58] These attacks were part of a large military campaign in the second half of 1946 planned by Chiang and executed by his generals in a bid to drive the CCP forces out of the war in China proper.[59] While the GMD forces suffered heavy casualties, the Nationalist records show that Chiang's all-out offensive failed to destroy the CCP's combat power, albeit it resulted in territorial gains.[60] The two warring parties together dragged China into the whirlpool of a full-blown civil war in the second half of 1946.

Hostages of the war

The most destructive aspect of an all-out war is when it becomes dominant and overrules the political, diplomatic and economic logics of the states or armed actors.[61] In the midst of the full-scale civil war, Chiang, Mao and even Marshall were almost simultaneously hijacked by the war they chose to fight or looked to mediate. In mid-July, overzealous Nationalist secret agents conducted two separate but fatal extrajudicial assassinations of prominent leaders of the Democratic League, Li Gongpu and Wen Yiduo, in the south-western China metropolis of Kunming. The Li and Wen assassinations immediately attracted condemnation of Chiang's repressive regime nationally and internationally. This topic has been widely discussed by a number of authors without a solid consensus over who was responsible for ordering the death warrants. Some suggest that the murders must have been incited or ordered at the top level of Chiang's regime, if not by Chiang himself. The assassinations must have been carried out in favour of a more explicit emphasis on the GMD's repressive policies, not to mention that the

---

58 Geng Routian, *Zhongguo jiaofei kanluan*, 2: 145–6, 150–3, 187–8; Guofangbu shizhengju ed., *Kanluan*, 7: 102–4; CMC to Chen Yi, Song Shilun and Central China Bureau, 11 September 1946, in *Chen Yi nianpu* [Chronological biography of Chen Yi], ed. Liu Shufa (Beijing: Renmin chubanshe, 1995), 1: 470.
59 See a synopsis of Chiang's war plan in *Chang Diary*, Folder 8, Box 45, esp. the point-form list of scheduled events of the month after the diary's retrospection log of July 1946.
60 Guofangbu shizhengju ed., *Kanluan*, 2: 33–4; Wang Chaoguang, *Zhonghua Minguo shi*, ser. ed. Zhongguo shehui kexue yuan jindaishi yanjiusuo Zhonghua Minguo shi yanjiushi, 11: 462–95.
61 Martin Shaw, *The New Western Way of War: Risk-Transfer War and Its Crisis in Iraq* (Cambridge: Polity Press, 2005), 55–6.

city of Kunming had been at the forefront of the student-led anti-GMD movement.⁶² Some contend that Chiang was unlikely to risk international censure by ordering the killing of the two minor party figures.⁶³

For Chiang, the assassinations happened at the most inopportune times, as he needed to play the blame-shifting game against the CCP about who was responsible for the outbreak of the full-scale civil war. The seriousness of the two assassinations was unprecedented. Wen was shot to death in broad daylight on his way home after attending the memorial service for Li, who had been assassinated four days earlier.⁶⁴ When the assassins fired the fatal shot at Wen, Li's murder had already created a furore. No government in its right mind would order extrajudicial killings under the circumstances.

An internal investigation carried out by the Nationalist government quickly solved the case. Two low-ranking army officers from the Kunming Garrison Command underwent a fast-track trial on 15 August. Both men received the death penalty and were allegedly executed in less than two weeks.⁶⁵ Chiang was angry at Huo Kuizhang, the garrison commander at Kunming and the alleged mastermind of the two assassinations. He nevertheless believed that Huo's many sins should have been forgiven under the circumstances.⁶⁶ Huo was dismissed from his job but was never prosecuted for his role in the Li–Wen case.⁶⁷

While political dissidents in GMD-held areas were living in fear after the assassinations in Kunming, the American mediators were unexpectedly pulled into a military conflict and became disputants themselves. On 29 July, a US Marine supply convoy clashed with CCP combatants in a deadly skirmish at the town of Anping about 60 kilometres south-east of Beiping. The US investigating officers reported that the marine-escorted trucks were en route to Beiping carrying food and supplies for the Executive Headquarters and the UNRRA when the marines were ambushed. A CCP report obtained by Zhou contradicted the Americans. It charged that the

---

62   Zhang Lan to Chiang Kai-shek, 18 July 1946, in *Zhongguo minzhu tongmeng*, ed. Zhongguo minzhu tongmeng zhongyang wenshi ziliao weiyuanhui, 198–9; Wang Chaoguang, *Zhonghua Minguo shi*, ser. ed. Zhongguo shehui kexue yuan jindaishi yanjiusuo Zhonghua Minguo shi yanjiushi, 11: 506–10.
63   Taylor, *Generalissimo*, 355.
64   Liang Shuming and Zhou Xinmin, 'Li Wen an diaocha baogao shu' [An investigation report on the Li–Wen assassinations], in *Liang Shuming quanji*, Liang Shuming, 6: 656–85.
65   Guo Tingyi, *Zhonghua Minguo shishi*, 4: 552, 556.
66   *Chiang Diary*, 19 August 1946, Folder 9, Box 45.
67   *Shilüe*, 66: 584.

incident was a combined invasion by the US Marines and the Nationalist armies of the CCP-held areas.⁶⁸ At Mao's suggestion, the CCP insisted upon the Americans firing the first shot.⁶⁹

The Executive Headquarters conducted an investigation into the incident but failed to reach a tripartite consensus over the three parties' role in the fighting. The disputes therefore remained unresolved. A study based on CCP sources, however, found that the tragic incident was a result of an ambush set up by the CCP forces just outside their territories in eastern Hebei. The Yan'an leadership had no prior knowledge of it. The US Marines in usual patrol formation did not raid any town, and there were no GMD troops on their team. The CCP local commanders and field team members resorted to contamination of vital evidence at the scene and abetting the making of misleading witness statements in the wake of the fighting. The military adventurism of individual CCP commanders was fuelled by a Mao-sponsored mass movement against US military aid to the GMD. As the movement was in full flight in June and coincided with the beginnings of the all-out civil war, it was almost impossible for grass-roots cadres to understand that Mao just needed them to rise up against the United States' 'erroneous policies' not kill US Marines.⁷⁰ This revisionist study contradicts popular notions in China, but it is well in line with what Zhou's associate Wang Bingnan privately told a US assistant naval attaché afterward.⁷¹

The Stuart Committee

The further acceleration of the military conflict convinced Marshall of the urgent need to bring an American with long experience in China to his mediation effort. At his suggestion, the US government appointed Dr John Leighton Stuart, a Chinese-born American missionary and former president of Yenching University at Beiping, as American ambassador to China on

---

68 Myers to Byrnes, 30 July 1946; minutes of meeting between Marshall and Zhou, 1 August 1946; record of meeting between Stuart, Zhou and Philip Fugn, 6 August 1946, *FRUS*, 1946, 9: 1418, 1427–37, 1452–60.
69 Yang Kuisong, '1946 nian Anping shijian zhenxiang yu Zhonggong dui mei jiaoshe' [The truth about the Anping incident of 1946 and the CCP–American negotiations], *Shixue yuekan* [History Monthly], 4 (2011), 60–74.
70 Yang Kuisong, '1946 nian Anping Shijian'.
71 Caughey to Robertson, 15 September 1946, *FRUS*, 1946, 10: 188–9; cf. Wang Chaoguang, *Zhonghua Minguo shi*, ser. ed. Zhongguo shehui kexue yuan jindaishi yanjiusuo Zhonghua Minguo shi yanjiushi, 11: 548–9.

11 July.[72] Stuart was knowledgeable about China, but not enough to pass Chiang's test of cultural competence; he failed to appreciate the imperial Chinese rulers' two-fold method of quashing revolts both by force and by pacification measures, which justified Chiang's civil war policy.[73] Stuart proposed the creation of an informal five-member committee equally represented by GMD and CCP members with Stuart as chairman.[74]

Marshall, Stuart and Zhou reached an understanding that the initial topics of discussion within the small group would be limited to the dispute over the State Council. The Americans nonetheless advised Zhou not to dictate the outcome of discussions in advance because it was impossible to guarantee anything before the convention of the committee, particularly over the issuance of ceasefire orders once the dispute over the State Council was settled.[75] The short-term committee would be convened on creating momentum for the peace talks via settling the dispute over the distribution of seats in the State Council. The value of the proposal rested not on providing ready-made permanent solutions but on its potential to create manageable stages on the way to long-term success.

Chiang did not seem to appreciate the value of the Stuart Committee. He expressed his support of Stuart's idea but set forth a list of prerequisites, which had to be accepted by the CCP beforehand. These requirements were of three sorts. They included the CCP's agreement to put the January ceasefire order into effect, the restoration of communications and the army reorganisation agreement. Even if the CCP was in full compliance with Chiang's prerequisites, Chiang would not support the committee unless the CCP accepted five extra conditions. Chiang's 'five demands' were even harsher than those he stipulated in June after the temporary ceasefire in Manchuria. Chiang now required, in addition to his previous request of the withdrawal of the CCP forces from areas situated in Shandong, Rehe and Manchuria, the withdrawal of the CCP troops in northern Jiangsu to the

---

72 Marshall, *Marshall's Mission to China*, 1: 186–92.
73 Stuart to Byrnes, 21 July 1946, *FRUS*, 1946, 9: 1388–93; *Shilüe*, 66: 387.
74 *China White Paper*, 1: 174–5.
75 Minutes of meeting between Marshall, Stuart and Zhou, 6 September; memorandum by Zhou to Marshall and Stuart, 6 September 1946, *FRUS*, 1946, 10: 153–8, 158–60.

territory located in the northern area of the Lanzhou–Lianyungang railway.[76] Chiang notified Stuart that he would unilaterally abort the negotiations if his demands were not met.[77]

The plethora of preconditions imposed by Chiang did not coincide with the idea of the Stuart-proposed informal group, which attempted to infuse more flexibility into the negotiation process. In particular, Chiang's entire proposal suffered from a lack of consistency. His attempted reinstatement of the January ceasefire resolution, which essentially restored the status quo of 13 January, and his demand for the CCP forces to withdraw from northern Jiangsu were utterly incompatible. Zhou, not unexpectedly, rejected Chiang's terms immediately.[78]

The Americans found no delight in their meetings with Chiang,[79] but the meetings with Zhou gave them no joy either. Zhou essentially demanded a comprehensive ceasefire and that all unsigned agreements before 30 June should be signed without delay. He requested the reorganisation of the current government so that resolutions could be reached on both the political and military issues simultaneously. If his demands were not met, Zhou maintained, it would have been only too evident that the GMD intended to extend the civil war.[80] The mandatory nature of Zhou's demands made them unlikely to become topics worthy of discussion for the Nationalists. In a meeting on 26 July, Marshall could not but ask Zhou, 'Who is to do the discussing?'[81]

The arms embargo

When the Stuart-proposed committee was in tatters before it had even begun, Marshall resorted to radical measures to revive his mediation position. He initiated a US arms embargo on China at the end of July with the support of the Truman administration in the midst of the CCP's prosecution of US military aid to the GMD. Export licence suspension

---

76 Marshall, *Marshall's Mission to China*, 1: 192; cf. Yu-ming Shaw, *An American Missionary in China: John Leighton Stuart and Chinese–American Relations* (Cambridge, MA: Council of East Asian Studies, Harvard University, 1992), 174.
77 *Shilüe*, 66: 491.
78 'Record of Conference at the Embassy in China, August 6, 1946', *FRUS*, 1946, 9: 1452–60.
79 Caughey's diary, 23 August 1946, *Marshall Mission to China*, ed. Jeans, 259.
80 Minutes of meeting between Marshall and Zhou, 1 August 1946, *FRUS*, 1946, 9: 1430.
81 Minutes of meeting between Marshall and Zhou, 26 July 1946, *FRUS*, 1946, 9: 1409.

and the resulting shutdown of shipments of arms and ammunition to the Nationalist government was put into effect from August, marking the beginning of an unprecedented nine-month ban on combat-type military equipment to China.[82]

In Washington, the chairman of the Nationalists' Chinese Supply Commission, Wang Shoujing, lobbied the US government to overturn the ban. The Americans deflected Wang's queries.[83] His efforts nonetheless exposed more problems with the GMD's excessive munitions import dependence and the capacity limits of the United States to maintain a reliable supply of sufficient munitions to Chiang's gigantic army in a nationwide civil war.

Current Chinese Civil War literature is divided over the issue. Some scholars argue that the embargo was designed for politics instead of policy and that the GMD had large stockpiles of weapons and ammunition.[84] Others maintain that the negative consequences of the embargo on the GMD forces was not noticeable until six months later.[85] It was unlikely that the Nationalists did not have war reserve ammunition in storage, given that a full-blown civil war was currently under way in China. It is notable, however, that the GMD military was facing an arms supply crisis even without an embargo. The Nationalists' capability to replace arms, equipment and ammunition for their US-armed elite forces was almost non-existent, as no appreciable quantity of these items was produced in China.[86] From the .30-calibre ammunition for their US carbines to small replacement parts, lubricants and coolants for their US military vehicles, the weaponry of Chiang's crack troops was import dependent. Major GMD arms depots had only a limited range of US military equipment in stock,[87] in part because the supply of certain items, such as automotive parts, was inadequate to meet the US Army's own demand.[88]

---

82 *China White Paper*, 1: 180–1, 354–6; Tsou, *America's Failure in China*, 428.
83 Cummins to Wang Shoujing, 23 August 1946, *FRUS*, 1946, 10: 757.
84 E.R. Hooton, *The Greatest Tumult: The Chinese Civil War, 1936–49* (London: Brassey's, 1991), 38, 50–2.
85 Hu Mei and Ren Donglai, '1946–1947 nian meiguo dui hua junhuo jinyun de jige wenti' [Issues about American embargo of arms and ammunition against China between 1946 and 1947], *Meiguo yanjiu jikan* [American Studies Quarterly], 3 (2007): 85–102.
86 Smyth to Byrnes, 7 June 1946, *FRUS*, 1946, 9: 994.
87 'Lianqin di yi, er junxie ku tiaozhi meixie chuyun zhuyuanbiao' [American munitions transportation and specifications of the first and second arms depots of the combined logistics command], n.d., *Juan 17/Quanzong* 774, Zhongguo dier lishi dang'anguan [The Second Historical Archives of China] (hereafter SHAC).
88 Lovett to Stuart, 31 December 1947, *FRUS*, 1947, 7: 939–40.

The .30 carbine cartridges were always in short supply at the rate of consumption of the GMD armies, even though they were the in-stock ammunition in the United States for the US forces. A US War Department document of 1947 has verified that the existing stocks and productive capacity of the .30 calibre ammunition in the United States was inadequate to meet the most basic needs of a country as big as China to wage an all-out war for six months. The sales of 'war surplus matériel' from the United States to the GMD regime had been the subject of severe criticism by the CCP.[89] According to the War Department's estimation, the total amount of the 'surplus' .30 cartridges could only meet 8 per cent of the Nationalists' needs in a six-month supply of ammunition. The remaining 92 per cent could be fully met only by reducing the stocks currently held for US strategic priorities in the Western Hemisphere and global military training programs by roughly 20 per cent.[90] As delivering a short-term supply of the .30 cartridges to the Nationalists was a near impossibility for the US government, solutions to a continuing supply would depend on the investment incentives of private US industries. The main obstacle was that almost all ammunition manufacturers in the United States were currently under contract to supply the US forces. These suppliers would be facing both production capacity and contract obligation difficulties in filling the Chinese orders.[91]

Unlike their elite counterpart, most of the GMD infantrymen predominantly used locally sourced arms and ammunition, but they did not fare better with the embargo. The most commonly used Chinese-made Zhongzheng Type rifles with the 7.92 x 57mm ammunition (also known as Generalissimo or Mauser ammunition) were not only inadequate in quantity but also in quality, which later became a subject of complaint.[92] While captured Japanese small arms of varying quality were used by the two warring parties on the civil war battlefield, such weapons also needed captured Japanese ammunition, specifically, 6.5 x 50mm and 7.7 x 58mm bullets. Counterfeit weapons and military equipment—such as customised small arms and

---

89 Mao, 'Wei Meiguo junshi yuanhua fa'an de shengming' [Statement opposing US military aid to China bill], 22 June 1946, in *Tingzhan tanpan*, 318–19.
90 Patterson to Marshall, 23 July 1947, *FRUS*, 1947, 7: 879–80.
91 Acheson to Marshall, n.d., *FRUS*, 1947, 7: 855–6.
92 'Binggong shu hefu ge junshi jiguan budui junshi jiantao huiyi ti'an' [Bureau of ordnance: A review on proposals from military review meetings of all military organisations and services], July–September 1948, *Juan* 219/*Quanzong* 774, SHAC.

substandard lubricants—were also being used on the battlefield. However, the GMD's Army Headquarters had raised the alarm over the danger of using fake products.[93]

In mid-August, the US State Department suspended an export licence for the shipment of 130 million rounds of Generalissimo ammunition to China.[94] This represented a massive reduction in ammunition supply for the GMD, as foregoing estimates carried out by US military intelligence indicated that the rifle ammunition consumption of Nationalist forces was approximately 110 million rounds per annum.[95] US forces did not use the Generalissimo ammunition, and a constant supply of it was by no means assured in the United States post-war. The 130 million rounds currently on the banned list were specially procured by the United States during World War II for China as military aid.[96] The ammunition had been in storage in the United States for many years and was due to expire. Even if the ban was lifted, the Nationalists had to send the bulk to a top ammunition manufacturer in Europe or the United States for inspection or recondition.[97]

The Generalissimo ammunition is a special cartridge of German origin, which had been widely used in Europe. Although a number of European countries still regarded Chiang as a friend, most of them could only offer uncertain ammunition supply to the GMD government. The Spanish Army, for example, had just begun to replace its old 7.00mm rifles with 7.92mm rifles and would have been reluctant to reduce the 7.92 x 57mm ammunition stock by sales abroad.[98] The Nationalists therefore tried desperately to purchase one-hundred million rounds of Generalissimo ammunition from independent manufacturers in Europe. Previous studies emphasise Washington's diplomatic victory in persuading Canada, the United Kingdom and other European countries to join the arms embargo

---

93   'Lujun zongsiling bu yinxing dongbei diqu bingqi shiyong zhi zhuyi' [Matters needing attention in using weapons and military equipment in the North-east: An army headquarters publication], March 1947, *Juan* 2546/*Quanzong* 774, SHAC.
94   Cummins to Wang Shoujing, 23 August 1946, *FRUS*, 1946, 10: 757.
95   Military Intelligence Division G-2, War Department General Staff to C.B. Smith, Department of State, Transmittal of information, 21 February 1947; 893.24/2–2147; National Archives Microfilm Publication LM 69, Reel 31; Records of the US Department of State Relating to the Internal Affairs of China (hereafter DOSIAC), 1945–49; RG 59; NACP.
96   Ringwalt to Vincent, 2 April 1947, *FRUS*, 1947, 7: 813–14; minutes of meeting between Marshall and Yu Dawei, 19 September 1946, *FRUS*, 1946, 10: 206–8.
97   Notes of meeting between Ringwalt and Wang Shoujing, 22 April 1947, *FRUS*, 1947, 7: 822–4.
98   Philip W. Bonsal to Marshall, 1 May 1947; 893.24/5–147; National Archives Microfilm Publication LM 69, Reel 31; DOSIAC, 1945–49; RG 59; NACP.

of China.⁹⁹ Nevertheless, the Belgians and the Danes had expressed genuine interest in exporting arms to China, since the embargo made little economic and political sense in post-war Europe.¹⁰⁰

The United States clamped down on attempts to sell arms and ammunition to the Chinese quite easily in the end. Declassified archival materials confirm that no European ammunition maker had the production capacity to supply such a great quantity of ammunition by itself, which precipitated the diplomatic triumph of the Americans. Leading firearms manufacturer Fabrique Nationale of Belgium was interested in selling one-hundred million rounds of Generalissimo ammunition to its Chinese buyers, but it could fill only half the order and needed to strike a deal with Winchester of the United States for supplying the other half. The deal was off in the end, owing in part to the disapproval of the US government.¹⁰¹ The Nationalists, for their part, apparently encountered difficulties in making payment to the Belgians. The letter of credit that the Nationalists needed for the big purchase was withheld for unknown reasons.¹⁰² This might not be a surprise, considering the GMD's dwindling war chest. Chiang therefore had only had two options. He could either keep fighting until ammunition and supplies were exhausted, or he could readjust his negotiation position in the hope that the Americans would reverse the embargo.

Perfect falling-out

On 10 August, Marshall and Stuart released a joint press statement in a bid to exert pressure on both parties for a settlement. The statement attributed the negotiation deadlock to both parties' failure to reach an agreement, particularly on issues related to the redisposition of troops and the CCP-held local governments.¹⁰³ Truman simultaneously sent a stern personal message to Chiang essentially telling him to find a peaceful solution to end the civil war or face loss of support from the United States.¹⁰⁴

---

99 Hu and Ren, '1946–1947 nian', 94.
100 Kirk to Marshall, 4 March 1947; 'Memorandum of telephone conversation, by the deputy director of the Office of Far Eastern Affair (Penfield)', 16 April 1947, *FRUS*, 1947, 7: 809, 820–1.
101 Exton to Cummins, 'Activities of Fabrique Nationale', 14 February 1947; 893.24/22–747; Cummins to Ringwalt, 'Ammunition to China', 10 February 1947; 893.24/2–1047; National Archives Microfilm Publication LM 69, Reel 30; DOSIAC, 1945–49; RG 59; NACP.
102 Alan Goodrich Kirk to Marshall, 28 March 1947; 893.24/3–2847; National Archives Microfilm Publication LM 69, Reel 31; DOSIAC, 1945–49; RG 59; NACP.
103 Joint statement by Marshall and Stuart, 10 August 1946, *FRUS*, 1946, 10: 1; Marshall, *Marshall's Mission to China*, 1: 205.
104 Truman to Gu Weijun, 10 August 1946, *FRUS*, 1946, 10: 2–3.

Zhou reacted first to the Marshall–Stuart media stunt, although the CCP propaganda published a defiant point of view against the statement.[105] Zhou told Stuart on 12 August that his party was ready to make offers vis-à-vis Chiang's demands, including a concession of troop withdrawal from positions occupied since 7 June in Shanxi Province.[106] The province had been experiencing the brunt of the full-scale civil war since July 1946 after a strong CCP force laid siege to the GMD-held strategic city of Datong near the northern border of the province. The CCP armies of 80,000 troops launched final assaults against some 20,000 desperate Nationalist defenders of the city in early August after severing the city's main railway to the GMD-held provincial capital of Taiyuan in the south. If Datong was captured, the CCP forces could combine their armies at Zhangjiakou to attack Beiping.[107]

If Zhou wished to maintain his tough negotiation stance, he could not propose a withdrawal from the siege because he regarded all CCP military operations as being initiated to counter or divert the GMD attacks.[108] Therefore Zhou's new offer expressed his intention to give a constructive response to the Marshall–Stuart joint statement. The problem was that Zhou was vitriolic towards Chiang, and the situation on the battlefield remained fluid.[109] If Chiang did not reciprocate quickly enough, Zhou might change his mind. Much to Stuart's vexation, Chiang did not shun his business-as-usual attitude. His message, delivered on 14 August commemorating the first anniversary of victory against Japan, was filled with predictable anti-Communist rhetoric.[110] Chiang might have argued that he was just trading insults with Mao. In Mao's latest smear campaign, the Nationalists were painted as 'paper tigers' and 'running dogs' of the 'US reactionaries'.[111]

On 26 August, Zhou told the press that the CCP would not enter into any negotiation until the Nationalists made a clear statement that they had relinquished Chiang's 'five conditions'.[112] Zhou was not wrong for seeking an unambiguous rhetorical shift on Chiang's part before making any decision, but once he made his position public, he set himself up, as

---

105 *Renmin ribao*, 14 August 1946, Handan.
106 Minutes of meeting between Stuart and Marshall, 12 August 1946, *FRUS*, 1946, 10: 7–8.
107 Guofangbu shizhengju ed., *Kanluan*, 6: 17–24; Geng Routian, *Zhongguo jiaofei kanluan*, 2: 221–7.
108 Minutes of meeting between Marshall and Zhou, 23 August 1946; Zhou to Marshall, 30 September 1946, *FRUS*, 1946, 10: 72–9, 258–9.
109 Minutes of meeting between Stuart and Marshall, 12 August 1946, *FRUS*, 1946, 10: 7–8.
110 *Shilüe*, 66: 529–54.
111 Mao, 'Smash Chiang Kai-Shek's offensive by a war of self-defence', 20 July 1946; 'Talk with the American correspondent Anna Louise Strong', August 1946, in *Selected Works*, Mao, 4: 89–95, 97–101.
112 *Tingzhan tanpan*, 214–20.

Chiang did, in an inflexible negotiation position. Zhou said repeatedly that he needed the Americans to give him two guarantees as conditions for him to enter the five-member committee: Chiang would drop the five demands, and a ceasefire would go into effect immediately after the meeting. Zhou asserted that the two prerequisites were needed in order to prevent Chiang from negotiating in bad faith and using peace talks as a cover for escalating violence.[113]

Marshall was disappointed, replying, 'If Doctor Stuart and I could guarantee the ceasefire, the fighting would have stopped months ago.'[114] Zhou was not convinced, arguing that he had the responsibility to ask for guarantees in order to avoid being forced 'step by step' into a concession that he was not ready to commit to. He told Marshall and Stuart that his agreement to consider joining Stuart's little committee constituted a concession already.[115]

Marshall paid a visit to Madame Chiang, telling her that the US military equipment had been fuelling Chiang's 'sense of false power'.[116] He successfully forced Chiang to back down on 9 September. Chiang agreed that a Committee of Three meeting would be held concurrently when the five-member committee met. The Committee of Three would discuss a new truce and all outstanding military issues, but the CCP must designate its representatives for the National Assembly and State Council before the announcement of the truce. Chiang also agreed to let the State Council settle all territorial disputes.[117]

However, the issue at play was not whether Chiang had retracted his 'five conditions' but Marshall's impression of Chiang's position during their meeting; Marshall informed Zhou of this in a memorandum dated 10 September. First, Marshall got the feeling that Chiang would not support governmental reforms before the convening of the National Assembly. Second, Marshall believed that Chiang was unlikely to withdraw from the places his armies had recently occupied.[118]

---

113 Minutes of meeting between Marshall and Zhou, 4 September 1946; minutes of meeting between Marshall, Stuart and Zhou, 5 September 1946, *FRUS*, 1946, 10: 117–29, 132–46.
114 Minutes of meeting between Marshall, Stuart and Zhou, 5 September 1946, *FRUS*, 1946, 10: 144.
115 Minutes of meeting between Marshall, Stuart and Zhou, 5 September 1946, *FRUS*, 1946, 10: 135, 140, 144.
116 Minutes of meeting between Stuart and Marshall, 10 September 1946, *FRUS*, 1946, 10: 170.
117 Marshall to Zhou, 10 September 1946, *FRUS*, 1946, 10: 168–9; *Chiang Diary*, 9 September 1946, Folder 10, Box 45.
118 Marshall to Zhou, 10 September 1946, *FRUS*, 1946, 10: 168–9.

Zhou was clearly preoccupied when he conferred with Marshall on 11 September. He steadfastly refused to participate in the five-member committee, declaring that Stuart's informal group was virtually a scam as long as the war continued. Zhou instead demanded that a formal Committee of Three meeting be called immediately in order to re-establish a ceasefire. Although Zhou labelled Chiang's entire proposal a breach of PCC resolutions, he admitted that Chiang's idea of settling disputes via the State Council was a topic worthy of discussion by the Stuart-led small group. In other words, Zhou refused to become involved in the Stuart Committee before Chiang halted all military operations, even though he still found common ground with Chiang on the State Council.[119]

Zhou's insistence on calling a Committee of Three meeting was at odds with Stuart's idea of turning the highly publicised but stalemated formal negotiations into a more informal one. From a negotiation view point, informal discussions are essential to increasing the likelihood of concession.[120] Given that both Chiang and Zhou agreed to take the dispute to the State Council, Stuart's informal group could have reinvented the entire negotiation in a less competitive environment before both parties gained enough momentum to resume formal negotiations. Instead, as Marshall noted, Chiang effectively botched the Committee of Three meeting from the start by knowingly restricting his negotiators' ability to make concessions. Zhou, for his part, could not even agree to give Stuart custody of a sealed envelope containing the CCP nominees for the State Council.[121]

Zhou was not interested in participating in Stuart's informal group before getting all the guarantees he requested. The problem was that Chiang had agreed to take the dispute over the CCP local government to the State Council. The offer observed the letter and the spirit of the PCC resolutions and fell within the scope of what Stuart's small group set out to discuss. Zhou was aware that if he walked away from the negotiation, he would be putting himself in an untenable position. 'I cannot refuse to consider anything', Zhou told Marshall.[122]

---

119 Minutes of meeting between Marshall and Zhou, 11 September 1946, *FRUS*, 1946, 10: 171–82.
120 Lewicki, Barry and Saunders, *Negotiation*, 340–1.
121 Minutes of meeting between Marshall and Stuart, 12 September 1946, *FRUS*, 1946, 10: 185–6.
122 Minutes of meeting between Marshall, Stuart and Zhou, 5 September 1946, , *FRUS*, 1946, 10: 138–9.

While Zhou's negotiation strategy was in limbo, Chiang provided all the help that Zhou could possibly get. Zhou went to press Stuart on 13 September that the CCP must be given ten seats in the State Council. As mentioned, the disagreement over the State Council seats could have been a non-issue if one of the parties intended to tone down the competitive dynamic in their post-treaty relationship. Although Zhou had been advised not to dictate the outcome of the discussions in advance, he told Stuart that if his request was not accepted beforehand, there was no need for the informal committee to convene. Simultaneously, Chiang's representatives informed Stuart that the GMD would not discuss the distribution of seats in the State Council in informal meetings, relegating the Stuart Committee useless. The sudden change of heart indicated that Chiang wanted to renege on his previous proposition.[123]

Chiang's latest backflip on the peace talks put Zhou in the perfect position to withdraw from the negotiations. Marshall's office received three strongly worded memoranda from Zhou on 16 September, asking Marshall to convene a Committee of Three meeting 'immediately' for a ceasefire. Zhou was unabashed in claiming that all other 'intricate' attempts to break the deadlock were 'non-instrumental'. He suggested that an impromptu Committee of Three meeting was the only hope left to provide 'a direct and simple' solution. After doubling down on his criticism on the US-sponsored peace talks, Zhou notified Marshall that he was leaving Nanjing for Shanghai and would not be back until the Committee of Three was called.[124]

Zhou made a public announcement in Shanghai about his withdrawal from the peace talks. He also delivered a bold statement, including a vow to continue fighting the GMD in the civil war.[125] By the end of September 1946, Zhou began to evacuate his intelligence teams secretly from the GMD-held cities. The aeroplanes of the Executive Headquarters and freighters of the UNRRA were used to ensure the success of the covert operations. Zhou reminded his staffers that the all-out civil war had reached the point of no return.[126]

---

123 Marshall, *Marshall's Mission to China*, 1: 254; Caughey to Marshall, 15 September 1946, *FRUS*, 1946, 10: 188.
124 *FRUS*, 1946, 10: 189–94, citations from 189, 191–2; Marshall, *Marshall's Mission to China*, 1: 256–7.
125 Entry 19 September 1946, *Zhou nianpu*, 692–3.
126 Zhou to CC, 27 September 1946, and excerpts from Zhou's talk after listening to reports from Lian Guan and Yang Lin, late September 1946, *Zhou nianpu*, 693–4.

While the negotiations stalled, the fierce battle for Datong continued to unfold. The CCP attack culminated in early September when the GMD troops were in danger of losing their last line of defence.[127] The Executive Headquarters and its field teams were powerless to halt the fighting.[128] The situation therefore continued to deteriorate. The Nationalists announced on 4 September that if the CCP did not lift the siege, they would retaliate by attacking CCP-held Zhangjiakou, even though Chiang had previously agreed to put it under CCP control.[129] The CCP combatants were forced to end the siege of Datong on 14 September after the Nationalists captured the CCP's rear base a hundred kilometres to Datong's north. Chiang's armies from North China and Manchuria formed a task force to attack Zhangjiakou after the relief of the siege.[130] The offensive was conducted on a grand scale despite repeated warnings from the CCP that it considered the attack to be a conclusive announcement of a total split.[131]

Marshall's embarrassment was made worse by the fierce military confrontations. He put in writing for the first time his intention to terminate the mediation mission to Chiang on 1 October.[132] On 6 October, Chiang agreed to halt the offensive against Zhangjiakou by issuing a ten-day and non-renewable truce for both parties to settle all the disputes within the truce period. Chiang made the offer after having some very unpleasant exchanges with Marshall.[133] Chiang did not regret it because he was expecting a refusal from the CCP.[134]

Chiang's predictions were right. The CCP saw his proposal as a threat and turned it down outright.[135] The rejection justified Chiang's decision to continue the offensive against Zhangjiakou. Marshall and Stuart called for desperate measures again and issued another joint statement on 8 October. It detailed the unyielding positions of the two warring factions and

---

127 Guofangbu shizhengju ed., *Kanluan*, 6: 27.
128 Robertson to Marshall, 10 August 1946, *FRUS*, 1946, 9: 1504–5.
129 Guo Tingyi, *Zhonghua Minguo shishi*, 4: 559.
130 Guofangbu shizhengju ed., *Kanluan*, 6: 28–32, 43–53.
131 Zhou to Marshall, 30 September; minutes of meeting between Marshall, Dong Biwu and Wang Bingnan, 1 October 1946, *FRUS*, 1946, 10: 258–9, 262–6.
132 Marshall to Chiang, 1 October 1946, *FRUS*, 1946, 10: 267–8.
133 Records of conversation between Chiang, Marshall and Stuart, 6 October 1946, *Shilüe*, 67: 231–41; Marshall to Carter, 6 October 1946, *FRUS*, 1946, 10: 298–9.
134 *Chiang Diary*, retrospection log after diary entry of 12 October 1946, Folder 11, Box 45; cf. Taylor, *Generalissimo*, 360–1.
135 'Oral Statement by General Chou En-lai for Ambassador Stuart', 8 October 1946, *FRUS*, 1946, 10: 310–11.

disclosed the CCP's rejection of Chiang's ten-day truce in full.[136] Marshall then departed quietly to Shanghai in an effort to persuade Zhou to return to the negotiating table.[137] This was the Americans' second attempt since August to break the negotiation impasse through the media. A party usually would not take its case to the public unless it wants to show toughness in a position.[138] When Marshall tried to use the same tactic to foster a reconciliatory atmosphere, he was taking a real risk.

Zhou's patience was now running out. When he met Marshall on 9 October, Zhou rounded on Marshall about the timing of the joint statements, complaining that they were always released after the CCP's rejection of demands from the GMD, leading the public to misunderstanding. Zhou went on to excoriate Marshall for his handling of the mediation, including certain expressions within the text of the second joint statement that Marshall deemed trivial.[139]

The Zhou–Marshall conference made no headway. The meeting nonetheless summed up all major differences between the two warring parties. On the question of a ceasefire, the GMD preferred a short-term truce and used it as a litmus test for the CCP's sincerity of resolving all unsettled issues. The CCP considered the temporary truce as military coercion, claiming that it would accept nothing but a permanent ceasefire provided for the restoration of the territorial status quo of 13 January in China proper and a GMD troop withdrawal to the positions held on 7 June in Manchuria.[140]

On the political issues, both parties implemented the PCC resolutions on their own terms. On the quota of seats in the State Council, the maximum concession on offer from the Nationalists was one non-partisan seat to be recommended by the CCP; adding that extra seat to the initial eight and four seats allotted to the CCP and the Democratic League, respectively, made a total of thirteen seats. The Chinese Communists ridiculed the GMD's 'concession'. They instead reiterated all the old arguments to justify their 'original right' of enjoying fourteen votes in the council with the Democratic League.[141]

---

136 Minutes of meeting between Marshall and Stuart, 8 October 1946; public statement by Marshall and Stuart, 8 October 1946, *FRUS*, 1946, 10: 311–12, 312–13.
137 Stuart to Byrnes, 9 October 1946, *FRUS*, 1946, 10: 330–1.
138 Lewicki, Barry and Saunders, *Negotiation*, 346–9.
139 Minutes of meeting between Marshall and Zhou, 9 October 1946, *FRUS*, 1946, 10: 332–41.
140 Ibid., 332–41.
141 Public statement by Marshall and Stuart, 8 October 1946; minutes of meeting between Marshall and Zhou, 9 October 1946, *FRUS*, 1946, 10: 312–13, 332–41, citation from 295.

On the convocation of the National Assembly, the GMD government had made a unilateral announcement on 3 July that the assembly would be held on 12 November 1946.[142] Chiang felt that he had every right to confront the obstructive tactics of the CCP and play a leading role in China's constitutional future.[143] The CCP in turn declared that it would neither submit names of delegates nor participate in the assembly and cited its 'two-stage' interpretation of the PCC resolutions to support the claim that the GMD's unilateral decision had breached its treaty obligations.[144]

Veto players and the third-party bloc

The GMD forces captured Zhangjiakou on 11 October after the CCP troops retreated to nearby rural areas.[145] The Nationalists' victory coincided with their announcement of the resumption of nationwide conscription.[146] The GMD's chief of general staff, Chen Cheng reinforced the already-prevalent war psychosis, declaring on 17 October that his armies would be able to win the civil war within months.[147] The Americans were willing to exhaust all means before withdrawing from the negotiations. Under the auspices of Stuart, leaders of the Democratic League, the Youth Party and non-partisan politicians formed a third-party bloc and intervened in the stalemated peace talks.[148] Zhou met delegates of the third-party alliance on 15 October, but he declined to comment on their request for returning to Nanjing.[149]

While Zhou was radiating his silent power, all parties deadlocked in the negotiations were trying to make sense of Stuart's move to deal the third-party bloc into the main game. The third-party bloc's meddling in the negotiations sent a strong reminder to the two warring sides and the Americans that the PCC resolutions were a deal done by four parties and independent political leaders. The Democratic League, the Youth Party and the non-partisan politicians had the right to interpret the resolutions in their respective ways. Most importantly, the third-party bloc could surpass the

---

142 *Shilüe*, 66: 277.
143 *Chiang Diary*, 1 July 1946, Folder 8, Box 45.
144 Minutes of meeting between Marshall and Zhou, 9 October 1946, *FRUS*, 1946, 10: 332–41.
145 Guofangbu shizhengju ed., *Kanluan*, 6: 44–62.
146 Guo Tingyi, *Zhonghua Minguo shishi*, 4: 570.
147 Li and Zhang eds, *Jiefang zhanzhen shiqi*, 268.
148 Stuart's first contact with the third-party members about the matter was made on 14 September. See Jiang Yuntian, *Zhongguo jindaishi*, 95.
149 Li and Zhang eds, *Jiefang zhanzhen shiqi*, 265.

military antagonism of the two belligerent parties as China's democratic third force.[150] This was what the American mediators were unable to do. Nevertheless, the third-party coalition could achieve this goal only in a multiparty bargaining environment.

The minor parties were being kept in the background after the PCC because the only two armed Chinese factions had vetoed agreements and returned to the battlefield. In the state of a civil war, only players who have armies powerful enough 'to avoid being soundly defeated by a united army in the aftermath of an agreement' have the ability to veto an agreement unilaterally. As David Cunningham identifies, these armed factions can become the 'veto players'.[151] The military might of the GMD and the CCP therefore made them the only two 'veto players' in the Chinese Civil War. As the general secretary of the Democratic League, Liang Shuming remembered, 'The overall situation has been dominated by the two big forces; others can do nothing against them.'[152]

On the contrary, if the third-party alliance succeeded in negotiating the two warring factions into peace agreements, the civil liberties endorsed by the PCC would have been set free. Once a multiparty bargaining environment was established, life for the two erstwhile belligerents would have been less straightforward. The GMD and the CCP would have had to woo minor parties and non-partisan members, who together would have potentially enjoyed twelve votes in the State Council, either for getting proposals passed or simply because of institutional constraints. Meanwhile, the third-party alliance had come into play. It made the CCP, the GMD and even the Americans simultaneously hold ambivalent attitudes towards the group. The Americans considered the group an alternative for resolving the impasse, but they trod carefully to avoid giving the wrong impression to the CCP that they were trying to win over the Democratic League from it.[153] Marshall was confronted with the brutal fact that the group was formed by independent yet ambitious politicians with somewhat unique personalities. Democratic League member Luo Rongji was a leader of the group, but his flamboyant personality did not earn more credibility for him. Marshall was troubled by Luo's habit of smearing things in his random talks with the press.[154]

---

150 Liang Shuming, 'Wo canjia Guogong hetan', 954.
151 Cunningham, *Barriers to Peace in Civil War*, 36.
152 Citation translated from Liang Shuming, 'Wo canjia Guogong hetan', 954.
153 Notes on meeting between Marshall, Liang Shuming and Ye Duyi, 17 October 1946, *FRUS*, 1946, 10: 385.
154 Minutes of meeting between Marshall and Stuart, 12 September 1946, *FRUS*, 1946, 10: 186.

Zhou was in less of a mood to reopen the peace talks. He rather used meetings with the third-party bloc to persuade the CCP's closest ally, the Democratic League, to boycott the National Assembly.[155] In general, Zhou believed that the third-party bloc needed to be educated because of their illusion of peace and ignorance of Chiang's conspiracy. The difficult part was that the Democratic League was a minor party alliance. It was not a disciplined Marxist–Leninist party like the CCP, even though the deputy general secretary of the league, Zhou Xinmin, was concurrently a senior CCP cadre.[156] The chairman of the league, Zhang Junmai, was a constitutionalist who played an important role in the CRDC.[157] The CCP quickly perceived that Zhang wavered over boycotting a constitutional assembly.[158]

League member Huang Yanpei was a respectable front man of the third-party bloc, a key CCP sympathiser and a member of the People's Political Council (*Guomin canzheng hui* 國民參政會)—a GMD-controlled advisory body—who received salary payments from the government. Although the GMD military police raided his home in January 1946, Huang did not stop receiving cash payments as gifts from the Chinese crime boss and Chiang's staunch ally, Du Yuesheng, who had been trying to lure Huang over to Chiang. Du paid Huang 4 million *Fabi* when Huang was actively involved in mediation efforts from October 1946 to January 1947. The relationship between the two was not limited to cold cash. The pair stayed in touch via correspondence even when Du was away. Huang might have needed to maintain a good relationship with Chiang's number one hired killer for financial reasons and safety concerns. However, it did not exonerate him from mismanaging conflicts of interest.[159]

Generally speaking, the Democratic League had certain incompatible views on the constitution and army nationalisation with the CCP, not to mention that the inability of many minor-party bloc members to resist corruption had been well recorded.[160] Given that oscillating political stances and personalities would be magnified in a multiparty bargaining environment,

---

155 Zhou to CC, 15 October 1946, *Zhou nianpu*, 698.
156 Zhou to CC, c/o Ye Jianying, 21 October 1946, *Zhou nianpu*, 700; Liang Shuming, 'Wo canjia Guogong hetan', 924.
157 Jeans, 'Last Chance for Peace'.
158 Entry 4 October 1946, *Zhou nianpu*, 695.
159 Huang's diary, 26 January, 26 July, 3 and 17 October 1946, 19 January and 25 February 1947, *Huang Yanpei riji* [The diary of Huang Yanpei], Huang Yanpei (Beijing: Huawen chubanshe, 2008), 9: 121–2, 179–80, 205, 244, 255 (hereafter *Huang riji*).
160 Jiang Yuntian, *Zhongguo jindaishi*, 56–7; Liang Shuming, 'Wo canjia Guogong hetan', 934–5; Eastman, 'China's democratic parties'.

it posted a challenge for the CCP in dealing with the third-party alliance in the State Council if a peace settlement could be materialised. The unpredictable interparty politics of a power-sharing government lent veracity to the old assumption that the CCP could conquer China faster by force than by political means.[161]

The Nationalists did not want the third-party bloc's direct involvement in the peace talks either. They did not have many friends in the group, as even their political ally the Youth Party had been critical of the GMD. Although Chiang had promised the Youth Party a democratic and constitutional government,[162] it still gave him a hard time during the PCC by advocating a quasi-cabinet system to rein in presidential power.[163]

Hence Chiang needed to put his proposal on the table first instead of allowing the third-party coalition to exert influence on the negotiations. He did it on 16 October in a public statement. It started with Chiang's usual anti-CCP rant, which the CCP considered bullying. The rest of the proposal was inversely related to its offensive rhetoric. It supported the Zhou-proposed formal meeting of the Committee of Three concurrently with a meeting of Stuart's informal committee, with eight conditions attached. Some of the stipulations in Chiang's proposal were either totally identical with or partially different from the CCP's demands. For example, Chiang's agreement to calling meetings of the CRDC was answering the CCP's call that a consensus on the constitution should be reached before formally passing it in the National Assembly. The suggestion for armies of the two warring factions to stay at their present localities pending further decisions was in essence supporting Zhou's call in August for an immediate nationwide ceasefire. Regrettably, Chiang threatened at the end of the proposal that he would not implement a ceasefire until the CCP accepted his eight conditions and announced its lists of delegates of the National Assembly.[164]

The CCP intended to reject Chiang's plan outright as it failed to address its 'two conditions', namely the restoration of positions occupied by the two opposing armies on 13 January and the implementation of PCC resolutions on the CCP's terms.[165] Another problem was that Chiang's proposal came

---

161 Tsou, *America's Failure in China*, 399.
162 Eastman, 'China's democratic parties', 190–1.
163 Jiang Yuntian, *Zhongguo jindaishi*, 57–8.
164 *China White Paper*, 2: 674–5.
165 *Tanpan shi*, 419–20.

only after the Nationalists invaded the CCP base in Jiangsu and captured its regional headquarters at Huaiyin city on 19 September. The CCP construed Chiang's proposal as a mockery of their defeat under the circumstances.[166]

Although leaders of the third-party alliance might tell the press that they were disappointed in Chiang's proposal,[167] they did not completely oppose it. Luo Rongji and Zhang Junmai found shortcomings in Chiang's proposal, particularly on the demand for the submission of the list of delegates of the National Assembly before the reorganisation of the government. Zhang nonetheless did not believe that these defects were as important as the ceasefire, because these 'outstanding points' were negotiable after a truce deal had been struck. Luo asserted that the CCP 'would be glad to have and had proposed' many of the ideas stated in Chiang's proposal. The problem was Chiang's attitude. According to Luo, Chiang's approach was like saying, 'I give you these terms; agree or not.' 'The Communists cannot accept that attitude … There is a matter of face there', Luo added.[168]

Given that the view of the third-party coalition on Chiang's 'eight points' was different from that of the CCP, it was likely to roll out an independent proposal in the event of the CCP refusal of Chiang's plan.[169] A third-party proposal could be something close to a fifty-fifty split—an approach that modern mediators have been advised to avoid—and unacceptable to both major parties.[170] However, the 'original right' of the group to put forward its own proposal would make it difficult for the two warring parties to dismiss it.

The CCP leadership quickly identified the problems. It advised Zhou to actively advocate the CCP's terms rather than insisting on getting 'guarantees' before attending meetings.[171] The instruction was similar to the advice from Marshall that Zhou refused to accept when they conferred in Shanghai.[172] However, the Yan'an leadership issued a public statement on 18 October.

---

166 Tong, *Fengyu sishi nian*, 465; Geng Routian, *Zhongguo jiaofei kanluan*, 2: 150–5.
167 Jeans, 'Last Chance for Peace', 305.
168 *Huang riji*, 18 October 1946, 9: 205–6; minutes of meeting between Marshall, Stuart and members of the third-party group, 22 October; minutes of meeting between Marshall and Carsun Zhang, 22 October 1946, *FRUS*, 1946, 10: 399–408, citations from 402, 404, 408.
169 For the mediation principles of the third-party bloc, see Liang Shuming, 'Wo canjia Guogong hetan', 957–8.
170 Gibson, Thompson and Bazerman, 'Shortcomings of Neutrality'.
171 *Tanpan shi*, 419–20.
172 Minutes of meeting between Marshall and Zhou, 9 October 1946, *FRUS*, 1946, 10: 332–41.

It contradicted Chiang's 'eight points' with its 'two conditions' after a fiery tirade accusing the GMD of waging civil war and treaty violations with the American accomplices.[173]

The third-party group were eager to get Zhou back to Nanjing. They drafted a basic proposal outline at Zhou's residence on 19 October 1946. The draft was written with inclusive rhetoric, but the article about the two opposing forces holding their current position in a nationwide ceasefire was borrowed from Chiang's 'eight points'. The group took the draft and brought Zhou with them to visit the Nationalists' PCC representative, Wu Tiecheng. The visit set up an informal meeting between representatives of the five signatories of the PCC resolutions. During the meeting, Wu promised to increase the openness of the negotiations, maintaining that Chiang's 'eight points' merely served as a basis for negotiations. The meeting ended with an agreement approved by acclamation that Zhou would return to the peace talks in Nanjing.[174]

The third-party bloc and Zhou met Chiang after arriving at Nanjing on 21 October. Chiang, who believed that Zhou and the minor party politicians had no sense of decency, did not throw support behind the group. The entire meeting lasted only about eight minutes, and nothing of any substance was achieved. Chiang left in a hurry for another inspection tour to Taiwan.[175] Chiang admonished his interlocutors not to circumvent his principle: there would be no ceasefire without the CCP accepting his terms. Also, he did not stop ordering his armies to intensify the offensive.[176]

Members of the third-party group were shattered when Chiang's representatives failed to live up to their side of the bargain by engaging in an open-minded negotiation. Some even began to realise that Zhou's return might be the political manoeuvre that preceded the CCP's pulling out from the peace talks.[177] The two warring sides simply reiterated their respective non-negotiable terms again and used them to attack each other.

---

173 Stuart to Byrnes, 19 October 1946, *FRUS*, 1946, 10: 390–3.
174 *Huang riji*, 19 October 1946, 9: 206; Jiang Yuntian, *Zhongguo jindaishi*, 101–4; minutes of meeting between Marshall, Stuart and members of the third-party group, 22 October 1946, *FRUS*, 1946, 10: 399–407.
175 *Chiang Diary*, 21 October 1946, Folder 11, Box 45; Tong, *Fengyu sishi nian*, 468.
176 Chiang to Chen Bulei, c/o Chen Cheng and Yu Dawei, 22 October 1946; Chiang to Chen Cheng, 23 October 1946, *Shilüe*, 67: 341–2, 357.
177 *Huang riji*, 21 October 1946, 9: 207; Liang Shuming, 'Wo canjia Guogong hetan', 954.

7. TOWARDS AN ALL-OUT CIVIL WAR IN CHINA

Disagreement over the allocation of state councillors' seats topped the list of the most contentious political issues between the two warring parties—a dispute over the deficit of one state councillor seat, to be precise.[178]

As discussed, the State Council had the authority to settle almost all the disputes between the two belligerent parties. Both parties could have adhered to the letter and the spirit of the PCC resolutions much better if they settled the conflict over the quota of the state councillors cooperatively with the third-party coalition and went to the inaugural session of the State Council to dispute all other outstanding issues. Although the third-party coalition members did not reach a consensus over the real causes of the two-party civil war, they agreed that the row over the single state councillor seat was a façade for the GMD and the CCP to hide their true objectives.[179] If Chiang ignored the CCP's boycott and went ahead with the assembly on 12 November 1946, it would put an end to their mediation efforts.

The Nationalists captured the CCP-held Manchurian seaport of Andong on 25 October. Zhou was furious about it and threatened to withdraw from the negotiation for the last time. Zhou requested the members of the third-party group, who prompted pleas for Zhou to stay, not to advance any proposal without his consent.[180] The demand meant that the group must take concerted actions with the CCP.

The third-party coalition was committed to a quick way to end the conflict. It defied Zhou's request and forwarded an independent proposal simultaneously to Chiang, the Americans and Zhou on 28 October. The terms of the ceasefire in the proposal were essentially what Zhou had been informed of in Shanghai, but it was the articles about the troop deployment in Manchuria that caused Zhou's fear. While the proposal recommended that the CCP forces would be redeployed to three cities in remote northern Manchuria, it virtually let the GMD have free access to most of the areas along the Chinese Changchun Railway.[181]

The proposal showed a clear intention to defuse the ticking Manchurian time bomb by separating the two opposing armies in the most obvious way. It was not at odds with the idea of having a provincial demarcation of

---

178 'Counterproposals by the Chinese Communist Party', 22 October 1946, and GMD's reply, n.d., *FRUS*, 1946, 10: 412, 417–18.
179 Jiang Yuntian, *Zhongguo jindaishi*, 105–7.
180 Entry 25 October 1946, *Zhou nianpu*, 701.
181 Notes on meeting between Marshall and Stuart, 29 October 1946, *FRUS*, 1946, 10: 445–8; cf. *Tanpan shi*, 422.

garrison lines for the two warring sides that Zhou initially proposed back in June.[182] The unfolding events proved that it might not be a bad idea, as the two opposing forces had committed to launch massive winter offensives in Manchuria.

The third-party bloc nevertheless seemed not to be taking the aggressive negotiating style of the two warring factions into account. The two heavily armed veto players in the Chinese Civil War would prefer the fighting to be sustained before moving into quid pro quo exchanges at the time of their choosing rather than accepting a truce brokered by a minor-party alliance.[183] Zhou met the third-party group representatives who brought the proposal to him. He threw tantrums to express his disappointment at not being consulted for an unfair deal. It caused huge embarrassment to everyone present, particularly to the group's leader, Liang Shuming.[184]

Chiang, freshly returned from Taiwan, capitalised on the misfortune of the third-party bloc. He made a couple of quick steps in the lead-up to the National Assembly that would end the Americans' and the third-party bloc's mediation attempts and precipitate the final split with CCP. Chiang met members of the third-party group right after their clash with Zhou. He asked them not to propose truce deals, stating that he would issue a ceasefire pending the minor parties' submission of the names of delegates for the National Assembly regardless of how the CCP reacted. The third-party coalition began facing the prospect of breaking up after the meeting.[185]

Chiang then rapidly informed the Americans that he was going to make further concessions, including a pledge that his force would stop expanding its territory along the Chinese Changchun Railway before the State Council was reorganised. As the concessions were a modification of the third-party group's proposal that Zhou deemed unfair, he could be sure that the latter would be too proud to accept them. Chiang noted privately that his concessions merely served the purpose of winning the minor parties over.[186]

---

182 Minutes of meeting between Marshall and Zhou, 12 June 1946, *FRUS*, 1946, 9: 1025–34, esp. 1031.
183 Marshall to Truman, 26 October 1946, *FRUS*, 1946, 10: 435–6.
184 Jiang Yuntian, *Zhongguo jindaishi*, 121–3; Liang Shuming, 'Wo canjia Guogong hetan', 960–1; *Tanpan shi*, 422; Tong, *Fengyu sishi nian*, 470–1.
185 Jiang Yuntian, *Zhongguo jindaishi*, 130–3; *Huang riji*, 6 November 1946, 9: 214.
186 *Chiang Diary*, 29–30 October 1946, Folder 11, Box 45; Marshall, *Marshall's Mission to China*, 1: 347.

On 8 November, Chiang issued an unconditional ceasefire order and a statement reiterated the opening of the National Assembly on the 12th.[187] Chiang's double-sided announcements incited the CCP to release a counterstatement scoffing at the unilateral ceasefire, particularly at the article about conducting self-defence. The CCP considered it the pretext for more military actions.[188] Meanwhile, the Nationalists conveyed messages to the Democratic League about a new formula of eight (CCP), five (Democratic League), four (the Youth Party) and three (independent) regarding the twenty non-GMD state councillors, and proposed once again that twelve votes were all it needed to veto decisions. However, the CCP had shifted its focus to delegitimise a Chiang-controlled National Assembly. Zhou admitted to the third-party bloc leaders that the quota of the state councillors was not an issue any more because the real veto power came from the CCP–minor-party bloc cooperation. He asserted: 'It's all the same to me now whether we will be allotted one more seat or one less.'[189]

On 11 November, the GMD government postponed the National Assembly for three uselessly short days.[190] The third-party bloc members were devastated. They believed that the dispute over the distribution of seats in the State Council had been completely resolved as the CCP–Democratic League bloc now had thirteen votes to veto decisions that required only twelve. Chiang could have reached out to the CCP and started restructuring the State Council instead of rescheduling the assembly to the 15th.[191] Chiang, however, had other ideas. The three-day postponement was his plan to isolate the CCP and split the Democratic League in order to make the National Assembly a GMD rubber stamp.[192]

The temporary alliance of the third-party group disintegrated when the National Assembly convened on 15 November 1946 amid a CCP–Democratic League boycott. The Youth Party and Zhang Junmai's associates, attended the assembly with some non-partisans.[193] They tried to make an impression, but the GMD was in full control in the end. The assembly (later known as the Constituent National Assembly 制憲國大) adopted

187 *Shenbao*, 9 November 1946.
188 Stuart to Byrnes, 9 November 1946, *FRUS*, 1946, 10: 499–500.
189 Jiang Yuntian, *Zhongguo jindaishi*, 145, citation translated from 147.
190 Marshall to Truman, 11 November 1946, *FRUS*, 1946, 10: 523.
191 Jiang Yuntian, *Zhongguo jindaishi*, 148–50.
192 *Chiang Diary*, 11 November 1946 and the retrospection log after entry for 2 November 1946, Folder 12, Box 45.
193 Zhang Junmai did not attend the Assembly. See Jeans, 'Last Chance for Peace', 321.

the new constitution of China on 25 December in basically the same form as initially presented, including the much-disputed articles about executive responsibility to legislature and the autonomy of provincial governments.[194] Zhou and key members of the CCP delegation departed for Yan'an on 19 November for the last time, after declaring in a public statement that the National Assembly was illegal.[195] A representative of the CCP's liaison office in Nanjing declared on 6 December that the CCP forces had launched pre-emptive strikes from all fronts in the name of the PCC resolutions.[196]

Marshall was recalled and returned to the United States on 8 January 1947 as chances to reopen negotiations were all but gone. The US government announced its complete withdrawal from the tripartite peace talks after Marshall's departure.[197] Marshall told Truman before his recall that the CCP definitely considered him to be *persona non grata*.[198] Marshall had guessed right. China was bracing for nationalist protests against the US military presence in January 1947, following the rape of a Chinese female student by US soldiers in Beiping.[199] A phased withdrawal of US forces soon followed, and by October 1947, US military personnel in China were reduced to 6,532 men, including 1,591 marines.[200]

The Nationalist authorities issued notices to enforce the withdrawal of all CCP representatives on 28 February 1947.[201] The door for negotiations was formally shut on 9 March after the last contingent of CCP delegates had left. In preparation for invasion by their ground forces, Nationalist aircraft bombarded Yan'an on 11 March, soon after the withdrawal of the US military observers team.[202] The Nationalists now faced a benign State Council as the

---

194 Stuart to Byrnes, 29 December, *FRUS*, 1946, 10: 665–6; Guo Tingyi, *Zhonghua Minguo shishi*, 4: 585–7. For the full translation of text of the constitution, see Marshall, *Marshall's Mission to China*, 2: 490–515.
195 Zhou Enlai, 'Statement on the Kuomintang's Convening of a National Assembly', 16 November 1946, in *Selected Works of Zhou Enlai*, Zhou Enlai, 1: 269–72.
196 Guo Tingyi, *Zhonghua Minguo shishi*, 4: 586.
197 Personal statement by Marshall, 7 January 1947; press release issued by the Department of State, 29 January 1947, *China White Paper*, 2: 686–9, 695.
198 Marshall to Truman, 28 December 1946, *FRUS*, 1946, 10: 661–5.
199 The rape case has been extensively studied by scholars. See Robert Shaffer, 'A rape in Beijing, December 1946: GIs, Nationalist protests, and US foreign policy', *Pacific Historical Review* 69, no. 1 (2000): 31–64; James A. Cook, 'Penetration and neocolonialism: The Shen Chong rape case and the anti-American student movement of 1946–47', *Republican China* 22, no. 1 (1996): 65–97; Suzanne Pepper, *Civil War in China: The Political Struggle, 1945–1949*, 2nd edn (Lanham, MD: Rowman & Littlefield, 1999), 52–8.
200 Forrestal to Marshall, 15 November 1947, *FRUS*, 1947, 7: 918–20.
201 Li and Zhang eds, *Jiefang zhanzhen shiqi*, 339–40.
202 Stuart to Marshall, 9 March 1947, *FRUS*, 1946, 10: 722–3; *Mao nianpu*, 3: 175.

CCP and Democratic League were out of the political picture completely. They successfully rammed a resolution on general mobilisation of Chinese society for a civil war against the CCP through the council in July 1947 before it was enacted into law in a GMD-controlled National Assembly on 18 April 1948. The resolution gave the Nationalists not only unlimited power to control all forms of labour, services and materials but also the authority to impose restrictions on freedom of speech and expression.[203] The CCP, on the other hand, had no need to enact legislation. It believed that it held the mandate of 'the people' to overthrow an oppressive government. The combat-ready armies of the two veto players of the Chinese Civil War were finally able to fight freely along the lighted path of an all-out war.

Marshall: 'The state of peace appears at times more difficult than the state of war'

In his meeting with Marshall, Hu Lin, one of the founders of the prestigious Chinese newspaper *Dagong Bao* (大公報, *Ta Kung Pao, Impartial Daily*), suggested that the difference between the GMD and the CCP was less stark than one would have imagined: both were revolutionary parties motivated by destructive impulses, and both adopted similar tactics against each other.[204] The Nationalists' chief of general staff, Chen Cheng, seemed to agree with Hu. He admitted privately that he learnt revolutionary ideas from the Soviets.[205] As discussed, the two veto players in the Chinese Civil War were equally capable of destroying each other on the battlefield. Chiang's two-fold strategy that prioritised quashing revolts by force was matched by Mao's all-out offensive approach. Both men virtually collaborated to make the civil war interminable, and they led their respective parties into a state of moral attenuation. As the civil war raged on, the two combatant parties became just what they were fighting.[206]

---

203 Stuart to Marshall, 21 July 1947, *China White Paper*, 2: 756–8; *Shilüe*, 70: 384–9, 74: 212–16.
204 Minutes of meeting between Marshall and Hu, 22 October 1946, *FRUS*, 1946, 10: 409–12.
205 Chen's diary, monthly retrospection log, January 1946, *Chen Cheng xiansheng riji* [The diary of Chen Cheng] (Taipei: Guoshiguan, 2015), 2: 693.
206 For the moral dilemma in human conflict, see Beth Fisher-Yoshida, and Hene Wasserman, 'Moral conflict and engaging alternative perspectives', in *The Handbook of Conflict Resolution*, ed. Deutsch, Coleman and Marcus, 560–81.

Thus, the two opposing forces became locked in a vicious cycle of attack and counter-attack. The Nationalists' offensive culminated in territorial gains, but the all-out attacks of the Chinese Communists succeeded in inflicting overwhelming Nationalist casualties. While triumph and disaster are two imposters, both sides' use of truce and peace talks as cover to prepare fresh attacks was astonishing. Chiang purposely omitted the deadline from his unilateral ceasefire order in furtherance of his offensive strategies. Chiang's tactic was countered by the CCP leaders' approaches to manipulate the ceasefire monitoring mechanism. The CCP's evacuation of non-combat personnel from its combat units in preparation for renewed fighting was a stunning example of using the agreed terms of ceasefire for prohibited purposes. Given that the evacuation of injured and sick soldiers can hardly be considered a hostile act, this unorthodox approach, even today, allows belligerent parties to circumvent truce agreements with a carefully crafted list of prohibited acts.[207]

The total war footing increasingly blurred the line between bellicose rhetoric and practical polices. Chiang might not have intended to make targeted killing the mainstay of his government, but his secret police apparently went astray in the midst of the war. In this sense, Chiang's decision to pardon the mastermind of the Li–Wen assassinations might have been justified: bad environments often make normal people commit atrocities. There was no evidence that leaders in Yan'an gave orders to attack the US Marines. Mao nonetheless deemed it necessary to shift the blame entirely to the Americans after the deadly firefight. Mao must have known that the barbarity of the full-blown civil war knew no boundaries, and no one had the power to contain the warlike populism of which he was the biggest patron.

The two belligerent parties were sceptical about the long-term value of agreements in the midst of escalated military confrontations. Both Chiang and Zhou stipulated harsh conditions and looked for guarantees of consensus even to enter negotiations. Chiang's and Zhou's concerns over the irrelevance of short-term success for a long-term win were not unwarranted. Scholars of today have confirmed that agreements have little long-term value if the relationship between disputants is built on mutual mistrust.[208] This perhaps explains why the present historical view in China of Stuart's

---

207 See the recommended list of prohibited acts from a ceasefire template provided by the Public International Law and Policy Group, *The Ceasefire Drafter's Handbook*, 17–19.
208 Dean G. Pruitt, Robert S. Peirce, Neil B. McGillicuddy, Gary L. Welton and Lynn M. Castrianno, 'Long-term success in mediation', *Law and Human Behavior* 17, no. 3 (1993): 313–30.

five-member committee is basically unchanged since Zhou considered it a scam in 1946.[209] It was not until the 1990s that conflict resolution theorists started thinking about long-term success at several intervals after mediation.[210] Stuart was therefore ahead of his time with his innovative ideas in peace negotiations. This raises the question of whether future studies of Stuart's contributions to the Marshall mission need to go beyond prior studies that focus on Stuart's pro-Nationalist stance and distrust of the CCP.[211] The successful implementation of the Stuart-proposed informal yet short-term committee relied on the disputants' appreciation of the potential of short-term agreements in creating manageable intervals for long-term success. This was exactly what contemporary scholars have set out to explore. Stuart's plan was snubbed by the two warring factions at the time, and his posthumously published embassy report is metaphorically titled *The Forgotten Ambassador*.[212] Given that modern negotiation studies have only begun to scratch the surface of the subject that Stuart raised more than half a century ago, perhaps one could hope that the forgotten ambassador might not be forgotten again.

Stuart's creative informal committee was the American mediators' last trump card.[213] When the plan failed even before it began, the Americans resorted to desperate measures. The arms embargo was perhaps the most extreme one. Despite early signs of success, the embargo failed to dissuade Chiang from using force to settle problems. Chiang literally ignored the arms embargo despite the fact that his armies were hit hard by it. The quantity of US ammunition held by the GMD Army had reduced to a dangerous level in April 1947, but Chiang kept his field commanders ignorant of this fact.[214] The Americans started to relax the arms embargo from April 1947 until it was unofficially ended by December of the same year after it was proved to be penalising only the GMD but not the CCP.[215] The arms embargo ended with the bitter triumph of Chiang's persistence and the Americans' failure to erase the stigma of their support of the Nationalists in the civil war.

---

209 *Tanpan shi*, 409–11.
210 Pruitt, Peirce, McGillicuddy, Welton and Castrianno, 'Long-term success'.
211 Yu-ming Shaw, *American Missionary in China*, 195–6.
212 Kenneth W. Rea and John C. Brewer eds, *The Forgotten Ambassador: The Reports of John Leighton Stuart, 1946–1949* (Boulder, CO: Westview Press, 1981).
213 Caughey's diary, 14 August 1946, *Marshall Mission to China*, ed. Jeans, 259.
214 Timberman to Butterworth, 22 April 1947; Stuart to Marshall, 23 December 1947, FRUS, 1947, 7: 821–2, 933–4.
215 Acheson to Smith, 2 April 1947; Lovett to Royall, 31 December 1947, FRUS, 1947, 7: 814–15, 938–9; 'Draft policy memorandum prepared in the embassy in China', 6 September 1946, FRUS, 1946, 10: 147–50.

Marshall and Stuart paid the price for their desperate move of publicising the inflexible stances of the two belligerent parties to the public. Perhaps Marshall's remark about the unyielding positions of both parties also applied to himself: '[The mistake was] a very human reaction, though a very short-sighted one.'[216] When the tide of war turned against the Nationalists in mid-1947, Marshall was singled out for censure, particularly for the GMD's defeat in Manchuria. Chiang's exercise in serial blame-shifting began with talks via diplomatic channels[217] denouncing Marshall to the GMD military leaders[218] and ended with the vilification of Marshall in his diary. Chiang's comments were well recorded, and they ensured that Marshall's name was tied to the Nationalists' debacle in the Chinese Civil War.[219]

Stuart claimed that he was aware of Chiang's psychology.[220] If so, he also must have been aware that both major parties considered the third-party bloc's intervention to be a problem. The question for the two warring sides was not whether the third-party group was able to broker a fair deal for them but whether they preferred to handle the politics in a more institutionalised, post-settlement environment. Tsou once hypothesised that the CCP would capture control of the government very quickly if the PCC resolutions were fully implemented.[221] However, this chapter shows that both the GMD and the CCP preferred a two-party civil war to a multiparty bargaining environment.

As Marshall presciently observed, 'The state of peace appears at times more difficult than the state of war.'[222] The vigorous political manoeuvring of Chiang and Zhou virtually killed off the third-party group's last-ditch mediation efforts in the end. Nevertheless, the third-party bloc's quixotic but futile efforts for peace contained a scathing indictment of the two warring factions. Liang Shuming had given Marshall a little insight into what was going on: 'Outside of the two principal contesting parties, all other parties and all the people of China unanimously wanted peace.'[223]

---

216 Minutes of meeting between Marshall, Dong Biwu and Wang Bingnan, 4 October 1946, *FRUS*, 1946, 10: 285.
217 Stuart to Marshall, 19 June 1947, *FRUS*, 1947, 7: 191–2.
218 Du Yuming, 'Liaoshen zhanyi gaishu' [An overview of the Liaoshen campaign], in *Liaoshen zhanyi qinliji*, ed. Zhongguo renmin zhengzhi xieshang huiyi quanguo weiyuanhui wenshi ziliao yanjiu weiyuanhui Liaoshen zhanyi qinliji shenbianzu, 24.
219 *Chiang Diary*, 3 October 1948, Folder 5, Box 47 and 7 August 1951, Folder 3, Box 49; Jiang and Liu, 'Yi zhu shi'.
220 Stuart to Byrnes, 7 August 1946, *FRUS*, 1946, 9: 1465–6.
221 Tsou, *America's Failure in China*, 408.
222 Marshall to Truman, 26 October 1946, *FRUS*, 1946, 10: 437.
223 Minutes of meeting between Marshall and eight delegates of PCC, 8 June 1946, *FRUS*, 1946, 9: 997.

Previous studies have justified Zhou's outbursts against the third-party coalition's lack of concern over the CCP's interests by rolling out an independent proposal.[224] Admittedly, the third-party group's failure to follow Zhou's script was unacceptable to the CCP. To put things into context, however, the third-party bloc, like Marshall, was seeking 'some quick way[s] to stop the fighting with a minimum of discussion'.[225] For them, everything else, such as whose army should be in which position on what date or who would get one more seat in the State Council, had become less important. At a meeting held after Zhou's outbursts, third-party alliance member Huang burst into tears when he talked about the suffering of the Chinese people in the civil war.[226] Everyone cries for different reasons.

When the entire nation was galloping blindfolded down the path of an all-out civil war, the third-party group's last-minute decision to join the peace talks raised the question of whether the two belligerent parties' tirades against each other's putative treaty violations were self-serving attempts to heighten the militancy of the negotiations. The increased competitive dynamic in the negotiations could only give the two veto players more excuses to intensify the war. The third-party bloc's query about the nature of the row over the one-seat deficit in the State Council shed some light on the convenient rhetorical façade designed for China to stay the course of a two-party civil war. To date, the third-party coalition's view on the polemic stands as an alternative to the long-running debate, with some pointing to the GMD's hypersensitivity about maintaining absolute power and others laying blame on the CCP's obstructive tactics.[227] Hence Zhou's confession to the minor party politicians about his obliviousness to the quota of the State Council is admirable, as he virtually admitted that the CCP used the disagreement as a tool.

---

224 *Tanpan shi*, 421–2; Wang Chaoguang, *Zhonghua Minguo shi*, ser. ed. Zhongguo shehui kexue yuan jindaishi yanjiusuo Zhonghua Minguo shi yanjiushi, 11: 519–20.
225 Minutes of meeting between Marshall and Zhou, 26 October 1946, *FRUS*, 1946, 10: 434.
226 *Huang riji*, 29 October 1946, 9: 211.
227 See, for example, Wang Chaoguang, *Zhonghua Minguo shi*, ser. ed. Zhongguo shehui kexue yuan jindaishi yanjiusuo Zhonghua Minguo shi yanjiushi, 11: 180–1; Wang Yunwu, 'Sue zai Zhongguo', 455–6.

Conclusion

Knowledge about negotiation is timeless. This book has demonstrated that modern negotiation literature can help us better comprehend China's postwar struggle between peace and war. But the dialogue between the present and the past is a two-way street in the study of history. Understanding the history of past peace efforts can influence present-day conflict resolution strategies. The futile peace attempts, made between 1945 and 1947, to find a settlement that would end the Chinese Civil War encourage us to reimagine those gruelling negotiations and mediations beyond a simple binary of success and failure. Any negotiation can lose momentum, reach a deadlock or collapse. Nevertheless, principles, verbal commitments and even the most minor areas of agreement may set the foundation for future negotiations, no matter the outcome of current ones.

Scholars John L. Graham, Lynda Lawrence and William Hernández Requejo use 'the way forward is in the rearview mirror' as a metaphor highlighting the importance of contemporary legacies of past negotiations.[1] Three facets of negotiation were highlighted in the GMD–CCP negotiations during the civil war: (i) making concessions and pushing for a deal; (ii) the difficulties in overcoming impasses in political, military and territorial power-sharing disputes; and (iii) managing biased mediators. These became shared knowledge for the many negotiators that followed, explaining why it was imperative for the PRC interlocutors to have access to archival negotiation records when preparing for meetings with their counterparts after 1949.[2]

The Americans' quest for an effective mediation strategy to end the Chinese Civil War within the framework of the US–GMD alliance is a major theme of this book. While the American lead mediators attempted to influence the

---

1 John L. Graham, Lynda Lawrence and William Hernández Requejo, *Inventive Negotiation: Getting Beyond Yes* (New York: Palgrave Macmillan, 2014), 10.
2 Wilhelm, *The Chinese at the Negotiating Table*, 43–4.

GMD–CCP peace talk outcomes, they took various measures to ensure that their mediation efforts were accepted by all parties involved in the civil war, and not only their Nationalist allies. The measures included ensuring the CCP negotiators' safety, adopting unanimous approval as the consent threshold in the tripartite truce supervision system and issuing public statements calling for the two warring parties to reach a settlement. None of these measures, however, had more chance of success than talks at the table; from here, the American mediators could convince the two opposing sides that they were offering impartial, rational advice and facilitating a mutually beneficial and integrative agreement.

Hurley's discussion with Mao regarding the CCP's commitment to reduce the size of its armed forces, albeit unpleasant, was crucial to the outcome of the Chongqing peace talks. While both belligerent parties were seeking an agreement to end the Mao–Chiang summit, it was Hurley's direct talks with Mao that leveraged into the latter's concession. Marshall did not conceal his biased mediation stance when he proposed Nationalist troop movement in Manchuria as a key term of the January ceasefire. Marshall's truce proposal convinced his ally Chiang, but it was Marshall's participation in the mediation meetings that helped the Chinese Communists determine that the ambiguous ceasefire agreement met their own need for free troop movement in Manchuria. In other words, this rare intersection of interests between the two parties—the key to the CCP's conditional acceptance of the Marshall truce—was becoming manifest at the bargaining table.

Marshall attempted to use American aid to generate more influence on both sides 'behind the table'—this was not as successful as his 'at-the-table' approach. His plan to offer military assistance to the CCP in the name of training programs was abandoned after Chiang's protests. Marshall departed for Washington in March 1946 to organise a substantial loan to the GMD, as this book discusses. Once Marshall left the negotiating table, he was unable to manage the pace of negotiations and made timely modifications against initial offers, as he had done so skilfully in the January truce.

When Marshall returned, the military situation in Manchuria had deteriorated to a point that compromised both his mediation position and ceasefire implementation mechanism. The arms embargo that Marshall imposed to curtail Chiang's military ambition can be seen as an overuse of a 'carrot-and-stick' approach in peace mediation: Chiang refused to soften his tough negotiation stance even though the embargo damaged his forces. The Americans were forced to end the embargo as it punished only their

GMD ally. This policy reversal, and Marshall's futile attempt to offer military aid to the CCP, substantiated the argument that material strength can be a powerful leverage for mediators to increase the likelihood of success, but it is not always beneficial.[3]

The American mediators' attempt to achieve peace in post-war China further demonstrates that resolving conflicts with all parties involved in a negotiation remains the most effective way to achieve positive outcomes in conflict resolution. This is perhaps the rationale behind Marshall and Stuart's motivation to rekindle the Committee of Three meeting through talking to each party separately and calling for informal tripartite meetings, even when hopes for peace were almost dashed by the continued escalation of fighting. The Americans' attempts to mediate a peaceful settlement of the Chinese Civil War failed in 1947, but their belief in achieving outcomes at the bargaining table, while acknowledging behind-the-table options, has influenced the strategies of generations of American negotiators, including Henry Kissinger and, more lately, Donald Trump.[4]

Chiang Kai-shek was a risk taker. At times, his risk-taking behaviour converged with some of his more innovative ideas on Nationalist appeasement with the Soviets over Manchuria, as this book illustrates. Chiang was well known for having a conservative leadership that included elements of nationalism, sovereignty and legality, and it was these that restricted him from taking a more robust approach to Soviet and CCP activities in northeast China. This profoundly affected the GMD's effort in the civil war, as it was incapable of winning the war by military means alone against the CCP armies' rapid force concentration and dispersal.[5]

While the nation-wide civil war raged, the situation on the Manchurian battlefield changed with amazing rapidity. The CCP continued its domination of the major shipping routes from Shandong Peninsula to the Liaodong Gulf. In mid-1946, the GMD leaders planned air strikes against the commandeered small craft ferrying CCP combatants to Manchuria. The Americans, concerned about the safety of US Navy vessels, rejected

---

3   Lindsay Reid, 'Finding a peace that lasts: Mediator leverage and the durable resolution of civil wars', *Journal of Conflict Resolution* 61, no. 7 (2017): 1408–10.
4   Eugene B. Kogan, 'Art of the power deal: The four negotiation roles of Donald J. Trump', *Negotiation Journal* 35, no. 1 (2019): 78.
5   Zheng Dongguo, 'Cong daju jingong', 576–84.

this plan.⁶ The GMD armies then tried to establish a quarantine line cutting through the southernmost tip of the Liaodong Peninsula, in order to seal off the CCP penetration by taking the considerable risk of mistargeting the Soviet garrison in the Lüshun–Dalian zone. With Soviet support, the resilient CCP fighters continued to hinder the GMD's efforts to stop them bringing in troop reinforcements.⁷ In April 1947, the CCP was capable of sending combatants from the Shandong Peninsula to debarkation ports in the Liaodong Peninsula via a huge flotilla of more than a hundred yachts.⁸ The fast-improving CCP sealift capabilities indicated that the tide of the civil war had turned in its favour. Manchuria soon became the main CCP base for the counteroffensive against the GMD.⁹

After suffering a series of humiliating defeats at the hands of the CCP, the GMD armies retreated into a few large Manchurian cities, where they were isolated and surrounded by CCP forces by the end of 1947.¹⁰ The quagmire the Nationalists faced in Manchuria came with huge financial costs. The Nationalists had to grapple with the logistic nightmare of transporting a massive amount of rice monthly from China proper to feed its armies in the north-east.¹¹ The Manchurian railway network also inflicted heavy financial losses on the GMD government. As sections of railway close to the northern border were in CCP hands, GMD–Soviet cross-border trade was virtually non-existent. Manchurian railways lost 2.5 billion CCNE per month by the end of 1946,¹² or a loss of 26 million CCNE per day, according to a source obtained by the Americans in early 1946.¹³ This is a far cry from what was intended. Given that agreements of joint ownership and operation of the Chinese Changchun Railway in the Sino-Soviet treaty had fallen apart after the Soviets withdrew, Moscow was justified in not meeting its treaty commitment to share such losses with the GMD.¹⁴ Zhang Jia'ao correctly observed, at the end of 1946, that the GMD's unsustainable

---

6   Smyth to Byrnes, 1 July 1946; 893.00/7–146; National Archives Microfilm Publication LM 69, Reel 4; DOSIAC, 1945–49; RG 59; NACP.
7   Fan Zhenchao, 'Jianchi Liaonan' [Keep up the resistance in southern Liaoning], in *Xueye xiongfeng*, Li Yunchang, 252–60.
8   Xiong's diary, 12 April 1947, *Xiong Papers*, Box 14, portfolio 2.
9   Westad, *Decisive Encounters*, 121.
10   Junshi kexueyuan junshi lishi yanjiu bu ed., *Zhongguo renmin jiefangjun*, 411–12.
11   Xiong's diary, 14 October 1946, *Xiong Papers*, Box 13, portfolio 2; Zhang Jia'ao's diary, 6 November 1946 and 24 January 1947, *Zhang Gongquan*, ed. Yao Songling, 1: 762–3, 2: 788–9.
12   Zhang Jia'ao's diary, 11 December 1946, *Zhang Gongquan*, ed. Yao Songling, 1: 773–6.
13   Josselyn to Byrnes, 26 March 1946, *FRUS*, 1946, 9: 600–1.
14   'Caojian: Zhi Sulian dashiguan jieliie' [Handwritten copy: A summary of the correspondence from the Ministry of Foreign Affair to the Soviet Embassy], 21 January 1947, *Xiong Papers*, Box 12.

military spending and economic losses in Manchuria would invariably trigger a currency downfall.[15] As is known, a sharp devaluation of currency in China in 1948 ultimately sank the nation into a total economic collapse in 1948 and 1949.[16]

While the prospect of the civil war looked grim to the GMD, its dispute with the Soviets over Dalian continued to unleash animosity. The Soviets allowed the Nationalists to send only a limited number of police to take over the city's local government.[17] The Nationalists, however, were not interested in any takeover without the presence of a strong GMD armed force. In mid-1947, the Nationalists acknowledged that it was not in their best interests to resume the exercise of sovereignty over Dalian. This was because the administrative takeover could not stop CCP forces from entering Manchuria. Besides, Dalian was no longer the perfect entry port to Manchuria for GMD troops, as some vital port equipment had already been removed by the Soviet forces.[18] In August 1947, the GMD government unilaterally declared the closure of Dalian's port to all foreign ships. Given that the GMD had no control over the area where this injunction had been introduced, the declaration was merely provocative political rhetoric that yielded little gain.[19] The Soviets rebuffed the GMD's unilateral act through an assertive communiqué in which they severely critiqued the GMD government's delay in implementing the agreement concerning Dalian.[20]

The GMD–Soviet dispute over Dalian finally faded when both sides severed diplomatic relations in 1949, after the Nationalists retreated to Taiwan in the wake of its defeat in the civil war.[21] However, resentment between the two governments lingered. In 1952, after a nearly three-year diplomatic campaign in the United Nations,[22] the GMD government

---

15 Zhang Jia'ao's diary, 11 December 1946, in *Zhang Gongquan*, ed. Yao Songling, 1: 773–6.
16 *China White Paper*, 1: 369–409.
17 *Zhonghua Minguo*, 7, book 1: 496–7, 518–19.
18 Dong Yanping and Zhang Jianfei, 'Lüda shicha tuan Dong Yanping Zhang Jianfei shicha baogao' [Report of Lüshun–Dalian fact-finding delegation by Dong Yanping and Zhang Jianfei], 17 June 1947; Chen Cheng to Wang Shijie, 24 September 1947, *Zhonghua Minguo*, 7, book 1: 521–39, 548–9.
19 Zhang Qun to Chiang Kai-shek, 15 August 1947, *Shilüe*, 70: 599–600.
20 Counsellor Fedorenjo to Wang Shijie (communiqué, Chinese translation), 22 December 1947, *Zhonghua Minguo*, 7, book 1: 554–5.
21 'Waijiaobu buzhang Ye Gongchao guanyu Zhongsu duanjue bangjiao zhi shengming' [A statement from Foreign Minister Ye Gongchao on China's severing of diplomatic relations with the Soviet Union], 3 October 1949, *Zhonghua Minguo*, 7, book 1: 848.
22 Jiang Tingfu, 'Sannian kong Su de fendou' [The three-year struggle in filing charges against the Soviet Union]; Wang Shijie and Hu Qingyu, 'Woguo xiang Lianheguo tichu kongsuan shimo' [An account of our nation's pursuing of charges against the Soviet Union in the UN], *Zhonghua Minguo*, 7, book 1: 825–44.

succeeded in pushing the United States to pass a General Assembly resolution. This concluded that the Soviet Union had 'failed to carry out' the Sino-Soviet treaty.[23] In the aftermath of the GMD's diplomatic success, Chiang Kai-shek signed off on a presidential directive abolishing the Sino-Soviet treaty.[24] The GMD-controlled Taiwanese media declared a victory for national dignity and the moral foundation of anti-imperialism,[25] making it an astonishing feat for Chiang's pro-Western regime at the height of the Korean War.

In November 1946, the United States signed the Treaty of Friendship, Commerce and Navigation with the GMD government. This treaty essentially granted the US free access to Chinese markets and opened most Chinese ports to US merchant vessels.[26] US businesses, however, struggled to enter the Manchurian market even after Soviet troop withdrawal. Historical documents show that unspecified large US companies had tried to import bristles and perilla oil from Manchuria in 1946, but no Chinese exporter accepted the orders, simply because the risk of doing business in the war zone was too high.[27]

Taking advantage of the GMD's foreign policy mishap, the CCP worked to establish economic ties with the USSR. In 1946–47, the Soviet Union was experiencing a devastating famine and urgently needed food imports.[28] CCP leaders quickly seized the opportunity by offering exports of Manchurian agricultural products to the Soviet Union. The two parties finally struck a barter deal by the end of 1946 for exports of Manchurian grains to the USSR.[29] Once started, the CCP–Soviet cross-border trade in Manchuria gathered pace quickly, as grain exports to the Soviet Union increased to 8 per cent of the total grown in CCP-ruled areas in 1947.[30] In exchange, the

---

23 United Nation General Assembly Resolution A/RES/505 (VI), 'Threats to the political independence and territorial integrity of China and to the peace of the Far East, resulting from Soviet violations of the Sino-Soviet Treaty of Friendship and Alliance of 14 August 1945 and from Soviet violations of the Charter of the United Nations', 1 February 1952, retrieved 30 May 2022; undocs.org/en/A/RES/505(VI).
24 'Zongtong mingling feizhi Zhongsu youhao tongmeng tiaoyue jiqi fujian wen' [A presidential directive for the abrogation of the Sino-Soviet treaty and the subsidiary agreements], 25 February 1953, *Zhonghua Minguo*, 7, book 1: 995–6.
25 *Zhonghua Minguo*, 7, book 1: 1000–14.
26 Westad, *Decisive Encounters*, 51.
27 'Guangfu hou Dongbei shuchuru maoyi zhi genggai' [A survey on export and import businesses in post-war Manchuria], c. 1947, *Xiong Papers*, Box 12.
28 Roberts, *Stalin's Wars*, 327–8.
29 Wang Shoudao, 'Dongbei jiefangqu renmin zhengquan de jianli ji caizheng jingji gongzuo' [The establishment of the people's regime and works on financial and economic affairs in the Northeast Liberation Area], *Liaoshen*, 2: 367–9.
30 Ibid., 367–9; Levine, *Anvil of Victory*, 178.

CONCLUSION

Soviets offered consumer goods such as salt and fabrics to the CCP; later, Lin Biao's Manchurian field forces started to obtain Soviet-made trucks (e.g. the GAZ-AA 1.5 tonne light truck). These Soviet military vehicles played a key role in making Lin's armies the most mobile CCP forces during the Chinese Civil War.[31] The close economic ties justified the favourable reports of the CCP-controlled media in Dalian about the Soviets, despite atrocities committed by the Red Army (e.g. theft and rape) against the local population.[32] From 1947/48 onwards, the Soviet Union became the largest trading partner of the CCP regime, ushering in a new era of Sino-Soviet economic relations.[33]

Despite the various setbacks, Chiang Kai-shek remained motivated. After the opening of the National Assembly in late 1946, the office of the assembly's secretariat hosted an opera to welcome delegates. This featured the maestro of Beijing Opera, Mei Lanfang. Jiang Yuntian attended the opera as one of the delegates who had defied the CCP's boycott calls. Upon arrival, he was ushered to a premium seat where he met Chiang, who was quite upbeat. Chiang felt that the passing of the constitution in the assembly he controlled would help the CCP realise its lofty socialist goal. Chiang asked: 'Well, why wouldn't they agree?' Jiang did not give Chiang any accolades. He insinuated that the Nationalist one-party rule was the barrier to democratic peace. The conversation ended with a displeased Chiang departing the opera prematurely. Jiang regretted his inability to communicate his despair about the death of peace in China more effectively to Chiang.[34] There was no immediate cure for Jiang's sadness, because he was one of the peacemakers from the minor parties who had been forced to pick a side in the civil war they had once tried desperately to avert. No one can win a peace that someone else has lost.

---

31 Wang Shoudao, 'Dongbei jiefangqu', 368–9; Yao Dezhi, 'Benchi zai zhanchang shang de qichebing' [Mechanized transportation corps in action on the battlefield], in *Xueye xiongfeng*, Li Yunchang, 566–70.
32 Tang Yunchao, 'Riben touxiang hou Su jun zai Dalian de qingkuang' [The Soviet forces in Dalian after the Japanese surrender]; Wang Shiming, 'Lüshun jiefang chuqi yu Su jun guanxi de huigu' [A review on the relationship with the Soviet forces in Lüshun at the beginning of the liberation]; Luo Peng, 'Xinsheng Shibao de shiba ge ban yue' [The eighteen and a half months of the *Xinsheng Daily*], in *Sulian Hongjun zai Lüda* [The Soviet Red Army in Lüshun-Dalian] (Internal circulation materials, 1995), 85–8, 111–16, 136–48.
33 Wang Shoudao, 'Cong zhanzheng zouxiang jianshe' [From war to economic development], in *Liaoshen Juezhan xuji*, ed. Liaoshen zhanyi jinianguan guanli weiyuanhui and Liaoshen juezhan xuji bianshen xiaozu, 451–67.
34 Jiang Yuntian, *Zhongguo jindaishi*, 151–2, citation translated from 152.

Bibliography

Archives

Chiang Kai-shek Collections, Academia Historica [Guoshiguan, AH], Taiwan:
- *Quanzong* [record group, QZ]: *Jiang Zhongzheng zongtong wenwu* [President Chiang Kai-shek cultural relic, JZZW]

Chiang Kai-shek Diaries, 1917–72, Hoover Institution Archives, Stanford University

Hsiung Shih-hui Papers, Rare Book and Manuscript Library, Columbia University

National Archives Administration, National Development Council, Taipei (NAA):
- *Quanzong* [record group, QZ]: *Guofangbu shizheng bianyiju* [Bureau of Historical Compilation and Translation, Ministry of National Defence]

National Archives of the United States, College Park, Maryland (NACP):
- Records of the US Department of State Relating to the Internal Affairs of China (DOSIAC), 1945–49; Record Group 59 (RG59); National Archives Microfilm Publication LM 69, Reels 4, 30–31
- Records of the US Joint Chiefs of Staff (JCS); Record Group 218 (RG 218)
  - 218.3 Records of the Chairman, Admiral Leahy, 1942–48
- Records of US Army Forces in the China–Burma–India Theaters of Operations (CBIT); Record Group 493 (RG 493)
  - 493.5 Records of Headquarters US Forces China Theater (CT)
  - 493.8 Records of Peiping Headquarters Group, 1946–47
- T.V. Soong Papers, Hoover Institution Archives, Stanford University
- United States Army Forces in China, *History, Peiping Executive Headquarters: Forces in China Theater, 1st–4th Quarters, January–December, 1946*. Washington, DC: National Archives of the United States, n.d.

Second Historical Archives of China [Zhongguo dier lishi dang'anguan]:
- *Binggong Shu* [Bureau of ordnance], 1928–49; *Quanzong* 774

Interview

Mr Wang Chuying, commissioner, Nanjing City Branch Committee, People's Consultative Conference, formerly head of the Operational Department, 14th Division, New 6th Army, National Army. Interviewed by Victor Cheng. Nanjing, 14 November 1996

Books, chapters and articles

Agawa, Hiroyuki. *The Reluctant Admiral: Yamamoto and the Imperial Navy*. Trans. John Bester. Tokyo: Kodansha International, 1979

Alitto, Guy. 'Chiang Kai-shek in Western historiography'. In *Proceedings of Conference on Chiang Kai-shek and Modern China*, ed. Compilation Committee of Proceedings of Conference on Chiang Kai-shek and Modern China, 1: 719–808. Taipei: China Culture Service, 1987

Almedom, Astier M. 'Re-reading the short and long-rigged history of Eritrea 1941–1952: Back to the future?' *Nordic Journal of African Studies* 15, no. 2 (2006): 103–42

Bai Xianyong and Liao Yanbo. *Beihuan lihe sishi nian: Bai Chongxi yu Jiang Jieshi* [Forty years of sorrow and joy: Bai Chongxi and Chiang Kai-shek]. Vol. 2. Taipei: Shibao chuban, 2020

Barbey, Daniel E. *MacArthur's Amphibious Navy: Seventh Amphibious Force Operations, 1943–1945*. Annapolis, MD: United States Naval Institute, 1969

Bazerman, Max H., Jared R. Curhan and Don A. Moore. 'The death and rebirth of the social psychology of negotiation'. In *Applied Social Psychology*, ed. Marilynn B. Brewer and Miles Hewstone, 268–300. Malden, MA: Blackwell Publishing, 2004. doi.org/10.1002/9780470998557.ch8

Benton, Gregor. *Mountain Fires: The Red Army's Three-Year War in South China, 1934–1938*. Berkeley, CA: University of California Press, 1992

—— *New Fourth Army: Communist Resistance along the Yangtze and the Huai, 1938–1941*. Berkeley, CA: University of California Press, 1999

Bercovitch, Jacob. 'Problems and approaches in the study of bargaining and negotiation'. *Political Science* 36, no. 2 (1984): 125–44. doi.org/10.1177/003231878403600203

Bingley, Richard. *The Security Consultant's Handbook*. Ely, Cambridgeshire: IT Governance Publishing, 2015

Blainey, Geoffrey. *The Causes of War*. New York: Free Press, 1973

Bland, Larry I., ed. *George C. Marshall's Mediation Mission to China, December 1945–January 1947*. Lexington, VA: George C. Marshall Foundation, 1998

Boikova, Elena. 'Aspects of Soviet–Mongolian relations, 1929–1939'. In *Mongolia in the Twentieth Century: Landlocked Cosmopolitan*, ed. Stephen Kotkin and Bruce A. Elleman, 107–22. Armonk, NY: M.E. Sharpe, 1999

Boorman, Howard L., ed. *Biographical Dictionary of Republican China*. Vols 1–2. New York: Columbia University Press, 1967–79

Brewer, Marilynn B. and Miles Hewstone, eds. *Applied Social Psychology*. Malden, MA: Blackwell Publishing, 2004

Chang, Jung and Jon Halliday. *Mao: The Unknown Story*. London: Jonathan Cape, 2005

Chang Yu-fa and Shen Sung-chiao, eds. *Tung Wen-ch'i xiansheng fangwen jilu* [The reminiscences of Mr Tung Wen-ch'i]. Taipei: Institute of Modern History, Academia Sinica, 1986

Chen Cheng. *Chen Cheng xiansheng riji* [The diary of Chen Cheng]. Vol. 2. Taipei: Guoshiguan, 2015

Chen Chunhua, trans. 'Sidalin yu Jiang Jieshi siren daibiao Jiang Jing'guo de huitan jilu (yi)' [Record of conversation between Stalin and Chiang Ching-kuo, the personal representative of Chiang Kai-shek, series 1], 30 December 1945; 'Sidalin yu Jiang Jieshi siren daibiao Jiang Jingguo de huitan jilu (er)' [Record of conversation between Stalin and Chiang Ching-kuo, the personal representative of Chiang Kai-shek, series 2], 3 January 1946. *Ming Pao Monthly* 32, no. 2 (1997): 47–56; no. 3 (1997): 44–51

Chen Lian. 'Jiefang zhanzheng guodu jieduan Zhonggong zhongyang lüequ Dongbei de zhanlüe fangzhen yu bushu' [The strategic principle and disposition of the Central Committee of the Communist Party of China on capturing the north-east in the transition period of the War of Liberation]. *Junshi lishi* [Military history] 2 (2002): 53–7

Chen Mingde, ed. 'Liu Yinxi he shouqiang dui' [Liu Yinxi and the handgun squad]. In *Hegang dangshi ziliao*, ed. Zhonggong Hegang shiwei dangshi gongzuo weiyuanhui, 2: 132–9. Internal circulation materials, 1986

Chen Tsun-Kung and Chang Li, eds. *Shijue xiansheng fangwen jilu* [The reminiscences of General Shih Chueh]. Taipei: Institute of Modern History, Academia Sinica, 1986

Chen Yi. 'Siping baoweizhan' [The battle of defence of Sipingjie]. In *Liaoshen juezhan*, ed. Zhonggong zhongyang dangshi ziliao zhengji weiyuanhui, Zhongguo renmin jiefangjun Liaoshen zhanyi jinianguan jianguan weiyuanhui and Liaoshen juezhan bianshen xiaozu, 1: 219–28. Beijing: Renmin chubanshe, 1988

Chen Zhiling and He Yang. *Wang Ruofei zhuan* [Biography of Wang Ruofei]. Shanghai: Shanghai renmin chubanshe, 1986

Cheng, Shiu Chiang. 'The escalation of hostilities in Manchuria, 1945–47: A study of strategic realities and normative guidelines in military conflict in the context of the Chinese Civil War'. PhD diss., University of Melbourne, 2002

Cheng, Victor Shiu Chiang. 'Imagining China's Madrid in Manchuria: The communist military strategy at the onset of the Chinese Civil War, 1945–1946'. *Modern China* 31, no. 1 (2005): 72–114. doi.org/10.1177/0097700404270549

—— 'Modern military technology in counterinsurgency warfare: The experience of the Nationalist Army during the Chinese Civil War'. *Working Paper in Contemporary Asian Studies* 20 (2007): 1–15. Centre for East and South-East Asian Studies, Lund University

—— 'Modern war on an ancient battlefield: The diffusion of American military technology and ideas in the Chinese Civil War, 1946–1949'. *Modern China* 35, no. 1 (2009): 38–64. doi.org/10.1177/0097700408318909

—— 'Rethinking the Chongqing negotiations of 1945: Concession-making, the trust/distrust paradox, and the biased mediator in China's post-war transitions'. *Journal of Chinese Military History* 9 (2020): 168–203. doi.org/10.1163/22127453-bja10004

Chiang Ching-kuo. 'Wo zai Sulian de shenghuo' [My life in the Soviet Union]. In *Jiang Jingguo xiansheng quanji*, ed. Jiang Jingguo xiansheng quanji banji weiyuanhui, 1: 1–90. Taipei: Government Information Office, 1991

Chiang Kai-shek. *Soviet Russia in China: A Summing-up at Seventy*. London: George G. Harrap, 1957

Chongqing Shi zhengxie wenshi ziliao yanjiu weiyuanhui [Literary–Historical Source Materials Research Committee of the PCC Chongqing City Branch] and Zhonggong Chongqing shiwei dangxiao [Chongqing Party School of the CCP], ed. *Zhengzhi xieshang huiyi jishi* [True history of the PCC]. Vol. 1. Chongqing: Chongqing chubanshe, 1989

Clubb, O. Edmund. *Twentieth-Century China*. 2nd edn. New York: Columbia University Press, 1972

Cohen, Raymond. *Negotiating across Cultures: International Communication in an Interdependent World*. Rev. edn. Washington, DC: United States Institute of Peace Press, 1997

Compilation Committee of Proceedings of Conference on Chiang Kai-shek and Modern China, ed. *Proceedings of Conference on Chiang Kai-shek and Modern China*. Taipei: China Culture Service, 1987

Cook, James A. 'Penetration and neocolonialism: The Shen Chong rape case and the anti-American student movement of 1946–47'. *Republican China* 22, no. 1 (1996): 65–97. doi.org/10.1179/repc.1996.22.1.65

Corbetta, Renato, and Molly M. Melin. 'Exploring the threshold between conflict management and joining in biased interventions'. *Journal of Conflict Resolution* 62, no. 10 (2018): 2205–31. doi.org/10.1177/0022002717720754

Cowley, Robert, ed. *What If? The World's Foremost Military Historians Imagine What Might Have Been*. London: Macmillan, 2000

Cunningham, David E. *Barriers to Peace in Civil War*. Cambridge: Cambridge University Press, 2011

Deane, John R. *The Strange Alliance: The Story of American Efforts at Wartime Co-operation with Russia*. London: John Murray, 1947

Deng Ye. 'A new exploration into the background and basic themes of the Chongqing negotiations'. *Social Sciences in China* 2 (2006): 115–27

—— 'Dongbei wenti yu Siping juezhan' [The question of north-east China and the decisive battle at Sipingjie]. *Lishi yanjiu* [History Studies] 4 (2001): 57–71

—— *Lianhe zhengfu yu yi dang xunzheng: 1944–1946 nian jian Guogong zhengzheng* [Coalition government and one-party political tutelage: The GMD–CCP political struggle 1944–46]. Beijing: Shehui kexue wenxian chubanshe, 2003

—— 'Lun Guogong Chongqing tanpan de zhengzhi xingzhi' [On the political nature of the Chongqing negotiations between the GMD and the CCP]. *Jindaishi yanjiu* [Modern Chinese history studies] 1 (2005): 30–64

Deutsch, Morton. 'Justice and conflict'. In *The Handbook of Conflict Resolution*, ed. Morton Deutsch, Peter T. Coleman and Eric C. Marcus, 43–68. San Francisco, CA: Jossey-Bass, 2006

—— Peter T. Coleman and Eric C. Marcus, eds. *The Handbook of Conflict Resolution: Theory and Practice*. 2nd edn. San Francisco, CA: Jossey-Bass, 2006

Dier jie jindai Zhongguo yu shijie guoji xueshu yantao hui [The second international symposium on modern China and the world], ed. *Dier jie jindai Zhongguo yu shijie guoji xueshu yantao hui lunwen ji* [Proceedings of the second international symposium on modern China and the world]. Beijing: Zhongguo shixue hui, 2000

Ding Xiaochun, Ge Fulu and Wang Shiying, eds. *Dongbei jiefang zhanzhen dashiji* [The chronology of the Manchurian Liberation War]. Beijing: Zhonggong dangshi ziliao chubanshe, 1987

Dong Biwu nianpu bianji zu [Editorial group of the chronological biography of Dong Biwu], ed. *Dong Biwu nianpu* [The chronological biography of Dong Biwu]. Beijing: Zhongyang wenxian chubanshe, 1991

Dong Xin and Mao Shuai. 'Dongbei jiu sheng liutongquan pingshu' [Observations on the Circulating Currency of the nine provinces of the North-east]. *Zhongguo qianbi* [Chinese coinage] 1 (2018): 44–56. doi.org/10.13850/j.cnki.chinum.2018.01.007

Dong Yanping. *Su e ju dongbei* [Soviet Russia's invasion of north-east China]. Taipei: Chinese Library, 1965

—— 'A report of the military mission of the Republic of China on the negotiations with the Soviet military authorities for the withdrawal of Soviet troops from the North-Eastern Provinces'. c. 1946. In *Hsiung Shih-hui Papers*, Box 3. Rare Book and Manuscript Library, Columbia University

Dong Zhanlin. 'Gongda Shanhaiguan qianhou' [The battle of Shanhaiguan and its aftermath]. In *Shanhaiguan zhi zhan*, ed. Yuan Wei, 73–84. Beijing: Junshi kexue chubanshe, 1989

Dongbei wuzi tiaojie weiyuanhui yanjiu zu [The study group of the North-east Goods and Materials Regulated Committee], ed. *Dongbei jingji xiao congshu: Meitan* [A concise compendium on the economy of the north-east: Coal industry]. Vol. 8. Shenyang: Dongbei wuzi tiaojie weiyuanhui, 1948

Dongfang jingji yanjiusuo [Eastern Institute of Economic Research], ed. *Dongbei jingji congshu* [The north-eastern economy series]. Vol. 3. (Shanghai: Dongfang shudian, 1946)

Druckman, Daniel. 'Turning points in international negotiation: A comparative analysis'. *Journal of Conflict Resolution* 45, no. 4 (2001): 519–44. doi.org/10.1177/0022002701045004006

Du Tao. 'Huiyi dang diyi ren shizhang de qingkuang' [As the first mayor for the city of Hegang: My recollections]. In *Hegang dangshi ziliao*, ed. Zhonggong Hegang shiwei dangshi gongzuo weiyuanhui, 2: 53–5. Internal circulation materials, 1986

Du Yuming. 'Guomindang pohuai heping jingong Dongbei shimo' [An account of the Nationalists' peace agreement violations and the offensive into the north-east]. In *Liaoshen zhanyi qinliji: Yuan Guomindang jiangling de huiyi*, ed. Zhongguo renmin zhengzhi xieshang huiyi quanguo weiyuanhui wenshi ziliao yanjiu weiyuanhui Liaoshen zhanyi qinliji shenbianzu, 514–64. Beijing: Zhongguo wenshi chubanshe, 1985

—— 'Liaoshen zhanyi gaishu' [An overview of the Liaoshen campaign]. In *Liaoshen zhanyi qinliji: Yuan Guomindang jiangling de huiyi*, ed. Zhongguo renmin zhengzhi xieshang huiyi quanguo weiyuanhui wenshi ziliao yanjiu weiyuanhui Liaoshen zhanyi qinliji shenbianzu, 1–46. Beijing: Zhongguo wenshi chubanshe, 1985

Eastman, Lloyd E. 'China's democratic parties and the temptations of political power, 1946–1947'. In *Roads Not Taken: The Struggle of Opposition Parties in Twentieth-Century China*, ed. Roger B. Jeans, 189–99. Boulder, CO: Westview Press, 1992

Fairbank, John K. and Albert Feuerwerker, eds. *The Cambridge History of China*. Vol. 13, pt 2. Cambridge: Cambridge University Press, 1986

Fan Zhenchao. 'Jianchi Liaonan' [Keep up the resistance in southern Liaoning]. In *Xueye xiongfeng: liu zai Dongbei zhanchang de jiyi*, Li Yunchang, 252–60. Shenyang: Baishan chubanshe, 1988

Fang Qiang, Wu Liangping, Liu Ying and Chen Bocun. 'Hejiang renmin de juexing: Yi Hejiang Sheng tugai yundong he genjudi jianshe' [Mass awakening in Hejiang: Remembering the land reform movement and the establishment of base areas]. In *Liaoshen juezhan*, ed. Zhonggong zhongyang dangshi ziliao zhengji weiyuanhui, Zhongguo renmin jiefangjun Liaoshen zhanyi jinianguan jianguan weiyuanhui and Liaoshen juezhan bianshen xiaozu, 2: 50–67. Beijing: Renmin chubanshe, 1988

Fang Zhongfu. 'Huiyi sanren xiaozu zai Shandong de huodong qingkuang' [A recollection of the field team in Shandong]. In *Shandong dangshi ziliao*, ed. Zhonggong Shandong shengwei dangshi ziliao zengji weiyuanhui, 4: 58–77. Jinan: Zhonggong Shandong shengwei dangshi ziliao zengji weiyuanhui, 1985

Fidlon, David, trans. *Soviet Volunteers in China, 1925–1945: Articles and Reminiscences* Moscow: Progress Publishers, 1980

Fisher, Roger. 'Fractionating conflict'. *Daedalus* 93, no. 3 (1964): 920–41

——, William Ury and Bruce Patton. *Getting to Yes: Negotiating an Agreement without Giving In*. 2nd edn. London: Random House, 1999

———, William Ury and Bert Spector. 'An interview with Roger Fisher and William Ury'. *Academy of Management Executive* 18, no. 3 (2004): 101–8. doi.org/10.5465/ame.2004.14776177

Fisher-Yoshida, Beth and Hene Wasserman. 'Moral conflict and engaging alternative perspectives'. In *The Handbook of Conflict Resolution*, ed. Morton Deutsch, Peter T. Coleman and Eric C. Marcus, 560–81. San Francisco, CA: Jossey-Bass, 2006

Follett, Mary Parker. 'Constructive conflict'. In *Dynamic Administration: The Collected Papers of Mary Parker Follett*, ed. Henry C. Metcalf and L. Urwick, 30–49. Bath: Management Publications Trust, 1941

Freedman, Lawrence D. 'Calling the shots: Should politicians or generals run our wars?' *Foreign Affairs* 81, no. 5 (2002): 188–94. doi.org/10.2307/20033277

Fussell, Paul. *The Great War and Modern Memory*. Oxford: Oxford University Press, 1975

Garver, John W. *Chinese–Soviet Relations, 1937–1945: The Diplomacy of Chinese Nationalism*. New York: Oxford University Press, 1988

Geng Biao. *Geng Biao huiyilu* [The memoirs of Geng Biao]. Beijing: Jiefangjun chubanshe, 1991

Geng Routian. *Zhonggou jiaofei kanluan zhanshi yanjiu* [A study of the history of bandit suppression in Republican China]. Vols 2–3. Taipei: Lujun zongsilingbu, Guofangbu zuozhan canmou cizhang shi, 1981

Gibson, Kevin, Leigh Thompson and Max H. Bazerman. 'Shortcomings of neutrality in mediation: Solutions based on rationality'. *Negotiation Journal* 12, no. 1 (1996): 69–80. doi.org/10.1111/j.1571-9979.1996.tb00079.x

Gillin, Donald G., and Ramon H. Myers. 'Introduction'. In *Last Chance in Manchuria: The Diary of Cheung Kia-ngau*, Zhang Jia'ao, ed. Donald Gillin and Ramon Myers, 1–58. Stanford, CA: Hoover Institution Press, 1989

Girard, Joe. *How to Close Every Sale*. New York: Warner Books, 1989

Graham, John L., Lynda Lawrence and William Hernández Requejo. *Inventive Negotiation: Getting Beyond Yes*. New York: Palgrave Macmillan, 2014

Gray, Colin S. *Defining and Achieving Decisive Victory*. Carlisle, PA: Strategic Studies Institute, US Army War College, 2002

Guo Dequan. 'Zhongsu youhao tongmeng tiaoyue qianding jingguo' [An account of the signing of the Sino-Soviet treaty]. *Zhuanji wenxue* [Biographical literature] (Taipei) 35, no. 2 (1979): 30–2

Guo Tingyi (Kuo Ting-yee). *Zhonghua Minguo shishi rizhi* [A chronological history of Republic of China]. Vol. 4. Taipei: Academia Sinica, 1984–85

——— Chia Ting-Shih, Ma Tien-kang, Chen San-Ching and Chen Tsun-Kung, eds. *Bai Chongxi xiansheng fangwen jilu* [The reminiscences of General Pai Chung-Hsi]. Vols 1–2. Taipei: Institute of Modern History, Academia Sinica, 1984

Guofangbu shizhengju [Bureau of historical compilation and translation, Ministry of Defense], ed. *Kanluan zhanshi* [A history of rebellion suppression]. Vols 2, 4, 6, 7, 9. Taipei: Guofangbu shizhengju, 1975–84

——— ed. *Suijing diyi nian zhongyao zhanyi tiyao* [A summary of major operations in the first year of the War of Pacification]. N.p.: Guofangbu shizhengju, 1948

Guomin zhengfu zhuxi Dongbei Xingyuan gongzuo baogao [The Nationalist government chairman's report: The North-east Headquarters]. N.p.: March 1947

Harbutt, Fraser J. *Yalta 1945: Europe and America at the Crossroads*. New York: Cambridge University Press, 2010

Heinzig, Dieter. *Soviet Union and Communist China, 1945–1950: The Arduous Road to the Alliance*. Armonk, NY: M.E. Sharpe, 2004

Hendon, Donald W., Matthew H. Roy and Zafar U. Ahmed. 'Negotiation concession patterns: A multi-country, multiperiod study'. *American Business Review* 21, no. 1 (2003): 75–83

Hobsbawm, E.J. *The Age of Extremes: The Short Twentieth Century, 1914–1991*. London: Michael Joseph, 1994

Holloway, David. *Stalin and the Bomb: The Soviet Union and Atomic Energy 1939–1956*. New Haven, CT: Yale University Press, 1994

Hooton, E.R. *The Greatest Tumult: The Chinese Civil War, 1936–49*. London: Brassey's, 1991

Hsiung, James C., and Steven I. Levine, eds. *China's Bitter Victory: The War with Japan, 1937–1945*. Armonk, NY: M.E. Sharpe, 1992

Hsü, Immanuel C.Y. *The Rise of Modern China*. 4th edn. Oxford: Oxford University Press, 1990

Hsüeh, Chün-tu, ed. *Dimensions of China's Foreign Relations*. New York: Praeger Publishers, 1977

Hu Mei and Ren Donglai. '1946–1947 nian meiguo dui hua junhuo jinyun de jige wenti' [Issues about American embargo of arms and ammunition against China between 1946 and 1947]. *Meiguo yanjiu jikan* [American Studies Quarterly] 3 (2007): 85–102

Hu Qiaomu. *Hu Qiaomu huiyi Mao Zedong* [Hu Qiaomu remembers Mao Zedong]. Rev. and enl. edn. Beijing: Renmin chubanshe, 2003

Hu Zhefeng. 'Shilun Siping baoweizhan zhong de Mao Zedong yu Lin Biao' [Mao Zedong and Lin Biao in the battle of defence of Sipingjie: An elaboration]. *Junshi lishi yanjiu* [Military history studies] 4 (1996): 1–12

Huang, Grace C. 'Creating a public face for posterity: The making of Chiang Kai-shek's Shilüe manuscripts'. *Modern China* 36, no. 6 (2010): 617–43. doi.org/10.1177/0097700410375405

Huang Kecheng. *Huang Kecheng huiyilu* [The memoirs of Huang Kecheng]. Vol. 1. Beijing: Jiefangjun chubanshe, 1989

Huang Yanpei. *Huang Yanpei riji* [The diary of Huang Yanpei]. Vol. 9. Beijing: Huawen chubanshe, 2008

Ihara, Takushu, ed. *Zhanhou Dongbei jieshou jiaoshe jishi—yi Zhang Jia'ao riji wei zhongxin* [True story of the post-war negotiation for the takeover of Manchuria: From the perspective of Zhang Jia'ao diary]. Beijing: Zhongguo renmin daxue chubanshe, 2011

Jeans, Roger B. 'Last chance for peace: Zhang Junmai (Carsun Chang) and third-party mediation in the Chinese Civil War, October 1946'. In *George C. Marshall's Mediation Mission to China, December 1945–January 1947*, ed. Larry I. Bland, 293–325. Lexington, VA: George C. Marshall Foundation, 1998

—— ed. *Roads Not Taken: The Struggle of Opposition Parties in Twentieth-Century China*. Boulder, CO: Westview Press, 1992

—— ed. *The Marshall Mission to China, 1945–1947: The Letters and Diary of Colonel John Hart Caughey*. Lanham, MD: Rowman & Littlefield, 2011

Jervis, Robert. *The Meaning of the Nuclear Revolution: Statecraft and the Prospect of Armageddon*. Ithaca, NY: Cornell University Press, 1989

Jiang Jingguo xiansheng quanji banji weiyuanhui [Editorial Group of the Collected Works of Jiang Jingguo], ed. *Jiang Jingguo xiansheng quanji* [The collected works of Chiang Ching-kuo]. Vols 1 & 15. Taipei: Government Information Office, 1991

Jiang Yongjing. 'Cong Wang Shijie riji kan Zhongsu mengyue de qianding' [The Sino-Soviet treaty in perspective: The diaries of Wang Shijie]. *Zhuanji wenxue* (Taipei) 56, no. 6 (1990): 29–36

—— and Liu Weikai, 'Yi zhu shi quanpan bai: Zhanhou Jiang Jieshi chuli Dongbei wenti de yipan daiqi' [One bad move is all it takes to lose a chess game: A chess blunder in Jiang Jieshi's handling of the Manchurian problem during the post-war period]. *Zhuanji wenxue* (Taipei) 97, no. 3 (2010): 25–38

Jiang Yuntian. *Zhongguo jindaishi zhuanliedian* [The turning point of modern Chinese history]. Hong Kong: Youlian chubanshe, 1976

Jiang Zhongzheng zongtong dang'an: Shilüe gaoben [The Chiang Kai-shek collections: The chronological events]. Vols 36, 62–67, 70. Taipei: Academia Historica, 2003–12

Jin Cha Ji ribao ziliao ke [The documentation section of the Shanxi–Chahar–Hebei Border Region Daily], ed. *Junshi tiaochu zhixing qingkuang huibian* [Executive Headquarters information publication]. N.p.: c. 1946

Jin Dejun. 'Jieshou Anshan Zhaohe zhigangsuo de huiyi' [Remembering the takeover of the Shōwa Steel Works], ed. Jiang Yanshi. In *Anshan wenshi ziliao xuanji*, ed. Zhongguo renmin zhengzhi xieshang huiyi Anshan Shi weiyuanhui wenshi ziliao yanjiu weiyuanhui, 1: 140–9. Internal circulation materials, 1986

Junshi kexueyuan junshi lishi yanjiu bu [Military history research department of the Military Science Academy of the PLA], ed. *Zhongguo renmin jiefangjun liushi nian dashi ji, 1927–1987* [Major events in the PLA's 60 years, 1927–87]. Beijing: Junshi kexue chubanshe, 1988

Kahn, Herman. *Thinking about the Unthinkable*. New York: Avon Books, 1968

Kan, Francis Yi-hua. 'The irreconcilable Chinese rival regimes and the weakening of the policies of neutrality of the great powers'. *Civil Wars* 3, no. 4 (2000): 85–104. doi.org/10.1080/13698240008402456

Keller, Jonathan W., and Yi Edward Yang. 'Leadership style, decision context, and the poliheuristic theory of decision making'. *Journal of Conflict Resolution* 52, no. 5 (2008): 687–712. doi.org/10.1177/0022002708320889

Kennedy-Pipe, Caroline, and Clive Jones. 'An introduction to civil wars'. *Civil Wars* 1, no. 1 (1998): 1–15. doi.org/10.1080/13698249808402364

Kissinger, Henry. *White House Years*. Boston, MA: Little Brown, 1979

Kogan, Eugene B. 'Art of the power deal: The four negotiation roles of Donald J. Trump'. *Negotiation Journal* 35, no. 1 (2019): 63–83. doi.org/10.1111/nejo.12265

Kotkin, Stephen, and Bruce A. Elleman, eds. *Mongolia in the Twentieth Century: Landlocked Cosmopolitan*. Armonk, NY: M.E. Sharpe, 1999

Kriesberg, Louis. 'De-escalating gestures'. September 2003. *Beyond Intractability*, ed. Guy Burgess and Heidi Burgess. Conflict Research Consortium, University of Colorado. Retrieved 28 May 2022. www.beyondintractability.org/essay/disarming_behavior

Kritek, Phyllis Beck. *Negotiating at an Uneven Table: Developing Moral Courage in Resolving Our Conflicts*. San Francisco, CA: Jossey-Bass, 1994

Kuniholm, Bruce Robellet. *The Origins of the Cold War in the Near East: Great Power Conflict and Diplomacy in Iran, Turkey, and Greece*. Princeton, NJ: Princeton University Press, 1980

Kurbalija, Jovan, and Hannah Slavik, eds. *Language and Diplomacy*. Msida: DiploProjects, 2001

Kurtz-Phelan, Daniel. *The China Mission: George Marshall's Unfinished War, 1945–1947*. New York: W.W. Norton, 2018

Kydd, Andrew. 'Which side are you on? Bias, credibility, and mediation'. *American Journal of Political Science* 47, no. 2 (2003): 597–611. doi.org/10.1111/1540-5907.00042

Lai, Sherman Xiaogang. *A Springboard to Victory: Shandong Province and Chinese Communist Military and Financial Strength, 1937–1945*. Leiden: Brill, 2011

Lary, Diana. *China's Civil War: A Social History, 1945–1949*. Cambridge: Cambridge University Press, 2015

Lee, Chong-sik. *Revolutionary Struggle in Manchuria: Chinese Communism and Soviet Interest, 1922–1945*. Berkeley, CA: University of California Press, 1983

Levine, Steven I. *Anvil of Victory: The Communist Revolution in Manchuria, 1945–1948*. New York: Columbia University Press, 1987

—— 'Soviet–American rivalry in Manchuria and the Cold War'. In *Dimensions of China's Foreign Relations*, ed. Chün-tu Hsüeh, 10–43. New York: Praeger Publishers, 1977

Levinson, Jay Conrad, Mark S.A. Smith and Orvel Ray Wilson. *Guerrilla Negotiating: Unconventional Weapons and Tactics to Get What You Want*. New York: John Wiley & Sons, 1999

Levy, Jack S. 'Loss aversion, framing and bargaining: The implications of prospect theory for international conflict'. *International Political Science Review* 17, no. 2 (1996): 179–95. doi.org/10.1177/019251296017002004

Lew, Christopher R. *The Third Chinese Revolutionary Civil War, 1945–49: An Analysis of Communist Strategy and Leadership*. New York: Routledge, 2009

Lewicki, Roy J., Bruce Barry and David M. Saunders. *Negotiation*. 6th edn. New York: McGraw-Hill, 2010

Li Bingling. 'Hengdu Bohai, jinjun Liaodong' [Cross the Bohai Sea and march towards Liaodong]. In *Xueye xiongfeng: liu zai Dongbei zhanchang de jiyi*, Li Yunchang, 41–5. Shenyang: Baishan chubanshe, 1988

Li Daren. *Dongbei kanluan huiyi* [Remembering the war of bandit suppression in the north-east]. Taipei: Boxue chubanshe, 1979

Li Disheng. *Guomindang xiaji junguan de riji: Cong Jiangnan dao Dongbei 1946–1948* [Diaries of the GMD's junior officers: From the south of the lower reaches of the Yangtze River to Manchuria 1946–1948]. Beijing: Huawen chubanshe, 2012

Li Jiexin. 'Guomindang xianbing silingbu pai zhu Guiyuan jingwei ban de huiyi' [My recollections as a member of the security squad of the GMD military police command at the Cinnamon Garden]. In *Chongqing wenshi ziliao xuanji*, ed. Zhongguo renmin zhengzhi xieshang huiyi Sichuan Sheng Chongqing Shi weiyuanhui wenshi ziliao yanjiu weiyuanhui, 1: 83–99. Chongqing: n.p., 1987

Li Jukui. 'Zai Beiping juntiao bu' [My days in the Executive Headquarters in Beiping]. In *Dangshi ziliao zhengji tongxun*, ed. Zhonggong zhongyang dangshi ziliao zhengji weiyuanhui, 6 (1985): 26–31. Beijing: Zhonggong dangshi chubanshe, 1985

Li Moan. *Shiji zhi lü: Li Moan huiyilu* [A walk through the twentieth century: The memoirs of Li Moan]. Beijing: Zhongguo wenshi chubanshe, 1995

Li Weihan. 'Renmin wu quan, dufu jiquan—wei xianfa de jia mianmu' [The people are powerless, but the dictators maintain their grip on power: The false front of the bogus constitution]. *Qunzhong* [People] 14, no. 3 (1947): 10–14

Li Xiannian. 'Yao zhengque pingjia zhongyuan tuwei' [Properly evaluate the Central Plain breakout]. In *Zhongyuan tuwei qianhou*, ed. Zhonggong Henan shengwei dangshi gongzuo weiyuanhui, 19–22. Zhengzhou: Henan renmin chubanshe, 1988

Li Xiannian zhuan bianxie zu [Editorial group of the Biography of Li Xiannian] and Er-Yu bianqu geming shi bianji bu [Editorial group of the revolution history of the Hubei–Henan border region], eds. *Li Xiannian nianpu* [The chronological biography of Li Xiannian]. Vol. 1. Beijing: Zhongyang wenxian chubanshe, 2011

Li Yong and Zhang Zhongtian eds. *Jiefang zhanzhen shiqi tongyi zhanxian dashiji* [A chronology of the united front in the period of the Liberation War]. Beijing: Zhongguo jinji chubanshe, 1988

Li Yunchang. *Xueye xiongfeng: liu zai Dongbei zhanchang de jiyi* [Heroic warriors in the snowy field: The north-east battlefield in our memory]. Shenyang: Baishan chubanshe, 1988

Li, Yuzhen. 'Chiang Kai-shek and Joseph Stalin during World War II'. In *Negotiating China's Destiny in World War II*, ed. Hans Van de Ven, Diana Lary and Stephen MacKinnon, 141–55. Stanford, CA: Stanford University Press, 2015. doi.org/10.11126/stanford/9780804789660.003.0009

Li Zhengguan and Chen Tongshen. 'Sui shangbing yuan lieche beishang tuwei' [Breakout to the north in the train with the ill and injured personnel]. In *Zhongyuan tuwei qianhou*, ed. Zhonggong Henan shengwei dangshi gongzuo weiyuanhui, 252–8. Zhengzhou: Henan renmin chubanshe, 1988

Li Zhisui. *The Private Life of Chairman Mao: The Memoirs of Mao's Personal Physician*, trans. Hung-chao Tai. London: Random House, 1994

Liang Jingchun. *Maxie'er shihua baogao shu jianzhu* [Marshall's mission to China: A commentary on the report]. Taipei: Institute of Modern History, Academia Sinica, 1994

Liang Shuming. 'Canjia jiu Zhengxie de jingguo' [An account of my work in the old PCC]. In *Zhengzhi xieshang huiyi jishi*, ed. Chongqing Shi zhengxie wenshi ziliao yanjiu weiyuanhui and Zhonggong Chongqing shiwei dangxiao 1: 728–39. Chongqing: Chongqing chubanshe, 1989

—— *Liang Shuming quanji* [Collected works of Liang Shuming]. Vol. 6. Jinan: Shandong renmin chubanshe, 2005

—— 'Tan guofu weiyuan ming'e fenpei wenti' [On the distribution of seats in the State Council]. In *Liang Shuming quanji*, Liang Shuming, 6: 686–89. Jinan: Shandong renmin chubanshe, 2005

—— 'Wo canjia Guogong hetan de jingguo' [An account of my participation of the GMD-CCP peace talks]. In *Liang Shuming quanji*, Liang Shuming, 6: 906–62. Jinan: Shandong renmin chubanshe, 2005

—— and Zhou Xinmin. 'Li Wen an diaocha baogao shu' [An investigation report on the Li–Wen assassinations]. In *Liang Shuming quanji*, Liang Shuming, 6: 656–85. Jinan: Shandong renmin chubanshe, 2005

Liao Yaoxiang. 'Jiangjun xin liu jun yuhui Sipingjie de jingguo' [An account of the flanking maneuver of Chiang Kai-shek's New Sixth Army toward Sipingjie]. In *Wenshi ziliao xuanji*, ed. Zhongguo renmin zhengzhi xieshang huiyi quanguo weiyuanhui wenshi ziliao yanjiu weiyuanhui, 42 (1980): 61–82. Beijing: wenshi ziliao chubanshe, 1980

—— and Du Jianshi. 'Guanyu Meijiang goujie de neimu' [A behind-the-scenes report of the Americans' collaboration with Chiang Kai-shek]. In *Wenshi ziliao jingxuan*, ed. Wenshi ziliao xuanji bianji bu, 12: 1–64. Beijing: Zhongguo wenshi ziliao chubanshe, 1990

Liaoshen zhanyi jinianguan guanli weiyuanhui [The Committee Board of the Museum of Liaoshen Campaign] and Liaoshen juezhan xuji bianshen xiaozu [The editorial group of 'Liaoshen Campaign, a supplementary volume'], eds. *Liaoshen juezhan xuji* [The Liaoshen Campaign, a supplementary volume]. Beijing: Renmin chubanshe, 1992

Liddell Hart, B.H. *Strategy*. 2nd rev. edn. London: Signet, 1974

Ling Shaonong. 'Yi Xinzhan, Lafa zhandou' [Remembering the battle of Xinzhan and Lafa]. In *Xueye xiongfeng: liu zai Dongbei zhanchang de jiyi*, Li Yunchang, 122–7. Shenyang: Baishan chubanshe, 1988

Liu Gangfu. 'Huiyi wo he Gao Jingting tanpan dacheng xieyi de jingguo' [An account of my experiences in negotiating and reaching an agreement with Gao Jingting]. In *Anhui Wenshi ziliao*, ed. Zhengxie Anhui Sheng weiyuanhui wenshi ziliao yanjiu weiyuanhui and Anhui Sheng shehui kexueyuan lishi yanjiusuo, 25: 17–30. Hefei: Anhui renmin chubanshe, 1986

Liu Shufa, ed. *Chen Yi nianpu* [Chronological biography of Chen Yi]. Vol. 1. Beijing: Renmin chubanshe, 1995

Lü Fangshang, ed. *Jiang Zhongzheng riji yu minguo shi yanjiu* [Chiang Kai-shek diary and the study of Republican Chinese history]. Taipei: Shijie datong, 2011

Lü Guangguang. 'Mao zhuxi tong Zhang Lan de huimian' [Chairman Mao's meetings with Zhang Lan]. In *Chongqing tanpan jishi*, ed. Zhonggong Chongqing shiwei dangshi gongzuo weiyuanhui, Chongqing Shi zhengxie wenshi ziliao yanjiu weiyuanhui and Hongyan geming jinian guan, 438–45. Chongqing: Chongqing chubanshe, 1984

Lü Zhengcao. *Lü Zhengcao huiyilu* [The memoirs of Lü Zhengcao]. Beijing: Jiefangjun chubanshe, 1988

Luo Longji. 'Canjia jiu Zhengxie de yixie huiyi' [Some of my recollections of the old PCC]. In *Zhengzhi xieshang huiyi jishi*, ed. Chongqing Shi Zhengxie wenshi ziliao yanjiu weiyuanhui and Zhonggong Chongqing shiwei dangxiao, 1: 704–27. Chongqing: Chongqing chubanshe, 1989

Luo Peng. 'Xinsheng Shibao de shiba ge ban yue' [The eighteen and a half months of the *Xinsheng Daily*]. In *Sulian Hongjun zai Lüda*, 136–48. Internal circulation materials, 1995

Luo Shiquan. 'Huiyi zai Hegang gongzuo de rizi li' [Remembering my days at Hegang]. In *Hegang dangshi ziliao*, ed. Zhonggong Hegang shiwei dangshi gongzuo weiyuanhui, 2: 62–5. Internal circulation materials, 1986

Lyudnikov, I.I. 'Internationalist assistance'. In *Soviet Volunteers in China, 1925–1945: Articles and Reminiscences*, trans. David Fidlon, 305–12. Moscow: Progress Publishers, 1980

Mackenzie, Dewitt. 'Chinese civil war is seen as world threat'. *Kentucky New Era*, 19 July 1946. Hopkinsville, KY: n.p.

Mao Zedong. 'Build stable base areas in the north-east'. 28 December 1945. In *Selected Works of Mao Tse-Tung*, Mao Zedong, 4: 81–3. Beijing: Foreign Languages Press, 1961–65

—— 'Concentrate a superior force to destroy the enemy forces one by one'. 16 September 1946. In *Selected Works of Mao Tse-Tung*, Mao Zedong, 4: 103–7. Beijing: Foreign Languages Press, 1961–65

—— 'Fu Chongqing tanpan qian zai Zhengzhiju huiyi shang de jianghua' [Speech delivered at the Politburo meeting before departing for Chongqing], 26 August 1945. In *Mao Zedong wenji*, ed. Zhonggong zhongyang wenxian yanjiushi, 4: 15–17. Beijing: Renmin chubanshe, 1993–99

—— 'On peace negotiations with the Kuomintang—Circular of the Central Committee of the Communist Party of China'. 26 August 1945. In *Selected Works of Mao Tse-Tung*, Mao Zedong, 4: 47–51. Beijing: Foreign Languages Press, 1961–65

—— 'On the Chungking negotiations'. 17 October 1945. In *Selected Works of Mao Tse-Tung*, Mao Zedong, 4: 53–63. Beijing: Foreign Languages Press, 1961–65

—— *Selected Works of Mao Tse-Tung*. Vol. 4. Beijing: Foreign Languages Press, 1961–65

—— 'Situation and our policy after victory over Japan'. 13 August 1945. In *Selected Works of Mao Tse-Tung*, Mao Zedong, 4: 11–26. Beijing: Foreign Languages Press, 1961–65

—— 'Smash Chiang Kai-Shek's offensive by a war of self-defence'. 20 July 1946. In *Selected Works of Mao Tse-Tung*, Mao Zedong, 4: 89–95. Beijing: Foreign Languages Press, 1961–65

—— 'Talk with the American correspondent Anna Louise Strong'. August 1946. In *Selected Works of Mao Tse-Tung*, Mao Zedong, 4: 97–101. Beijing: Foreign Languages Press, 1961–65

—— 'Wei Meiguo junshi yuanhua fa'an de shengming' [Statement opposing US military aid to China bill]. 22 June 1946. In *Tingzhan tanpan ziliao*, 318–19. Chengdu: Sichuan renmin chubanshe, 1981

Marolda, Edward J. 'Through a long glass: US naval leaders and the Chinese Civil War, 1945–1950'. *Journal of Strategic Studies* (UK) 15, no. 4 (1992): 528–47. doi.org/10.1080/01402399208437497

Marshall, George C. *Marshall's Mission to China, December 1945–January 1947: The Report and Appended Documents*. Vols 1–2. Arlington, VA: University Publications of America, 1976

Mburu, Nene. 'Patriots or bandits? Britain's strategy for policing Eritrea 1941–1952'. *Nordic Journal of African Studies* 9, no. 2 (2000): 85–104

Melby, John F. *The Mandate of Heaven: Record of Civil War, China 1945–49*. New York: Anchor Books, 1971

Metcalf, Henry C., and L. Urwick, eds. *Dynamic Administration: The Collected Papers of Mary Parker Follett*. Bath: Management Publications Trust, 1941

Ming Pao Monthly. 1997. Hong Kong

Miscamble, Wilson D. *From Roosevelt to Truman: Potsdam, Hiroshima, and the Cold War*. Cambridge, NY: Cambridge University Press, 2007

Moore, Christopher W. *The Mediation Process: Practical Strategies for Resolving Conflict*. 2nd edn. San Francisco: Jossey-Bass, 1996

Murdock, Michael G. 'Exploiting anti-imperialism: Popular forces and nation-state-building during China's Northern Expedition, 1926–1927'. *Modern China* 35, no. 1 (2009): 65–95. doi.org/10.1177/0097700408318986

Nakayama, Takashi. *Manshū, 1945.8.9. Sorengun shinkō to Nihongun* [Manchuria, 9 August 1945: The Red Army against the Japanese forces]. Tokyo: Kokusho kankokai, 1990

New York Times. 1945–46. New York

Nie Rongzhen. *Inside the Red Star: The Memoirs of Marshal Nie Rongzhen*, trans. Zhong Renyi. Beijing: New World Press, 1988

Nikolopoulos, Andreas. *Negotiating Strategically: One Versus All*. New York: Palgrave Macmillan, 2011

Nishimura, Shigeo. 'Cong Xiong Shihui riji kan Guomin zhengfu jieshou Dongbei shi "xiangchang" de zhengzhi maodun' ['On-the-scene' political conflict of the Chinese Nationalist government's takeover of Manchuria: From the perspective of Xiong Shihui diary]. In *Zhanhou Dongbei jieshou jiaoshe jishi—yi Zhang Jia'ao riji wei zhongxin*, ed. Takushū Ihara, 190–207. Beijing: Zhongguo renmin daxue chubanshe, 2011

Niu Jun. *Neizhan qianxi: Meiguo tiaochu Guogong maodun shimo* [At the eve of the civil war: An account of the United States' role in mediating the GMD–CCP conflicts]. Taipei: Babilun chubanshe, 1993

—— 'The origins of the Sino-Soviet alliance'. In *Brothers in Arms: The Rise and Fall of the Sino-Soviet Alliance, 1945–1963*, ed. Odd Arne Westad, 47–89. Washington, DC: Woodrow Wilson Center Press, 1998

Pan Liangui. 'Zhongyang yinhang dongbei jiu sheng liutongquan ge'an yanjiu' [Case studies on the Circulating Currency of the Nine Provinces of the Northeast of the Central Bank of China]. *Qianbi bolan* [Coin expo] 3 (2009): 11–16

Pauley, Edwin W. *Report on Japanese Assets in Manchuria to the President of the United States*. July 1946. Washington, DC: n.p., 1946

Pehar, Dražen. 'Use of ambiguities in peace agreements'. In *Language and Diplomacy*, ed. Jovan Kurbalija and Hannah Slavik, 163–200. Msida: DiploProjects, 2001

Peng Zhen. 'Dongbei jiefang zhanzhen de tou jiugeyue' [The first nine months of the Liberation War in the north-east]. November 1988. In *Liaoshen juezhan xuji*, ed. Liaoshen zhanyi jinianguan guanli weiyuanhui and Liaoshen juezhan xuji bianshen xiaozu, 3–19. Beijing: Renmin chubanshe, 1992

—— 'Wo men de renwu shi zhengqu quan dongbei' [Our responsibilities for dominating the whole north-east]. 26 October 1945. In *Peng Zhen wenxuan*, ed. Zhonggong zhongyang wenxian bianji weiyuanhui, 103–5. Beijing: Renmin chubanshe, 1991

Peng Zhen zhuan bianxie zu [Editorial group of the biography of Peng Zhen], ed. *Peng Zhen nianpu 1902–1997* [Chronological biography of Peng Zhen 1902–1997]. Vol. 1. Beijing: Zhongyang wenxian chubanshe, 2002

Pepper, Suzanne. *Civil War in China: The Political Struggle, 1945–1949*. 2nd edn. Lanham, MD: Rowman & Littlefield, 1999

―― 'The KMT–CCP Conflict 1945–1949'. In *The Cambridge History of China*, ed. John K Fairbank and Albert Feuerwerker, 13, pt 2: 723–88. Cambridge: Cambridge University Press, 1986

Pi Dingjun. *Pi Dingjun riji* [The diaries of Pi Dingjun]. Beijing: Jiefangjun chubanshe, 1986

Pruitt, Dean G., Robert S. Peirce, Neil B. McGillicuddy, Gary L. Welton and Lynn M. Castrianno. 'Long-term success in mediation'. *Law and Human Behavior* 17, no. 3 (1993): 313–30. doi.org/10.1007/bf01044511

Public International Law and Policy Group. *The Ceasefire Drafter's Handbook*. Washington, DC: PILPG, 2013. Retrieved 22 May 2022. static1.squarespace.com/static/5900b58e1b631bffa367167e/t/5b730a224fa51ab1083c22bb/1534265892577/PILPG+Ceasefire+Drafter%27s+Handbook+%28Including%2BTemplate%2BCeasefire%2BAgreement%29-2.pdf

Putnam, Linda L. 'Challenging the assumptions of traditional approaches to negotiation'. *Negotiation Journal* 10, no. 4 (1994): 337–46. doi.org/10.1111/j.1571-9979.1994.tb00033.x

Qin Xiaoyi, ed. *Guofu Quanji* [The complete works of the father of the country]. Vol. 1. Taipei: Jindai Zhongguo chubanshe, 1989

―― ed. *Zhonghua Minguo zhongyao shiliao chubian—Dui ri kangzhan shiqi* [A first selection of important historical materials of the Republic of China—The period of the war of resistance against Japan]. Vol. 3: *Zhanshi waijiao* [Wartime diplomacy]: book 2; vol. 5: *Zhonggong huodong zhenxiang* [The truth about the CCP's activities], books 1–4; vol. 7: *Zhanhou zhongguo* [China in the post-World War II period], books 1–2. Taipei: Zhongguo Guomindang zhongyang weiyuanhui dangshi weiyuanhui, 1981–88

Qing, Simei. *From Allies to Enemies: Visions of Modernity, Identity, and US–China Diplomacy, 1945–1960*. Cambridge, MA: Harvard University Press, 2007

Raiffa, Howard. *The Art and Science of Negotiation*. Cambridge, MA: Belknap Press, 1998

Rapoport, Anatol. *The Origins of Violence: Approaches to the Study of Conflict*. New York: Paragon House, 1989

Rea, Kenneth W., and John C. Brewer, eds. *The Forgotten Ambassador: The Reports of John Leighton Stuart, 1946–1949*. Boulder, CO: Westview Press, 1981

Reid, Lindsay. 'Finding a peace that lasts: Mediator leverage and the durable resolution of civil wars'. *Journal of Conflict Resolution* 61, no. 7 (2017): 1401–31. doi.org/10.1177/0022002715611231

Ren Zhibin. 'Zhongyuan tuwei de zhandou lichen jiqi zhanlüe zuoyong' [The empirical process of the battles and the strategic significance of the Central Plain breakout]. In *Zhongyuan tuwei qianhou*, ed. Zhonggong Henan shengwei dangshi gongzuo weiyuanhui, 1–18. Zhengzhou: Henan renmin chubanshe, 1988

Renmin Ribao [People's Daily]. 1946. Handan

Roberts, Geoffrey. *Stalin's Wars: From World War to Cold War, 1939–1953*. New Haven, CT: Yale University Press, 2006

Royle, Trevor, ed. *A Dictionary of Military Quotations* New York: Simon & Schuster, 1989

Ryan, Mark A., David M. Finkelstein and Michael A. McDevitt, eds. *Chinese Warfighting: The PLA Experience since 1949*. Armonk, NY: M.E. Sharpe, 2003

Schoppa, R. Keith. 'Diaries as historical source: Goldmines and/or slippery slopes'. *Chinese Historical Review* 17, no. 1 (2010): 31–6. doi.org/10.1179/tcr.2010.17.1.31

Scott, David. *China and the International System, 1840–1949: Power, Presence, and Perceptions in a Century of Humiliation*. Albany, NY: State University of New York Press, 2008

Shaffer, Robert. 'A rape in Beijing, December 1946: GIs, nationalist protests, and US foreign policy'. *Pacific Historical Review* 69, no. 1 (2000): 31–64. doi.org/10.2307/3641237

Shao Lizi. 'Zhengfu yu Zhonggong daibiao huitan jingguo' [An account of the meetings between the government and the representatives of the CCP]. 12 January 1946. In *Chongqing tanpan jishi*, ed. Zhonggong Chongqing shiwei Dangshi gongzuo weiyuanhui, Chongqing Shi zhengxie wenshi ziliao yanjiu weiyuanhui and Hongyan geming jinian guan, 357–62. Chongqing: Chongqing chubanshe, 1984

Shaw, Martin. *The New Western Way of War: Risk-Transfer War and Its Crisis in Iraq*. Cambridge: Polity Press, 2005

Shaw, Yu-ming. *An American Missionary in China: John Leighton Stuart and Chinese-American Relations*. Cambridge, MA: Council of East Asian Studies, Harvard University, 1992

Shenbao [Shanghai News]. 1946. Shanghai

Sheng, Michael M. *Battling Western Imperialism: Mao, Stalin, and the United States*. Princeton, NJ: Princeton University Press, 1997

Shi Liang. *Dongbei de kuangye* [The mining industries in the north-east]. Dongbei jingji congshu [The north-eastern economy series], ed. Dongfang jingji yanjiusuo, vol. 3. Shanghai: Dongfang shudian, 1946

Shi Peimei and Zhen Zaiming. 'Deng Baoshan zai Yulin he Zhonggong tuanjie kangri de pianduan' [A page in the history of Deng Baoshan's anti-Japanese alliance with the CCP in Yulin]. In *Gansu wenshi ziliao xuanji*, ed. Zhongguo renmin zhengzhi xieshang huiyi Gansu Sheng weiyuanhui wenshi ziliao yanjiu weiyuanhui, 25: 112–19. Lanzhou: Gansu renmin chubanshe, 1987

'Sino-Soviet Treaty of Friendship and Alliance: Treaty of Friendship and Alliance between the Republic of China and the USSR'. *Department of State Bulletin* 14, no. 345 (1946): 201–8

So Wai Chor. 'The making of the Guomindang's Japan policy, 1932–1937: The role of Chiang Kai-shek and Wang Jingwei'. *Modern China* 28, no. 2 (2002): 213–52. doi.org/10.1177/009770040202800203

Soni, Sharad K. *Mongolia–China Relations: Modern and Contemporary Times*. New Delhi: Pentagon Press, 2006

Stein, Janice Gross, ed. *Getting to the Table: The Process of International Prenegotiation*. Baltimore, MD: Johns Hopkins University Press, 1989

——— 'Prenegotiation in the Arab–Israeli conflict: The paradoxes of success and failure'. In *Getting to the Table: The Process of International Prenegotiation*, ed. Janice Gross Stein, 174–205. Baltimore, MD: Johns Hopkins University Press, 1989

Stoler, Mark A. 'Why George Marshall? A biographical assessment'. In *George C. Marshall's Mediation Mission to China*, ed. Larry I. Bland, 3–14. Lexington, VA: George C. Marshall Foundation, 1998

Sulian Hongjun zai Lüda [The Soviet Red Army in Lüshun-Dalian]. Internal circulation materials, 1995

Sun Yueqi. 'Huiyi wo yu Jiang Jieshi jiechu er san shi' [Remembering a few things in dealing with Chiang Kai-shek]. In *Wenshi ziliao xuanji*, ed. Zhongguo renmin zhengzhi xieshang huiyi quanguo weiyuanhui wenshi ziliao yanjiu weiyuanhui, 84 (1982): 113–34. Beijing: Wenshi ziliao chubanshe, 1982

Svensson, Isak. 'Who brings which peace? Neutral versus biased mediation and institutional peace arrangements in civil wars'. *Journal of Conflict Resolution* 53, no. 3 (2009): 446–69. doi.org/10.1177/0022002709332207

Tang Kai. 'Wei jiefang Dongbei juxing dianjili' [Strengthening the foundation for the liberation of the north-east]. In *Shanhaiguan zhi zhan*, ed. Yuan Wei, 40–53. Beijing: Junshi kexue chubanshe, 1989

Tang Yunchao. 'Riben touxiang hou Su jun zai Dalian de qingkuang' [The Soviet forces in Dalian after the Japanese surrender]. In *Sulian Hongjun zai Lüda*, 85–8. Internal circulation materials, 1995

Tang Zong. *Zai Jiang Jieshi shenbian banian: Shicongshi gaoji muliao Tang Zong riji* [Diaries: My eight years as Jiang Jieshi's confidential secretary], ed. Gonganbu dang'an guan [Archives of the Public Security Bureau]. Beijing: Qunzhong chubanshe, 1991

Tanner, Harold M. 'Guerrilla, mobile, and base warfare in communist military operations in Manchuria, 1945–1947'. *Journal of Military History* 67 (October 2003), 1177–222. doi.org/10.1353/jmh.2003.0340

—— *The Battle for Manchuria and the Fate of China: Spring, 1946*. Bloomington, IN: Indiana University Press, 2013

—— *Where Chiang Kai-shek Lost China: The Liao-Shen Campaign, 1948*. Bloomington, IN: Indiana University Press, 2015

Taylor, Jay. *The Generalissimo's Son: Chiang Ching-kuo and the Revolution in China and Taiwan*. Cambridge, MA: Harvard University Press, 2000

—— *The Generalissimo: Chiang Kai-shek and the Struggle for Modern* China. Cambridge, MA: Belknap Press of Harvard University Press, 2009

Tian Liang. 'Xingshan Shi jiefang chuqi de wuzhuang jianjun gongzuo' [Establishing armed forces in the city of Xingshan during the early years of liberation]. In *Hegang dangshi ziliao*, ed. Zhonggong Hegang shiwei dangshi gongzuo weiyuanhui, 2: 140–2. Internal circulation materials, 1986

Tian Yushi. 'Dongbei jieshou sannian zaihuo zuiyan' [An avowal of guilt: The three-year misfortunes in the takeover of Manchuria]. *Zhuanji wenxue* (Taipei) 35, no. 6 (December 1979), 19–29; 36, no. 1 (January 1980), 65–71; 36, no. 2 (February 1980), 80–6; 36, no. 3 (March 1980), 97–104; 36, no. 4 (April 1980), 103–7; 36, no. 5 (May 1980), 85–9; 36, no. 6 (June 1980), 82–8; 37, no. 1 (July 1980), 100–6; 37, no. 3 (September 1980), 113–19, 37, no. 4 (October 1980), 114–18, 37, no. 6 (December 1980), 109–14; 38, no. 1 (January 1981), 58–63; 38, no. 2 (February 1981), 92–6; 38, no. 3 (March 1981), 125–8; 38, no. 4 (April 1981), 101–4

Tingzhan tanpan ziliao [Source materials on cease-fire negotiations]. Chengdu: Sichuan renmin chubanshe, 1981

Tong Xiaopeng. *Fengyu sishi nian* [A forty-year tribulation]. Beijing: Zhongyang wenxian chubanshe, 1994

Tsou, Tang. *America's Failure in China, 1941–50*. Chicago: University of Chicago Press, 1963

Tu, Chuande. 'The 1945–1946 GMD–CCP peace talks and the origins of the Chinese Civil War'. PhD diss., University of Wisconsin—Madison, 2000

United States Department of the Army. *US Army Guerrilla Warfare Handbook*. New York: Skyhorse, 2009

United States Department of State. *Foreign Relations of the United States: Diplomatic Papers, the Far East, China*, 6 (1944), 7 (1945), 9–10 (1946), 7 (1947). Washington: United States Government Printing Office, 1967–72

—— *The China White Paper, August 1949*. Vols 1–2. Stanford, CA: Stanford University Press, 1967

—— *The Conference of Berlin (The Potsdam Conference), 1945*. Vol. 2. Washington, DC: Government Printing Office, 1960

van de Ven, Hans. *China at War: Triumph and Tragedy in the Emergence of the New China, 1937–1952*. London: Profile Books, 2017

—— Diana Lary and Stephen MacKinnon, eds. *Negotiating China's Destiny in World War II*. Stanford, CA: Stanford University Press, 2015. doi.org/10.11126/stanford/9780804789660.001.0001

Waijiao yanjuhui [The association for the study of diplomacy], ed. *Dongbei zhanlüe tieluwang* [Strategic railway network in Manchuria]. N.p., 1936. Available at Ministry of Justice Investigation Bureau, Taipei; call no. Diao (調)527.254.7445

Waldron, Arthur. 'China without tears: If Chiang Kai-shek hadn't gambled in 1946'. In *What If? The World's Foremost Military Historians Imagine What Might Have Been*, ed. Robert Cowley, 377–91. London: Macmillan, 2000

Waltz, Kenneth N. *Theory of International Politics*. Boston: McGraw-Hill, 1979

Wan Yi. *Wan Yi jiangjun huiyilu* [The recollections of General Wan Yi]. Beijing: Zhonggong dangshi chubanshe, 1998

Wang Chaoguang. *1945–1949: Guogong zhengzheng yu Zhongguo mingyun* [The GMD–CCP political struggle and the fate of China, 1945–1949], overseas rev. edn. Hong Kong: Hong Kong Open Page, 2011

—— 'Guogong neizhan chuqi de Dongbei zhanchang yu Jiang Jieshi de junshi jueche' [The Manchurian theatre in the initial stage of the Chinese Civil War and the military decision-making of Jiang Jieshi]. In *Jiang Zhongzheng riji yu minguo shi yanjiu*, ed. Lü Fangshang, 519–54. Taipei: Shijie datong, 2011

―――― *Zhonghua Minguo shi* [A history of republican China]. Vol. 11 (1945–47). Ser. ed. Zhongguo shehui kexue yuan jindaishi yanjiusuo Zhonghua Minguo shi yanjiushi. Beijing: Zhonghua shuju, 2011

―――― 'Zhan yu he de bianzou: Chongqing tanpan zhi Zhengxie huiyi qijian de Zhongguo shiju yanbian' [A variation on war and peace: The evolution of China's political situation from the Chongqing negotiations to the Political Consultative Conference]. *Jindaishi yanjiu* 1 (2002): 14–42

―――― 'Zhanhou Zhongsu Dongbei jingji hezuo jiaoshe yanjiu' [A study of the Sino-Soviet economic cooperation negotiation in Manchuria after the war]. *Jindaishi yanjiu* 6 (2002): 58–88

Wang Chen-main. 'Marshall's approach to the mediation effort'. In *George C. Marshall's Mediation Mission to China*, ed. Larry I. Bland, 21–43. Lexington, VA: George C. Marshall Foundation, 1998

Wang Qiqing. 'Dui jieshou Hegang meikuang de huiyi' [My recollections on the takeover of the Hegang coal mines]. In *Hegang dangshi ziliao*, ed. Zhonggong Hegang shiwei dangshi gongzuo weiyuanhui, 2: 50–3. Internal circulation materials, 1986

Wang Shijie. *Wang Shijie riji* [The diary of Dr Wang Shih-chieh] Vol. 5. Taipei: Academia Sinica, 1990

Wang Shiming. 'Lüshun jiefang chuqi yu Su jun guanxi de huigu' [A review of the relationship with the Soviet forces in Lüshun at the beginning of the liberation]. In *Sulian Hongjun zai Lüda*, 111–16. Internal circulation materials, 1995

Wang Shoudao. 'Cong zhanlüe shang renshi Zhongyuan tuwei de zhongyao yiyi' [A strategic perspective on the significance of the Central Plain breakout]. In *Zhongyuan tuwei qianhou*, ed. Zhonggong Henan shengwei dangshi gongzuo weiyuanhui, 27–8. Zhengzhou: Henan renmin chubanshe, 1988

―――― 'Cong zhanzheng zouxiang jianshe' [From war to economic development]. In *Liaoshen Juezhan xuji*, ed. Liaoshen zhanyi jinianguan guanli weiyuanhui and Liaoshen juezhan xuji bianshen xiaozu, 451–67. Beijing: Renmin chubanshe, 1992

―――― 'Dongbei jiefangqu renmin zhengquan de jianli ji caizheng jingji gongzuo' [The establishment of the people's regime and works on financial and economic affairs in the Northeast Liberation Area]. In *Liaoshen juezhan*, ed. Zhonggong zhongyang dangshi ziliao zhengji weiyuanhui, Zhongguo renmin jiefangjun Liaoshen zhanyi jinianguan jianguan weiyuanhui and Liaoshen juezhan bianshen xiaozu, 2: 361–75. Beijing: Renmin chubanshe, 1988

—— *Wang Shoudao huiyilu* [The memoirs of Wang Shoudao]. Beijing: Jiefangjun chubanshe, 1988

Wang Yizhi. 'Bayiwu qianhou de Dongbei kangri lianjun' [The North-east Anti-Japanese United Army before and after the V-J Day]. In *Liaoshen juezhan*, ed. Zhonggong zhongyang dangshi ziliao zhengji weiyuanhui, Zhongguo renmin jiefangjun Liaoshen zhanyi jinianguan jianguan weiyuanhui and Liaoshen juezhan bianshen xiaozu, 1: 156–66. Beijing: Renmin chubanshe, 1988

Wang Yunwu. 'Su e zai Zhongguo du hou gan' [Impression after reading *Soviet Russia in China*]. In *Xiulu lun zheng*, Wang Yunwu, 454–7. Taipei: Faling yuekan she, 1964

—— *Xiulu lun zheng* [Writing political commentary at my mountain abode]. Taipei: Faling yuekan she, 1964

Wedemeyer, Albert C. *Wedemeyer Reports!* New York: Holt, 1958

Wei, William. *Counterrevolution in China: The Nationalists in Jiangxi during the Soviet Period*. Ann Arbor, MI: University of Michigan Press, 1985

Weiss, Joshua N., and Sarah Rosenberg. 'Sequencing strategies and tactics'. September 2003. *Beyond Intractability*, ed. Guy Burgess and Heidi Burgess. Conflict Research Consortium, University of Colorado. Retrieved 29 May 2022. www.beyondintractability.org/essay/issue-segmentation

Wendt, Alexander. *Social Theory of International Politics*. Cambridge: Cambridge University Press, 1999

Wenshi ziliao xuanji bianji bu [Editorial group of the literary–historical source materials collections], ed. *Wenshi ziliao jingxuan* [A selection of literary–historical source materials]. Vol. 12. Beijing: Zhongguo wenshi ziliao chubanshe, 1990

Westad, Odd Arne, ed. *Brothers in Arms: The Rise and Fall of the Sino-Soviet Alliance, 1945–1963*. Washington, DC: Woodrow Wilson Center Press, 1998

—— *Cold War and Revolution: Soviet–American Rivalry and the Origins of the Chinese Civil War, 1944–1946*. New York: Columbia University Press, 1993

—— *Decisive Encounters: The Chinese Civil War, 1946–1950*. Stanford, CA: Stanford University Press, 2003

White, Theodore H., and Annalee Jacoby. *Thunder Out of China*. 2nd edn. New York: William Sloane, 1961

Wilhelm, Alfred D. *The Chinese at the Negotiating Table: Style and Characteristics*. Washington, DC: National Defense University Press, 1994

Wise, Laura. 'Territorial power-sharing and inclusion in peace processes'. PA-X Report, Power-sharing Series, 1–47. Edinburgh: Global Justice Academy, University of Edinburgh, 2018. Retrieved 24 May 2022. www.politicalsettlements.org/wp-content/uploads/2018/07/2018_Wise_PA-X-Territorial-Power-Sharing-Report.pdf

Womack, Brantly. 'Asymmetry and systemic misperception: China, Vietnam and Cambodia during the 1970s'. *Journal of Strategic Studies* 26, no. 2 (2003): 92–119. doi.org/10.1080/01402390412331302995

Wortzel, Larry M. 'The Beiping–Tianjin campaign of 1948–1949: The strategic and operational thinking of the People's Liberation Army'. In *Chinese Warfighting: The PLA Experience since 1949*, ed. Mark A. Ryan, David M. Finkelstein and Michael A. McDevitt, 56–72. Armonk, NY: M.E. Sharpe, 2003

Wu Huanzhang. 'Kangzhan shengli hou jieshou dongbei de huiyi, shang' [Recollections of the takeover of north-east after the end of the War of Resistance against Japan, Part 1]. *Zhuanji Wenxue* (Taipei) 24, no. 2 (1974): 33–9

Wu, Tien-wei. 'The Chinese Communist movement'. In *China's Bitter Victory: The War with Japan, 1937–1945*, ed. James C. Hsiung and Steven I. Levine, 79–106. Armonk, NY: M.E. Sharpe, 1992

Wu Xiuquan. 'Peihe Sujun jiefang dongbei' [Liberating the north-east in coordination with the Soviet Army]. In *Liaoshen juezhan*, ed. Zhonggong zhongyang dangshi ziliao zhengji weiyuanhui, Zhongguo renmin jiefangjun Liaoshen zhanyi jinianguan jianguan weiyuanhui and Liaoshen juezhan bianshen xiaozu, 1: 145–55. Beijing: Renmin chubanshe, 1988

—— *Wo de lichen* [A look back over my career]. Beijing: Jiefangjun chubanshe, 1984

Xiao Hua. 'Hengkua Bohai, jinjun Dongbei' [Cross the Baohai Sea and march towards the north-east]. In *Liaoshen juezhan*, ed. Zhonggong zhongyang dangshi ziliao zhengji weiyuanhui, Zhongguo renmin jiefangjun Liaoshen zhanyi jinianguan jianguan weiyuanhui and Liaoshen juezhan bianshen xiaozu, 1: 206–16. Beijing: Renmin chubanshe, 1988

Xiao Jiansheng. *Zhongguo wenming de fansi* [Chinese history revisited]. Hong Kong: New Century Press, 2009

Xiao Jinguang. *Xiao Jinguang huiyilu* [The memoirs of Xiao Jinguang]. Beijing: Jiefangjun chubanshe, 1987

'Xingshan Shi jiuge yue de zongjie baogao 1945.12.20–1946.9.25' [A summary report for the nine months in the city of Xingshan from 20 December 1945 to the period ending 25 September 1946]. In *Hegang dangshi ziliao*, ed. Zhonggong Hegang shiwei dangshi gongzuo weiyuanhui, 2: 20–49. Internal circulation materials, 1986

Xinhua ribao [Xinhua Daily]. 1945. Chongqing

Xiong Shihui. *Haisangji: Xiong Shihui huiyilu, 1907–1949* [An insider's account of modern Chinese history: Memoirs of governor and general Hsiung Shih-Hui, 1907–1949], ed. Hong Chaohui. New York: Mirror Books, 2008

Xu Jie. 'Si jin gang cheng' [Our four campaigns for the steel city]. In *Anshan wenshi ziliao xuanji*, ed. Zhongguo renmin zhengzhi xieshang huiyi Anshan Shi weiyuanhui wenshi ziliao yanjiu weiyuanhui, 1: 1–92. Internal circulation materials, 1986

Xu Yongchang. *Xu Yongchang riji* [The diary of Xu Yongchang]. Vol. 8. Taipei: Institute of Modern History, Academia Sinica, 1991

Xue Xiantian. 'Sulian chaiyun Dongbei jiqi shebei shuping' [Critical comments on Soviet removal of industrial equipment in the north-east]. In *Dier jie jindai Zhongguo yu shijie guoji xueshu yantao hui lunwen ji*, ed. Dier jie jindai Zhongguo yu shijie guoji xueshu yantao hui, 639–51. Beijing: Zhongguo shixue hui, 2000

'Yalta Agreement on the Kuriles: Text of the agreement'. *Department of State Bulletin*, 14, no. 347 (1946): 282–3

Yang Jingbin, ed. *Wushierjun kanluan zhanyi jishi* [True history of the 52nd Army in bandit suppression battles]. Taipei: Beida shuju, n.d

Yang Kuisong. *Shiqu de jihui? Kangzhan qianhou Guogong tanpan shilu* [Lost opportunity? A true record of the GMD–CCP negotiations during the period before and after the War of Resistance]. Guilin: Guangxi Shifan Daxue chubanshe, 1992

—— 'Yijiusiliu nian Guo-Gong Siping zhi zhan ji qi muhou' [The KMT–Communist battle at Sipingjie in 1946: Behind the scenes]. *Lishi yanjiu* [Historical research] 4 (2004): 132–52

—— *Zhonggong yu Mosike de guanxi, 1920–1960* [The Chinese Communist Party's relations with Moscow, 1920–1960]. Taipei: Dongda tushu gongsi, 1997

—— *Zhongjian didai de geming: Guoji da beijing xia kan Zhonggong chenggong zhi dao* [Revolution in the intermediate zone: The Chinese Communist victory in an international context]. Taiyuan: Shanxi renmin chubanshe, 2010

—— '1946 nian Anping shijian zhenxiang yu Zhonggong dui mei jiaoshe' [The truth about the Anping incident of 1946 and the CCP–American negotiations]. *Shixue yuekan* [History Monthly] 4 (2011): 60–74

Yang Shengqing, ed. *Zhongguo gongchan dang tanpan shi* [A history of negotiations of the Chinese Communist Party]. Vol. 1. Beijing: Zhongyang wenxian chubanshe, 2005

Yang Tianshi. *Jiang Jieshi zhenxiang* [The truth about Chiang Kai-shek]. Taipei: Fengyun shidai, 2009

Yao Dezhi. 'Benchi zai zhanchang shang de qichebing' [Mechanised transportation corps in action on the battlefield]. In *Xueye xiongfeng: liu zai Dongbei zhanchang de jiyi*, Li Yunchang, 566–70. Shenyang: Baishan chubanshe, 1988

Yao Songling, ed. *Zhang Gongquan xiansheng nianpu chugao* [A draft chronological biography of Zhang Jia'ao]. Vols 1–2. Taipei: Zhuanji wenxue chubanshe, 1982

Yu, Maochun. *OSS in China: Prelude to Cold War*. New Haven, CT: Yale University Press, 1996

Yuan Wei, ed. *Shanhaiguan zhi zhan* [The battle of Shanhaiguan]. Beijing: Junshi kexue chubanshe, 1989

Zagare, Frank C., and D. Marc Kilgour. 'Alignment patterns, crisis bargaining, and extended deterrence: A game-theoretic analysis'. *International Studies Quarterly* 47, no. 4 (2003): 587–615. doi.org/10.1046/j.0020-8833.2003.00280.x

Zartman, William I. 'Prenegotiation: Phases and functions'. In *Getting to the Table: The Process of International Prenegotiation*, ed. Janice Gross Stein, 1–17. Baltimore, MD: Johns Hopkins University Press, 1989

—— ed. *International Multilateral Negotiation: Approaches to the Management of Complexity*. San Francisco, CA: Jossey-Bass, 1994

Zeng Kelin. 'Huoyue zhanlüe quanju: yi gongke Shanhaiguan zhi zhan' [A critical turning point: recollections of the battle of Shanhaiguan]. In *Shanhaiguan zhi zhan*, ed. Yuan Wei, 31–9. Beijing: Junshi kexue chubanshe, 1989

—— 'Jinjun Dongbei de zuichu shike' [Marching into the north-east: The initial stage]. In *Xueye xiongfeng: liu zai Dongbei zhanchang de jiyi*, Li Yunchang, 8–15. Shenyang: Baishan chubanshe, 1988

—— *Zeng Kelin jiangjun zishu* [An autobiography of General Zeng Kelin]. Shenyang: Liaoning renmin chubanshe, 1997

Zhang Heming. 'Guanyu Shanhaiguan baoweizhan de zongjie baogao' [A report on the battle of defence of Shanhaiguan]. C. 1946. In *Shanhaiguan zhi zhan*, ed. Yuan Wei, 160–77. Beijing: Junshi kexue chubanshe, 1989

Zhang, Jia'ao (Cheung Kia-ngau). *Last Chance in Manchuria: The Diary of Cheung Kia-ngau*, ed. Donald Gillin and Ramon Myers. Stanford, CA: Hoover Institution Press, 1989

Zhang Jiuru. *Hetan fuzhe zai Zhongguo* [The disastrous road towards peace talks in China]. Taipei: Lianjing chuban shiye gongsi, 1981

Zhang Keliang. 'Guomindang jieshou Angang mianmianguan' [The GMD takeover of the Anshan Iron and Steel Company in perspectives]. In *Anshan wenshi ziliao xuanji*, ed. Zhongguo renmin zhengzhi xieshang huiyi Anshan Shi weiyuanhui wenshi ziliao yanjiu weiyuanhui, 1: 150–82. Internal circulation materials, 1986

Zhang, Suchu. 'Why Marshall's mission failed'. In *George C. Marshall's Mediation Mission to China, December 1945–January 1947*, ed. Larry I. Bland, 45–62. Lexington, VA: George C. Marshall Foundation, 1998

Zhang Zengjie, ed. 'Huifu he fazhan meikuang shengchan zhiyuan jiefang zhanzheng' [Supporting the war of liberation: Resuming and developing coal production]. In *Hegang dangshi ziliao*, ed. Zhonggong Hegang shiwei dangshi gongzuo weiyuanhui, 2: 188–93. Internal circulation materials, 1986

Zheng Dongguo. 'Cong daju jingong dao zhongdian fangyu' [From massive attack to the defence of key points]. In *Liaoshen zhanyi qinliji*, ed. Zhongguo renmin zhengzhi xieshang huiyi quanguo weiyuanhui wenshi ziliao yanjiu weiyuanhui Liaoshen zhanyi qinliji shenbianzu, 565–84. Beijing: Zhongguo wenshi chubanshe, 1985

——— *Wo de rongma shengyai* [My army life]. Beijing: Tuanjie chubanshe, 1992

Zheng Hong. 'Chongqing tanpan jilüe' [A summary of the Chongqing negotiations]. In *Chongqing wenshi ziliao xuanji*, ed. Zhongguo renmin zhengzhi xieshang huiyi Sichuan Sheng Chongqing Shi weiyuanhui wenshi ziliao yanjiu weiyuanhui, 1: 1–56. Chongqing: n.p., 1987

Zheng Shaowen. 'Balu Jun Xin Si Jun Zhongyuan Junqu Wuhan banshichu dui Mei-Jiang de douzheng' [The struggle against the Americans and the Nationalists in the Wuhan branch office of the Central Plain Military Region of the Eighth Route Army and the New Fourth Army]. In *Wuhan wenshi ziliao*, ed. Zhengxie Huibei Sheng Wuhan Shi weiyuanhui wenshi ziliao yanjiu weiyuanhui, 5: 1–10. Hankou: Zhongguo renmin zhengzhi xieshang huiyi Wuhan Shi weiyuanhui wenshi ziliao yanjiu weiyuanhui, 1981

Zhengxie Anhui Sheng weiyuanhui wenshi ziliao yanjiu weiyuanhui [The literary–historical source materials study committee—An affiliate of the Anhui Provincial Committee of the Chinese People's Political Consultative Conference] and Anhui Sheng shehui kexueyuan lishi yanjiusuo [Institute of historical studies, Anhui academy of social sciences], eds. *Anhui Wenshi ziliao* [Literary–historical source materials of Anhui]. Vol. 25. Hefei: Anhui renmin chubanshe, 1986

Zhengxie Huibei Sheng Wuhan Shi weiyuanhui wenshi ziliao yanjiu weiyuanhui [The literary–historical source materials study committee of the Wuhan city committee of the Hubei Province of the Chinese People's Political Consultative Conference], ed. *Wuhan wenshi ziliao* [The literary–historical source materials of Wuhan]. Vol. 5. Hankou: Zhongguo renmin zhengzhi xieshang huiyi Wuhan Shi weiyuanhui wenshi ziliao yanjiu weiyuanhui, 1981

Zhonggong Chongqing shiwei dangshi gongzuo weiyuanhui [The committee of party history of the CCP Chongqing branch], Chongqing Shi zhengxie wenshi ziliao yanjiu weiyuanhui [The literary–historical source materials study committee—An affiliate of the Chinese People's Political Consultative Conference, Chongqing branch] and Hongyan geming jinian guan [Hongyan Village Revolutionary Memorial Hall], eds. *Chongqing tanpan jishi* [The true story of Chongqing negotiations]. Chongqing: Chongqing chubanshe, 1984

Zhonggong Hegang shiwei dangshi gongzuo weiyuanhui [Committee for party history compilation of the Hegang City branch committee of the CCP], ed. *Hegang dangshi ziliao* [Source materials for party history of the city of Hegang]. Vol. 2. Internal circulation materials, 1986

Zhonggong Hegang shiwei dangshi yanjiushi [Research office for history of the CCP Hegang City branch committee], ed. *Hegang dangshi ziliao*. Vol. 11. Internal circulation materials, 1990

Zhonggong Henan shengwei dangshi gongzuo weiyuanhui [The party history working committee of the Henan provincial committee of the CCP], ed. *Zhongyuan tuwei qianhou* [The central plain breakout, before and after]. Zhengzhou: Henan renmin chubanshe, 1988

Zhonggong Jiangsu shengwei dangshi gongzuo bangongshi [Office for party history of the Jiangsu provincial committee of the CCP], ed. *Su Yu nianpu* [Chronological biography of Su Yu]. Beijing: Dangdai zhongguo chubanshe, 2006

Zhonggong Kaifeng shiwei dangshi bangongshi [Office of party history of the Kaifeng City branch committee of the CCP] and Zhonggong Shangqiu diwei dangshi bangongshi [Office of party history of the Shangqiu County branch committee of the CCP], eds. *Yudong zhanyi* [The eastern Henan campaign]. Zhengzhou: Henan renmin chubanshe, 1988

Zhonggong Shandong shengwei dangshi ziliao zengji weiyuanhui [Committee for compiling materials on party history of the Shandong provincial committee of the CCP], ed. *Shandong dangshi ziliao* [Materials on the party history of Shandong]. Vol. 4. Jinan: Zhonggong Shandong shengwei dangshi ziliao zengji weiyuanhui, 1985

Zhonggong zhongyang dangshi ziliao zhengji weiyuanhui [Committee for compiling materials on party history of the Central Committee of the CCP], ed. *Dangshi ziliao zhengji tongxun* [Newsletters for compiling materials on party history]. Vol. 6. Beijing: Zhonggong dangshi chubanshe, 1985

——— Zhongguo renmin jiefangjun Liaoshen zhanyi jinianguan jianguan weiyuanhui [The founding committee of the PLA's Liaoshen Campaign Museum] and Liaoshen juezhan bianshen xiaozu [The editorial group of Liaoshen juezhan], eds. *Liaoshen juezhan* [The Liaoshen Campaign]. Vols 1–2. Beijing: Renmin chubanshe, 1988

Zhonggong zhongyang wenxian bianji weiyuanhui [Historical source materials compliance committee of the Central Committee of the CCP], ed. *Peng Zhen wenxuan* [Selected works of Peng Zhen]. Beijing: Renmin chubanshe, 1991

Zhonggong zhongyang wenxian yanjiushi [Research office for documentation of the Central Committee of the CCP], ed. *Liu Shaoqi nianpu 1898–1969* [The chronological biography of Liu Shaoqi, 1898–1969]. Vols 1–2. Beijing: Zhongyang wenxian chubanshe, 1996

——— ed. *Mao Zedong nianpu 1893–1949* [The chronological biography of Mao Zedong, 1893–1949]. Vol. 3. Beijing: Renmin chubanshe and Zhongyang wenxian chubanshe, 1993

——— ed. *Mao Zedong wenji* [Collected works of Mao Zedong]. Vol. 4. Beijing: Renmin chubanshe, 1993–99

——— ed. *Zhou Enlai nianpu, 1898–1949* [The chronological biography of Zhou Enlai, 1898–1949]. Beijing: Zhongyang wenxian chubanshe, 1989

——— ed. *Zhu De nianpu (xinbian ben) 1886–1976* [The chronological biography of Zhu De, new edn, 1886–1976]. Beijing: Zhongyang wenxian chubanshe, 2006

Zhonggong zhongyang wenxian yanjiushi [Research office for documentation of the Central Committee of the CCP] and Zhonggong Nanjing Shi weiyuanhui [The CCP Nanjing branch committee], eds. *Zhou Enlai yijiusiliu nian tanpan wenxuan* [Selected essays of Zhou Enlai in the peace negotiations of 1946]. Beijing: Zhongyang wenxian chubanshe, 1996

―― and Zhongguo renmin jiefangjun junshi kexue yuan [PLA Academy of Military Science], eds. *Mao Zedong junshi wenji* [Collected military papers of Mao Zedong]. Vol. 3. Beijing: Junshi kexue chubanshe and Zongyang wenxian chubanshe, 1993

Zhongguo dier lishi dang'anguan [The second historical archives of China], ed. *Kangri zhanzheng shiqi Guomindang jun jimi zuozhan riji* [Confidential field diaries of the GMD armies during the War of Resistance against Japan]. Beijing: Zhongguo dang'an chubanshe, 1995

Zhongguo minzhu tongmeng zhongyang wenshi ziliao weiyuanhui [The literary–historical source materials committee of the Central Committee of the Chinese Democratic League], ed. *Zhongguo minzhu tongmeng lishi wenxian* [Historical materials of the Chinese Democratic League]. Beijing: Wenshi ziliao chubanshe, 1983

Zhongguo renmin jiefang jun junshi kexue yuan [PLA Academy of Military Science] and Mao Zedong junshi sixiang yanjiu suo nianpu zu [The editorial division of chronological biography of the institute of Mao Zedong's military thought], eds. *Mao Zedong junshi nianpu 1927–1958* [The chronological military biography of Mao Zedong, 1927–58]. Nanning: Guangxi renmin chubanshe, 1994

Zhongguo renmin jiefang jun zhengzhi xueyuan diyi junshi yanjiaoshi [The first unit for teaching and research on military affairs, PLA Institute of Politics], ed. *Zhongguo remin jiefangjun zhanyi zhanli xuanbian* [Selected case studies of the operational history of the PLA]. Vol. 2. Beijing: Zhongguo renmin jiefangjun zhengzhi xueyuan chubanshe, 1984

Zhongguo renmin zhengzhi xieshang huiyi Anshan Shi weiyuanhui wenshi ziliao yanjiu weiyuanhui [The literary–historical source materials study committee of the Anshan City committee of the Chinese People's Political Consultative Conference], ed. *Anshan wenshi ziliao xuanji* [A collection of selected literary–historical source materials of Anshan]. Vol. 1. Internal circulation materials, 1986

Zhongguo renmin zhengzhi xieshang huiyi Gansu Sheng weiyuanhui wenshi ziliao yanjiu weiyuanhui [The literary–historical source materials study committee of the Gansu provincial committee of the Chinese People's Political Consultative Conference], ed. *Gansu wenshi ziliao xuanji* [A selection of literary–historical source materials of Gansu]. Vol. 25. Lanzhou: Gansu renmin chubanshe, 1987

Zhongguo renmin zhengzhi xieshang huiyi quanguo weiyuanhui wenshi ziliao yanjiu weiyuanhui [National committee of literary–historical source materials study committee of the Chinese People's Political Consultative Conference], ed. *Wenshi ziliao xuanji* [A selection of literary–historical source materials]. Vols 42 and 84. Beijing: Wenshi ziliao chubanshe, 1980 and 1982

Zhongguo renmin zhengzhi xieshang huiyi quanguo weiyuanhui wenshi ziliao yanjiu weiyuanhui Liaoshen zhanyi qinliji shenbianzu [The editorial group of 'The Personal Accounts of the Liaoshen Campaign' of the literary–historical source materials study committee of the national committee of the Chinese People's Political Consultative Conference], ed. *Liaoshen zhanyi qinliji: Yuan Guomindang jiangling de huiyi* [Personal accounts of the Liaoshen Campaign by former Guomindang generals]. Beijing: Zhongguo wenshi chubanshe, 1985

Zhongguo renmin zhengzhi xieshang huiyi Sichuan Sheng Chongqing Shi weiyuanhui wenshi ziliao yanjiu weiyuanhui [The literary–historical source materials study committee of the Chongqing city committee of the Sichuan Province of the Chinese People's Political Consultative Conference], ed. *Chongqing wenshi ziliao xuanji* [A selection of literary–historical source materials of Chongqing]. Vol. 1. Chongqing: n.p., 1987

Zhongguo shehui kexue yuan jindaishi yanjiusuo Zhonghua Minguo shi yanjiushi [Department of Research in Republican Chinese History, Institute of Modern History, Chinese Academy of Social Sciences], ser. edn. *Zhonghua Minguo shi* [A history of Republican China]. Vol. 11. Beijing: Zhonghua shuju, 2011

Zhongyang dang'anguan [Central Party Archives], ed. *Zhonggong zhongyang wenjian xuanji* [Selected documents of the Central Committee of the CCP]. Vols 14–16. Beijing: Zhongyang dangxiao chubanshe, 1989–92

Zhongyang ribao [Central Daily News]. 1945. Shanghai

Zhou Enlai. 'Statement on the Kuomintang's Convening of a National Assembly'. 16 November 1946. In *Selected Works of Zhou Enlai*, Zhou Enlai, 1: 269–72. Beijing: Foreign Language Press, 1980

—— 'Statement on the Second Plenary Session of the Sixth Central Executive Committee of the Kuomintang'. In *Selected Works of Zhou Enlai*, Zhou Enlai, 1: 250–7. Beijing: Foreign Language Press, 1980

—— *Selected Works of Zhou Enlai*. Vol. 1. Beijing: Foreign Language Press, 1980

—— *Zhou Enlai shuxin xuanji* [Selected correspondence of Zhou Enlai]. Beijing: Zhongyang wenxian chubanshe, 1988

Index

administrative inspector, 67–8, 74
aggressive behaviour in negotiation, 63
Andong, 39, 231
Anhui, 62, 68, 202, 204–5, 207
Anping incident, 211–12
Anyang, 204–5
arms embargo, 214–18, 237, 242

Bai Chongxi, 101, 185–6
Baotou, 84
Barbey, Daniel, 40
Beiping, 51, 101–2, 114, 145, 152, 186–7, 211–12, 219, 234
Beiping–Guisui railway, 84
bias of US negotiator, 3, 14, 16, 50, 54, 67, 74, 109, 134, 174–5, 242
biased mediator, 64–5, 241
Bengbu, 205
Benxi, 93, 177–8, 183–4, 187
Birch, John, 76
Bohai Sea, 78
Byroade, Henry, 115, 176–7, 191

calculated incompetence, 68, 74
calculated passivity *see* withdrawal tactics
Central Executive Committee (CEC) of the GMD, 130–3, 139, 163, 175
Chahar, 78, 101–11, 113, 115, 196
Changchun, 30–1, 34, 38–40, 43–5, 92, 95, 143–7, 149–54, 162, 164, 165–7, 171, 178–80, 182–4, 186–8, 190–1, 193–5

Chengde, 35, 79, 201
Chiang Ching-kuo, 29, 33–4, 37, 44–5, 147–8, 150–1, 162, 168
Chiang Kai-shek:
 anti-communist rhetoric, 61, 219, 228
 army reorganisation, 129
 and ceasefire, 108–9, 111–13, 180–2, 184, 187, 196, 199, 202, 213–14, 220, 228–33 *passim*, 236, 242
 and Chinese sovereignty, 21, 37, 243
 Chongqing peace talks, 54–5, 65, 72
 and diary, 2, 10–12, 61
 GMD troop entry to Dalian, 22–3, 34, 36–9
 and Japan/Japanese, 22, 26, 219
 and Mao, 21, 47, 52–4, 59, 61, 72, 76
 and Marshall, 106, 108–11, 113, 120, 134–5, 138, 150, 163, 168, 187, 189, 202, 195, 220, 238, 242
 payout plan for the Soviets, 17, 148–51, 167, 169
 and Political Consultative Conference, 105, 113, 138–9, 221, 228
 post-war territory recovery, 45–6, 51

283

and Sino-Soviet economic
cooperation, 22, 145, 148–51,
155–6, 161–2, 166, 168–70
Sino-Soviet Treaty (1945), 24–7,
42–4
Sipingjie offensive, 18, 177–80,
184–5, 194
and Soviets, 37–8, 43–5, 143–52,
163–4, 167–70, 178–9
Chiang, Madame, 151–2, 168, 220
Chifeng, 79, 111–13, 115–17, 136,
152
China Democratic League, 29, 75,
123–5, 139, 182, 186, 210, 224–7,
233, 235
China Soviet Union Treaty of
Friendship and Alliance *see* Sino-
Soviet Treaty
Chinese Changchun Railway, 27, 30,
93, 153, 170, 231–2, 244
Chinese Civil War (1945–49), 107,
134, 135, 166, 195, 209
attack and counterattack cycle, 236
Mao's strategy, 208–9
outbreak of full-scale conflict, 203,
206, 211–12, 235
and retaliatory military actions,
195–6
US Marines, 51, 190, 211–12,
234, 236
See also Manchurian civil war; veto
players; Zhou Enlai; *and specific
topics*
Chinese Communist Party (CCP),
1, 22
Anshan, 157, 159, 187
armed forces, size of, 56–8, 60–4
passim, 72, 74, 126–9
army food and clothing supply, 53,
87–8, 205, 206–7
Birch murder, 76
ceasefire, 113–15, 116, 233
Chongqing negotiations, 48–69
passim

Dalian dispute, 22–3, 45
Datong, battle for, 219, 223
Democratic League, 75, 123–5,
224, 233, 235
Double Tenth Agreement, 70–1,
203
Duolun, 111–13, 136
Fengman Hydroelectric Power
Plant, 156
former Japanese territories, 64
guerrilla forces and tactic, 18,
52–3, 57, 77, 83, 85–6, 88–9,
91–2, 107
Hegang Coal Mine, 155–61, 169
and Hurley, 53–4, 61, 64–7, 73–4
Jiangsu victories, 209
Liberated Areas, 49, 56, 61, 66–7,
71, 75–6, 82, 86, 131, 205
Manchuria, war in, 78–104 *passim*
(*see also* Mao Zedong)
and Marshall *see* Zhou Enlai
as Marxist–Leninist party, 227
military expansion (1937–45), 48
military strategy after World War
II, 52–3
National Assembly, 121–2, 123–4,
130–1, 137, 139, 220, 225,
227–8, 232–5
rejection of truce, 223–4
Sipingjie *see* Sipingjie, battle of
Stuart Committee, 212–13, 221–2
territorial recovery after World War
II, 47, 51
Tianmu Mountain, battle of, 53
United Front with GMD, 22, 28,
50
US forces, 211–12
US Navy, 40
and USSR, 38, 45, 80–1, 113,
246–7
as veto player, 226
Zhang Xinfu murder, 153–4
Chinese Nationalist Party *see*
Guomindang

Chongqing negotiations, 13–14, 73, 242
  aggressive behaviour, 63
  deadlock, 74–5
  and Hurley, 54, 61, 64–7, 73–4
  near breakdown, 63–4
  and traffic accident, 69–70
  whipsaw approach, 64
Circulating Currency for the Nine Provinces of the North-East (CCNE), 17, 103, 149, 150, 167, 244
civil war *see* Chinese Civil War, 1945–49; Manchurian civil war

Dalian, dispute over, 28–34, 38–9, 44, 245
Datong, battle for, 219, 223
Dong Yanping, 36–7, 142–3, 145, 152–3, 162, 164
Double Tenth Agreement (1945), 70–1, 74, 106, 122, 134, 203
Du Yuesheng, 227
Du Yuming, 39, 40, 46, 94, 99, 104, 116–17, 185–6, 187–8

Executive Headquarters, 114–15, 118–19, 121, 128, 135, 176–7, 181, 191, 200, 202, 211–12, 223

field teams, 114, 116–18, 175–7, 191, 196, 200, 204–6, 212, 223
Follett, Mary Parker, 133–4, 136
fractionating approach, 50
Fushun, 153–5, 165–6
Fussell, Paul, 195
Fu Zuoyi, 51

Gillem, Alvan, 174–5, 181
Guangzhou, 172
Guomindang (GMD), 1, 22
  army reorganisation agreement, 126–30

attempts at seaborne landing of troops, 39–41
CCP alliance and negotiations, 467, 53, 71, 241
CCP territorial claims, 55–6, 67
ceasefire violations, 116–19
Chongqing negotiations, 47, 53–7, 64–5, 67, 72, 74, 76
Dalian, 13, 17, 22–3, 25, 28–3, 41, 43–5, 245
economic negotiations with Soviets, 141–70
highball negotiation technique, 58–9
and Hurley, 54, 64–5, 76
Japanese properties in Manchuria, 17, 143
and Marshall, 107–15
National Assembly, 67, 70, 138, 225, 233, 235
negotiating team, 55
passivity in negotiation, 144–5
payout plan for the Soviets, 150–1, 167
Political Consultative Conference, 109, 132–3, 137, 139
post-ceasefire differences, 133–9
pre-emptive concession, 59–60, 72
Sino-Soviet economic cooperation, 141–70 *passim*
Sino-Soviet Treaty, 23–8, 42–6
size of CCP army, 58–9
Soviet military threat, 144
truce, 110–15, 134, 190–1, 197
and US alliance, 32, 163, 169, 241–2
See also Chiang Kai-shek; Chiang, Madame; Manchurian civil war; Sipingjie, battle of

Haicheng, 187
Handan, 204
Hangzhou, 53, 62
Harbin, 95, 179, 186–7, 190, 192

285

Hebei, 77–9, 84–5, 87–9, 91, 99, 138, 205, 207, 212
Henan, 84, 204–5, 207
Hetao region, 51
highball negotiation tactic, 58–9
high-pressure tactics, 73, 135
Huaiyin, 229
Huang Kecheng, 88, 184, 194
Huang Yanpei, 227, 239
Huludao, 33, 38–40, 92, 102, 172, 182
Huo Kuizhang, 211
Hu Qiaomu, 66, 70
Hurley, Patrick, 50, 76, 105
  as mediator and negotiator, 53–4, 61, 64–7, 73–4, 134, 242

Japanese assets in Manchuria, 17, 141, 161, 167
Jiangsu, 62, 68, 71, 87, 201–2, 205, 207–9, 213–14, 229
Jiang Yuntian, 47–8, 247
Jinzhou, 34, 80, 84–5, 87, 89, 92–4, 97, 99–100, 104, 145

Kissinger, Henry, 59–60, 72–3, 243
Kuming, 210–11

Lafa, 191
Lanzhou–Lianyungang railway, 61, 70, 202, 214
Li and Wen assassinations, 210–11, 236
Li Xiannian, 203–4, 205–7
Li Yunchang, 78–9, 85
Liaodong Gulf, 33, 45, 243
Liaodong Peninsula, 31, 159, 161, 244
Liaoxi, 79
Liddell Hart, B.H., 7
Lin Biao, 18, 84–5, 88, 90–3, 98, 101, 118–19, 131, 177, 179, 182, 183–5, 188, 190–1, 195, 247
Liu Shaoqi, 82–4, 91–8, 118–19, 131–2, 135, 191

Luo Rongji, 226, 229
Lüshun, 27, 36, 39, 45, 244

Mackenzie, Dewitt, 2
Malinovsky, Marshal Rodion Yakovlevich, 30, 32–6, 39–41, 43–4, 143, 148, 151–2, 160–1, 170
Manchurian civil war, 78–104 *passim*
  and Guomindang (GMD), 88–90, 99–104, 171–4
  and Mao, 84–8, 90–2, 97–9
  and US equipment, 88, 94, 171–3
Mao Zedong:
  and ceasefire, 115
  and Chongqing negotiations, 47–8, 52–5, 57–61, 72, 76
  and Hurley, 61, 64–7, 73–4, 242
  illness, 92, 97
  and Kissinger, 59, 72–3
  and Manchurian civil war, 78–9, 84–8, 177, 179, 186, 191
  and Marshall, 134, 179, 180
  as military planner, 52–3, 57–8, 84–8, 90–2, 97–9, 177, 183–4, 191, 193–4, 203, 206, 208–9, 235
  as political leader, 86–7, 97–9
  and Sipingjie, 177, 179, 183–4, 192–4
Marshall, George C., 15–16, 242–3
  and army reorganisation, 127, 130
  as biased third party, 134, 174, 242
  ceasefire negotiations, 108–15, 179–82, 196, 197
  and Chiang Kai-shek, 108–11, 150, 163, 168, 180, 187, 189, 195, 220
  and Committee of Three, 109, 181, 196, 243
  and Mao, 134, 179, 180
  mission goals and objectives, 105–6
  and Political Consultative Conference, 110, 120–1, 124, 135

recall, 234
truce, 110–15, 186–7, 190–1, 200–3, 242
and Zhou Enlai, 108–9, 131, 190, 221, 224
mediators, American, 134, 212, 241–3
See also Hurley, Kissinger, Marshall
Mongolian People's Republic (MPR), 25–6

Nanjing, 12, 62, 148, 187, 190, 208, 222, 225, 230, 234
National Assembly, 67, 70, 106, 121–4, 130–1, 137–9, 220, 225–9, 232–5, 247
North-East Bureau (NEB), 82, 95–7, 192
North-East Democratic United Army (NEDUA), 118–19, 171, 175–80, 182–90, 193–5
and Sipingjie, 177–85
North-East Headquarters (NEHQ), 28–30, 32, 142, 145–6, 153, 182
North-East People's Autonomous Army (NEPAA), 84–5, 90, 92–4, 118

packaging concessions, 112
passivity as negotiation technique, 144–5
Pauley, Edwin, 157, 167
peace bid, last ditch, 200–2, 212–33
Peng Zhen, 82–3, 90–1, 95, 98
Petrov, Appolon Alexandrovich, 30, 36–8, 45, 162–3, 165–6
Political Consultative Conference (PPC), 67, 70, 75–6, 106, 108, 121–2, 124–6, 130, 134, 136, 138, 202, 221, 224–6, 228, 231, 234, 238
army reorganisation agreement, 126–7
resolutions, 16, 120–6, 130–4, 136–9, 221, 224–5, 228, 230–1, 234, 238
pre-emptive concession, 60, 72

Qingdao–Jinan railway, 192
Qinhuangdao, 41, 46, 78, 89, 102, 107
Qiqihar, 201

Rehe, 35, 78–9, 81, 94, 99, 101, 104, 111, 113, 115–16, 118, 135, 196, 213
Robertson, Walter, 115

Shandong, 45, 62, 78, 82, 138, 158, 178, 192, 196, 201–3, 205, 210, 213, 243–4
Shanghai, 62, 107, 208, 222, 224, 229, 231
Shanhaiguan, 46, 79–80, 84–5, 87–90, 97, 144–6
Shanxi, 51, 64, 71, 76, 205, 219
Shenyang, 33–5, 79–82, 84, 93–6, 99, 104, 119, 145–6, 153, 164–5, 171, 182, 185–9
Shi Jue, 90, 116
Sino-Soviet economic cooperation, 141–70 *passim*
Sino-Soviet Treaty, 23–32, 42–3, 45, 78, 116, 142–3, 146, 152–3, 169, 244, 246
Sipingjie, battle of, 18–19, 171, 174, 177–85, 188, 192, 193–5
Sladkovsky, M.I., 143–50, 156, 158–60, 164, 169
Song Ziwen, 21, 24–7, 43, 146, 170
Soong, T.V. *see* Song Ziwen
State Council, 122–4, 137, 139, 231–4
and dispute resolution, 220–1, 231
distribution of seats, 213, 222, 224, 226, 233
and third parties, 228, 232, 239
Stuart Committee, 212–14, 221–2
Stuart, John Leighton, 212–14, 218–23, 225, 236–8
Suiyuan, 51, 84, 94
Sungari River, 186, 189–90

Sun Liren, 171, 188
Sun Yat-sen, 21, 132
Sun Yueqi, 154–6, 168

Taiwan, 230, 232, 245
Tangshan, 107
territorial claims, 56, 67–8, 74
third-party bloc, 225–33, 238–9
third-party intervention, 5, 54, 65, 73–4, 110–11, 180
Tianjin–Pukou railway, 192
truce, China proper, 118, 134–5, 224
truce, 15-day *see* truce, Manchuria (June 1946)
truce, Manchuria (January 1946), 108–9, 113–15, 154
   Committee of Three, 109, 111, 114, 176–7
   and Mao, 115
   and Marshall, 106, 109–10, 117–19, 134, 180, 242
   Political Consultative Conference, 113, 120, 126
   truce teams (field teams), 114, 116–18, 174, 175–7
   violations of, 116, 118, 176, 196
truce, Manchuria (June 1946), 185–93, 195–6, 199, 223–4, 236
   Committee of Three, 181, 196, 200, 202, 204–5, 208, 220–2, 228, 243
Truman administration, 106, 167, 214
Truman, President H., 43, 105–8, 121, 130, 134, 234
   and Chiang Kai-shek, 218
Tsou Tang, 16, 148, 169, 238

United States Marines, 51, 116, 190, 211–12, 234, 236
United States military forces, 41, 173, 189, 216–17, 234
United States Navy, 39–41, 171, 189, 216–17

veto players, 20, 226, 232, 235, 239

Waldron, Arthur, 100
Wang Qiuhua, 42
Wang Ruofei, 55, 58–60, 67, 71
Wang Shijie, 25–7, 42–3, 55–6, 146, 162–3, 165–6, 169–70
Wang Shoujing, 215
Wang Tianming, 208
Wedemeyer, Albert, 41, 53, 66, 76, 101–2, 110, 127, 136, 171
Weihaiwei, 196
Westad, Arne, 23
whipsaw approach, 64
Willkie, Wendell, 29
withdrawal tactic (calculated passivity/withholding), 144–5
Wuhan, 203, 208
Wuhe, 204–5

Xi'an incident, 22
Xiao Jiansheng, 133
Xiong Shihui, 27–36, 38–41, 43–4, 143, 152

Yalu River Hydroelectric Power Plant, 155
Yantai, 196
Yan Xishan, 51, 64, 71
Yan'an, 47, 52
   leadership, 58, 60, 62–3, 77–8, 81–2, 92, 96, 115, 126, 129, 131, 133–4, 203, 209, 212
   orders and directives from, 51, 59, 77–9, 83, 95, 207, 236
Ye Jianying, 115, 117–18
Yellow Sea, 39
yesable proposition, 160, 165
Yingkou, 33, 38–41, 84, 104, 118–19

Zeng Kelin, 79–82
Zhang Jia'ao, 28–30, 32–4, 44, 143–50, 153–6, 160–2, 164–9, 170, 244

INDEX

Zhangjiakou, 117, 127, 138, 201, 219, 223, 225
Zhang Junmai, 29, 227, 229
Zhang Qun, 55, 60, 64, 111–13, 127, 135–6
Zhang Xinfu, 153
Zhang Zhizhong, 54–5, 58, 62–3, 67–8, 74, 127, 181
Zhou Enlai, 55, 129, 211, 220, 233, 237
    army reorganisation, 127, 129
    calculated incompetence, 74
    CCP army size, 58
    ceasefire (January 1946), 107–8, 111, 114, 116–18, 135–6, 196
    Chongqing peace talks, 55–76, 82
    Committee of Three, 111, 204–5, 221–2, 228
    field teams, 116–17
    and Guomindang, 63, 112–13, 133, 135–6, 139, 214, 236
    last-ditch peace bid, 200–5, 213–14, 219–22, 224–9, 234, 236–8
    and Marshall, 108–10, 112–13, 116–17, 127, 135, 138, 174, 181–4, 190, 192, 200–3, 213, 219–22, 224
    Political Consultative Conference, 67, 76, 105, 130–3, 139, 230
    and Sipingje, 177, 181–2
    third-party bloc, 225, 227, 229, 230–3, 238–9
    truce, Manchuria (June 1946), 174–5, 187, 190–2, 196
    and Zhang Qun/Zhang Zhizhong, 67–8, 74, 111–14, 127
Zhou Xinmin, 227

www.ingramcontent.com/pod-product-compliance
Lightning Source LLC
Chambersburg PA
CBHW070754230426
43665CB00017B/2352